A WAGER on DEATH

The Vittorio Messori Series
edited by Aurelio Porfiri

Hypotheses about Jesus

A Wager on Death

VITTORIO MESSORI

A WAGER ON DEATH

The Christian Proposal: Deception or Hope?

The Vittorio Messori Series
edited by Aurelio Porfiri

Translated by Nicholas Reitzeg

SOPHIA INSTITUTE PRESS
Manchester, New Hampshire

Copyright © 2021 by Edizioni Ares, Via Santa Croce, 20/2, Milano, Italy 20122.

English translation copyright © 2024 by Sophia Institute Press.

First published in Italian as *Scommesa Sulla morte* in 1982 by SEI, Turin.

Printed in the United States of America. All rights reserved.

Cover by LUCAS Art & Design / Jenison, MI

Cover image: *Field-flowers-fantasy-nature* (Pixabay 54722420) and *Sunrise* (Pixabay 287097).

Scripture quotations are from the ESV® Bible (The Holy Bible, English Standard Version®), copyright © 2001 by Crossway, a publishing ministry of Good News Publishers. Used by permission. All rights reserved. The ESV text may not be quoted in any publication made available to the public by a Creative Commons license. The ESV may not be translated in whole or in part into any other language.

No part of this book may be reproduced, stored in a retrieval system, or transmitted in any form, or by any means, electronic, mechanical, photocopying, or otherwise, without the prior written permission of the publisher, except by a reviewer, who may quote brief passages in a review.

Sophia Institute Press
Box 5284, Manchester, NH 03108
1-800-888-9344
www.SophiaInstitute.com

Sophia Institute Press is a registered trademark of Sophia Institute.

paperback ISBN 979-8-88911-006-4

ebook ISBN 979-8-88911-007-1

Library of Congress Control Number: 2024937871

First printing

Lord,
have mercy on the Christian who doubts,
on the incredulous who longs to believe,
on us prisoners of life,
who grope onward, alone in the night,
under heavens no longer illuminated
by the torches of an ancient hope.

Joris-Karl Huysmans

Contents

This Volume ix

Introduction 3

PART I
Causes

1. Cards on the Table 9
2. A Skeleton in the Closet of the East 19
3. A Skeleton in the Closet of the West 33
4. The Triumph of Death 57

PART II
Effects

5. A Social Scourge 69
6. Crimes and Punishments 81
7. The Door upon the Mystery 101
8. A Risk, A Search 125

PART III
Choices

9. At the Bazaar of Religions 137
10. The Divided Christ 171
11. With Which Church? 191

PART IV
Reality

12. Words and Things 225
13. Not to Die 265
14. Life Among Us? 301
A Short Valediction 349
About the Author 355

This Volume

As many will know, my first book was titled *Hypotheses about Jesus*, and had surprising success not only in Italy but around the world. From the moment the original and its translations came out, readers began sending me letters requesting me to continue my religious research by publishing another book. In reality, I disappointed them and kept silent for several years, and in the end disappointed my publisher as well, presenting him with a title judged scandalous: *A Wager on Death*. At that explicitly Catholic press, a cover with salacious references would probably have led to less indignation. But in the end, they asked: how can we refuse a text by an author so in demand, not only in Italy but around the world?

Despite some scandalized clerics, the unforeseen materialized. After the surprise of the first readers (many of them secularists, but also some believers), word of mouth spread and the circulation was surprising this time as well, as the reprints over the course of the years demonstrate, including this one after four decades. Not a fan of summaries, I will stop here, grateful to Stefano Chiappalone for his pertinent observations on the text.

Each reader is free to continue reading or to put the book down. Nevertheless, the theme confronted here is, objectively speaking, the only one that all of us without exception will have to face — a theme that concerns "eternity" even.

Regardless of the hypotheses each reader might have, he must, like it or not, choose whether an everlasting eternity awaits him or not. Thus, it is worth the effort to give the issue some serious thought, as this book seeks to do.

Vittorio Messori

A Wager on Death

Introduction

TRY TO IMAGINE THIS situation.

A young journalist publishes his first book, in which he recounts the route he took in his research into the figure of Jesus, a Jesus whom he had just rediscovered, had just come to know. He did not hang much hope on the text, but it seemed important for him to write it, and thanks to his journalistic connections, he was able to find an editor, a Catholic one at that, who would publish it for him. He believed his book would be important above all for himself, and then for those few benevolent readers who would condescend to read it.

Despite his skepticism, once published, the book became an amazing success, a bestseller that over the years would sell more than a million copies around the world and would be officially translated (and pirated as well) into more than fifty languages. Returning to the early days of this unbelievable success, the editor who found the "hen that laid golden eggs" in his hands obviously did not think twice about asking the author for another book. You have to make hay while the sun shines, as we say. And naturally there were also readers asking for another text after his fine book about Jesus, which took them by the hand in rediscovering the person of the Nazarene, so often hidden by theological grandstanding, and now instead portraying Him through recourse to the good sense that is fortunately innate in each of us, though often hidden by false reasoning.

But our author was not in a hurry, wanting to take his time, and after a fairly long period, he presented the editor with another text, bearing the title *A Wager with Death*. Death? Of course, the Catholic publisher was a bit perplexed, because the theme did not seem to encourage readers to buy the book, death being one of those topics we prefer not to discuss, possibly not even to mention. But Vittorio Messori, the journalist in question, was nonetheless sure that the text would do well. He was right: the book proved to be a phenomenal success.

The situation described above is the story of the book you now hold in your hands, a situation the author mentions in his own introduction.

Surely, it took courage to choose as his theme one of the deepest taboos of our age, the topic we all think we can eliminate by not talking about it. I too join Vittorio Messori in understanding the embarrassment, the discomfort, the difficulty that speaking about death arouses in people. Obviously, we are all instinctively attracted to life, not to the end of life.

When this topic comes up in conversation, we are often told not to think about it, but the problem is that death, nevertheless, thinks about us. Even if we act as if it did not exist, all of us must come to terms with it one day or another. This is what makes Messori's attempt understandable, and I think successful: to face the matter head on, investigating the reasons why this topic is so often removed from our existential horizon.

One response to this query could be that death frightens us. This is true. We see it as the end of everything, the moment at which we lose the ability to enjoy the people around us and the pleasures that life offers us. And we cannot help thinking, as we see others confronting that supreme moment, that death is often accompanied by suffering, and no one likes to suffer. Quite often we have experienced this suffering indirectly through someone dear to us, and how well we know that this suffering that precedes the final passage is painful for us, at times excruciating.

Hence we must be clear about it: we have every reason to see in death an unwelcome guest. It does no good to deny death, however, pretending it is not part of life. Let us be frank: it will come. About this, unfortunately, there can be no doubt.

Thus, it is better to try to comprehend this passage that we so fear.

The book you are about to read is not an easy book.

Do not hope for a consoling read, filled with green pastures and fluttering angels. Sure, Christian hope is presented, but this does not mean that the reality of death is omitted. It is presented in all its drama. As the author says, "Certainly: the force I sought to give to the argumentation is proportional to the importance of the subject matter. Anyone preferring softer tones, *chiaroscuro*, compliments, ceremonies, or diplomacy will find some pages to be brutal. But I hope this is a brutality similar to that of the surgeon who cuts the swollen pus boil without hesitating at the patient's protests." Certainly a bit brutal, this image, but I believe it serves to understand that reading this book will perhaps be shocking for some, but necessary precisely because of the argument it treats.

On the occasion of the death of the great Italian intellectual Umberto Eco, Vittorio Messori wrote an article in the popular newspaper *Corriere della Sera*, recalling his encounter with Eco, who in his youth had been a fervent Catholic, only to arrive at what he defined as "apostasy" from all faith. Recalling this encounter, Messori mentions the moment when, without rhetoric, the topic of death was confronted. Umberto Eco was not a believer, but was certainly a man of great intelligence, and it's worthwhile to consider the following passage from that article written by Messori in 2016:

> We spoke about death: a drama that lived in his flesh, he told me, ever since his father died unexpectedly. "Many years have passed since then, but I think about it every day. I don't seek, like Freud, to avenge myself on my father, but to vindicate him. Here too can be seen the reason for my professional activity. Me, a collector of honors, as someone said? No, rather someone who wants to give to his father the satisfaction that he hoped to have from his son but didn't." I asked him where his father is now. Where are all the dead? Where will all of us be, too? He answered: "Beyond those bronze doors is chaos, darkness. Or there's nothing, or a flat and desolate desert with no end." Death, I reminded him, is the greatest of wagers, open to many possible outcomes. And what if those who say that Jesus Christ will come to us were right? As one who had often thought about this, he did not hesitate in answering. "Listen, if by chance the Nazarene truly exists and wants to whip up a case against me, I would tell him more or less the things I'm telling you: I've reasoned this and that, and I've come to the conclusion that you would not be there waiting for us. I believe we could come to a reasonable settlement. If instead he is the cruel, vindictive God of certain Protestant sects, then it's better to have nothing to do with him. Send me to Hell, then, where there will at least be good people." A pause, and then: "But look, I am convinced that if there really were a God, he would be the one of that St. Thomas with whom, if he were alive today, I would have argued, but who was a man who, despite everything, one could reason with over matters that count." Now, even Umberto Eco "knows." And as for the respect which such a diligent life merits

from everyone, believers will say a prayer, with discretion equal to their conviction, before the coffin of the man who, coherently and without hypocrisy, did not want a religious presence.

I find this passage is so beautiful because of the frankness and concreteness of Messori's manner of speech, but also because of the intelligence and subtle humor (the daughter of intelligence) demonstrated by Eco in his conversation with the journalist. Believer or non-believer, it is always nice to deal with intelligent people who can nourish a serious conversation, especially when descending to the concrete level, as our journalist does. You will find Messori's concrete style of speaking in this book, as well.

Messori (whose biographical information can be found in my introduction to *Hypotheses about Jesus* published previously with Sophia Institute Press, or — for those who know Italian — in a booklet I wrote about him under the title *Et Et: Ipotesi su Vittorio Messori*), as I have said, does not split hairs. The book reads smoothly thanks to Messori's journalistic style, which keeps the reader constantly interested, but it is also a difficult read because of its subject matter. As Messori writes, the topic embarrassed the book's author too, because if we consider it seriously, it is certainly an issue that makes us very, very tense.

Yet I would like to think that after reading this book you will also feel relieved by the fact that you have finally had the possibility to face one of your greatest fears, your fear of death. *The* greatest fear, in fact. You will no longer be satisfied with avoiding the topic with a nervous shrug of the shoulders, for you will have looked it in the face, trying to understand better what awaits us all. At least we might meditate on our common destiny by staring it in the face.

— *Aurelio Porfiri*

PART I
CAUSES

A curious adventure came our way: we had forgotten that we have to die. This is what historians will conclude after having examined all the written sources of our age. An investigation into about one hundred thousand non-fiction books of the past twenty years will demonstrate that only two hundred (a percentage, therefore, of 0.2%) confronted the problem of death. Including medical books.

Pierre Chaunu

CHAPTER 1

Cards on the Table

A Problem, a Killjoy

WE'VE TAKEN A WRONG turn. No one will come out alive from the adventure of life.

At birth there is no remedy: from the cradle we find ourselves on death row in a land where pardons are unheard of.

The Argentine writer Jorge Luis Borges says, "Death is a custom that all, sooner or later, must respect." Among contemporaries, the French-Romanian Emil Cioran echoes this: "Death is the most solid and secure thing life has invented up to now."

Three centuries ago, a man with no fear of words, Blaise Pascal, cut to the quick: "As beautiful as the comedy was at any rate, the last act is always bloody. In the end, dirt gets shoveled on the head. And that's it, forever."

No, we have not become eternal, not even in the age of technological prodigies. Do not allow yourself to be fooled by the blinking red lights on your electronic contraptions. Do not be fooled by the so-called "triumphs" of medicine. Little or nothing has changed here in the last twenty-five centuries, since the Psalmist wrote, "The years of our life are threescore and ten / or even by reason of strength fourscore / ... they are soon gone and we fly away" (Ps. 90:10).

Statistics show that, in all, we can count on about twenty-five thousand days; a few thousand more for some. But afterward, there will be no more. For no one. Yes, for the author of these lines as well, and for you who read them, it will soon be evening.

And yet, despite everything, today something seems different. "All men are mortal. I am a man. Therefore, I too am mortal": the famous ancient syllogism has lost nothing of its logical strength. But if this were evident, a given to all who have preceded us, it seems for many today it has become bad news of the type one must keep to oneself; or better yet, apply one's ingenuity to denying or at least hiding.

I refuse to play that game. I am a journalist; I am obliged to communicate the news as I see it, whether good or bad, insofar as it has been ascertained. And this is the most certain of news. To be a killjoy is, at times, a duty.

I am not a politician who must flatter, beg, or promise always and everywhere to win your trust, to get a vote. I am not a writer of romance novels or a screenwriter of soap operas obliged to provide a happy ending. Nor am I a sociologist, a jack-of-all-trades for every emergency, paid in cash and in ephemeral fame to distract you with superficial digressions as long as my guise is pedantic and pseudo-scientific.

Here too I ply my thankless trade of a peddler of news, knowing the great risk I run. I am violating the pact spoken of by the French anthropologist Luis Vincent Thomas, the pioneer of the disquieting school of "thanatologists," scholars of contemporary aspects of death: "In today's societies and among intellectuals there exists a tacit agreement. 'I'm counting on you,' say readers, 'that you will provide me with instruments for forgetting, masking, denying death. If you don't carry out this task I've entrusted you with, you'll be fired: I won't read you anymore.'"

Morbid?

On the contrary: I am afraid you really need to read what I have to say, and not because I presume these pages are worth your time. I do not take myself that seriously; it is the topic I am placing before you which is serious. Though difficult, it is necessary to consider, sooner or later, a reality that belongs to us — whatever it is, and without pious lies.

I know well your resistance in the face of the terrible but unavoidable *Thing* upon which I am inviting you to reflect. That resistance, that defensive instinct I have found in myself, too. I have had the luxury to experience it in every form during the years in which I have been forcing myself to sit down and write these pages.

I believe it behooves you not to set this book down, not hiding even the title with that little word (*death*), one simple monosyllable. I believe it behooves you not to escape to some place where you can justify yourself saying that entreating this topic is morbid, neurotic.

Philippe Ariès,[1] another thanatologist, a man who dedicated his life to reflecting on this theme, came to a conclusion that closes off this exit strategy: "What is truly morbid is not speaking about death, but keeping silent about it as people do today. No one is more neurotic than the one who considers facing the question of the end to be neurotic."

As a consolation to the reader, I will show my cards right from the start: in reality, helping death come out of hiding means helping life. As Ariès says, "To forget death and the dead means rendering a terrible disservice to life and the living."

I recognize your defense mechanism (which is mine too) because I know your anguish (this, too, is mine). It hides in the depths perhaps, but it is there; it acts, even if you deny it. Neither does it vanish if you try to hide it even from yourself.

In any case, there is no shame in that anguish: on the contrary, it is the tragic sign of the greatness and the misery of man; it is the onerous nobility of the only living being that knows it must die. He too, *Homo sapiens*, is capable of not knowing why he lives and dies. But he knows, and he alone, that living every day he must die. That anguish is, paradoxically, the guarantee of balance and mental health. Carl Gustav Jung, one of the fathers of psychoanalysis, often repeated, "A man who does not consider the problem of death and does not perceive the drama, is in urgent need of treatment." He caringly placed on his couch the fools and hypocrites who thought it was an "adult" thing, perhaps "modern" or "elegant," to act as if it were not important.

Repression is the worst therapy for any problem, especially if it is a tormenting problem. There is no way out but to confront it.

For what it is worth, the bottom line of my long experience sleuthing in such dark regions is that, if one does not try to escape, if one can overcome the resistance, if as a spelunker one descends into the chasm as far as one can — well, precisely at that moment, unexpectedly, the lump in one's throat begins to dissolve. If one accepts the duty to live (and so, to walk toward death) with open eyes, one might find not further fears and torments, but serenity and consolation. I would say even joy, if it did not smack of bloated rhetoric.

---

[1] Editor's Note: Philippe Ariès (1914–1984) was a French medievalist and historian.

At any rate, I am not revealing anything new. I am simply confirming with personal experience what the true sages of every time and culture have always taught. It is a truth that is silenced or denied only by certain lugubrious contemporary "masters," according to whom accounting for one's own humanity would count as lugubrious; according to whom penultimate concerns (and never the ultimate ones) would count as important.

Here I must confess that this book has helped the one who wrote it. He would like nothing more than to help those who read it, whatever the conclusions they might draw from it. The prospect of consolation is not only for the one who believes he can give a satisfying, resolute response at the end of the investigation to the brutal questions death poses. There is also dignity in seeking, with honesty and tenacity, even without finding an answer.

Always and everywhere, every man tends toward one objective only: being happy; or at least, being as little unhappy as possible. Even the one who sets off to hang himself aims at this. In this case, the lesser evil, the choice that renders him less unhappy, is not to escape but to face; not to allow one to be dominated by "destiny," but to try to interpret it.

Com-patire or compassion (in its original sense of "to suffer together") will save me from transforming into "author" or "theologian." I place myself entirely next to the reader, and not out of vanity or self-satisfaction, but because I cannot do otherwise. The reader is human just like me, in this moment is alive like me, is *still* alive, too. He is my companion in the adventure (not always exhilarating) of a life we have not asked for and of an end of life that has been imposed on us as well.

"Don't take me for a 'doctor'" Eugène Jonesco, the French comedy writer, has one of his characters say. "I'm just someone who asks the questions out loud that others ask under their breath."

This path is not only difficult but also risky: when one decides to ask these ultimate questions out loud, the profound discussion one would like risks sliding into the trite at every step, if not even into *kitsch, pompier*. Or even worse, into preaching.

I attempted to defend myself by clinging to the only profession I know: not that of teaching, but informing; not of demonstrating, but narrating.[2]

---

[2] While working on *Hypotheses about Jesus*, I had the experience of a child in the German story who, pulling on a rope under the portal of a church, set in motion

HITTING A WALL

After long searching and comparison (I continue to show my hand) in this book I believe, in the end, one can glimpse a possible solution to the obligatory wager with life and death, advancing a proposal which seeks nothing else than to be a finger pointing in one direction: "There!"

In this matter at least, I recognize myself in Hans Küng, the famous Swiss-German theologian: "This book has not been written because the author considers himself a good Christian. But because he discerns that being a Chrisitan is a particularly positive value." In these pages one finds not the person I am, unfortunately, but the one I would like to be.

Although at times I risk being a judge, I remain always the accused, and I never forget that. It would be ridiculous of me to seek to convert the reader while, if anything, I am trying to convert myself. We must remember that "conversion," according to its etymology, means to "turn myself together" toward Something, or better yet, Someone.

Thus, there is a *you* that runs through these pages, from these very first ones. I have not repressed it, but have preserved how it spontaneously emerges from the depths.

That *you*, in fact, is not a literary expedient. More than a hypothetical reader, it addresses me. The me of yesterday who knew of many books but not what they call "the books" (*biblia*) by definition. The me of today, with whom I start afresh a dialogue every morning that often degenerates into a quarrel.

"For all my life," the poet Eugenio Montale confided in his last days, "I have been hitting a wall, trying to discover what is, if anything, on the other side of the wall, convinced that life must have a meaning that escapes us. I have knocked ever more desperately, like one who waits in vain for an answer."

In its impotence, this book is also a stubborn pounding on that wall, like those hypotheses that preceded it. But it is also the testimony of an experience different from that of Montale, perhaps one more fortunate than the poet's and

---

the church bells, to his fright. Thousands of readers from all over the world took up my appeal to send me their criticism, suggestions, confirmations, which I would eventually take into account in a future edition (which came out in 2019). I responded to all of them, a bit embarrassed by the praise, but very grateful for the many suggestions and criticism. "Many," someone said, "write books because it's the only way to talk without being interrupted." As far as I'm concerned, I desire nothing better than to be interrupted and, better still, contradicted.

in any case more problematic, and which frees one of all arrogance and presumption: the experience of one who seemed to hear some sort of echo in response to that bashing against the wall that inexorably crosses each person's path.

An echo, a sound both clear and confused, that promises the hope beyond all hope in this our desert where all wells have run dry and all oases are mirages; a possibility of a victory for life in a world where death reigns; a hope of being forgiven and saved in a society that denies sin but anxiously asks what those scourges are, those "mysteries of iniquity" that devastate it.

A RED FLARE

The pages that follow are the result of an adventure that was unforeseen at the beginning. My intent was in fact this: to point out how today's dominant culture, however verbose, is silent (and it could not be otherwise) about the problem of the meaning of life and death; to examine if and in what way the ancient Christian eschatology might still be a credible answer to those questions.[3] I intended, therefore, to discover (above all for myself, and then to propose the results to the reader) what is truly behind those old words that today have become nearly unpronounceable even for many believers: "Paradise," "Hell," "Purgatory," and even "devil," "angel," and so forth.

I have worked on this project for years, with the effort of one who is aware of the terrible complexity of the problem; with the drudgery of one who wants to, and *must*, popularize, but at the same time abhors the slapdash simplicity of the dilettante.

After I finished the first draft, I realized that having worn out the author, such a book risked wearing out the reader as well, with its heft. And so, I put off for another occasion, if that would be granted me, a detailed analysis of the contents of the Christian afterlife.

I shall not tarry in further explanations: all will be much clearer for those who make it to the final part. There, one shall see how (through opening into an explicitly Christian discussion) one can cling to the *here and now* more than

---

[3] *Eschatology* is a word composed of two Greek terms: *éscata*, last things; and *logos*, discourse. Since the end of the seventeenth century, *eschatology* has come to mean that aspect of religious messages (not only of the Christian message, therefore) that attempt to penetrate the "last things": the end and the goal of each human being (individual eschatology) and of humanity, the world of the entire cosmos (general or collective eschatology).

escaping into the *afterlife*. Namely, how one can engage the concrete efficacy of the gospel message of hope; of the relationship between the things one sees and hears, and the words and practice of the Church. This, nonetheless, is not a "volume one," even though another might be added to go beyond the discussion about the content of Christian hope. This is an entirely autonomous volume because, I hope, it will perform on its own the function for which it was conceived and written.

It should be like a flare shot into the darkness surrounding us, to indicate the existence of a problem hidden and remote, but one which concerns us most intimately; to point out, willingly or not, that we need to set off in search of a solution without which we are all exposed to personal and social disasters; to indicate a possible path we might set out upon; and finally, to describe a place, a Church, where our problem is confronted and combated by remedies that have shown their validity over many centuries.

Truth be told, someone dear to me who proofread the manuscript suggested that this is not an unoffensive flare, but a punch to the gut.

Certainly: the force I sought to give to the argumentation is proportional to the importance of the subject matter. Anyone preferring softer tones, *chiaroscuro*, compliments, ceremonies, or diplomacy will find some pages to be brutal. But I hope this is a brutality similar to that of the surgeon who cuts the swollen pus boil without hesitating at the patient's protests.

"Punch me if you so desire," says Plutarch's Themistocles to his interlocutor, "but first hear me out."

Clearly, I have it out not for those with whom I debate, but with the inhumane ideologies they represent.

If I seem to go *against*, it is because I attempt to go *beyond*. I do not rejoice when hopes are dashed; if anything, I realistically acknowledge that they point toward a Hope that might not delude.

By his own powers, no one can give to others faith in God; everyone, however, can work at spoiling faith in the many obsessions and idols of our day.

To do this, it is important to avoid subduing the passion within us, the fervor, though always subjected to reason and to an even higher judgment (at least for the believer): as Pascal reminds us, "truth without charity is not God but an idol." It would be strange if, in order to destroy idols, we created another one.

With due caution, I love the verses of Nazim Hikmet, the poet of that enormous religious movement that was the Soviet revolution (at least at its beginning): "If I do not burn / and you are not on fire / if both of us do not catch fire / who will ever dissipate the darkness?"

Here, the fire is already in the very object of the discussion. The more I moved forward, the more I realized that the liminal situation of death is truly like a brazier that fuses all the rest and leaves only the metal, if there is any. And when there is metal, it distinguishes infallibly the noble from the vile. Reflection, here, means burning every wrapping, however attractive it might be, to lay bare the content. Meditation, here, means uncovering what is worthy and what is unworthy, getting to the bottom of things, reestablishing the right scale of values.

Pornography

Let us return to where we were: even today, despite living amidst the prodigies of science and technology, everyone will still die; and that old usage by which ancient despots strangled the bearers of bad tidings would serve no purpose. Nor does it solve anything to habituate ourselves passively to the current practice of keeping silent and dismissing the matter.

I do not know what can be done if we remain reluctant, despite the positive reassurances and the warnings of the wise to move forward and face the problem.

I do not know what can be done because it was not me who decided that, every day and every night, for sixty thousands of our colleagues in humanity, the hypothesis become a certainty and the wager with death is decided, crossing the threshold of the afterlife in which there can be All or Nothing.

It is not my sadistic inspiration to remark that we, provisionally alive, are but a scant minority.

The ancient expression that defines "the world of the majority," that of the dead, is based on an objective fact. As we too await our turn to become part of that world, we live treading on what remains of the hundred billion of our peers who have preceded us in the mere four thousand years of history that can in some way be reconstructed. If someone were to assign shadows, behind each one of us there would be thirty ghosts.

The obsessive French refrain is repeated: "The marionettes / go, go, go / three little rounds and then they're gone."

Before the lights of the ephemeral proscenium go out definitively for us as well, it might be worthwhile to stop for a moment and reflect. Better still: it might be worthwhile to make room in our lives, every day, for the awareness that this life is not unlimited, it has a boundary. Only in this way can the living hope to become truly human.

"Would be," "might be": there is a precise reason why I use the conditional. Death is a certain fact with an uncertain date. And yet, (as we have already seen) precisely this event, the only foreseeable one securely in everyone's future, is the one most tenaciously ignored by this society of futurologists, planners, programmers, and organizers of the future.

It happens in the East as in the West, among communists and capitalists, in the First World as well as in the Second World, awaiting in hiding and in denial of death. These markers of "progressive" and "advanced" societies are exported to the Third World and Fourth World, as well, which in some ways remain faithful to the wisdom of the ancients.

Never had it happened before in all history: the morbid silence, the neurotic denial of the same human condition are absolute novelties introduced by contemporary culture. Never as today has the bitter irony of Pascal sounded so relevant and caustic:

> Men, not capable of curing death and hoping for greater happiness, have decided not to think about it. This is all they have been able to contrive to console themselves. But this is a miserable remedy because instead of confronting evil, they want only to hide it as long as they can.

The observation has been made numerous times, but it is worth repeating: the ancient social prohibition on speaking about sex and genital functions has shifted to death and the dead.

Our culture, which we call "rational," "liberated," "adult," has brought down (and not without good reason) the taboo that rendered unmentionable man's sexual dimension. But this is the same culture that has created a new taboo, defended by an even more obsessive scrupulosity.

The Pornography of Death is the apt title chosen by the Englishman Geoffrey Gorer for his study on society and how the sanctions foreseen by the old codes for so-called "obscene actions" have shifted to whomever challenges the new neuroses. And the punishment is worse than the prison of former times: excommunication, isolation, and the social ghetto.

A Wager on Death

Do not be fooled if in recent years various books have arrived in the bookshops on the taboo or problem. If those pages speak of death, it is almost always with the aim of convincing you to put on the underwear which we have taken off.

CHAPTER 2

A Skeleton in the Closet of the East

Page Ten-thousand, Line Three

The decree on the pornography of death creates a common bond between West and East, "capitalism" and "socialism." Both regimes divided up the world and find no other equilibrium than in the reciprocal threat of death, but have not learned to come to terms with death.

They have not learned; or better, have not been able to: as will become abundantly clear, coming to terms would have meant disintegrating systems that lurched forward precisely by insisting on denying the most profoundly human of humanity's problems. Both the East and the West truly have the proverbial "skeleton in the closet" suggested by the title of this chapter and by that which follows. Shall we begin with a few samples, based on facts and only facts, of the vast, variegated but (at least in this case) uniform world of Marxism?

There are few who have read the more than ten-thousand printed pages of Karl Marx's *opera omnia*. Those who have can testify that in those millions of lines, three, and only three, are dedicated to dying. It was in an aside in the *Economic and Philosophic Manuscripts of 1844*, where he mentioned distractedly the fact that "death appears as a harsh victory of the species over the individual." But this shadow is too awkward, and Marx tries immediately to chase it away, denying its very existence. He writes, "The determinate individual, nevertheless, is nothing but a generically determined being, and as such is immortal."

It is not clear what he means by this; in less vaguely embarrassing words, it seems to mean that man dies but that the species, humanity, is immortal. It is the naïve faith of a man of the 1800s who exulted in the puffs of smoke of the first steam engines, and did not suspect the quite different mushroom cloud that would arise at 8:15 in the morning on August 6, 1945, above a remote city called Hiroshima. But it is also the baffling superficiality (or hypocrisy?) of one of the most venerated "wisemen" and "masters" of history who ignores (or pretends to ignore) what death truly means for a specific man, not for an abstract "generically determinate being."

Nevertheless, Marx would not touch that thorny button again until thirty years later, in 1878, in a letter to a friend who had lost a family member. Neither does he offer here a word other than "forget," "hide," "act like nothing has happened": "It is life that helps us, with all of its little joys and boredoms, and its many worries." Odd: the great "master of reason" has no other counsel than to adapt to the bitter moral of *Candide* by that other untiring "reasoner" Voltaire: *"Travaillons, sans raisonner,"* "We work, without reasoning."

The silence of the Founder is not fortuitous, but provided a teaching moment:

> In all the classic works of Marxism one finds the same negligence and the same embarrassment before the problem of death, leading one to think that it is not a matter of forgetfulness but of a necessity imposed by the logic of a system that cannot bear to be confronted with a question that is insoluble for him.

So wrote Joseph Gevaert, a contemporary Flemish philosopher.

The Slavic scholar, Marxist, and member of the Italian Communist Party, Vittorio Strada, confided, "One must recognize, however, that facing the problem of death, the Marxist is defenseless; he cannot offer one single authentic response."

The silence, the embarrassment, the escape are so flagrantly evident that they are almost ill at ease to make it known. One feels like a delinquent when denouncing this flaw (unfixable if not by deconstructing the entire edifice) in the Marxist catechism, which seeks to explain everything. With a similar forgetfulness, it ends up unable to explain anything that truly counts not to the anonymous "masses of workers" but to the concrete "worker."

Such an important part of man escapes this system that boasts of being the one true "total humanism," to the point of justifying the irony of Edgard Morin, a communist sociologist, whose book on death was not unrelated to his leaving the party: "Marxism, my dear, has studied the economy, the market, and social laws. Marxism is magnificent. Too bad it forgot to study man."

WORD GAMES

Marxism is the last and most fortunate heir of a long series of efforts trying to exorcise death by means of word games.

Ludwig Feuerbach, the German philosopher who in many ways was a teacher to his fellow German Marx, was deluded by thinking one could dissolve the inevitable "accident" by denying its very existence: "Death is a phantom, a chimera, a nothing," he insisted. "Its reality is imaginary; it arises only in our ideas."

Alberto Moravia[4] was among the most zealous Italian writers to substitute genitals for death; he was the most listened to among the criers of this ideological pastiche, a hybrid pseudo-cultural cocktail in which Marxism is preeminent, at least insofar as it was useful to fawn over it. Moravia says, "Death? It does not exist. According to Einstein, there is no end, there is no beginning. Death is simply the transformation of certain forms of life."

Happy are they who can be content with what they have, assures the proverb. As for us, we are more demanding and never content with anything. Thus, these verdicts which ought to be definitive seem the pathetic word games of those trying to convince themselves, first of all.

Besides, the consoling citation of Moravia ("according to Einstein...") is inappropriate. Instead of the modern physicist (whose name is invoked perhaps to give the illusion of "scientific" to the strange ultimatum) our poet ought to have invoked Epicurus, the ancient philosopher at the origins of the cultural tradition that gave rise to Feuerbach and Marx. "What does death matter to us?" asks the fragment of Epicurus. "Death does not exist. When we are present, she is not. And when she is present, we are not."

This *calembour*, Epicurus's word game, is as brilliant in appearance as it is empty upon reflection and illusory upon factual verification.

Here we see the superficial conception of death as a destination separated from life: like a problem that arises only when, suddenly, it stops in front of us; on the other hand, according to the well-known medical definition, life is only "the totality of the functions that oppose death."

Whether on the physiological level or on the philosophical or psychological level, death is not *at the end*, but *within* life itself. It is not an annoying

---

[4] Editor's Note: Alberto Moravia (1907–1990) was one of the most influential Italian writers of the 20th century. He is the author of several works, also translated into English.

formality discharged on some remote day: it is a daily reality, the possibility of every instant, on which its request for meaning is projected. Newly born, we are old enough to die. As soon as we reach full development, dissolution begins: by our twenty-fifth year, a hundred thousand brain cells die every day without being substituted; the last day is, therefore, only an end of dying.

According to Martin Heidegger, the master of German existentialism and one of the greatest philosophers of the twentieth century, man is but a *Sein-zum-Tode*, a "being-toward-death." At this point, the mortal condition, far from being a "nonexistent nothing," puts its stamp on every hour of life; it gives life a different meaning according to the answers we offer it.

Not only Heidegger, but all the existential philosophers have placed their finger in the wound; thus, although some professed to be Marxists like Jean-Paul Sartre, they enraged Marxist dogmatism. Existentialism observes, "If death makes no sense, then life makes no sense. The search for a direction to give to life must always be preceded by the search for the meaning of death, as distant as it might be."

A logical, reasonable observation, but prohibited by Marxism, which can be taken seriously only when it feigns belief that death is a secondary matter, a trivial accident that has nothing to do with life and its commitments, which in any case is a "natural" event, about which it makes no sense questioning, or questioning oneself.

But then: there is not only *my* death. If one accepts that my death does not concern me ("When we are present, she is not"), there remains the fact that others die, too: our parents, our children, our friends, those we love and who love us.

We are not dead, not yet. But around us, nearby, very near to us, people die. Here too, "when she is present, we are not"?

There was a time when, like all newspaper journalists, I was obliged to frequent the morgue. I swear I never thought about citing Epicurus, Marx, Feuerbach, or Moravia to parents, wives, husbands, children, or brothers dumbfounded and screaming before the marble table on which a mangled cadaver lay.

In those grim basements, when a journalist perceives with discomfort that his presence is like a vulture that descends upon a corpse, never did it come to mind to demonstrate to those poor desperate relatives that "in reality death does not exist"; that as Marx assures, "man is a generically determined being and as such is immortal"; that "according to Einstein…"

The line of Eugenio Montale states, "If one dies it matters to no one / as long as he is unknown and far away."

THE STRESS MEASUREMENT

We now know that it is the body itself that contradicts the hypocrites and the superficial who, in order to save their ideological dogmas, would reduce man to a level lower than that of bovines that balk at the doors of the slaughterhouse. Not even for such beasts is death "a natural fact."

The intensity of bodily stress in the face of the facts of life has been established, therefore. With sophisticated instruments, the breadth of the hormonal tempest has been measured, the adrenaline release, the physiological modifications set off under the impulse of external circumstances.

As can be easily foreseen by anyone who reasons in terms of humanity and not in terms of blind or hypocritical propaganda, stress with a much greater intensity (conventional measurement: 100) can be verified in situations of mortal danger for the subject. Slightly lower (98) is the stress produced by the death of an immediate family member. Following close behind (90), the death of a relative or an intimate friend. The classification stops at a score of 10: "Stress from a traffic violation."

In this list there is no trace of stress related to political events which have no impact on our lives or on our private interests. This "political" stress, say the researchers, "appears to be barely relevant and therefore is not measurable."

No hormonal or adrenaline release, then, for a decline in votes for one's party during an election, or for a change in political leader, or a shake up in the government. Strange, isn't it? With respect to Marxist dogma, only politics should matter to man; while death, a non-political, individual reality if there ever was one, would be irrelevant. Is there not some disconnect here with what is written in the depths of our bodies? The suspicion is important and is worth considering at a later moment.

Antonio Gramsci,[5] the founder of the Italian Communist Party, admonished the party militants, saying, "to ask questions about death is not modern," and exhorted them to "eliminate such inferior manifestations, these inorganic residuals of obsolete states of mind."

---

[5] Editor's Note: Antonio Gramsci (1891–1937) was an influential Italian Marxist philosopher and writer.

Many decades have passed since that appeal, but people persist in not being as "modern" as Gramsci would have liked them to be. Some try to act as if nothing had happened, inventing ways to eliminate "inferior manifestations," "obsolete states of mind": but their very bodies find ways of betraying them, as the diabolical stress-measuring machines reveal.

A man for whom death is not a problem, according to "atheistic" psychoanalysis, in reality does not exist; and if he did exist, he would need to be cured as Jung asserted, in agreement with all his colleagues of every psychological school. Indeed, more than "ill," perhaps he would not even be human, but an inhumane monster. Those explorers of the depths of the subconscious teach that in each of us there acts what they call "the two basic anxieties": the anxiety of folly; and the more common and primordial anxiety of death.

The thanatologist Louis V. Thomas writes:

> Despite the abundance and the wealth of studies by psychologists and psychoanalysts on the anxiety of death, we are not always capable of defining what it actually consists of. What we do know is that it is universal, and it acts upon children and adults alike, upon illiterate and professors, upon the "primitive" as well as the "evolved."

We know that the more one tries to repress it, to deny it, to hide it, the more that anxiety becomes intolerable. In fact, the efforts of Marxism and of every other contemporary ideology to remove it reveals its strength. Every repression is dictated by distress; we do not repress what we consider to be pleasant or at least indifferent, merely "natural."

Ernesto De Martino was a Marxist, an ethnologist, and a scholar of myth, religion, and folklore. The aim of his work was precisely to confirm Marxist prejudices through his studies. He observed with indulgent detachment, examining through the lens of the sage the religious views on death, these pathetic "derangements," these "prescientific superstitions."

But the moment arrived in which, cleaving to the theory, the Marxist would have to come full circle, in unperturbed awareness that man returns to the material from which he came through a series of extraordinary cases; but that Humanity, the Class, the Proletariat, the Party, and the Cause remain immortal and continue to march, bare chested and flag waving in the wind, toward their certain Destiny.

In theory this is all well and good. In practice, it is a bit different from the slogans, as De Martino and many others came to learn:

> If someone has cancer and knows he must die, he can be sure that the death of an individual is a natural thing and almost irrelevant. But the temptation to ask questions, to rebel, is great. Unfortunately, this is not written in Marx.

Such was the concern of this famous scholar in a final, heart-rending letter to a friend.

ALWAYS, NEVER

Death is not natural; natural is the desire to live, the survival instinct, the hope of defeating the annihilation that threatens us. Not one culture exists, not one society, that has not rebelled against death, perceiving it as a violence, as radically unnatural.

If archaeology is above all the study of the tomb, it is because this is the most constant, the richest of artefacts, constructed with the most solid and resistant of materials. At least by means of a lasting sepulcher one can challenge the destruction of one's entire life. Divided in all other matters, races and civilizations are united by the same revolt, by the same stubborn hope of victory, in some form, in the battle against the enemy, the Grand Intruder.

Having children is not justifiable, on a purely rational plane, in our society, where the sexual act can be easily separated by technical means from reproduction, and where extra hands and arms are not needed to help in the fields, nor as support for the elderly and retired. One child, today, is not as it once was: a cruelty of fate, or an indispensable helper. It is, if anything, the opposite.

One child is *also* the loss of liberty, an expense, a worry, anxiety. It is *also* insomnia, excrement, urine, a problem of space in tight urban dwellings. Raised at the price of such great inconvenience, a child is *also* rebellion against parents, the need not to thank but to kill, at least symbolically, the one who gave him life. Sigmund Freud and his followers did not appear in vain: every parent–child relationship is an intertwining of both magnanimous and homicidal impulses.

Yet, despite all of this, despite the protest of pure reason, not only do we continue to procreate, but the more a society is rich and evolved, the more the black market of adoptions develops, the black market of children. Reading through women's magazines, one finds with dramatic frequency the letters of aspiring mothers rendered desperate by sterility. They do not write from impoverished regions but from post-industrial metropolises.

The fact is that not our reason, but some hidden, profound, inextirpable impulse leads us to try to live through our children something of ourselves, our name, the remembrance of our ephemeral passage. Having children has always been, and still is today, a protest against death; it is the effort to deny and overcome what we ought to await serenely, because, according to the latest teachers of humanity, "in reality it does not exist."

They are masters in humanity, like that well-known Italian Marxist scholar who recently deigned to admit that psychoanalysis might be right; that yes, "the fundamental anxiety" before the prospect of the end might exist and persist.

Nevertheless, assures the professor, the motive is to be found in the "lack of urban reform" that "renders out cities sepulchers."

So, this is the mechanism: one goes out for a walk, the sight of architectural monsters created by real estate speculators leads one to thoughts of the tomb, of death, and from this we are filled with anxiety. Courage! Just pass some laws that might better regulate the exploitation of available land, and the problem of dying will disappear like snow under warm sunlight.

Yet we are told that this anxiety persists even amid the green lawns of Scandinavia, or in Anglo-Saxon garden cities; or, if they existed, Soviet gardencities. Crude and heartless propaganda, true for some militant, honey-tongued survivor; words that recall the ancient Castilian saying: *Palabras y plumas, el viento las lleva*, "Words and feathers, the wind blows them both away."

Well-meaning Marxist friends tried to console the writer Dino Buzzati,[6] who was dying of cancer, with the few doubtful medicines in their cabinet: politics and social causes, the immortality of human work, the irrelevance of death. The writer left them one last note, written with a shaky hand:

---

[6] Editor's Note: Dino Buzzati (1906–1972) was an Italian writer, journalist, and painter.

And you want me to be concerned about the Middle East, the Soviet Union, the United States? Go break your necks and die, I don't care the least about anything. Don't make me laugh, my lips are chaffed.

Tragically, just one more confirmation, seen up close, that death incinerates many words and many remedies based only on reforms, urban renewal, and such like.

Even the elderly, those who by now should be "full of days," perceive death as a violence, rebelling against it. The old man who calmly approaches his end is a consoling invention of the young. Contrary to what one might think, surveys show that the elderly attempt to repress death much more than the young. The former think about it much more than the latter. Is this not because for the latter it is an improbable event, distant, almost impossible, while for the former it is a concrete, imminent reality?

"Young I exalted death; old, I exalt life." These are the words of Ludwig Feuerbach approaching seventy, the one who a few decades earlier had proclaimed death to be "a phantom, a chimera, a nothing." Arthur Schopenhauer, the German philosopher, wrote books to deny the will to live. The theoretical scholar held this; the concrete man (according to his biographers) was terrorized by the idea of dying and proposed to "live at least until ninety." He passed away desperate, still greedy for life, struck by pneumonia at seventy-one.

"Dying a natural fact?" asked William James, the American philosopher. "That might be, but the older I get, the less I believe it; because the more I age, the more I feel ready to live."

Did not Shakespeare say that "as to youth love is attributed, so to the aged avarice"? What is this clinging to "stuff," this longing (often more pathetic than detestable) of accumulating and having, if not the need to hold on to being which escapes us?

No need to deceive ourselves, no need for others to deceive us. There are two words that emerge spontaneously in those who experience love, in those inserted into the very mystery of being. Those words, those two adverbs are: *forever, never*. "I want to live with you *forever*;" "I will *never* leave you."

The need to deny death as testified by lovers is the same that runs throughout history: from the myth of the fountain of youth, to the medieval alchemist's dream of creating the elixir of everlasting life; even to the re-emergence in thousands of forms of this instinct in our technological society: in theories like Marxism that transfer the dream of immortality from the individual to the species, from the single to the masses, from the militant to the party, from the citizen to the city. Perhaps precisely here, in this proposal of immortality, however illusory it might be, is one of the reasons for the fascination and fortune of a system that has been proven false numerous times by history. But here too is one of the reasons for its irreversible crisis.

"FASCIST"

Christa Wolf, a writer in East Germany, wrote a fine novel later to be suppressed, *Reflections on Christa T.*. The reason for this drastic censure was the choice of protagonist: a young woman who died of leukemia at thirty. One who knew such regimes well observed the following:

> In the view of Eastern bureaucrats, this confiscation was entirely legitimate. Wolf had violated one of the main taboos of Marxism-Leninism, making death the principal subject of her book. For communist propaganda death is an irrational and inexplicable rupture in the march (which one must feign is unstoppable) toward happiness and the perfection of the socialist Paradise. Therefore, a book that speaks about death is by nature "counter-revolutionary," an "enemy of socialism," "fascist": thus, the censorship was legitimate.

Death was banned not only for petrified Marxists of the Soviet bloc, but also by many Western forms of Marxism, be they orthodox or heretical. Death must disappear everywhere because it always destroys the happy ending of the fairytale. It is always the killjoy that confuses the refined plans of theorists.

This is how Herbert Marcuse, the Western Marxist theorist to whom all sorts of revolutionary groups turned, consoled himself: "Death is an invention of the managerial middle classes." One of his probable disciples wrote on a wall at the University of Paris, "Death is fascist."

Jean Ziegler belongs to this school, a Swiss Marxist who titled one of his books *Essay on Death in Capitalist Countries* to make it immediately clear that in non-capitalist countries death, if not altogether unheard of, is at least something entirely different.

The irony is not too subtle. Michel Verret, a name we shall meet again as the renowned author of various Marxist pamphlets, wrote in all seriousness, "Only the bourgeois die. The revolutionary is eternal." In fact, Verret continues, repeating the phrase we have come to know, "We need to think of death on the level of species. My end, absurd scandal on the individual level, acquires its meaning on the level of species. I grow old and die, but humanity enjoys an eternal youth."

Jean-Paul Sartre, above reproach in these matters, had already observed, "Revolution, politics, can take from man the fear of living. But they do not free him from the fear of dying."

In Wonderland

At any rate, there is a strange logic to these Marxist consolations in their referral to politics, social action, and the collective. According to that ideology, the only thing that counts is life *here*, on *this* earth, which after all is the only life that exists. And yet, entire generations are asked to sacrifice themselves and die for future generations, hoping that at least they will see the golden age through the efforts of the many who have died.

It is a well-known model of society, at least among entomologists. In the anthill, or the termite nest, or the beehive, the present generation sacrifices itself in a systematic way in favor of successive ones so that they too can sacrifice themselves in turn. But man is neither an ant, nor a termite, nor a bee. It is therefore inevitable that he reconsiders the matter, especially after decades of increasingly intense disappointments. Might the hypothetical happiness of grandchildren comfort the sacrifice of grandparents and parents? Has that sacrifice, then, truly paved the way toward the Promised Land?

Sartre, in one of his last interviews, in light of the failure of all he had believed in and had fought for, recalled his phrase about "revolution that takes away man's fear of living, but not his fear of dying," confiding bitterly: "In reality, now I cannot even see how revolution might liberate us from the fear of living, seeing that it has come neither to my country nor to any other in the world." In response to the sacrifice of life required of so many men, there arise screams from gulags, and from the archipelago of imprisoned European, Asian, or African states — or from entire populations literally walled-in (a unique achievement in all of human history) within their own borders. "Proletariat of the world, forgive me!" says a caricature of Marx by a clandestine Polish labor union.

The myth has been revealed for what it was: messianism, a religion which lacked an answer to the problem of death (and therefore a response to the question about the meaning of life) that all other religions possess and propose. Thus, after having denied and hidden death from man, Marxism was now obliged to face an even more embarrassing fact: the prospect of its own death.

But if so-called "scientific" communism had been right, if the Marxist utopia had truly been feasible, would the problem of death not have become even more tragic and insoluble? The French writer André Malraux put in the mouth of one of his characters, "Nine months are not enough to make a human being; one needs sixty years of sacrifices, will power, and so many other things. And when this human being has been made, when he is finally a man, then he is only good to die."

Would not this absurdity be even more desperate for the citizen of the mythical society of "*de facto* communism," that earthly Paradise without alienation, where to each is given according to his need, where work is joy, where war and tensions have disappeared forever? For the citizen of this wonderland dreamed up by the Marxist, would not dying be even more absurd? If it is really that difficult to leave this world of "alienation," of "surplus value," of "contradictions," what could it possibly be to leave the world envisaged by the Jewish fantasy of Karl Marx, that world where the earth will drip with milk and honey?

Although a heretic in the eyes of Soviet officialdom, the Marxist philosopher Ernst Bloch once said:

> It might make sense to die for the realization of communism. But what sense does it make to die when communism had already been realized? At that time, death would become even more unbearable, because after having abolished poverty and alienation, there would be an immense range of human possibilities, such that no one could die with the feeling of having lived all that a man can live.

"But Humanity Shall Live!" Shall It?

Digging even deeper: will there be a future, whatever it might be, perhaps not even a luminous one, to console the death of the militant communist? Unfortunately, reciting "if man dies, humanity lives" has lost its comforting effect:

if the death of a human being has never been in doubt, for the first time in history the death of humanity has also become probable.

Since the beginning of the atomic age, no one can speak with certainty of the future of society: the power accumulated in nuclear arsenals can destroy not one but a thousand earths. At this moment, it seems there is the equivalent of three tons of TNT ready for each of us. This world wears on its face the wrinkles of old age and, perhaps, the end. It is not the usual pathetic religious visionaries who say this, but lay experts, adding that to bring down the curtain on history definitively, we do not even need the earthshaking scene of nuclear apocalypse. The daily malfunctioning of "progress" and "development," which are the heart, the hope, the life of modern ideologies beginning with Marxism, will be enough. In any case, the apocalypse is a well-founded scientific hypothesis today, not only a religious prospect.

Well now: if humanity should disappear from the face of the earth, how can we deny that all the immense efforts and the unprecedented suffering, requested by the "avant-garde of progress" from so many hidden, enthusiastic, or reluctant men, have been in vain? In the words of Joseph Gevaert:[7]

> That the end will come early or late makes little difference. Science says this will happen sooner or later, that the human race will not last as long as the dinosaurs. But science is invoked by these men only when it behooves them. Thus, for Marxist thinkers, not only the end of man, but also the prospect of an end of humanity is taboo.

Beyond the slogans and the dialectical ruses that enchant fewer and fewer people (especially fewer and fewer youth, instinctively in need of sincerity and truth), reason seems to be on the side of Ernst Bloch. This great philosopher, though a tormented Marxist, was expelled first from his East German university and then from East Germany itself, accused of "corrupting the youth"—the same accusation hurled at Socrates before he was forced to drink the hemlock.

Bloch was banished (and his disciples sent to jail) because he dared to remind them of truths such as this:

---

[7] Editor's Note: Joseph Gevaert (1930–2019), Salesian priest and scholar in the field of catechetics.

Death is a radical anti-utopia. Death is the terribly realistic warning for one who believes he can explain everything with dogmatic formulas; for one who believes in "scientific readings of history" that resolve every problem; for one who believes he can give answers to all the questions that emerge from the heart of man with economic and social reforms. Death is the insurmountable contradiction for the powerful who delude themselves thinking they can eliminate every unpleasant reality by pulling the only levers at their disposal: politics, economy, and law enforcement.

CHAPTER 3

A Skeleton in the Closet of the West

Styles

THEY WOULD GLADLY HAVE fired at death from the guard towers of the Iron Curtain, from the rooftops of the offices of every communist party in the world, if only to force it into hiding.

But neither in the West, the so-called "free world," would they grant death a passport.

Death is the grand asylum-seeker of our time, banished desperately from both unions, the North American and the Eurasian, which have dominated with armaments and with the force of their ideologies, apparently opposing each other, but which to the attentive observer reveal themselves to be quarrelsome daughters of the same mother. We shall see this more clearly, pointing out that the confrontation with death immediately reveals the truth: in this case, the brotherhood between Washington and Moscow.

But the disturbing stranger is not concerned about these groups; borders do not exist for him. "Against all that is an enemy, it is possible to procure a defense. Then there is death. Death is what makes us all live in an unfortified city." This is what Epicurus acknowledged, the same one who deluded himself into erecting a fortress denying the reality of the enemy. Things have not changed: not even a barrage of missiles could possibly keep the disturber of every system at bay.

The West: that part of the world whose symbols and myths, besides Coca-Cola and the heroine needle, can be found in *Playboy*, a magazine for the average frustrated man.

The shiny monthly published in Chicago allows intellectuals to look at naked women, a pleasure for nearly all men, whether college graduates or illiterates, without feeling less intelligent and well-educated. It is a symbol of America such that (the story is true, not a joke) the federal government financed a braille edition for the blind. Hugh Hefner, legendary founder and director of *Playboy*, obliged the innumerable international editions throughout the West to use a stylebook, a manual with mandatory rules for putting the magazine together. That stylebook states in its general introduction: "In *Playboy*, it is prohibited to talk about children, prisons, disasters, the elderly, illness. But above all, it is strictly forbidden to talk about death."

Like the silence of Marx, the prohibition of Hefner is neither isolated nor random: it is the same that holds in every advertising agency. And publicity is the very soul of the West: without it, the entire productive mechanism would get jammed up. Just as in Moscow or Beijing, so in New York, Frankfurt, or Milan, one cannot concede space to a reality that is in irreconcilable contradiction with the entire system.

If someone were not to follow the rules of the game that Hefner had the merit of clarifying, and the forbidden questions were allowed, in the East the police would be in the streets, whereas in the West a team of specialists would be sent into action ready to diagnose a "nervous exhaustion," prescribe powerful tranquilizers, and above all counsel "distractions."

In fact, only the most naïve still suggest a period of rest in such cases. One now understands that there can be no therapy worse than allowing a man time to think. "A king," observed Pascal, "left to reflect on what he is and what he shall be, would become in a brief time the most unhappy of the most miserable of his subjects who works and is distracted." Stopping to reflect is the worst condemnation for citizens of societies that are based on the refusal to face the reality of the human condition.

It is true, as Pascal notices, that "all our problems derive from the fact that we do not know how to be still in a room." But the reality is that we cannot be still, because "he who wants to forget about death, though it is certain and inevitable, must avoid rest and must look for nothing more than agitation."

This is an agitation that Pascal calls *divertissement*, "di-version" understood in its etymological sense of "divert" or "distract" or "lead away" or "turn in another direction;"[8] another direction, namely, than that which leads toward the end, raises unresolvable questions both in the East and in the West. Thus, on one side, the ideal is Stakhanovism, the worker who has no free time; on the other side, the proposed ideal of advertising is the "dynamic lifestyle" in which there is not one moment to stand still.

It is no wonder that in the logic of things, Western society is and will always be a "society of di-version/entertainment." It is the society that demonizes solitude, a dangerous luxury that only the sage, the hermit, the monk can be allowed; or, on the contrary, the madman, the fool—namely, only the ones who have fully come to terms with themselves, or those who cannot.

It is a society that promotes (increasingly on the public dime) the old *circensis*, the spectacles offered by the empire to the Roman plebians to keep them under control, ennobling the din of today with definitions of odd and conformist jargon like "emerging question of new culture." Giuseppe Prezzolini confirms this, though he should be taken with due caution: "Men who entertain become celebrities, the Benjamins of the crowd, and are considered benefactors of the human race: they help us to forget for several hours that we must die."

This is the society that placed its technological resources at the service of a mission that speaks volumes: the mission to kill silence. Silence is a friend only to those who "re-flect," of those who bow down to examine themselves; it is the terrible enemy, on the other hand, of those who want to turn in another direction to be entertained.

There is an attempt here to pass off as a sign of "cultural progress" the programmed uproar, always and everywhere agitated by the incredible increase in musical consumption, the more appreciated the louder it is.

In reality, whoever is not blinded by superficial slogans feels pity more than admiration for the unfortunate youth who, leaving his room where the full volume hi-fi sound system or the transistor radio have accompanied his every moment, then pulls his headphones over his ears and hurries to the dance club. And tomorrow it starts all over, as soon as the alarm clock goes off.

---

[8] [Translator's note: The Italian word *divertimento* has as its primary meaning "entertainment, amusement, fun," which is reflected in the second entry found in the Webster English Dictionary under "diversion": something that diverts or amuses; a pastime.]

Konrad Lorenz, the wise, old Nobel Prize winner, a specialist in the behavioral study of animals (and isn't man part of the animal kingdom?), says, "This rampant need for noise can be explained only by the need to suffocate something."

Thus, in the pity for the youth dazed by the noise, one can add the adult businessman as well, smoking a cigar and always running after the presumed "spontaneous fashions" of the new generations and speculating on the need to assassinate the silence. He too, the poor devil, another victim of a culture that can survive only by dulling itself and others with noise, even if it is "musical," with drugs and alcohol, or perhaps with travel.

Suspicious Cults

Yes, precisely those trips that are another of the biggest businesses in the West and whose boom, equal to that of TV shows and entertainment of every type, is considered with a tender eye by sociologists and journalists (either too clever or too naïve) who see there, or act like they see, only "cultural motivations."

As displayed with monotonous constancy by all surveys, asked about what he most desires, the average man throughout the West puts one verb alone at the top: *to travel*. Among our obsessions, travel is truly at the center of a new cult.

And yet, the old universal saying reminds us that what really counts is not so much seeing as knowing the world. And if one must set off on a journey to see it, to know it one must simply stand still and observe the life of a village. The greatest thinkers and the most famous sages were sedentary.

One often forgets that travel as it is conceived today, without any other purpose than amusement and distraction, is an entirely new phenomenon in history. As long as life is lived within a system of values in which one finds answers (true or not, but at least real answers) to the questions about living and dying, man did not feel the need to escape. Not by chance is the English word *travel* the same as the Italian word *travaglio* (suffering; anguish, distress; birthing labor) and the French word *travail* (work, job, profession); travel was understood to be an exertion, something risky, an expense to be faced only for good reasons — pilgrimage, business, instruction — and never simply as "distraction" or "evasion," as is said quite meaningfully.

To explain this total upheaval of perspective, it seems inadequate merely to cite the revolution in transportation that has rendered faster, easier, and safer what once was slow, uncomfortable, and dangerous.

There must be something more, perhaps the something that Martin Heidegger referred to: "Today's man is on the run." Heidegger was convinced, as we know, that all of life stands under the sign of the prospect of death and that the worst, most illusory remedy is the non-acceptance of reality. "To be on the run means always admitting that one is aware of an imminent danger and a threat." The most dangerous danger, the most threatening threat is the end that is incumbent upon all of us.

At any rate, how is it that phenomena like the superstitious elevation of the *weekend* to the status of an idol (all the more so insofar as a society is wealthy and "advanced") escape reflection? There are many, serious studies that show how, around this new obsession, typical religious attitudes have been coagulating: *human* sacrifice, if it is true that those who set out on the roads every Friday evening in the United States are blithe to the fact that at least fifteen thousand of them will not return and another thirty thousand will be injured in accidents of every type; *economic* sacrifice, the tithe, the offering of money, as demonstrated by the fact that Europeans and Americans say they are willing to renounce every other expense except that for their car and for gas to go out on the weekend; *bodily* sacrifice, the "mortification" that leads one to place on the altar of the idol even one's health, as occupational health workers attest on Monday morning in the increase in physical and psychic exhaustion.

Also suspect and irrational is another of the many religious cults of societies that consider themselves secular and "liberated," but which, denying death, have become neurotic, looking for escape in any direction. The cult, also unheard of throughout history, of the young and of youth—namely, of what is farthest from death. It is a cult that, like all religions, demonizes the idol's adversary—in this case, the elderly and old age.

One seeks to render the new cult credible by presenting it as "progressive" or "left-leaning," and therefore good and appropriate. Actually, there is an illuminating booklet penned by one Dr. Joseph Goebbels, the Nazi Propaganda Minister of the Third Reich. The title is *Youth on Parade*, and it begins this way: "The youth is always right. The elderly have no right to exercise influence over them." History eventually revealed just how right the Hitler Youth would be. On the other side of the Alps, Fascism had chosen as its hymn a song called *Giovinezza* (*Youth*).

In these decades, beyond the borders of East and West, the Nazi–Fascist cult of youth has not only been perpetuated, but even exalted. In reality, there is ever greater need to exorcize (by means of whatever is young, whatever is new) the nightmare of death, and to hide the old which, by its mere presence, warns of what awaits us all. Any attempt to moralize, invoking the usual reforms and organizing the usual inconclusive conventions on "the condition of the elderly," is useless: this is the logic of present-day fascist, socialist, and capitalist cultures.

What remains is the enormous injustice committed against the elderly by these generations, by these regimes; it will be worthwhile to revisit this cruelty, one of many, of our barbarism toward the human countenance.

"Sadistic, Cruel, Traumatic"

If in the West one is concerned about death and the dead, it is only for the sake of business: the best-selling books, in America and in Europe, are detective and spy novels, where at least one corpse is indispensable. The same holds for films and TV series: death is entertainment — the death of others, at least — as long as it's fiction.

In real life, however, death must not exist.

Just as I was working on writing these pages, the TV was flooded for two days with the direct transmission of emergency crews trying to rescue a child who had fallen down a well. This anguishing "spectacle" was interrupted by commercials, water polo matches, and adventure series. When it was announced that the rescue efforts had failed and that the child had died, an outraged mob assailed those responsible for the operation, attempted to lynch the rescue crews, and the next day the newspapers asked for the resignation of the commander of the fire department, responsible only for not having done the impossible, for not having performed a miracle.

As in the pages of the *Reader's Digest* (together with *Playboy*, a magazine emblematic of the West), life must be a pleasant fairytale with a happy ending. Pouncing on the firemen and demanding their exemplary punishment, the commoners and journalists were really protesting against the poor child, guilty of having reminded them that death *still* exists, despite every technological prodigy.

But whoever recalls this harsh truth is lost, as Professor Herman Feifel can testify. This American psychologist, rebelling against the behavior of so many of his colleagues who labeled as "mental breakdown" the curiosity to ask the wrong questions out loud, was among the first to break the conspiracy of silence. And so, challenging the taboo, he came out with a volume on his despised specialization: the psychological behavior of the dying and of those who, in some way, are in direct contact with death.

The revenge of a system that cannot bear to be disturbed was unleashed upon Feifel: his university dismissed him, protesting that his research was not "scientific," but rather sadistic, cruel, and traumatic. His own colleagues, some threatening to drag him into court accusing him of "inhumanity," proposed that he be expelled from the professional guild, preventing him from doing any further research.

Although doctors often project upon themselves many religious (or better, superstitious) needs in a society that seeks to venerate in them the wizards and shamans of the past, doctors are not demigods descended from the heavens: they are products of our culture.

They are the ones, then, who do not mention death to the students in their departments, with the excuse that death is a "philosophical" problem; they are the ones (beginning with the so-called "family doctor") whose choices result in ninety percent of their cases ending their days in a hospital ghetto rather than at home, where death would be more humane for the assisted and less costly for society, but more disturbing for those who wish to hide it.

It is doctors who, obsequious to mass conformity as is everyone, have purged their terminology: death (the greatest challenge to their power) they have never called by its true name, but have always defined it using Latin and thus obfuscating reality: *exitus*, "end," "exit." Now, even the dying person has lost his status, being modestly called a "terminal patient."

EXORCISMS

Such "modesty" is just one aspect of a general phenomenon. Our culture has created the most terrifying instruments of extermination in history and has literally invented the formerly unknown concept of "mass death," not only with the various bombs (atomic, hydrogen, neutron) but with the various genocides of the twentieth century. And yet, precisely in this culture of death, there is a race to be the most delicate, genteel, and compassionate when one is forced to allude to death.

One of the modern synonyms for death, cancer, has become an "incurable disease," "unforgiving disease," or in a scholarly manner, using the Greek, "neoplasia," while the cancer doctor hides behind the label "oncologist."

Who in the obituaries (or using the less explicit "necrologies") is capable of finding just one, simple, terrible, and true "died"? One will find many "has left us," "is no longer with us," "passed away," or even, with a more deprecatory than religious intent, "still lives."

Gorer, the sociologist who described the pornography of death, remarked that in English, supposedly the most "evolved" language in the world, the expression "dead person" used to indicate a cadaver is gradually disappearing. Doctors, nurses, relatives prefer to use the term employed for the sick: a *patient*.

In this abuse of a euphemism (from the dictionary: "A rhetorical figure that aims at attenuating the crudeness of a specific idea of a specific fact"), "adult" society brings back some decrepit superstitions: it is for so-called "primitives" that pronouncing an unpleasant word draws near the reality.

Behind such euphemisms there is not only a superstitious terror; there is also a good dose of hypocrisy, of egoism masked as "charity." Linguists report that this masked exorcism of the euphemism is used only apparently out of respect toward *the one of whom it speaks*; in reality, it is aimed at protecting *the one who speaks*.

Thus, for example, the elderly are persecuted, reduced to rubbish by the same society that would never call them "old people," but rather contritely calls them "elderly." Out of due respect, to be clear! Old age? What a brutal, impolite word! Good mannered as we are, we should rather say "senior citizen," or even "in one's golden years."

By using these delicate words, these euphemisms, we are certainly not protecting old people, but ourselves. We exorcise death with the help of this vocabulary to *our* advantage, not for the sake of the "elderly," for whom our reverence immediately diminishes as we pass from words to deeds.

Thus, social services throughout the West struggle to cover the demand for home health care for the elderly, regardless of the unemployment rate. We must understand: who would gladly work in daily contact with one who warns you today of what you too will be tomorrow? Seeing this, you are made to understand that after the "golden years" there are no more years left.

For the same reason the category of hospital nurses is, throughout the world, the most turbulent on the level of trade unions, with continual turmoil and very high absenteeism.

"It's strange," confessed the newly appointed Minister of Health in Italy, "the more you give them, the unhappier they are." The blessed innocence of a politician who thinks he's clever! Those working in close contact with death need to be given something quite different than what ministers and union leaders are able to give.

To Hide, to Hide Oneself

"Advanced" societies and their prophets have, for some time now, imposed their teaching upon children of everything that can be known about coitus and its techniques. And who today would deny that sexual education is appropriate and important? Who could ignore the decisive space of sex in human life? But why hide, and with so much snarly zeal, from those preparing for life, another aspect equally important and real in each person's life?

And so, on the thresholds of hospital morgues (where the terrible, solitary "death behind closed doors" of technocratic societies takes place), severe pedagogues keep watch, having decreed the absolute untimeliness that anyone should see this sight, especially children. These latter must know everything about how a younger sibling came into the world, but must know nothing about how and where grandma left it.

In the United States (where, by law, minors of fourteen can get abortions, but cannot enter a hospital ward) there are countless successful divorce cases against a partner accused of mental cruelty for having allowed their child to see a dying relative, or worse, their corpse.

The sight of death has become so obscene that the dying are isolated from all eyes that are not coldly professional technicians. One expires abandoned to specialists; alone, even if, in more sophisticated cases, in the midst of a crowd of mercenaries. Calculations of the German Health Ministry show that, over the course of twenty-four hours, more than forty experts circulated around the beds of an intensive care ward.

In this aseptic environment, amid the buzzing of devices and the flashing of colored lights, the eternal mystery of dying has been debased, and by cruel irony, is more debased the more the society is wealthy and "advanced." The bare technical fact of death is reported on a monitor, by electronic sounds, by curves on a graph.

The patient is asked to respect a precise code of etiquette, the acceptable style of facing death — "acceptable," one must understand, by the healthy, who demand that the patient does not disturb them. The moribund must not complain, ask questions, feign ignorance of the truth, but must die without ever mentioning death. Above all, he must try to end it during the normal working hours of the staff.

Given that some will insist on dying, they can at least show good taste and do so without creating a fuss, like polite people; or better, clandestinely, hiding themselves in an arranged placed — just like when one needs to urinate or defecate, we lock ourselves into the toilet.

If the moribund is indecent, he will be even more obscene when dead. Just as those dying should act like they are not dying, so the cadaver should not seem dead.

In America, the problem has been solved at funeral homes, specialized in the technique of "final make-up." Thanks to specialized cosmetics, the face of the cumbersome corpse will rediscover its true colors, its body will assume real-life positions — working, relaxing, at the desk or on the recliner, perhaps smoking a pipe or a cigar.

Beware of laughing: these are not macabre Yankee antics, curious American fixations. Rather, these are the desperate defense mechanisms of a society obliged to expel what it has no room for, arriving at the logical conclusions. Beneath the expensive rites at those funeral homes one finds the same force that led to the previously unheard-of usage of building modern homes with doors and stairs too narrow to pass a coffin through. Thus it happens that those few who have not been hidden in time in the designated hospital morgues have to be lowered from the windows of their homes, constructed under the presupposition that those who live in them will never have to die.

FIVE STAGES OF DYING

For some time now, a few have begun to rebel. Through the breach opened by the persecuted Herman Feifel, a team of doctors, psychologists, and theologians — guided by Elisabeth Kübler-Ross, a Swiss-German psychiatrist working in Chicago — was able to sneak through. The group interrogated thousands of dying people, clashing with the furious resistance of doctors (as was foreseeable) who, according to Kübler-Ross, "reached the point of denying that there were people close to death in their wards." The conclusions of that courageous research are disturbing: from the very first suspicion of death, in every man and woman, violent reactions are unleashed.

There are four phases through which we must all pass.

The first phase or stage is that of denial: "That's not possible!" The second phase is that of rebellion: "Why me?" The third phase is that of pleading with God and with destiny: "Just give me another year!" The fourth is that of depression and desperation.

"Only in the best of cases," Elisabeth Kübler-Ross writes, "does one arrive at a *fifth* phase, that of acceptance: 'I'm ready.'"

Analogous and parallel phases are lived out by the family of the dying. They, too, often do not reach the last phase of acceptance, and they pay the unfathomably high human price.

Against the doctors who wanted to impede it, the work of Kübler-Ross's team was defended by the patients themselves. "We are grateful to you," repeated the unfortunate.

> We can finally talk about the drama we are forced to live through alone, in silence, because that's what the doctors and our relatives want, saying we shouldn't talk about death. Every time we try to mention it, we are silenced, and they refer us to hopes that we know are illusory.

Kübler-Ross writes, "If many are not able to die in peace but go angry and rebelling, this is due to the hospital staff and to the family members with their attitude of neurotic denial of reality."

This is how one dies in the proud, expensive hospitals, in the "temples of knowledge": alone, behind closed doors, and desperate, with one's face to the wall.

The Chicago researchers conclude:

> The fear of talking about death is a fear imposed by this society. Once the conspiracy of silence is broken, the dying find great comfort. Even more: to the final and optimal stage, that of acceptance, only the patients and relatives who can speak freely about death will arrive. Better yet, and infallibly, those few arrive at this who, since childhood, have been habituated to confronting their own finitude. If, from when one is young and healthy, one reaches the state of acceptance of one's own inevitable death, not only would passing away be easier and human, but we would live a richer life, with true values, we would truly know what the joy of living is all about.

Not by chance have the books of Elisabeth Kübler-Ross sold millions of copies in the United States alone, confirming a profound and immutable need, despite the violent repression and protests of the establishment.

In the Freezer

Ivan Illich, a writer and Catholic priest who fought to denounce what was hiding behind the shiny Western display cabinet, wrote, "Only the pain that one considers remediable shows itself to be unbearable."

One must presume, then, that the most atrocious of all is the death of those wealthy Americans who, under the illusion that they can prove wrong the age-old wisdom ("There's a remedy for all things, except for death"), have recourse to so-called cryogenic technology.

This is the extreme expedient for denying reality. After signing agreements and disbursing large sums of money, when the moment comes, specialized companies freeze-dry the cadaver in liquid nitrogen, as anti-freeze is injected into the arteries. After this treatment, the corpse is placed into a refrigerator tomb (the "cryo-cryptoriums") in confident hope that "science" and "progress" will perform the miracle of finding a cure for whatever caused the person's death. Then the cadaver would have to be thawed, reanimated, cured, and returned like new to carry on with business.

This is not the isolated oddity of some eccentric: the cryogenic business is thriving in profits and development. It is sustained by the ranting of the usual professors of futurology, who hypothesize a society organized around gigantic refrigerator crypts while technicians work on the new science of resurrection.

There is, in fact, a theologian (among the odious traits of our time is the theologian who competes with the sociologist and the op-ed page in supporting whatever people want to hear) who foresees in the near future "a guaranteed victory over death thanks to the technical improvements of organ transplants."

Too bad the Reverend forgets that (besides every other consideration) in order to transplant into a living body a heart, liver, or brain, one needs a heart, liver, or brain from a dead body. And that dead body will remain just that, because he was deprived of his organs for the good of another human being. Assuming a victory of this sort over death, it would be the victory of some thanks to the definitive death of others.

Everything, even the denial of rationality, can serve for the consolation of these sons of the "culture of reason."

"Sixty-Eight"

I brought up this hysterical denial that unites East and West (provoking social problems that we will analyze in greater depth in subsequent chapters) to a colleague once, a well-known commentator in Italy taken seriously by his readers.

Though superficial, this friend was honest and this topic must have interested him, because a few days later he made a cautious exploration in the "enlightened" newspaper he collaborated with. Grappling with yet another analysis of the "youth situation," he reiterated that today's society does not offer ideals nor does it offer them meaning in life or in death. Death, in fact, "if it were the case," he asked, "that we progressive secularists, should begin to face the problem, and stop acting as if it didn't exist?" My colleague did not go any further than formulating this cautious question. But having become an expert from the many preceding experiences, I awaited a reaction amused and ironic. I didn't have to wait long: the reply, quick as it was irascible, arrived the next day. In that same newspaper, another famous journalist with sociological ambitions, another "maestro," scolded wildly the sacrilegious hand that wrote those lines daring to include the prohibited word.

"Death," began this journalist, with a predictable script, "is a problem for adolescents." But he continued unexpectedly, "If 1968 taught us anything it's that we have to avoid consolations." Verbatim: "1968," "consolations."[9]

Actually, the article under accusation did not ask at all for "consoling" answers; it only proposed a question, everyone being free to draw their own conclusions.

Would it be, then, a "consolation" unworthy of an adult to accept the human condition, welcoming the questions that it arouses? While avoiding even just the thought, would mentioning what is unpleasant qualify as "being adult," a being in need of "the lessons of 1968"? As always, to expect logic is to expect the impossible: deluding oneself with being able to discuss as an intellectual problem

---

[9] [Translator's note: In Europe, "1968" in this sense refers not to the year itself but to the broad revolutionary cultural movement that swept through the continent, nearly causing a revolution in France and generally challenging social mores throughout Western Europe. It signifies not a point on the calendar so much as a cultural moment. It serves as a similar signifier to "the counterculture" in English.]

what, for those "teachers," is, in reality, a psychological problem, is simply naïve. What is logic worth in the face of neuroses?

The Frenchman Roland Barthes, one of the most revered masters of 1968, was asked, "Why is it that in all your books you avoided the problem of death?" The oracle's response was the following: "I am a subject of language. For me, therefore, death is in language. Language is the space of death. On one side, language as absence; on the other side, death is in the fact that language is the gaze of the basilisk that crystallizes and fascinates." The interviewer, head of the culture section of one of the most prestigious international weeklies, was contrite as he registered these clear and tonic words for the reader whom he imagined in devoted expectancy. Behold, the masters who teach us to avoid consolations, who demonize them in order to find others hidden behind the smoke screen of their incomprehensible chatter.

Pierre Chaunu, a Christian and a famous historian of culture at the University of Paris, wrote:

> In the East as in the West, not being able to chase death away from life, it was decreed that it is shameful, it is unworthy of us, that it must be driven out of our thoughts. They threw excommunication at it because it destabilizes all of the hegemonic cultures of our time. Incapable of giving it a place, they hid it, banished it, prohibited it. But they are not deceived, these powerful masters of thought of the present moment: it is not that easy to put death to death.

BOURGEOIS AND RADICAL

To the East, in the countries of so-called "real socialism," Marxism had already been dead for some time in the heart of the people; it survived as a power structure, as an imperialism equal to its American counterpart.

As I write, the results of a survey were published, semi-clandestine but reliable, in parts of the Eastern bloc. It turned out that, if there were to be free elections, the local communist parties would have the vote of three out of every hundred electors. This was even fewer than the percentage of those who directly or indirectly worked for those parties.

Ernesto Balducci, an Italian essayist and one of the most attentive to movements in contemporary society, an openly left-wing theologian, recognized one of the causes of this Marxist ideological collapse in the fact that they carried out "a revolution without appropriation of the problem of death." In this way, he said, what one can create, at most, "is an old man within a new economy." "New" meaning the inept, ferocious State-run capitalism which we have seen as the concrete result of so many promises. But hope is evergreen...

"To find a Marxist still around, you have to leave Marxist countries and look to the capitalist ones," Alain Besançon, perhaps the leading Kremlinologist of our time, ironically noted. "Only in the West can you still find someone who places his hope in Marx, Stalin, Lenin, Mao and in what they represented." But also in the West, the myth of "scientific" communism, with all of its variants, is lost among those who were excited about it: the youth, the intelligentsia, the bourgeoisie. Not among the working classes, who were never Marxist, if one looks beyond the narrow province of ex-Catholic countries (Italy, France, Spain) and simultaneously excludes the Third World, with its problems of underdevelopment. In countries with a solid, long-standing industrial tradition (United States, West Germany, Great Britain, Switzerland, Scandinavia), even with millions of workers, the Marxist-Leninist parties are irrelevant, or they simply do not exist for a lack of adherents.

The empty place left by the decline of this political mythology in countries where it had taken hold, or the "eclipse of the sacred" from the religious crisis in other countries, is occupied by a culture generically called "radical." Its influence is enormous and growing, and goes well beyond its meager electoral results: it is, in fact, more a state of mind than a structured ideology, although its characteristic traits are easily recognizable.

Here, in this so-called "radical area," are gathered the movements that most characterize the contemporary world: feminism, homosexuality, objectors of every sort, nudists, drug cultists. Here, for a lack of better merchandise at the myth market, one finds the youth of our day, who merit much more than this ambiguous cocktail of ideologies.

And yet, precisely due to this confusing radical culture so representative in the West today, one of the essential vital necessities is the legalization of euthanasia.

We shall try to explain this by remembering that there are at least two types of euthanasia.

There is one type which the conformists of the "radical area," draped in all things alternative and subversive, condemn as "inhumane." But there is another type that the same conformists define "humane," "progressive," and for the sake of which he is ready to fight against obscurantism, naturally the clerical type.

In reality, the profound motivations of both types of euthanasia are the same: in both cases embarrassing and obscure.

The first type of euthanasia (the "bad" type) is called "social," and is what was practiced in our time on an industrial scale by the Nazis. It must not be overlooked that these malefactors enjoyed abundant sponsoring. In the 1920s, Alexis Carrel, Nobel Prize winner for medicine, proposed the suppression of entire social categories: from the elderly, to the mentally infirm, to the incurables. But even Plato, in the *Republic*, recommended the same: "Citizens who are not healthy in body are to be left to die." The second type of euthanasia (the "good" type) is called "agonic," and is advocated by the same people who are horrified by the appalling "social hygiene" practiced by Hitler's SS. This type is "criminal" while the former type is "civil progress," because it is aimed at avoiding the useless suffering of the dying. Beneficent even in its name: *euthanasia*, namely "good death," "death through pity," "through love."

On the contrary, next to death and abortion, euthanasia in its "agonic" variant is the third, inevitable ring that completes the chain that modern cultures parade around their neck. Euthanasia is the Third Person of the Trinity of those radicals who (despite their pathetic efforts to be considered "left-wing," to share that magical title "companion") are none other than the legitimate children of the West's capitalist, bourgeois liberalism. At the most, if they really insist, they can be granted the title "liberals of the left."

Not by coincidence do the bigger bourgeois newspapers, those bloated with expensive, full-color advertising, frequent the radical camp; while the mere sight of one of these gentlemen unleashes virulent eczema on the skin of a Marxist. In the West, in the battles over divorce, abortion, and euthanasia, it is the radicals who drag forward the communists who, in their own countries, recognize that trinity in their legal codes, but at the same time do all they can to inhibit their subjects from worshipping that god. From its Judeo-Christian origins, Marxism has preserved a sense of sociality, the sentiment of being part of a collective solidarity.

Radicalism, on the other hand, bears the Original Sin of that bourgeois capitalist liberalism that generated it and which makes it prosper: individualism which necessarily degenerates into violent egoism. The heart of the liberal radical's message is, as he himself says, "the right to my happiness." Everything that contrasts with this program must be attacked as detrimental: *mors tua, vita mea*.

Behind this culture that exalts divorce and abortion there is a precise egoistic motive, however much it might be drowned in a flood of noble words. What we really want is to liberate ourselves with as little effort as possible (and with the blessing, and its contribution to the expenses, of society) from our spouses, our unborn children, and our unwanted hindrances.

Behind the Noble Battles

The same individualism that is behind the exaltation of divorce and abortion is behind the typically liberal capitalist radical struggle to legalize euthanasia. Once again (as for the spouse or the fetus that are in our way) what we want is the elimination of our problem by eliminating the other.

The request is that society must eliminate those who in bad taste refuse to die, those whose impudence has demonstrated through their agony that something similar awaits us, too. Nothing is more unbearable to this culture than such a spectacle.

Behind this "noble battle" for euthanasia, behind its "highly civil and humanitarian" motivations, there is also this snake pit. At the level of concrete facts, there is the same impulse that, on the level of words, pushes the use of a euphemism: protect *us* and not "the old person" or "the sick person in the terminal phase"; save *us*, we who are still healthy and vital, rather than the dying.

Whether they are aware or not, these courageous paladins of euthanasia want the state's help, coupled with that of modern medicine and its techniques of rapid suppression, out of compassion for *themselves* more than for those in agony. One wants to terminate this indecent scene right from the start. One wants to be liberated as soon as possible, in a hypocritically clean and legal manner, from the questions that arise from the beds of the dying, and to which one is impotent to respond.

It is the same need to terminate those questions, suffocating the one expressing them through their suffering, that pushes for an emergency remedy in those countries in America and Northern Europe where euthanasia has not yet been legalized. Not able to inject that poison into the veins of patients, they use drugs that transform their cries of pain into cries of hilarity. Agony is transformed into euphoria — to the benefit, it is clear, not of the one robbed of his death. The mysterious nobility of dying is transformed into a lugubrious circus; but it is all to the benefit of the one otherwise condemned to witness it.

A document of the German episcopate, which we cite here not for its religious content (the time has not yet come) but for the spark of human truth it contains, states: "The greatest difficulty in assisting the dying consists in the fact that the death of a person requires the one assisting him to face his own death, too."

Who can stand this encounter? How can the sons of this culture do what the culture itself has organized in order to avoid it? Will the radicals be able to bear it with their mystical understanding of "partying" and "gaming" and "entertainment" and "health" and "beauty"? The one who (it's enough to flip through their magazines and look at the ads) proclaims that the only life worth living is the one that gives full satisfaction? The one who decrees that pleasure must be exhibited and tears hidden? That radical who, even when he fasts for his "humanitarian causes," seems to do so only to trim down a bit?[10]

[10] As I write, the leader of the Italian radicals, with an initiative contested even within his own party, promoted a raucous campaign urging Parliament to allocate millions "to save the lives of the hungry in the Third World." The initiative moved some goodhearted simpletons, but could not deceive those who still know how to reflect. In fact, it does not deny but rather confirms the petty, bourgeois, and individualist character of this way of thinking that is called "radical." We see here the typical capitalist mentality that thinks it can resolve everything (that it can, therefore, eliminate even a resurgence of a sense of guilt) by throwing money at it. Money is taken as the omnipotent divinity, as the prodigious wonderworker for every evil, physical or moral.

In reality, the dramatic problem of human misery demands a conversion, a personal sacrifice. The many Christian missionaries and lay volunteers have understood this better than anyone, who spend their lives day after day next to the marginalized, sharing their sufferings, doing what they can to alleviate them, ensuring at least a "presence," not merely economical, which is at the opposite pole from the comfortable hypocrisy of the radical. The latter would like to appease his conscience in some way, without touching his own life or his own wallet. On one side, the greatest "sacrifice" the radical submits to is the sit-in in front of a television station to grab an interview for propaganda purposes for himself or the party, or for its "generous causes." On the other side, he asks for the allocation of public funds that, belonging to everyone, are considered to belong to no one by the bourgeois mentality and thus also by the radicals.

Strange help: granted by the benevolence of Western countries that, after having disturbed the millenarian balance for their economic interests, now they would like to resolve the dramas they have provoked and are daily making worse. Countries that carry out every year the systematic destruction of enormous quantities of foodstuffs (fruit, eggs, wine, and meat) to maintain prices at higher levels, while sending food to the hungry. Everyone knows (and everyone acts as if they didn't) that this "aid for the poor" is only gifts between politicians, to the avaricious leaders of Third World countries who steal significant proportions

If no one can get involved in that confrontation with one's own death, which alone makes it possible to help others confront *their* deaths, then euthanasia is a necessary choice: provide it as soon as possible, for their deaths are indispensable to protect the living, who are frantically immersed in organizing conferences, festivals, "clear-headed moments," shows in town squares, "intelligent vacations," non-competitive marches, telethons, and so forth.

The agony we and others will have to face is the moment of nakedness, of complete truth. How can we pretend that those who have chased after "truths" can bear the prolonging of that agony, in the moment those "truths" are revealed as partial, superficial, and at any rate impotent to explain or console?

This is why the liberalization of euthanasia will invariably find a place in our legal codes (as it has at any rate in many countries), next to divorce and abortion. This is why the usual, unfaltering Catholic opposition will be defeated as usual by the next referendum. What use is it to fight for particular aspects of a culture, which, to survive, must neurotically suffocate everything that is unbearable to it? They cannot do otherwise, prisoners of their own premises.

Organic and logical in its consequences is a "religious" vision of man and of the world that goes so far as to reject euthanasia. But equally organic, equally logical in its consequences is the vision of man that goes so far as to

---

of these funds. The crumbs that arrive to the truly needy often aggravate the problem. But what does it matter? What matters is certainly not the poor, but the motives of politicians, their interests, their propaganda, and their stuffy bourgeois attitudes.

Besides an obscure sense of guilt, besides their outrageous hypocrisy, demagoguery, business deals, behind the propaganda of their "altruism," of which the radical is the standard bearer, there are also less transparent motivations. There is the ancient, often unconscious fear of the well-off white man before the masses of black people, of foreigners, of homeless, who one day might mobilize and, like modern-day barbarians, invade the kingdom of Western opulence. The unconfessed hope of those "heroes" is to keep the danger at bay, entrusting himself to the protection of the god of money. While the protest for "aid" that protects their well-being makes them feel generous, costs them nothing, and resolves nothing concretely, they repeat obsessively that the threatening "others" should be convinced to be castrated and sterilized, and to take birth control pills and increase the number of their abortions. They say they are pro-life, but they are for as few lives as possible. While they call a crusade for an uncertain salvation of the living, they advocate the certain massacre of the unborn. It is today's logic: protect those already safe, those who already have a job, those already under a roof, those already born.

remonstrate with it. Every tree bears its fruit, it cannot do otherwise: "Are grapes gathered from thorns, or figs from thistles?" (Matt. 7:16).

What good can come of trying to demolish a few unpleasant points in light of the enormous iceberg that is running its course (a question I ask perplexed Catholics who still trust in elections, judges, legal codes, and law enforcement)? What good can come of going to war with dull swords against inevitable aspects of an entire system?

Is there any sense in trying to impose some aspect of a *moral system* without first proposing a *faith*? And, with that faith, a vision of man that, despite certain appearances and the broad reassurances of the easy-going, the superficial, the theologians of the "warm and fuzzy," is antithetical to those who dominate the communist and bourgeois worlds?

In the religious perspective, there is a place for sin; there is a place for what is otherwise absurd: evil, pain, death. All of these are realities that Marxism and capitalism (in all their variants) must hide or promise to eliminate through social reforms and salary increases.

They have oriented their house toward what they say is the south, while the religious person says that there has been a misunderstanding: it is actually the north. And when winter comes, they will die of cold. If they fail to convince them to change the entire orientation of the house, taking away from them something like euthanasia would be like trying to take from them their windows or wood for their stove. This would mean unleashing a desperate fight for survival, as was seen in Italy and around the world in the virulent campaigns to legalize divorce and abortion — and, as we shall soon see, to legalize euthanasia.

Have I mistaken the diagnosis? Have I deceived myself? Here, as always, I am sincerely open to self-examination: it would not be a new experience for me. Elsewhere I have subjected myself to questioning when it was shown to be needed. I try never to forget that, according to every psychologist, the presumption to be right all the time is a sure sign of mental instability.

Why Now?

Certainly: there are hidden motives in the protesters who line the streets advocating the liberalization of euthanasia; but the drama of the dying and of their suffering is also tragically real. *Who knows how we will behave when it is our turn?* Reasoning calmly, seated in good health at a table in a peaceful room, is not exactly watching yourself die in physical and psychological conditions we have never experienced. "The suffering of a dying person cries out, and crying out cannot be explained; at the most it can be listened to, but always from the other side, enclosed in impotence and dismay" (Carlo Bo). On his deathbed, Cardinal Jean Villot repeated, "Churchgoers and believers should speak less of suffering. They often do not know what it really is."

I write this in distress, anguished by the terror of moralism, the hypocritical and cruel mask of the prig who pontificates on the pain of others while smoking his cigar after a fine meal. Yet is that pain perhaps prolonged and intensified by modern medicine, common to Marxist and capitalists, who glory in themselves and violate people by preventing them from dying when and how nature would like?

Is this not the usual tangle of contradictions of societies that ask to interrupt through euthanasia the suffering they themselves have created with medical technology where every form of "progress" is automatically considered positive?

Instead of helping man, it aggravates his situation, rendering a truly "natural" death a rare event (with intensive care units, resuscitation rooms, and pharmaceutical prolongation of life).

In this way, many today no longer fear death as much as they do the interminable dying to which indifferent modern medicine condemns us. But man has always suffered and died: why has the euthanasia question exploded now precisely, and only now, when it should be less urgent than ever?

For the one who is passing away, along with callous medical technologies, there are painkilling therapies and medicines available that were unimaginable until recently. *For the one who stays behind,* the strategy of hospital hiding, forced reclusion of the dying in a technocratic ghetto, ought to render less urgent the moral pain.

But why exactly now? A perceptive answer was suggested by Ivan Illich:

> Modern medical civilization tends to transform pain and death into a technical problem and, in this way, strips suffering of its intrinsic personal meaning. Religious cultures faced pain and death but interpreted them as challenges that demanded a response to the individual in difficulty. We have created, however, a society based on the idea that the individual does not even need to face pain and death personally. The modern medical

enterprise represents an attempt to do on behalf of others what they, thanks to their genetic and cultural patrimony, were able to do for themselves up to that point.

Once upon a time, Illich continues, the man who has now been transformed into a "consumer of anesthetics and analgesics" was reared in the truth, not in hypocrisy or dreams:

> The fact was not hidden from him that life is hard and that death is inevitable; he was called to learn the art of living in a world where suffering and the end cannot be eliminated.

WHAT IS MISSING

They say, with the aggressive air of those who possess a monopoly on the defense of human rights: "If it is the same sick person asking to be spared suffering, it would not be cruel to refuse him this act of pity." We will now consider one of the most respected and authoritative voices on this matter, Cicely Saunders, the English doctor who, shocked by the barbarous condition of the dying in her country, founded the St. Christopher Hospice in London.

Having understood that the only revolution possible is a return to tradition, this woman attempted to surround the last days of her patients (almost all in the terminal stages of cancer) in a climate of humanity that had been lost in the labyrinth of healthcare reforms, desired and constructed by politicians and union leaders.

At hospice, the dying receives opportune, effective remedies for his pain, but hospice bans all mechanical devices that do violence to nature, that force one who has concluded his life to vegetate indefinitely. Based on her profound experience of humanity, Saunders says, "This is what we have learned: if a patient invokes euthanasia, it is always because he is missing something or someone."

He is missing (in other words, *it was taken from him*) the capacity to live confronting reality with the joys and dramas of which Ivan Illich speaks, confirmed in the words of Balducci: "The stronghold of pedagogy these days has become the repression of death and any image of it. This has generated a psychic fragility that reacts in an irrational, hysterical, infantile way in the face of every threat."

He is missing a coherent, organic vision that gives space to laughter and tears, joy and pain, birth and death; a vision according to which no suffering was to be judged useless. That vision was not substituted by another one; no, it was prohibited, under pain of social ostracism, leaving one to look for some other meaning to life and death that would replace the traditional ones.

He is missing the human solidarity that had always alleviated the solitary drama of death. Solidarity and compassion that cannot come from a more efficient doctor or a more affectionate relative, as today often happens, if they have not even come to terms with their own death.

Everything and everyone are missing to the one making this appeal because they were "suicides" that the culture of the age is ready to harvest. Bernard Häring, one of the most renowned Catholic moral theologians, writes:

> The principal cause of freely accepted euthanasia, the reason why some desire to be killed with the omission of medical treatment or with the direct application of measures for suppressing them, is the sensation of being socially dead—the sensation that, for others, they are already dead and buried, from the moment in which they refuse fundamental social communication.

In the face of an undesired pregnancy, the elimination of the fetus is the easiest solution, but also the most superficial; likewise in this case, given the difficulty of accepting and facing death, the easiest and most superficial solution is suppressing the dying person, boasting in his magnanimity: "He wanted it, would it not have been cruel to deny him that?"

In reality, the truly humane solution would lead in the direction suggested by Häring:

> It has been thoroughly verified that requests for euthanasia (as with every attempt at suicide, of which willed euthanasia is just one aspect) are a last, desperate invocation of the suffering person for heartfelt attention to be shown him, a more intense love, a more efficacious assistance.

The true solution passes through the cross that consists in examining oneself once more, conversion to human compassion, accepting every inevitable reality however cruel; but this is uncomfortable and difficult. It cannot be expected of the paladins of the right to happiness; from the crusaders of a right never to suffer; from people who believe they have understood everything and do not understand that to avoid pain leads to more pain, denying evil accumulates more evil, hiding death causes more death.

No, euthanasia is not a *right* as is written on the placards of those protesting in the streets. To them, euthanasia is much more than a right: in their vision of life and of man it is, in fact, a *duty*.

CHAPTER 4

The Triumph of Death

WHEN THE GODS FALL

IF THE HEAVENS ARE emptied of God, said the great theologian Karl Barth, the earth is populated with gods. This is what has happened in the past few centuries: man in the secular city is not an *atheist*, as he believes he is; in reality, he is an *idolater*.

But now, in the East as in the West, all the gods that had substituted God are in agony: the idol of progress of ever greater and more widespread affluence; and of the arrival on earth of the kingdom of liberty, justice, and absolute peace. Every other obsession is in agony, created out of the clay that characterizes every contemporary culture: the negation of sin and thus "man is good in his natural state," corrupted only by a poorly organized society; the omnipotence of science and the economy guided by politics; and then, its final result, the earthly Paradise.

The great mountains have given birth to a mouse, or one could say, a monstrous rat. There is not one hope that has not been betrayed: *science* was supposed to liberate humanity, and instead it has created the instruments of its destruction; *technology* was supposed to humanize nature, and instead has devastated it; *history* was supposed to show its true character as the path of liberation, and instead has ended up behind barbed wire.

The promised kingdom of life and peace is in fact a world that survives only thanks to a frightful and precarious balance of terror. Next to the *threat* of death we find death *achieved*: in the twentieth century, deaths in war were ninety out of a thousand, against the fifteen out of a thousand in the less advanced nineteenth century.

Where has faith in the god of progress gone when, according to all surveys, the overwhelming majority of people foresee that in ten years' time the quality of life will not be better but in fact worse? It is precisely the failure and the fall of the gods that, stealing our hope in the future, render more arduous and solitary both life and death.

We have seen that capitalist bourgeois radicalism is the final refuge today for widows and orphans of the many cultural and political idols — so much so that it has become the exemplary ideology, the most significant in today's West, such that much of what seems alive and vibrant today ends up under the roof of its vast bazar.

Yet the heart and soul of radicalism, together with the ferociously logical individualism we shall analyze, is the act of placing progress in doubt. Precisely *this* was the heart and soul of Marxism and of classical bourgeois thought; in a word, what is the heart and soul of the same modern world. In all its confusing variations, radicalism, though prospering in the post-industrial world and drawing from it all possible personal advantages, yearns for a "return to nature," "genuine food," "therapeutic herbs," "medicine and not technology," "a village economy," "local handicrafts." It dreams of the good old days to the point of violent protesting against nuclear energy, the very symbol of modern progress (for better or worse), and proposing in exchange a return to ancient sun worship.

SURVIVING, LIVING

We are not so foolish or Manichean as not to recognize, behind the death of the god of progress, the genuine and undeniable progress achieved in past centuries.

But for those who can see into the problem, much of this progress (the extraordinary increase in average income, the decrease in working hours and the exertions of work, the increase of free time) contribute to intensifying the unanswered questions of man about himself and his destiny, and thus aggravating his situation. Having resolved the problem of survival, man has time and energy to examine life and living. As Joseph Ratzinger (the German theologian, philosopher, and eventual pope Benedict XVI) said, "death is the true problem of life."

Among the many things foreseen neither by Marx nor by any other architect (left or right) of the ideological cathedrals of our time, there is the question of the meaning of life and death, which became more pressing as the pressure of material needs was attenuated. Every increase in salary exacerbated the crisis of systems that have many answers to man's immediate future, but have nothing to say about his "absolute" future.

The hungry man answered one who wanted to argue with him about certain theoretical problems: "Talk to me about philosophy and maybe theology after I've eaten." But now, in America as in Europe or in the Soviet Union, there is plenty to eat. The moment is arriving in which people might want to "talk about philosophy or maybe theology." They might want to ask questions about the meaning of eating, drinking, sleeping, working, living, and perhaps even death.

In this case, the dominant systems, here too essentially equal, worry about fostering and organizing the "entertainment society" we have already discussed. The system seeks to occupy the time of its subjects who, for the first time in history, have been liberated from the struggle for survival.

The old Prussian military codes, inherited by the Nazis and used as a model throughout the world, said, "The troops must never be left to boredom. Boredom leads to reflection, and reflection generates a lack of discipline." The message was well-assimilated by those in power: after-work activities were an important invention for right-wing as for left-wing totalitarian regimes. As soon as he was elected president of France, François Mitterrand hastened to create a Ministry of Free Time. The Italian Communist Party organizes twelve thousand *"Feste dell'Unità"* (Unity Parties) every year: a thousand per month.

Capitalism is more refined, but also more brutal. It has no need for thugs to work at keeping its subjects from idleness; it's enough to foster the free market. One example: state-run and private television in Italy in the 1980s poured into the airwaves day and night nearly ten thousand movies per month. Add to that the imposition of the previously unheard-of need called hobbies: it was decreed that everyone must have at least one of these to fill the few free moments between work and the television orgy: "Boredom leads to reflection, and reflection to a lack of discipline."

We will not treat a phenomenon that we have already mentioned. Note, however, that despite every organized effort to remove idleness, and thus reflection, from the life of humanity, there are questions that filter through nonetheless and are a source of problems as salaries and free time increase. Although dazed and confused, people are aware of the distress which the elderly English Catholic Malcom Muggeridge writer identified thus:

It is true that throughout my life progress has achieved a greater understanding of the universe and improvement in the material conditions of life than in all preceding history. But this does not excite me at all. The atom has been split, the universe has been dented by spaceships, incomes have multiplied by ten since the Victorian age. But none of these propaganda achievements has any relation to the problem that, as a man who wants to be worthy of the name, interests me most: what is the meaning, if there is one, of my little and transitory passage through this place? Lengthening the average lifespan from thirty-five to seventy years, thanks to antibiotics and the disappearance of infant mortality, changes nothing; it only postpones the problem for a time. Instead, it dilates it, giving us more time to think about it.

A wonderful thing, scientific achievements, above all those in medicine (although, so it seems, what is given to one end is taken from the other) — but what Blaise Pascal once said remains as apropos as ever, this man from the age of leeches and enemas: "Doctors can cure you. But in the end, you will die." Or again, the Psalmist going back another two thousand years, *Dies hominis umbrae, umbrae quae transeunt*, "Man is like a breath, his days are like passing shadows" (Psalm 144:4).

And when all these shadows will have passed, though they were filled with pastime parties, with tasks about little problems and ephemeral problems like those about which politicians are concerned — what then?

Never So Victorious

Behind the façade, all illuminated and cheery thanks to the easy music offered by the ministry and the bureaucrats, with the blessing of the intellectuals of the regime, there stands a man never so alone in the face of his destiny, a man alone as never before.

In pre-Christian paganism, the individual was inserted into scared nature. The enigma of his fate, of his appearance and of his rapid disappearance, found a response, a solution, at least a consolation, however dubious and insufficient, in the awareness of the natural and immutable cycle of which he felt he was an integral part.

For the pagan, surviving in fullness of life beyond the threshold of death was an exceptional gift reserved to demigods and heroes. For the rest, there was the resigned wait to be reabsorbed by eternal nature. The tomb inscriptions of the Greco-Roman world and the sculpted countenances that adorn them watch us with eyes that express melancholy and dark sadness, but not with desperation or anguish.

And then came Christianity. For a long series of centuries, Western man was integrated into a system that (whatever one's judgment regarding its truth claims) gave precise answers as never before and never since to questions about the meaning of life and death.

The Church might often have forgotten to contribute to the betterment of man's earthly, material condition. But no one can deny that it has offered man a proposal, perhaps the most effective in history, for taming death, for transforming it from a nightmare into a hope, from an abyss into a doorway, from failure into fulfillment. And in this sense, despite it all, it has improved man's quality of life.

"Fewer churches, more hospitals," goes the slogan sprayed on walls. Those who study the times are a bit less drastic and simplistic, perhaps: if one were to make a hypothetical, impossible assessment of "happiness," who knows if today's hospital would help mankind in its depths as much as yesterday's churches did? An attempt at a response to this question will occupy the last part of this book.

And now? Now the man of the crowded train running through the dark tunnels beneath New York and Moscow has been stripped of both the natural cycle of the pagan and the liturgical cycle of the Christian. He has been conditioned, like Pavlov's dogs, to be interested only in what he sees and hears, without worrying about anything else. He has been told that there is nothing beyond the sensible and visible.

But in a universe without the invisible, it is only the visible — death — that exists. It is this same death that has never been so triumphant as it is now, in a society where one is alone and mute, though surrounded by a multitude where everyone clamors to cover the din of questions arising in each. And if those questions were expressed (though psychiatrists and law enforcement guard against this), some would offer politics, others technological developments; some parties and protests, others goods and consumption.

That's something, but it's certainly not the whole answer we need here.

Running, but Where To?

Twenty centuries of Christianity have not passed under the bridge without effect. They have left their profound mark on the earth that is now subjugated to new teachers. The wellspring has been deviated, declared no longer potable. But what remains exacerbates our anguish even more.

Olivier Clément, a writer calling attention to the tradition of Eastern Orthodoxy, once wrote:

> Christianity has taught man that he is a unique being and that he must rise again. The secular cultures of today have preserved from Christianity only the conviction that man is a unique being, forgetting about or rejecting the Resurrection. For this reason, death has never been so barren and terrible as it is now. If man is unique, he will perceive with inconceivable force the anguish of dying. Once the ideologies of the species and of progress have fallen, only the person, the individual, unarmed in the face of his end, remains.

Under the stimulus of Christianity, the modern world has exalted one of the characteristics of man: that he cannot live without being projected into the future.

"We never live, but we hope to live," said Pascal. If we were to scrutinize ourselves, we would realize that we are never resting in the present moment, although it is the only real one, the only one that belongs to us; we are always projecting ourselves into the future, of which we have, however, no certainty.

Have you ever seen a busload of tourists drive by? Very often, from behind the windows, they do not watch the road, the buildings, the monuments seen for the first time. Instead of entrusting these things to their eyes, they entrust them to the lenses of their cameras. Instead of enjoying the present moment, an obscure instinct drives them to invest in the future moment: they take pictures and make videos, hoping they will be able to enjoy them later, once returned home, looking at the filmed images.

Though taken from the daily routine, this too is a sign of our objective condition. This spontaneous projection toward the future has been enhanced to the extreme for two thousand years by the Christian message, which sees the history of man and society as an arrow aiming at a target.

The fulfillment of my story and that of the world is ahead of us. As St. Paul wrote to the Philippians:

> I may attain the resurrection from the dead. Not that I have already obtained this or am already perfect; but I press on to make it my own, because Christ Jesus has made me his own. Brethren, I do not consider that I have made it my own; but one thing I do, forgetting what lies behind and straining forward to what lies ahead, I press on toward the goal for the prize of the upward call of God in Christ Jesus (Phil. 3:11–14).

From the biblical message, modern culture has preserved only this "being stretched out toward the future," declaring at the same time the inexistence, or rather perniciousness, of the goal toward which it is running, the "prize" as St. Paul understood it.

Other content has been attributed to that goal, to that prize, content entirely within history. "The phrases of the intellectuals and politicians of today are immediately recognizable," someone said, "by the fact that they all use verbs in the future tense."

The spontaneous longing of man for the future has been entirely hijacked into the *collective future*: the thousand-year reich; the kingdom of realized-communism; the society of unlimited consumerism and well-being. On the contrary, the questions about a *personal future* have been repressed, demonized, accused of "individualism," of "alienation."

But precisely in these years, the day of reckoning has arrived.

The modern proposals for the collective future have been revealed for what they are: naïve and deceitful utopias, myths, fairytales for children who thought they were grown-ups and considered others infantile.

And so, there remains only the impulse that urges us forward. But whither do we go? Toward which future, if the collective one designed by those prophets revealed itself to be only an illusion? And if the individual future is closed by death and its wall on which none of those graffiti artists knows how to paint anything, where do we go?

A WITNESS

Marcel Proust's *A la recherche du temps perdu* (*In Search of Lost Time*), the immense literary cycle which perhaps more than any other marked the end of the nineteenth century, comprises an enormous fifteen volumes.[11]

---

[11] Editor's Note: While now typically published as a seven-volume work, Proust's *In Search of Lost Time* has also been divided into a fifteen volume work, which the author references.

As always happens, art (which is sincerity and mysterious authenticity, often well beyond the intentions of its author) once more unmasks triviality, lies, and the hypocrisy of the clever and the mediocre.

Thus, Marcel Proust gave witness as an artist (and paid the price) to the anguish of a culture that, in the face of death, has no other remedy than to hide or trivialize, but is instead tormented more than any other culture in history because no other has ever been this impotent. Proust is among the greatest examples of how dramatic it is today to become radically aware of what once was a given, serenely accepted by everyone: we are precarious, finite, inexorably condemned to disappear.

With the exasperated, refined sensibility of an artist, a Jew, a homosexual, a neurotic, a citizen of metropolitan Paris, and an intellectual of the world, Marcel Proust was literally grabbed by the throat (he suffered terrible psychosomatic asthma attacks) by the anguish of his age, which he said "escapes like sand, quickly leaving the hand empty."

"I hated death," he wrote in a confession that served as the guiding motivation of his laborious work, "but that thought adhered so tightly to the deepest layer of my being that I could not concern myself with anything without it being shot through with the intuition of the end."

As with all of us, he could not live without tending toward the future; but more intensely and painfully than we do, he perceived that this future crashes against a wall, and that death, bare and brutal, cannot be a worthy destiny. Tormented thus by the passing of hours without return, he frantically put his hand to the pen: "He worked," said his waiter, "as if he were to die the next day."

He tried to halt the fleeting moment, embalming it in literature, rendering it immortal and incorruptible on ink-stained paper, because, he said, "one is seen to die not in that instant but years before, after death has announced that he has come to take a place within us."

Proust lacks "religious" consolation; neither does he have political consolations, however. In the thousands of pages of his *Recherche*, the name of God is never to be found linked to a possible faith. Nor are there traces of modern surrogates of God: no political themes, no social concerns. No hope for a personal future in him; but not even any illusion of saving something in a collective future. Time, for Proust, is truly "lost." Thus, decades ahead of the common condition, he is the man of our days who naked must confront a mystery, an absurdity no longer domesticated.

What the writer can try to place in safety from a shadow that widens every day is only his little "private" experience: his days, with their routine, their words, their smells and sounds, their gestures; it all seems insignificant but instead it is unique and unrepeatable because it will never return again.

Time fades forever; but could it not in some way be recovered by going on "search" through the use of memory? If the future is closed off to us by the dark, why not try to find some comfort by saving at least the past from the darkness that already covers it? But the anguish, implacable despite the swelling effort of pathos to sublimate it in literature, explodes in thousands of tormented forms: from asthma, a bodily sign of an interior fatigue, to indomitable insomnia.

All of *Recherche* was written at night: only at dawn, closing against the light the heavy curtains of the elegant building on Boulevard Haussmann, could the writer finally sleep. There was in him, say the many who have examined his exemplary case with the instruments of psychology, the terror of the nighttime darkness, felt as the image and metaphor of death. It is the anxiety of dying that impeded him from abandoning himself to sleep until the appearance of the first light that would bring hope: for another day the enemy, the devourer of days, could perhaps be kept at bay.

Asthma, insomnia; the extreme of his well-known need to imprison memories in the room that a thick cork wall cover insulated from the outside. Not the picturesque eccentricity of the artist, but the last, touching defense, the attempt to close out the world, to isolate oneself from history, hoping to close out death as well, the uncontested queen of the world and of history, where nothing and no one can escape her power.

We are discussing Proust at length because the testimony of Marcel Proust concerns not only him but seems exemplary of what it means to live, and so to go toward the encounter with death, in the current solitude.

This contributes to the making of a witness ("martyr" in the etymological sense) of our drama. Not by chance, therefore, is his book (interminable, often prolix, apparently useless, wherein nothing extraordinary occurs, where not even a plot can be found, without any explicit eroticism) among the most widely read, loved, and influential of the century of which it is a symbol. "The book of the century," as it has been termed for the often-subterranean mark that it continues to leave, although the many intellectuals that continue to admire it ignore the drama that lies at its origins — a drama which, whether we like it or not, is also theirs.

The same intellectuals show astonishment because, for years, the finalists and winners of all the major literary prizes are almost always autobiographies, memoirs. This is the literary genre of the century: it is, was, and always will be the attempt to stop time by going in search for it, the effort to oppose an absurd, mysterious, merciless future by going back to the past. It is the only consolation possible along the same path that Proust trod.

Because, in a world in which the ancient hope has been given up for dead and new hopes are moribund, death triumphs and rages with its anguish. Despite it all, the memory that mercifully gathers memories fails to soothe, "leaves floating off a submerged forest which is the life behind our backs."

PART II
EFFECTS

Rem viderunt, causam non viderunt.

St. Augustine

*The boss said to his employee:
"I forbid you to think about death
during working hours."*

Cesare Zavattini

CHAPTER 5
A Social Scourge

An Indispensable and Impossible Reform

THE MOST INDISPENSABLE OF all reforms is in reality impossible: it is not and can never be found in the platform of any political party. Yet, among the many reforms invoked, planned, and threatened, this would truly be the most urgent and necessary: namely, to change society and culture, which is organized to prevent man from taking notice of his condition, making him live an incomplete, maimed life.

Parties and movements invite us to sign an infinite number of appeals and protests, from the nuclear threat to the extinction of seals; they have us fill the streets with signs denouncing oppression and violence. Rightly so. But it is not fair that they allow the most violent of violences, the most oppressive oppression to prosper and go unpunished: the ferocious, neurotic taboo against death, whose effects (some, at least) we shall point out in this second part.

We will still be speaking on the "non-religious" plane, to continue describing and denouncing an objective situation without reference to faith or unbelief.

For all of us, it is a matter of becoming aware of a reality: that it is an authentic social scourge to deny, hide, or declare obscene death and all that it recalls.

The psychoanalyst Erich Fromm notes, speaking not as a believer, but as the secular humanist that he was: "The current repression erodes love of life: it does not lead to euphoria but to necrophilia. Thus, societies today are vitalists in their intentions and death-bearing in their actions."

Although hidden from the pedants on their university chairs, there is a close, direct link between refusal of death and refusal of life, whose "quality" (spoken of tirelessly by politicians, sociologists, urban developers, and psychologists) is derived from reforms of transportation, healthcare, the schools. *Also*; but not *only*.

"Quality of life" depends in fact on a vision of the world and of man; those visions that dominate us today are inhumane, lacking as they do an essential dimension. Their man is "one-dimensional," to use a phrase from Herbert Marcuse, who enflamed so many tender hearts on university campuses.

But against what this German-American philosopher wanted his students to believe, it is not only bourgeois capitalism, but also every form of socialism the world has yet known that shuts us into the cage of one-dimensionality.

Thus, in a way unsuspected by the prophets of social causes, today one of the greatest social projects must be facing a problem that utopians and political shamans have wanted us to see as the most anti-social of all.

No doubt, this is the true reform of all reforms, but it is the only socially impracticable one. Sandro Spinsanti, a researcher of these issues, observes that "death's hunting party is a structural characteristic of contemporary societies, belonging to their load-bearing model." This is not a matter of marginal adjustments or even difficult changes, even when possible — what is at stake here is the entire orientation.

There is no need for a tormented, morbid return to the nightmare of the end. What is needed is not the skull sitting on the desk, nor even a coffin in place of one's bed, as described by certain ancient penitents and ascetics.

Nor would we counsel, as a profitable use of one's free time, the assiduous visitation of the morgue or the funerals of complete strangers. Direct contact with the death of others can have a liberating, educational function, but not always.

If it happens according to the dominant vision, the results are the opposite of what is needed. It seems that the highest rate of criminality is registered in settings that revolve around so-called funeral parlors. Cadavers, caskets, and tombs are privileged objects of sanguinary rackets and mafia. Whoever has had to frequent morgues for anatomical dissections, perhaps for medical school, knows that those places are often the theater of obscene and lugubrious "jokes" that signal the gravity of the unresolved psychological problems of these sad pranksters.

What is needed, what liberates, is not "touching death." As James Gevaert writes:

> It is not death per se that is instructive, because death is a tearing from the human world and the threat of the extinction of all

meaning. What performs the educational function is rather becoming aware of our mortal condition. That this condition would not be repressed but received willingly and freely.

If the great French anthropologist Louis V. Thomas dedicated his life to studying and speaking about death, it was not for edifying motives, but rather for concrete social reasons. Not with the aim of stimulating moralism or devotions did he found his *Société de thanatologie*, which has the explicit goal of renewing in Western culture the conversation on death.

Thomas (and others with him) decided to do this after having lived for years among the so-called savages in sub-Saharan Africa, among the last people not yet devastated by the "development" imported forcefully by the "secular and enlightened" Western powers.

These nations export death under the form of arms, alcohol, drugs, prostitution, automobiles, pesticides, insecticides, and pharmaceuticals, and call this "civilization." Furthermore, with these instruments of death, they export their culture, which produces death to the degree that the exporters are traumatized by death. Thus, in the words of Ivan Illich, "they impose on everyone the image of death proper to the modern white man, offering a top-quality contribution to the cultural colonization and to the neurosis and unhappiness of those peoples."

Upon his return to Europe, Louis Thomas gave this assessment:

> There are societies that respect man: those where life, following the wisdom of the ages, protects itself by giving space to the idea of its own end. And there are necrophiliac societies, on the other hand, devastated by pathological obsessions: our societies, the cultures of a death denied and buried with the same care given to burying cadavers. The concrete experience of the anthropologist shows that denying death generates more death.

Should we welcome a return to the forest, to the cave, to the tribe then, with their complex funeral rites? Certainly not. We would like simply to open eyes: one can be most inhumane precisely when trying to be considered humane. Does the attempt to set in motion every means for avoiding unpleasant thoughts for ourselves and our peers seem humane? Here, it suffices to inject a bit of suspicion: what if "adult" societies are really the most immature in all history? What if "rational" cultures are revealed to be in fact the most irrational?

"DARE TO KNOW!"

There is surely a good reason to ask these questions. Despite their different appearances, both Western society and the communist East have a common root: the eighteenth-century European Enlightenment, prolonged in the following centuries down to our day under the form of positivism, scientism, rationalism, and so forth. Ruthless, bourgeois liberalism as well as bloody, messianic Marxism come from there, from the Enlightenment.

If we wanted to search even deeper for today's roots, we must go beyond eighteenth century France, Germany, and England, all the way back to the fifteenth and sixteenth centuries in Italy. To the Renaissance, that is: this is the name we have given (for several centuries now) to the movement of emancipation from the formally "Christian" Middle Ages, though it was an emancipation that, rather than moving forward, went back fourteen or fifteen centuries, to the rediscovery of Greco-Roman paganism, which did not enjoy great success in its day; in effect, it reverted into the irreversible crisis that gave way to Christianity. The latter did not kill the classical world, but rather relieved a world that had already become gangrenous. The horrors of imperial decadence, to which the gospel contrasted as something new and fresh, were the natural solutions of a culture that modern historians (to the disgrace of the breathless poets of "classicism") characterize as "an infernal circle." The point of departure: slavery, the irreplaceable pilaster of every pre-Christian society. Slavery produced wealth, wealth produced luxury and immorality, these in turn lead to prostitution, and prostitution again reproduced slavery.

Yet the term *Renaissance*, like *Enlightenment*, has a clearly polemical ring to it: the former, a *rebirth* after the death imposed by the Church, the latter, the *lights* ignited in the night of Christian superstition, the torch of reason held high to illuminate life and render it truly free and worthy.

And so, today's cultures, so diverse and yet so united in their premises, methods, and outcomes, have followed the exhortation of one of the great masters of the Enlightenment, Immanuel Kant, the German philosopher: *Scire aude*! Dare to know! Run the risk of the truth! Make the most use of your reason possible! Rebel against the prohibition on seeking, imposed by religious dogmatism!

This Kantian exhortation was taken seriously. However one might judge the results, no one will deny modern culture the anxiety of a search driven to the extreme consequences, nor the label of "courageous," "audacious." Recent centuries have undoubtedly been characterized by one of the greatest and most terrible adventures of the human spirit and of human liberty.

But this formidable recommendation to investigate has been exercised in all directions except for one, in which explicit voluntary ignorance has been recommended and practiced. This has been no small oversight: the refusal to face man's entire reality — his life and, therefore, his death — has resulted in deforming all the rest of his attributes.

Contradicting their "dare to know!," all contemporary cultures have capitulated without a fight only in the face of the problem that interests us here; this reveals something important. Only here have thought systems, founded though they were on the fight *against* resignation, surrendered *to* resignation, as if it were better to dodge than to confront this essential aspect of human reality.

Insoluble or Non-Existent?

Even if one admits that the problem of death is seen as insoluble with the mere means that one believes, he is authorized to employ his own reason.

An Italian writer of the twentieth century, Arrigo Cajumi, a declared "illuminist" and a "libertine" in the classical sense of one who loves and defends his intellectual liberty, writes:

> We do not know the reason for our living and dying, we do not know what we have come to do down here: so, we try to pass the time in the way most consonant with our tastes. I have no other ethic, in fact; I am ready to applaud the person who, born to collect stamps or porcelain, has but that one aim in life.

This position seems honest and entirely legitimate, given the premises of a culture that says, "We want to trust and rely upon reason alone, and reason, as is well-known, confronted with the question why we live and die, is incapable of giving a decisive response. Why bother ourselves, then, if the problem is insoluble with the only instrument worthy of man?"

Only faith, they continue, could affect that step beyond reason which has shown itself insufficient for dedicating one's life to stamps and porcelain. Only faith, giving meaning to dying, might give a different meaning to living. And faith is like the courage of Don Abbondio in Manzoni's *Promessi Sposi*: those without it cannot give it to themselves. Is it not believers who affirm that their faith is a mysterious gift of God?

In reality, following the apparent logic of Cajumi, whom we take here as exemplary of a widespread mentality, there is the naïve concept (more than naïve: mythological, superstitious) of "reason" proper to all illuminists. They do not understand that the greatness of their goddess Reason (placed literally on the altars of the French Revolution, where it all began) can also consist in objectively recognizing its limits, recognizing in this way the true human condition. Reason elevated to obsession can lead (as it has led), in the material order, to inhumane science and homicidal technology, with the double threat of atomic and ecological extermination; and in the epistemological order, to the depths of profundity, but also to the heights of triviality and pedantic superficiality.

But beware of the logical leap: an unsolvable problem is not for this reason a non-existent problem. A question we cannot resolve does not cease for this reason to be a real question.

Yet this is precisely what has happened in the prideful culture of the "dare to know": from the verification that the problem and the questions posed by death seem irresolvable, one has made the leap to a denial of the very problem and question.

Death, therefore, has not at all been set in the most visible place on the shelf where one collects and keeps under watchful eye the unanswered questions. On the contrary, it has been hidden under the bed, buried in some inaccessible place, concealed behind a rag like a stack of obscene magazines. One has forgotten its existence, or one has at least sought to disguise it in the soothing clothes of an irrelevant "natural reality."

This has actually taken place in societies based on reason and courage: not the serene, diligent acceptance of an enigma regarding the human condition, but the neurotic negation of the enigma and, from there, of the human condition itself.

Ideologies and Wisdom

The fact is that the Enlightenment gave birth to "ideologies," a term we have employed several times already. What is behind this term? Liberalism, capitalism, and radicalism are all ideologies, as are the totalitarianisms of the right that rage in the West, and the forms of Marxism or the totalitarianisms of the left that dominate in the East and that struggle for power wherever bourgeois "shopkeeper societies" are still in authority.

"Ideology," says one acceptable definition, "is an a priori vision of the world, used as a constant filter between the one who accepts it and reality."

Thus, the follower of ideology does not reason based on the criteria of truth, humanity, rationality, or simple good sense, but judges everything through his "filter." What characterizes the ideologue or his disciple is contempt and denial of reality if it does not agree with his framework. If the facts do not pass through the filter and threaten to disturb his a priori vision of the world, then the motto of the ideologue and his followers rings out: "All the worse for the facts!"

Furthermore, modern ideologues, whether on the right or the left, all share the presumption of having science on their side, while their aims are simply political: power and domination.

According to capitalist liberalism, "the immutable laws of the market economy" are "scientific," to which, it logically follows, man must be sacrificed. The Marxist reading of history, in the face of which the concrete person must be immolated, is, according to Marxism, "scientific." The racist doctrine that, according to Nazism, justifies the concentration camps is "scientific." And so on. In reality, what they really want is not to explain life and its mystery, but to try to dominate the lives of others.

Wherever the Enlightenment ideologies have claimed victory (at least for the moment and at least in the "advanced" world), what has come to pass could not have been otherwise: can death and the questions it raises not adapt to the system? Are they blocked by the filter? Then they are declared inexistent or rejected. "Does death exist? All the worse for it!"

In reality, it has been all the worse for us.

Future historians (if there will be any) will be forced to recognize that our culture is radically different from all other preceding cultures.

By means of ideologies (and therefore of filters, prohibitions, contempt of facts, political censure, the logic of power), a historical fracture has been inflicted with devastating consequences. For millennia, the world changed, societies followed one after another, but never had the dialogue with death been interrupted, which was perceived always and everywhere as essential for the individual and for society.

Socrates, the wisest among men, said, "Our entire life must be a reflection upon death and a preparation to face it."

If this universal wisdom is rejected, as it has been for the first time in recent centuries, there can be as much technical development imaginable, and *knowledge* can grow infinitely, but there will never be true *wisdom*.

Such a maimed and crippled culture can produce, at the most, men of *expertise*, and it produces too many; it will never produce men of true *wisdom*. It can give birth to professors, but not teachers. There can be no wisdom where the very source of human knowledge has been forgotten, hidden, despised.

That this is the root of wisdom is the conviction expressed with amazing unanimity throughout the ages on every continent.

After the words of Socrates, exemplary of Western tradition, here is one other example from an Eastern culture, from Japan.

Yagyu-Tajiama-no-kami, the ancient, most famous, venerable teacher of the emperor, refused to receive among his students in the ring with sword and archery a samurai who, as the Zen texts say, "from his early childhood struggled with thoughts of his own mortality, learning to tame them." "What else can I teach you?" said the master, refusing the aspirant, "You have already attained the heart of wisdom: every other art is included in the art you have learned, including that of the bow and sword." "Because," added the master addressing his disciples, "he who knows death, knows life. And he who disregards death, disregards life."

Is the growing number of people who throng to the doors of the teachers of ancient traditions not attracted perhaps by this wisdom, the most fundamental of all and yet which is lacking in our opulent modern world?

To Become Adults

To face death, to "domesticate" it, is an obligatory condition not only for attaining wisdom, but also, more modestly, for passing from the infantile stage to the adult stage.

The Spanish philosopher Miguel de Unamuno writes, "It is the discovery of death that accompanies peoples and individuals into spiritual maturity."

The secular author André Malraux confirms this:

> The thought of death is the thought that makes a man. The day on which one has reflected for the first time on death ought to be

celebrated, because it marks the passage into maturity. Man is born when, for the first time, he murmurs in front of a cadaver: why?

Psychology and psychoanalysis confirm the intuition of philosophers and writers, suggesting that the life of man can be divided into two periods: before and after the emergence and acceptance of the thought of our mortal condition. One who does not pass from the first to the second phase, these modern sciences add, has no hope of ever becoming an adult.

What is true of the individual is true of society as well. Thus, there is no hope of maturation for these our cultures which proclaim to be the quintessential adults with an ingenuousness equal to their arrogance.

Consider what Elisabeth Kübler-Ross has to say about this matter, this courageous woman who proved once again that courage is not only a "manly" virtue:

> There came a time in my life when I realized that I had brought two children into this world, that I had given them well-being, upbringing, and an education; and yet they were empty, empty like a can of beer already drunk. I said to myself that I had to do something for them that was not merely material. Thus, in agreement with my husband, we welcomed a guest into our home: a seventy-four-year-old man whom the doctors had given no more than two months left to live. I wanted my children to be close to him during his path toward death, that they would see and touch with their hands the most important experience in the life of a human being. The guest stayed with us not two months, but two and a half years, welcomed in all things as a member of the family. Well, that experience gave my children incredible spiritual wealth. Those thirty months matured them in an extraordinary way. In that previously unknown brother who came to die among them, young and healthy, my children discovered a new meaning to life; they truly became adults. And he, that poor old man, gave us an incredible gift, not us to him, although we cared for him and assisted him with all the love we could give.

Is it not alarming that this experience of "getting to know death in order to know life," of "making room for dying in order to become adults," is reduced to the eccentricity of an American psychologist, when in every culture before ours it was not some privilege of the children of some non-conformist intellectual, but common experience of the poor even more so than the rich?

Dishonored, Dishonors

With maturity, it is a person's dignity itself that is placed in danger by the current situation.

Dishonored, death dishonors. Sages have always repeated that not only do wisdom and maturity depend on the confrontation with death; rather, the uniqueness, the dignity, and the nobility of man all depend on it. Of all that lives and dies on the earth, we alone know that we must die: it is our miserable lot, but it is our greatness as well.

> Man is but a reed, a cane. A thinking reed. There's no need for the entire universe to take up arms to crush him: a mist, a drop of water are enough to kill him. But also, if the entire universe took up arms to crush him, man would still be more noble than that which kills him. Because he knows he must die. The universe, however, knows nothing of this.

Thus reads a famous *pensée* of Pascal.

On the other hand, we have the objective aimed at today: to distract us by every means from thoughts that (again it is Pascal who repeats it) "constitute our entire dignity." After having robbed us of the rest, they attempt to rob us of death as well, with all that this signifies for our humanity.

"Animals and machines ignore their death," wrote an Italian author, Fausto Gianfranceschi, "They promise us the 'new' man. But is he 'new' because he will not know that he must die? This, if anything, is an old man, regressed to what is below his destiny, his dignity." He continues:

> We were the masters of our death and of its circumstances for millennia, while today we are no longer. Once upon a time, those about to die recognized their conditions: either because they understood with simplicity the signs or because someone near them was obliged to warn them. Stronger than the fear of dying was the fear of being deprived of one's death, of not being able to participate in it with awareness and the right state of mind. Now, it is quite normal to withhold the truth from

someone mortally ill. One says that this practice is suggested by humanitarian intentions. But it is an inhumane rule because it admits the resignation of the spirit. Because to die without knowing it is a double death.

Notice, for example, a traditional piece of wisdom, one of the most familiar in the West: Christian wisdom. And notice once more what is generically human in this message, beyond the religious significance.

For millennia, the Catholic Church has suggested an invocation in the Litany of Saints: *A subitanea et improvisa morte libera nos, Domine!* (Free us, O Lord, from a sudden death, that which takes us without our knowing it!)

If that is what one prayed, it was not only to be granted time to receive the sacraments *in extremis*. That might benefit the eternal salvation of the one dying, but the Church, in its authentic faith, has never overestimated this aspect. It has always known and preached that we die as we have lived, that our God is not deceived at the last moment with sacraments understood as magical rites.

One prayed to be liberated from a death *"subitanea et improvisa"* also because this type of end was considered a tragedy for the entire person, not only for his "soul." To die without being aware of it meant being robbed of the highest peak of human experience, of the summary of all of one's existence.

Man was the master of his death and he did not want to renounce this privilege, tragic yet precious. He did not want to have happen to him what now, with grotesque misrepresentation, is presented as a fortune: not that we are masters of our own death, but death is *our* master.

"Progressive" cultures have impeded for us the possibility of becoming adults; "rational" cultures impede us from becoming wise; "free" cultures have conducted us into this servitude. Only the technician, the doctor that guards the warehouse, the hospital ghetto of the dying, holds all knowledge and therefore all power, including that of stealing from the dying person his awareness and thus his dignity.

I have tried to identify a situation with a few initial consequences, some first effects.

But the journey must continue; we must continue to see how psychological imbalance and ideological hatred crash against men and things, against the living and the dead: from the grotesque fight against cemeteries, to the persecution of the elderly and whoever is stricken by grief. Other aspects need to be denounced, at least the most conspicuous, of this war unleashed against all that reminds us of the most dangerous enemy to our new masters.

Yes, a war. And just like every war, a social scourge whose highest price, as always, is paid by the defenseless and the innocent.

CHAPTER 6

Crimes and Punishments

War on Cemeteries

THE ENLIGHTENMENT, OF WHICH we are all children (in America, as in Europe and in the Soviet Union), came to political power at the end of the eighteenth century, first with the American Revolution and then, above all, with the French Revolution.

As soon as they had attained the power to impose laws, our forefathers hastened to decree an important measure: the expulsion, urgent and forceful, of any and every tomb from inhabited areas. It was as if, not able to abolish by law the cause (namely death), laws could at least render invisible the effect, the cemetery.

Understand: we know well the "serious hygienic reasons" put forward by those good men to justify their measures, presented, obviously, as a "sign of progress."

But there is always some conceited or indiscrete figure on the horizon. In this case, the killjoy is again Louis V. Thomas, the anthropologist who studied the cemetery laws of the new Europe after the revolutions: "After those apparently rational provisions, there is actually a neurotic alibi invented by a society trying to dodge its anguish." This is the conclusion of the contemporary scholar after analyzing secular funerary dispositions. These were nothing else than the translation into law of the appeal made by one of the most prestigious fathers of the new culture, Goethe.

"Away with the tombs! Away with the tombs!" exhorted this great figure, nostalgic of paganism and its superstitions. Instead of going forward, here too one went backward, returning to the terrors of the ancients, for whom the mere sight of a sepulcher was enough to strike them with the *fascinum*, by curses, the evil eye, and jinxes.

Were the cultures of reason born, then, with irrational attitudes? Did the new cultures actually rediscover something that was old?

Confirming this suspicion, the cemeterial provisions of the world that was finally enlightened all have one point in common: to avoid allowing the houses of the dead to be visible from the houses of the living. To attain this result, the precautions never seemed enough: the Jacobins of the French Revolution and, after them, Napoleon, established a distance of cemeteries first of two hundred twenty meters, and then five hundred meters from the first inhabited houses.

During the entire nineteenth century and into the early twentieth century, continuous fervor led to the construction of special railroads to reach the necropolises, the cities of the dead, relegated to remote areas, solitary and inaccessible. In society, where people died of pellagra, malaria, and starvation, where there were no railroads and streets for the living, great sums of money were spent to carry out these projects, incomprehensible and senseless only to those who cannot discern the anxiety that drove them to put their hand to their wallets.

In some cases, the authorities, anxious to employ in those inaccessible necropolises the meager national resources, were dissuaded only by popular revolt: less neurotic than their masters, the "common" people (or "normal" as is said with an indicative term) were not about to have their deceased stolen from them as well.

But not because of this did the powerful shelve a need vital by now to all, but above all to them: they fell back on the rigid, already existing laws. It happened in France, for example, when, in 1936, the Popular Front government took power, that famous coalition of communists and socialists that had a brief and tormented duration. It was not short enough, however, to avoid inserting among the most urgent points of its platform the question of cemeteries, considered still too visible.

Impetuously, the Front approved a decree that was as ridiculous as it was pathetic.

An obligatory high wall was to hide the cemetery from sight. But was it not better to hide the wall as well? It was thus ordered that the stone wall was to be doubled with a barrier of trees, compulsory evergreens so that not even the falling of the leaves nor the change of seasons would leave openings on a view intolerable to the regime.

The Jacobins had hidden the tombs with a wall; the socialists and communists hid the wall with trees; the radical bourgeois could not refrain from pushing the matter to an extreme: making tombs, walls, and trees disappear. In fact, cutting-edge architects now propose (and when they can, realize) the excavation of a great trench in the earth; within it, invisible to passersby, those cursed tombs that insist on tormenting us are dumped.

"Here," says Thomas commenting on the decree of the Popular Front and the projects of the new architects:

> The problem is not protecting the physical hygiene of citizens but protecting the mental hygiene of its leaders. We see here a hysterical reaction dictated by a hidden evil that torments precisely the ones who are most strident about being free of every obscurantist fear.

A Fistful of Ashes

We continue with the petulant questions: Are not the cultures that descend from the Enlightenment the ones that hold most dear the idea of incinerating cadavers? "Cremation societies" are among the most constant and perhaps picturesque of the "emancipation from religious darkness," above all in the nineteenth century but even today.

The headings of their bulletins almost always bear the word *reason* with a definite polemical function.

Certainly, reason here is at the service of "scientific hygiene motivations" as well. But in the face of the missionary zeal of the many apostles of cremation, the mischievous cannot but foster the usual suspicions. Is this not (as with the *fascinum*, the evil eye of the tombs) an expected return of ancient beliefs? Namely, the impure, polluting cadaver that must be purified by fire; the corpse as a repugnant object to be transformed as soon as possible into a handful of aseptic ashes. We throw into the flames, along with the cadaver, the disturbing questions that arise around it, while ridding ourselves of the tomb, reducing it to a little urn or even dispersing the ashes at sea or in a river. It is finished: nothing is left to disturb one's sight; out of sight, out of mind.

To these reasons of hygiene (quite difficult to justify given the extraordinary measures taken to isolate cemeteries), the missionaries of the most secular, most rational cremation societies add considerations regarding the excessive space the tombs occupy. This could be true; but here too one must raise suspicions, seeing that one of the most active of these cremation societies operates in Australia, a country with little more than one inhabitant per square kilometer.

The reality, once again, seems to be the same: the culture of the age of steam engines wanted to burn cadavers to conceal death along with them; the culture of rockets and space travel wants to freeze them to deny death. The motive and the roots are the same; what changes is only the technological development at the service of an unresolved psychological problem. It does not change (nor can it change) that lump in the throat, the voice that breathlessly accumulates reasonings; but the attentive ear can hear it marred by anxiety.

A further chance confirmation among the infinite possible ones? Here it is, plucked from an unsuspecting text: the *Guida d'Italia* of the Touring Club of Italy, first edition, 1914.[12] For visiting Milan, the guidebook recommends at least three days for the "rushed tourist." Of these three days, an entire morning is occupied by a visit to the Monumental Cemetery, with what the anonymous editor defines as "its enormous artistic treasures." The latest edition of this guide available came out about seventy years later; every mention of that cemetery is gone, not only for the "rushed tourist," but even for those who intend to dedicate not three, but a good seven days to visiting Milan.

Have "artistic treasures" dwindled in that place? No, over so many decades the treasures have greatly increased. But in those same years neurosis has also increased, the taboo against death has grown worse, travel has increasingly assumed the function of escape from the most unpleasant of all realities. The serious, programmatic Touring Club is right: those who travel for "entertainment" keep well away from tombs, from every tomb, even artistic ones.

Old, Therefore Leprous

Cadavers and tombs bear witness to death, as do (we mentioned this when talking about euthanasia) the seriously ill and the agonizing, so all these have to go.

But the elderly? Do they not remind us of the same reality, do they not send us the same intolerable signals just by looking at them? They have to go, too: "Raus!" as the Nazis yelled to those who disturbed their economic and ideological system.

I am not exaggerating; here too I am trying to cling to the objective facts. The unresolved neurosis that drives us toward the unprecedented, maniacal

---

[12] Editor's Note: A popular book for tourists on the main attractions of the "bel paese."

cult of the young as the ones farthest from death forces us (it cannot do otherwise) to demonize the elderly and senescence in general. We have already anticipated some of this.

Perhaps even more than women (half of humanity), the elderly (now almost a fourth of humanity) are the new "oppressed proletariat," both in the East and in the West.

We have seen how, out of hypocritical respect, they are called "elderly"; how old age has become "retirement age" or even "one's golden years" according to an ad campaign that tries to extort consumption to the very end, admitting them into extremely expensive private care homes.

In reality, such fragile, defenseless cultures could not have come about otherwise: the old person had to assume the part of the new leper; the plague-ridden one had to be quarantined often physically, always psychologically; taking our hat off to them as they go out the door, though.

We Western Europeans are now subjects in provinces on the outskirts of the Holy American Empire. The United States anticipates by a few years what, without escape, will become the prevalent custom here as well. It is this situation that leads us to turn often to the facts, numbers, and names of that country which, geographically and culturally, is the "Extreme West," the place where the ideologies of the West are driven to their ultimate consequences.

According to a census in those fifty states, more than ten percent of citizens has no contact with their parents, does not know if they are alive or dead, nor are they concerned to know. This is another phenomenon, one of many, that has come about for the first time in history. Here too, however, moralistic imprecations against these presumed "unnatural children" would serve no purpose: the actions of men, caution the wise, are to be neither judged nor despised, but if anything understood, interpreted. These Americans are neither worse nor better than those before them: they are children of a society that wants to have nothing to do with death and those nearing death; they are both the protagonists and the victims of a serious cultural neurosis.

On the other side of the Iron Curtain was the other great empire that had invested itself with the messianic vocation of teaching the populations subjected to it an entire way of life and customs. In the Soviet Union, the party published propaganda journals for every social category. For all, that is, except one: it goes without saying that the one social category overlooked was that of the elderly, who, in that immense country, counted more than fifty million.

This is an entirely logical oversight, not worthy of our surprise or scandal: a journal for the elderly could not speak only of victories, five-year plans carried out or soon to be. It would have to talk about problems, too. And this was not possible within the cage of a dogmatic power that programs the future of the "people," of "humanity," but that must make people forget that those abstract entities are composed of concrete men whose future, if they are old, is not ushered in by song and the glorious sunrise of the official mythology, but more realistically, the tomb.

Comrades heading toward their end could not and must not exist, with their economic and social problems, and especially their psychological problems, raising questions insoluble for the Central Committee. *Pravda*[13] (literally, "The Truth") could write anything except that one truth that puts to the test every other truth: we are not eternal; we are mortal.

Let them stay in a ghetto without newspapers, those killjoy retirees: they would sabotage with their mere presence a well-ordered system where only the "worker" (the industrious one portrayed in kitsch art of Socialist Realism) had a right to full citizenship.

And let Western retirees likewise keep silent and hidden, because they do not conform to the ideal of a "consumer group" theorized by the marketing men: he and she, young with two children, a boy and a girl, so that their purchases are diversified according to their sex.

Perhaps the only true "revolution" that draws together communism and capitalism is this: the transformation of the old person from an honored member of society to an embarrassing rejection, a shame to be covered up as often as possible.

The Fate of the Ex

It is not only the social expulsion of those approaching death that renders their condition much crueler than in any previous historical epoch. All the social services, the retirement funds (if there are any), are nothing but the miserable substitute of a condition that has continued from time immemorial, until the terror of death and the consequent cult of youth swept it away.

Family and society always had their place in all age categories. Children gave hope, adults the manpower, the elderly experience, a wealth ignored and

---

[13] Editor's Note: Official newspaper of the Communist party in Russia.

despised by societies that have become neurotically obsessed with appearing young, and so refuse to have a "memory."

It is the exact opposite of the times in which the elderly were protected by divine authority: "You shall arise before the hoary head, and honor the face of an old man, and you shall fear your God: I am the Lord" (Lev. 19:32). "A hoary head is a crown of glory; it is gained in a righteous life" (Prov. 16:31).

To live as a human means giving and taking, offering and receiving. Now it is forbidden to the elderly to offer the only thing they have: experience, wisdom. "Thus," says Kübler-Ross, based on her research, "the desire to die is generated in many because, not having anything more to give, life is no longer worth living."

While on one side we work to prolong the average lifespan, on the other side we seek a lowering of the retirement age. If experience counts for nothing, the magical slogan is: "Rejuvenate! Rejuvenate!" They must be dumped as soon as possible in the landfill.

In what condition, then?

Man today, though he goes into retirement early and unceremoniously, has been pushed since his childhood to "become someone" in an economic and social sense: school is now entirely a function of the job market.

Once again for the first time in history, the aim of education is no longer the formation of a complete person, but only the development of some of his occupational capacities. The prospect of possessing goods makes one look with compassion upon the being that sustained every educational system. Here was born the hatred, the iconoclastic fury against the old "humanistic" school, burdened no doubt by many errors and faults but oriented toward a less imbalanced formation than that oriented toward "profit" and "production."

The principal question is no longer "what must I learn and know to become a complete human being?" but "what must I learn to be well-paid some day and, as such, become a citizen with full standing in our consumeristic society (or in the society of workers)?"

All of this has a human cost to be paid by everyone when the tab comes: entering into the productive cycle, man is driven by an implacable mechanism to seek the greatest "success" possible. But all careers are devised in such a way as to expel you (retirees before their time, in order to make way for the new victims that push from below) when you have reached, if you have survived, that finish line you have been fighting to reach all your life: to "arrive." But where?

So look at you, not only kicked out by what had become your entire world, but suddenly and cruelly confronted by that *being* they tried to hide from you your whole life. They trained you to have a ferocious myopia, making you see *possession* as your only future, the next stage in your career or salary promotion. And now that your career is over, now that the next stage is decline, sickness, and death? After having confronted so many little, partial futures, what will you do now that you have time to confront a mysterious absolute future, one that draws nearer every day?

It is a future you will have to deal with without any preparation: the inexorable wheel of your career forced you to concentrate on the company's problems (whether private or public), or on your problems, but only in economical terms, on work contracts or your position in the corporate structure. What now, now that all of these problems have shown their relativity and have left space to the one true problem, that of your destiny as a man, and not merely as a worker and consumer?

They led you to believe that everything was resolvable in social terms; but now society is abandoning you. And not only does it abandon you because you no longer have a place in the productive process of the state or the multinational, nor are needed for the "progress" of the community (of which you constitute what is defined as "a dead weight"); not only have you been abandoned because your consumption is reduced or because you contradict by your mere existence the sacred texts of all ideologies.

It has also and above all abandoned you because the problem incumbent upon your future can only be faced in solitude. "Dying," wrote Montaigne to those who might have forgotten, "is each time a drama with just one protagonist."

"We die alone," repeats the contemporary theologian Hans Urs von Balthasar, "while life, from the mother's womb, is always communion (such that an isolated human 'I' can neither be born nor exist and cannot even be imagined); death momentarily suspends without time the law of communion." Each of us must come to terms with death and these terms are one-on-one, in an obligatory face-to-face.

Blaise Pascal pushes this reality to its logical conclusions, as is his habit. Pascal is not afraid of noting, "We are quite ridiculous when we seek comfort in our peers: miserable as we are, impotent as we are, they cannot help us. We shall die alone."

You will have to get by alone with death, the greatest of individual problems, and (as if that were not enough) this problem has been isolated and chased away to the end of life. It is forbidden to think about it before its time, when it still seems far off; forbidden in all phases of preceding life, even just to take account of our mortal condition, drawing the conclusions therefrom.

Expelled from the wheel of economic history, the only wheel that counts today, without anything more to distract you, a problem that is eternal presents itself to you as if it were new, fearful in its concreteness and solitude.

Years to Life, Not Life to the Years

Who can you confide in, who can help you to attenuate a bit the anguish and solitude?

Is it the psychologist who has or will have, sooner or later, your same problem, and in his briefcase has only soothing chatter for a fee? Is it a psychologist who was formed by what Balducci termed that "modern psychology developed not to reconcile with the prospect of death subjects afflicted by anguish, but to cleanse them of this anguish and return them to playing the games of the society of consumption and hedonism"?

Will you turn to the politician, the union leader, the sociologist? But all these are peddlers of theories and strategies only for the strong, the healthy, the young. The old and his perspective on death are doubly taboo, because they confound their power and their souls: what will become of their authority and their words when they too are nothing but "ex"?

Consider one of the new, truly powerful figures of Western society: the union boss, at least in certain contemporary Italian versions (though this might not be the case in past versions, or those in other countries where unions might no longer be necessary because the workers are already in power).

On this topic, there is a risk of scandal: unions and their leaders, according to the imposition of revered dogma, can be spoken of only in glowing terms. They can only be considered as noble, disinterested paladins of the ideal, spotless, and fearless knights of humanity.

But I laugh at those who shatter the statuettes of old saints to make themselves new ones. I refuse to consider categories or people not case by case, on an objective basis, but based on prejudices, whether favorable or unfavorable. I recognize no human institution as sacred: if I want the sacred, I know where to look for it; I prefer the original, not its imitations.

So, we must reason without tearing our garments ("Sacrilege!"): What does an old retiree matter to our unions (I am speaking about their management, not of course about their base) when their power is based on the membership cards of active workers and their strikes? The retiree no longer works; *therefore*, he can no longer strike, except against himself. *Therefore*, he does not ensure the power of the tycoons of cards and strikes. *Therefore*, if it does not exist for the "master," neither does it exist for the foremen of the "representatives of the workers," despite every hypocritical recitation to the contrary.

Moreover, they organize a fine debate for the elderly on the theme: "The Condition of the Elderly in the Local Area," a stimulating conference that assures money, publicity, and satisfied vanity for the speakers: all of them "inconvenient," "courageous," as well as the young or at the most the middle-aged. Otherwise, who would invite them?

In the end, the conference is over, and the elderly have been duped. My friend, our society is based on politics, rights, claims; all matters connected by their nature to force. Those who do not have it are recognized neither as citizens nor as being fully human.

Bosses and union leaders hold positions that are only apparently in opposition, but in reality, are united in the same logic: that of possession, money, and things. The bosses want to hold on to these as long as possible, while the union leaders want to get as much of it as they can. Both are legitimate attitudes, certainly, but they will not solve your problem, which might be economic, but in no case can be resolved only by means of some hypothetical increase in social security checks.

Should you throw your anxieties on your children, then, in your need for continuance, for defeating death? This has always been the most valid, natural strategy against the personal ruin that awaits each of us. We have already mentioned how strong this instinct still is today.

But it is a nearly impracticable route: the society of the seekers of eternal youth has fostered the widening of a chasm between parents and children. Hostility, diffidence, fear toward the old, even toward our old relatives, are behaviors widely reinforced by our dominant culture. It needs fresh blood: for production, for consumption, for the class struggle, for union militancy, maybe even for "liberation theology."

The new recruits must be forcibly removed from proximity, whether physical or emotional, to the elderly, to avoid running the risk of being distracted by reflections dangerous to the well-oiled social machine or to our complex utopian architecture, so perfect in theory.

Not by chance, young South American protesters march to slogans suggested by their directors: "*Del Viejo, ni el consejo,*" from the elderly we accept nothing, not even their advice. In this way, they can consider themselves "revolutionaries" too, but the logic is the same as their bourgeois counterparts.

Simon de Beauvoir, the companion of Jean-Paul Sartre, fought her entire life, in good faith, to foster a culture in which slogans such as this might constitute the model.

Then, Beauvoir, like Sartre, was obliged to confess that the idols in whom she had believed had been shattered on the ground. To her ideological disenchantment was added her advancing age, the fact of touching with her own hand what it means to grow old in a society that demands that you bare your breast, grasp the hammer and sickle, or more simply dive into the pool after cocktails. And what if the age of arthritis has already set in?

And so, one of Beauvoir's last books was titled *La vieillesse, The Old Woman*. It is an investigation into the present cruelty toward the non-young: we recommend it to those who suspect us of exaggerating the tone in the hope of demonstrating preconceived notions.

Here, we can only report the conclusions reached by Beauvoir, active in causes whose relative importance had been demonstrated by her life experience, yet (differing from many others) still capable of self-criticism:

> When we come to realize what the condition of the elderly is today, we can feel no satisfaction simply asking for reforms — a more generous political stance, better pensions, decent housing, and organized outings. It is the entire system that is under discussion, and our demand can only be a radical one: change life itself.

A noble appeal, but incapable of being realized, at least on the social level.

The bitter reflection of one of the most famous gerontologists, the American Edward L. Bortz, will be valid for a long time to come: "We have succeeded perhaps in adding more years to life. But we have not in the least given more life to the years."

THE CRIME OF MOURNING

But for the old there is at least one consolation.

No one today, not even the young person, is safe from the danger of social ostracism. Neurosis can strike implacably even the "non-old" and the "non-sick."

This happens when death touches us closely, striking someone near. A prohibition — another! — has been thrown at those who mourn and mourning itself, decreeing its obscenity, as for everything that smacks of death, and canceling it through the force of social customs.

Sandro Spinsanti says, "Mourning has become a socially deviant, criminal behavior, which our society, based on the trinity of health-youth-happiness, no longer tolerates."

I have grown weary of reporting that certain facts have taken place for the first time in history, but what can I do if here as well we have one such case? Neither does this seem a great sign of progress.

If someone tried to challenge social prohibition today, insisting on showing his grief in an external manner, he would be immediately punished by a void being created around him. There is a hiding place, never invisible enough, for tombs; there is a ghetto for the dying, for the old; but there is also a leprosarium for sending into quarantine anyone who, touched by death and wounded in the affections, has the impudence not to pretend that he is just fine.

Am I exaggerating here, too?

Among the many possible examples, I refer you to the recent experience of a journalist and writer I have already cited, Fausto Gianfranceschi, who underwent the terrible trial of the death of his twenty-year-old son. This man of vast experience discovered for the first time a reality that he euphemistically defined as "strange," and which led him to reflect and write:

> It was very difficult for me to talk about what had happened with others. I analyzed my difficulty and understood that it did not depend on my reticence (almost inexistent, especially at the beginning) as on the sensation that I was causing embarrassment (if not downright annoyance and the desire to hide) in the people to whom, in the first days, I naïvely confided this disaster. I noticed while talking it was as if I were breaching a taboo, as if I were committing something unbecoming that rendered me unpleasant.... People today distance themselves from one who

is in mourning, or they worry about avoiding the least allusion to the loss suffered.... And yet, this does not mean that people are heartless or were not moved: on the contrary, the more they are touched the more they try to hide their sentiment, obeying an unspoken but urgent censure that obliges us to speak as if death did not exist.

AND YET, EVEN PROFESSOR FREUD...

It was Sigmund Freud himself, the atheist founder of psychoanalysis, who warned against the dangers of a prohibition on mourning. According to Freud, as for all his colleagues after him, the mental health of all society is threatened by the prohibition of crying for one's dead. The suffering for the loss of a person dear to us needs to manifest itself in an external, social dimension as well. This is true of all that is authentically human (beginning with love) which has a need to shout out in public, to receive social approval.

And what else is mourning if not love for the one who has loved us, for the one we have loved? Snatching from us those who are nearest to us, death opens a profound wound within us. Like physical wounds, a psychological wound must be tended and cured to be able to heal little by little. Not incidentally, rites and customs of mourning are a constant in all societies — that is, in all societies except our own.

Freud speaks of an indispensable, liberating *Trauerarbeit*, the "work of mourning": if this is missing, as is often the case today, because it is tacitly (though not less cruelly) prohibited, not only does the suffering of those already wounded by death multiply, but a serious element of imbalance is added throughout society.

The father of psychoanalysis warned of this danger in Vienna, where the "work of mourning" was still tolerated.

Of course: that was already "bourgeois death," polluted by self-righteousness and individualism. From something authentically social, as it was in the preceding centuries, it now closed itself off within the nuclear family; but the shreds that remained of the millennial wisdom inherited from the tradition seemed sufficient to render it more bearable and more human.

We urge caution on those who try to justify the prohibition of traditional mourning, with its rhythms and rites, saying that it was the hypocritical decorum of a hypocritical society. In reality, more than a question of *savoir vivre*, at play here are the inalterable exigencies of our deepest humanity.

What, then, was that death like that at the turn of the twentieth century celebrated its last rites before the prevalence of the "thanatophobia" neurosis canceled everything, creating quite different neuroses? This is not a question of Christian (or religious in general) death and mourning, which we shall consider at the appropriate time. We are talking about "social," "secular" customs, practiced by believers and non-believers in the name of man, not necessarily of man in his relationship with God.

What those liberating rites, so rooted in history, were really like I cannot say from direct experience. For a long time now they have been superseded, at least in the places and settings I have known. Like many of my generation, I have to reconstruct traditional mourning rites based on written sources or on the remembrances of the elderly.

Except in rare cases, life ended where it had been lived, at home, in one's own setting, surrounded by relatives and friends who, by helping one to die, learned how to die as well. Having reached the end, funerary decorations would be brought out, black or violet, in the rooms and on the doors, for a necessary exterior manifestation of the interior grief. Man also needs signs and colors to bring out his *pathos*. It is this need that moves those in a protest march to wave a red flag, tinged with the ancient religious significance of ardor, courage, vitality; or that moves fans to wave the banners of their team; or moves the lover to dress instinctively in lively clothes.

The West chose black to manifest bereavement, while the East opted for the other extreme of the chromatic scale, white. It was not only a question of colors, but of symbols that best correspond, according to the different cultures, to a common need of every human being. Thus, even the disappearance of the decorations and the dark clothes "of mourning" marked the repression of an authentic need. And no repression, whether psychological or political, was ever positive.

After the decorations followed the sorrowful rite, though necessary and liberating, of the washing and dressing of the corpse. What was once entrusted to the merciful hands of relatives and friends is now outsourced (with hidden repugnance) to the mercenaries of specialized companies. In the "secular" world, the primitive belief in the impurity of the cadaver has returned in force: whoever sets eyes upon, or worse, lays hands upon the corpse, enters into contact with the divinities of death and contaminates himself and others among the living.

But even that contact with the corpse of a beloved person responded to the ineradicable need of gestures, of corporality, to externalize emotions.

There seem to have been visits called "perfunctory," which, as the name indicates, might have been subjectively hypocritical, but not for this reason less objectively necessary. In fact, they bore witness to the social dimension of every death.

One dies alone, but death does not concern only the individual: it involves the entire community; it is a drama both personal and social.

Those visits fulfilled a double function: they helped those receiving the visitors, showing them the solidarity of the community. But they helped the visitors as well, allowing them to consider the inevitability of death and therefore to give occasional and discrete vent to the anguish that is always present in us.

A liberating function was exercised also by the actions following the rite; first, the vigil around the coffin consisting in the prayers of the believer or the remembrance of the deceased for the non-believer. When the shadows of death fall on a person, his loved ones need the help of the group to confront at least the darkness of the first night. And they need friendly words, or just silent solidarity.

Then, the funeral procession: crowded, on foot, slow, because the mournful do not run. The scared run. Not by chance is the modern funeral characterized by haste, by the hearse that darts through traffic as fast as possible. These hasty funeral services are another revealing sign of a society that wants to get through it quickly because it is afraid. Evaluating man's capacity to produce and consume, it does not want to waste time with one who can never work or consume again, and therefore is of no use.

Economic exigencies, with the consequent necessity of not blocking traffic, have so easily prevailed over respect for the mystery of death, prohibiting funeral processions by police ordinance.

The circulation of people and goods today can be blocked only for "important" dead people, for the powerful deceased — namely, those who are still useful to the powerful, those who can reiterate their authority doing homage to the caste, only *they* are worthy of stopping even our automobile obsession.

After the funeral, there followed for the spouse a period of mourning, with a duration and severity that decreased according to the degree of kinship or friendship: from a completely black wardrobe to the black armband, or the button in the grommet; from months, perhaps years of bereavement to just a few days.

Of course, here too a suspicion arises (if not the certainty) of formalism. But it seems that not only propriety was at work here: different degrees and durations of mourning responded to a millennial experience, to the different intensity of the "work" required to heal the wound.

The most stricken, the immediate family, added to this adaptation of apparel the suspension of activities considered "worldly"; but the "world" did not forget them, but rather made visits, sent cards and letters. Before returning to normal life, a wise realism imposed the recognition of death's presence, power, and rights.

THE FORTUNE OF BEING BLACK

Quite different is the code of a culture that considers itself advanced because it first requires the dying to go with as little disturbance as possible and then imposes on the survivors not to disturb anything or anyone at all.

The more "advanced" this code is, the more it severely prohibits exterior manifestations, from crying to laments to (horror!) yelling, which remind us that death is near, that it wounds us still, and that it is not at all as "natural" as we are supposed to believe.

Who of us in the Northern Hemisphere, in industrial, modern regions, has not felt the disturbance, discomfort, if not even scorn and contempt, for the funerary customs of those in the Southern Hemisphere? Scorn toward, that is, the cultures that have preserved something of the authenticity and wisdom of ancient traditions, and who therefore give space to crying and shouting, to spontaneity in the face of tragedy.

This is not a question here of dignity, but of humanity. Those who are scandalized by these "backward customs" are often the very same people who rediscover the techniques of bodily expression (mime, dance, or even singing), who pay abundantly to learn them, but who refuse to admit that in the face of death as well (above all) man's whole being, and therefore also the body, can and must express his interiority.

Because our needs remain despite every repression, insult is added to injury with the commercial exploitation of a frustrated instinct. In the United States alone, enormous financial interests move behind funeral homes, which guarantee another service: for a congruous sum and under the direction of a stuffy funeral director, in well-hidden back rooms, relatives can give vent to their pain. There and only there, far from the eyes and ears of others, is it allowed to bear witness with voice and body how deeply death wounds us.

Once the shouting and crying are finished, the director fulfills needs that have been declared "surpassed" by the dominant culture, but evidently so little surpassed that they make rich the merchants who exploit them. The funeral parlor functionaries assure a minimum of the ancient social participation, comforting those present with words more or less prolonged according to the agreed upon tariffs. If requested, they can also recite "philosophical" or "humanistic" discourses, good for all faiths and incredulities, that recall the deceased and their merits. This takes place in a room with heavy black drapery, socially prohibited elsewhere. This is simply a grotesque surrogate of the comfort assured by traditional funerary rites. In any case, it is another of the privileges that "democratic" societies reserve for the wealthy, who can afford the services of funeral homes.

The poor know how to get revenge, however. Research by the few American thanatologists shows that the more modest the social class, the more humane the condition of the elderly, the dying, and those mourning their loss. It seems, in fact, that African Americans are the only group in the United States for whom death has a less ferocious countenance. Remembering in some way their ancient culture, they have preserved a familial and public dimension in death and the proper place of bereavement. The worst possible death, say the thanatologists, is a clandestine one, cursed, incomprehensible among the homes and deserted parks of the golden suburbs of the well-off. Who said it was advantageous to be among the "upper classes"? Extreme situations like death are capable of reestablishing truth and justice.

THE IGNORED GURUS

The taboo against death is so rigorous and entrenched that even the venerated oracles, those modern gurus called psychologists and psychoanalysts are not even given credence. Philippe Ariès says:

> The appreciation of mourning and its indispensable role on the part of psychologists is exactly opposite to that of society. The latter considers mourning to be morbid, while for psychologists it is the repression of bereavement that is morbid and causes morbidity. It is a unique case. In fact, all the other ideas of psychologists and psychoanalysts (on sexuality, child development, and so forth), whether correct or incorrect, have been disseminated and assimilated by Western society. Only their ideas on mourning and its beneficial function have been ignored by the

public and hidden by those who control the mass media. In the face of death, even the new teachers are impotent.

Only in this case do we plug our ears, while the "experts," otherwise given obsequious hearing elsewhere, remind us in vain:

> The abolition of the signs linked to death creates an unbearable tension, an authentic individual and social pathology of unresolved suffering that gives rise to depression, suicide, or manifestations of collective violence, which newspapers go on to define as "inexplicable." Like the negation of any reality, the negation of mourning and of what it represents weighs upon the subconscious and is among the factors of suffering and imbalance in the individual as in the community.

Those "experts" observe: the weight of suffering is more bearable insofar as the shoulders that must carry it are wide. Now, small nuclear families, broken relations with relatives, and the atomization of social relationships all make the terrible emotional weight unleashed by death a burden to be carried by a few, a burden that crushes them.

One does not have to be a psychologist to understand what the death of parents means to an only child, isolated in the big city, with just a few superficial acquaintances more than friends; and what the death of a member of a more well-structured and branched out family, inserted into a supportive community would mean. Ariès writes:

> Once, the death of a person dear to us was spread out over many. Furthermore, it did not destroy one's entire affective life, substitutions were in some way possible. Now there is little if anything left of this. And, as a final blow, one adds the prohibition of any funerary rite meant to lighten the psychological impact.

LAUGHING AT THE "BIG PEOPLE"

Do we need to list other banes brought upon us by that crime of which we have been guilty for several centuries now? It would certainly not be difficult to lengthen the chain or add more links; the identity of that social scourge is now clear. It is also equally clear that denouncing it is a duty, but we must do this without deceiving ourselves. There is no remedy for death; nor is there a remedy for the death of death decreed in "developed" countries, none excluded.

Neither do we have anything good or helpful to expect from our political, economic or cultural masters. There is a radical incompatibility between every power and every liberating rediscovery of death.

"*Qui a appris à mourir, a desappris à servir,*" one who has learned to die has unlearned to serve. Montaigne said it. Today more than in his time, breaking a prohibition can be the most revolutionary choice.

Nothing is as revolutionary as irony, which is the gift born of the attitude which the ancients called *contemplatio mortis*, the contemplation of death, or in today's terms, the realistic awareness of the human condition.

To the contrary of what the usual rumors repeat, this *contemplatio* (if properly understood) does not lead to alienation. If anything, it leads to the opposite: whether a believer or not, to be conscious that the time allotted us is not infinite stimulates us to live the present more fully, to take seriously every minute, every hour, every day.

In due time, one must denounce the widescale and false propaganda according to which "whoever thinks about death cannot think about life." Instead, it is precisely the person who is aware of the temporal limit of his existence who lives profoundly in the here and now.

But in the person who has faithfully given space to the end, his and others', appropriate seriousness coexists with an equally appropriate, liberating irony. And irony is precisely what is unbearable to the powerful of any sort (minister or industrial leader, celebrity or intellectual) who can tolerate aggression but not demythologizing.

What unites all the presumed "great of the earth" is that they take themselves seriously and expect others to do so as well. What infuriates them most is the joke, the ironic one-liner that reduces them to their true proportions. They can defend themselves from the terrorist's guns, but they are impotent before the smile of the ironic man — namely, of one who is aware that nothing is absolute because nothing is eternal.

"Religions are like the undertaker: they live upon death," says the Marxist Michel Verret. There is some truth here: too many "religious authorities" throughout history have had close ties with Caesar, placing at his disposal ambivalent theologies that help to keep their subjects at bay thanks to the bogeyman of death and Hell.

This has happened even in the Christian tradition, but it happened in the past. What about today? Is it not the new "horizontal religions" of today, the political ideologies, that live by imposing a censure on what they deem unpleasant? Do we not see how the corridors of power can be shored up not only by speaking too much about death, but also by not speaking about it and impeding others from speaking about it?

The awareness that we all have an end leads to a healthy irony, enemy of every caste and regime, because the "Great Democracy of Death" heeds no one, and it reestablishes and teaches absolute equality. Death is the one that no bodyguard can stop, that guides the most radical of revolutions eliminating every difference. Before it, everyone is revealed to be equally miserable and impotent, whatever their social class, whether dominant or subaltern.

These are such obvious observations of such elementary truths that they seem prosaic. One would be reticent about repeating them, were they not so thoroughly forgotten.

Thus, thanks to that forgetfulness, "thanatophobic" cultures, as well as the "thanatophilic" cultures of today, fall into one more contradiction. On one side, they claim the most radical democracy possible; but on the other side they forget that it has been historically proven that the first suspicion of equality among men, and thus the first seed of democracy, popped into the head of the one who reflected on the fact that the king and the slave both share the same destiny. How could one continue to believe that the radiant, omnipotent emperor, whether he sits in Rome or in Versailles, in the White House or in the Kremlin, is equal to us subjects if we fail to remember, and to remind him, that he too is mortal, like us and like all men?

It is a truth, I repeat, that is self-evident. But it is curious and disturbing that precisely those who shout the loudest that they want to combat the powerful and the domineering then fall enthusiastically into the trap of those same potentates, aiding them in burying ever deeper the Enemy that menaces everyone. But who menaces above all those who have bedded their nest so well here as to consider the greatest tragedy to be the inevitable end of their dominance.

This contradiction is glaring, but the use of reason is not the strong suit of the culture of reason.

CHAPTER 7
The Door upon the Mystery

The End or the Beginning?

WE ENDED THE PRECEDING chapter discussing, a bit disheartened, one of the many contradictions of the thought system and way of life to which we have been subjected.

We are the ones who insist on erring, when presuming to remain on the rational level. We do not want to convince ourselves that it is useless to appeal to our interlocutor's reason when their problem is not logical but rather psychological.

If we consider the psychological point of view, what once seemed senseless reveals a distorted justification. The immense apparatus erected from Los Angeles to Vladivostok, passing through Eastern and Western Europe to hide reality, shows itself for what it is.

Namely, it is the only wisdom possible for one who can do nothing but pass the time collecting stamps and porcelain; for one who wants to be absorbed by the little problems "downstream," because he cannot enquire into the big problem "upstream"; for the one who must concentrate his attention and that of his subjects on *current events* so as not to think about fearful *eternity*, which, however things turn out, awaits us with certainty. "The masters and teachers of today," says Konrad Lorenz, "in the end are not at all diabolical manipulators of consciences, or supermen with Luciferian intelligence. Perhaps they are only poor victims, all too human, of their inhumane doctrines."

They are poor people who, though without ever confessing it, do not in the least ignore the fact that death is a merciless meatgrinder where their chatter comes to an end, as do their consolations and alibis.

They know well that death is the door that opens fearfully onto an inviolate and inviolable mystery.

They know well that death is the unknown; that it is the enigma of the unexplored; that behind it can be the all or the nothing. Whatever happens, it drags us with it into the eternal: Will it be light or darkness, interminable life of total extinction? Is it an end or a beginning?

Quoting oneself is a bit ridiculous, but at times it is convenient. I quote myself, therefore, given that no one among the many critics on various continents has demonstrated that what I wrote in this paragraph on the first pages of *Hypotheses about Jesus* was wrong:

> The Problem behind the questions often ridiculed, almost as if to be left to adolescents, unworthy of adults: Who are we? Where do we come from? Where are we going?
>
> Is there a future for us, beyond the horizon that collides ineluctably against the wall of death? Or truly, as Ettore Petrolini sang under his breath bitterly, are we just packages, specimens of no value, which the obstetrician sends to the undertaker? Before the obstetrician and after the undertaker, life is open to two mysteries. Before birth and after death, on both extremities, our existence is immersed in the unknown, in the eternal: The Eternal, the nothing from which we came, perhaps. The Eternal, the nothing into which we shall sink.
>
> Those who compare our condition to a man awakening on a train rumbling through the night are probably not far off the mark. From whence did that train we are riding on (we know not how or why) depart? Where is it going? Why on this train and not another?
>
> There are some who are happy to inspect their compartment in the train, to check the dimensions of the seats, to analyze the materials. Then they fall back asleep peacefully: they are aware of the environment around them, and that's enough, the rest is not their business. If the anguish of the unknown clutches their throat, there is always a way of chasing it away by thinking of something else. As Carducci says, "better forgetful action without investigating this mystery of the universe." ... Returning to the image of the train, even the most arrogant have but one certain fact to offer: that the train will end up entering a dark

tunnel without the possibility of disembarking beforehand. But what lies beyond the entrance to that mysterious tunnel they do not know.

"There is nothing, there is only darkness," some say.

A respectable opinion. Unfortunately, however, it has the defect of lacking truth. No one has come back to give us an account of the journey beyond the *Todeslinie*, the line of death.

THE AFTERLIFE, OBVIOUSLY, DOES NOT EXIST

Several decades have passed since I wrote those lines. Since then, nothing seems to have changed: no one has come back yet from this one-way journey. Since the dawn of time, not only has man had the terrible habit of dying, but he insists on not wanting to cross back over that mysterious border to give us news.

Some exceptions — one in particular — come to mind. But the moment to talk about that has not yet come; this is still the time of remaining on the plane of facts verifiable by anyone, without appeals or reference to faith.

Alberto Moravia, the Roman writer, bored and dogmatic, reassures himself and those who take him seriously, saying, "Eternity, obviously, does not exist."[14]

Because we are neither Moravia nor one of his disciples (and God save us from that), we prefer to respect the reality of matters, recalling that no one can concede any "obviously" regarding what lies beyond the doors of death.

No one, I repeat — neither believer nor non-believer; neither can affirm nor deny. Here there can be nothing obvious, because there is nothing objectively demonstrable. There is no certainty here, expect to faith.

Speaking of Moravia, Saul Bellow, the Noble Prize-winning novelist, asked, "Why do these 'masters' refuse so obstinately to speak in terms of truth and humanity?" In reality, they cannot, prisoners that they are to the role bestowed by a society neurotically terrorized by the mystery of death.

Men like Moravia (one among many possible names) are for our time what the Pythias were to classical antiquity, the priestesses of the temple of Apollo at Delphi. As then, so today men run to consult the oracles to reassure themselves, to placate their anxieties.

---

[14] The trust of the reader in the textual exactness of the quotes can have a just limit. All quotes are presented faithfully, as in *Hypotheses* and as those who took the effort to check can testify. But, given the singular grotesqueness of Moravia's words, here *una tantum*, is the reference: *L'Espresso* no. 44 (November 6, 1977).

"Master, is it true or not, that after death there is nothing?" ask journalists on behalf of everyone, in the periodic rite of the superstitious interview with Moravia, or with whomever might be on the hotseat. "True indeed," confirms the master, pensive and paternal, "Most true. Keep calm. Write that there is nothing, tell this to the people. There is nothing. I assure you; I give you my word."

Alessandro Manzoni, in his novel *Promessi Sposi*, described Don Ferrante, the intellectual exorcist of the day, as the Pythia of the seventeenth century, the one who tranquilizes himself, demonstrating by means of dialectical passages that the plague does not exist. Manzoni says that, in those noble verbal efforts, "Don Ferrante always found an attentive, well-disposed ear: because one cannot explain the greatness of the authority of a professional scholar when he wants to demonstrate to others the things about which they are already convinced," or of which they want to be persuaded.

"*L'enfer n'existe pas, Sartre l'a prouvé*," (Hell does not exist, Sartre proved it) proclaimed a famous slogan in France a few years ago.

Every country, every century has its oracle, its Pythia, its teacher in consolations.

Sure, it's a shame that reality is different from how these oracles swear it is: there is here, unfortunately, no "obviously." No one has ever proven, nor will anyone prove anything regarding the "afterlife," "eternity."

SAVAGES, ENGINEERS, PHILOSOPHERS

Do not allow yourself to be enchanted by the consoling chatter of those dubious teachers. And do not allow yourself to be blinded by the control panels of all the computers and technological merchandise. The super technician in a white lab coat projecting, constructing, and manipulating those gadgets knows as much about the enigma of his destiny and that of his peers as the illiterate or the caveman.

The aerospace engineer at his base in California and the "savage" of the last surviving tribe in the South Seas are united by the same ignorance in this matter. In fact, it seems that the so-called savage might know much more than the engineer. Surely, that "primitive" is much better equipped than the American (or Russian, or European) to master the anxiety born of the mystery to which death gives access.

Only a coarse propagandist like Michel Verret can show off in phrases like this: "Science impedes one from attributing the least objective consistency to the religious fairytale about the afterlife."

Here is the attempt to transform a hope into a reality. Science and the problem of death (and what comes after, the "religious fairytale of the afterlife") are on two different, parallel planes that never meet. Bridging the two dimensions is not possible if we do not wish to become the worst of scientists, or something other than scientists.

Science can progress as much as it wants, but the mystery that concerns us here remains intact. Closed in its radiant spacesuit of technological marvels, the astronaut can die next to his prodigious space shuttle on the most distant of planets. But neither his fellow astronauts nor the technicians at the prodigious space center on earth will be able to say something credible, based only on their scientific knowledge, on the true meaning of that death.

You must guard against the misunderstanding into which they want you to fall. You must hold firmly that no science, no technological progress will ever be able to dent a mystery that is situated outside of its reach. It lies on another plane that does not belong to the same dimension.

But remember to be wary of those who would free themselves of the mystery using in an equally abusive way the means of research available to man: philosophical reflection. Joseph Gevaert is a Flemish philosopher we have already quoted. On par with his colleagues who have not renounced their role as "thinkers" by transforming themselves into propagandists, Gevaert denounces what he characterizes as "a situation that is disturbing and, from a philosophical point of view, completely intolerable." He observes: "Almost all philosophers who present death as the last word on human existence do so as if it were an absolutely evident given and not susceptible to discussion." In reality, he continues, "we have before us a pure and simple gratuitous affirmation, without the least attempt to base it on critical hypotheses."

Thus it happens, continues Gevaert, that "great thinkers, beginning with Karl Marx, Friederich Engels, and many others, do not show the least doubt about the radical and total disappearance of personal existence after biological death. But who gave them this self-assurance? It must be said: prejudice, nothing else but prejudice."

Two Faiths

This is the reality: the so-called men of reason are nothing but men of religion. To say that everything ends with death is precisely the same as positing "something" beyond that threshold, some continuation, God.

Both affirmations are indemonstrable on a concrete level: both depend not on experience or reason, but on a faith, a certainty that can never be *objective* but remains always confined in the *subjective*.

The believer in a "vertical" religion says in a traditional sense, "Beyond death there is God who awaits His creatures. Death is the last stage only in appearance, but in reality, it is the penultimate stage. Life is a gift that will be preserved for us."

The "free thinker," the bourgeois "strong spirit," or the Marxist "dialectical materialist," all believers in one of the new horizontal religions cloaked in science or "objective philosophy," all say: "There is no God, we are products of chance, evolution, biological necessity. In death, every one of us returns to the deaf and blind matter from which we came. Life is an accident, a chance occurrence which will end in dissolution."

Both affirmations are merely expressions of two faiths, contrary but equal.

In fact, if one looks closely, the "traditional" believer, the one who does not hide the fact that he is speaking in the name of faith, reveals an attitude of greater humility and logic. If he is an authentic believer and does not degenerate as well into a propagandist, he will confess that his faith is not *contrary* to reason, but that it *exceeds* reason, that "it has not been given to all to understand this word."

The "new" believer, the one wrapped in the garb of objectivity and science (and unjustly proud of it), will say that he, and only he, has on his side reason properly understood. Thus, having power at his disposal, he will lock up in a concentration camp or in a criminal asylum whoever dares to observe that (as demonstrated by the logic of the problem but also by the experience of the ages) reason alone is not capable in the least of responding to the question: *What is death? Is it an end or a beginning?* If the police do not answer his call, he will have recourse to cultural intimidation, ideological terrorism, declaring traditional believers deprived of rights to cultural citizenship, followers of old fairytales, folkloristic wrecks of a dying world.

On the Analyst's Couch

The victims of this type of terrorism might also rejoice because it prevents them from confusing themselves with personalities of whom the psychoanalyst Giacomo Dacquino[15] speaks in this way: "Much atheism is neurotic, not in the least

---

[15] Editor's Note: Giacomo Dacquino (1930–2021) was a psychiatrist, psychotherapist, and writer.

motivated by rational considerations. This is demonstrated by the fact that, though it is often incarnated in intelligent people, they carefully avoid verifying its reasons out of fear."

Dacquino was a psychoanalyst with a Christian orientation. Do you not trust him, suspecting partiality? Here, in reinforcement, is the testimony above suspicion of Cesare Musatti,[16] that was the dean of Italian psychoanalysts, one of the most respected specialists in Europe, a scholar with Jewish origins but who has never hidden his radical atheism. "It is easily demonstrable," says Musatti, "that the most violent deniers of God are those in whom the sense of divinity is strongest. Under these forms of atheism lies in reality a serious religious neurosis."

Could it be due to observations such as these that "truly socialist" countries have banned psychoanalysis for the same reason used by the Nazis: "Zionist and degenerate pseudo-science, expression of bourgeois decadence"?

One must proceed more cautiously with the contemptuous certainties that faith in a God behind the appearance of things (and therefore in an "afterlife," whatever it might be, behind the appearance of death) is always and only an expression of hidden alienation, of dubious unsatisfied desires.

These arguments are a boomerang that could return dangerously against the imprudent one who has thrown it. It is undeniable that much religiosity in the traditional sense can be and is pathological; that there can be a dark room behind the supposedly respectable façade of many "believers," of many crusaders for the faith.

But if certain champions of "non-belief" (namely of a religion like any other, with its myths and rites, its often-irrational dogmas that remain always indemonstrable) were to lie down on the psychoanalyst's couch, they might happen to discover in the depths not the rational motivations they boast about, but a basement full of embarrassing rubbish. Trust, if you wish, their conviction that behind death there is only death. But realize that in this way you adhere to a faith like any other, you take part in a religious wager.

On this topic, the highest proposal to man's reflection, there are no shortcuts, infallible weapons or secrets that will give you a sure victory. No one can be deceived in this matter: there is no victory.

---

[16] Editor's Note: Cesare Musatti (1897–1989) was a psychologist and psychoanalyst.

The Afterlife, Obviously, Exists?

If we want to stay faithful to all that we know about the history of mankind, from its murkiest beginnings to the present; if we want to move forward step by step, clinging to the facts and not to the *ipse dixit*, "he said it," the statement by Moravia could, if anything, be turned around: "Eternity, the afterlife, obviously exist." We are cautious in saying this, clearly, in the name of all the considerations just made. But some good reasons might not be lacking. In fact, ethnologists, anthropologists, and historians have been looking into these reasons for some time now: all cultures, every one of them, have believed, in various ways, that death is a continuation, not an end, to the human adventure.

As far back as one can push the investigation, at the root of every society, one finds a cult of the dead: namely, the certainty that the deceased in some ways are still alive, that there exists a mysterious exchange with them, that not everything has terminated with the gases and liquids of decomposition. This is a certainty that runs through all of history, without exception, uninterruptedly. It runs from primitive man down to us with immutable force, whatever might be said to the contrary.

There are good reasons, therefore, if many of our contemporaries (especially among those who consider themselves shrewd and emancipated, having studied a few years at university) run to find reassurance in their oracles, who know less about these issues than their domestic workers paid by the hour.

They seek contrived confirmations because they are aware that the idea of death as the end of everything is disoriented throughout history.

This is a new conviction, and in the minority even today; nor is it well established among those who say they share it.

Ernst Bloch was upset during his youthful fervor as a bigoted Marxist when he learned that on their deathbeds, most of the party bureaucrats set aside their sacred texts and secretly called for a priest or the pope. Arriving at that threshold beyond which there is only mystery, it seems then that no dialectic, however sophisticated, is enough to reassure. Placed concretely before the enigma, not even the custodians of atheist orthodoxy trust in their faith.

One can understand their doubts, seeing that, in one of its most renowned explanations, Marxism seeks to justify the universal belief in the afterlife referring to the experience of ancient hunting societies: "Noticing the indefinite renewal of game, however much they killed it, those primitives convinced themselves that life defies death and so arrived at the belief in a type of survival."

This, and many others I will spare you, is an explanation that might make an impression on militants with low expectations in a sub-branch of some Balkan province. But that it fails to convince even its proponents if, when words give way to anguish and the torment of the mystery, they inconvenience in the dark of night clergy who come with their answers derided in public and persecuted as mythological.

Irony in the face of theories is an easy out, theories like that of the hunters and their game, produced a posteriori to justify the a priori ideological theories. The millions of young workers, students, intellectuals, and professionals who disturbed the sleep of the aristocrats in the East do not seem to belong to "hunting societies." After so many decades of persecution and propaganda about after-death-nothing-as-science-says, the result was that the percentage of religious faithful in the Soviet Union was higher than percentages in France or Italy. Even higher in the land of insistent "scientific atheism" was the number of those who wanted religious funerals for themselves and for their beloved.

Before the mysterious anguish of death, Leonid Brezhnev, the leader of the Soviet Union, threw to the wind the many volumes edited by the Leningrad Institute for Atheism and, on par with pilgrims to Lourdes, Epidaurus, Varanasi, or Mecca, he gladly returned to what his propagandists called the "prescientific mentality."

To drive away the specter of the end, Comrade Brezhnev, the high priest of orthodoxy, entrusted himself to a team of healers, clairvoyants, gurus, and shamans: all people who, with their powers true or presumed, go well beyond the soothing materialistic theories, opening strange perspectives onto "another" dimension which the ingenuous nineteenth-century positivism of Marx and Lenin ridiculed. Even Leonid Brezhnev was tempted to mock them, but only from the podium of the Central Committee, when death was still far away; not in private, when the mystery was imminent.

The Priest and the Prostitute

There is a "Union of Atheists" whose headquarters is in Paris. At the most recent congress of the association, the president reminded everyone that "as far as we know, the oldest profession in the world is not, as is believed, prostitution, but rather the priesthood." Professor François Perrin, president of those atheists and a famous scholar, believed he was reiterating in this way his disdain for every religion.

But his words can be read differently.

It is not accidental if the priest appears immediately wherever there is an embryonic society, and he is always connected to the omnipresent culture of the dead. If men choose him from among them with such haste, it is because they are driven by the profound need to make sense of life by giving meaning to death. They ask the priest assistance in exorcising the usual, great question: *What is this mystery that surrounds us, and where are we going?*

It is an eternal need that continues to be quite strong today. Our cities are crowded with new and ancient priests to besiege with anxious questions: they are called "experts," "psychologists," "sociologists." Next to them are the sibyl-intellectuals, astrologers, seers. They are all simply the extension of the sacerdotal role of the past: the one who exorcises, placates, intercedes, explains, helps against the mystery of which death is the apex.

H. L. Mencken is a well-known name in the United States. He wrote the *Treatise on the Gods*, perhaps the most widely read anti-religious manual in America. As the editor defines it after so many reprints, this is "a secular and rational *summa* that dissolves all the fogs of superstition."

Mencken writes, "It is surprising to see how men, otherwise highly esteemed, attach themselves to ideas, like survival after death, that date back to the infancy of the human race."

Similar to the French Perrin and his Union of Atheists, not even the American is aware of the ambivalence of his words. How is it that "since the infancy of the human race" everyone has believed (and the belief still continues) in "survival after death"? How is it that this "idea" was so spontaneous that it leapt out of man's head the moment he started to reflect, as soon as he asked "why?" before the first cadaver, in Malraux's words?

There is an old rule that says: "When the majority is convinced of a reality, the burden of proof lies with the minority that denies it."

We shall use an example to explain this: the majority of physicians is convinced of the existence of a direct relationship between certain eating habits and the development of certain diseases. In many cases the conviction is based on statistical data and not on irrefutable scientific demonstration of cause and effect.

A minority of other physicians can then deny that relationship. Now, the burden of proving this denial lies with the minority.

Returning to our discussion: Not simply the majority but the *totality* of cultures of all times and places have been convinced that death is not the end of everything. Staying within the bounds of logic, there are a few who, only recently, have opposed this conviction, which should justify their thesis: the burden of proof, here, falls on those who stop at appearances and say that the cadaver exhausts the entire reality of death. But now we know that for some, logic is valid only when it places them in the right; it is worthless when it might cause them problems.

Thus, as Joseph Gevaert denounced above, one continues to take for granted, without a serious inquiry, what is not only indemonstrable, but which contradicts a universal conviction.

Let it be said: that this conviction is general and dates from as far back as history and anthropology can reach is not proof that Something truly "exists." On one side or the other, there is no certainty here if only in the risk of a wager either on God or on Chance. But this conviction is at least proof of the instinctive rebellion of man throughout time and place in the face of the idea of vanishing forever. This rebellion is so deeply rooted that, as Freud says, "at the bottom of the unconscious, no man is truly convinced of dying."

Would this tenacious and violent rebellion perhaps be a clue to a profound instinct that, like every natural instinct, corresponds to something that truly exists? The instinct to drink corresponds to water; the instinct to eat corresponds to food; the instinct to love corresponds to the other. Is only the instinct to avoid death for everyone everywhere illusory, without any corresponding reality? Among all the impulses, all of humanity's universal beliefs, is only faith in survival after death truly unfounded?

The centuries after the Enlightenment, as we have seen, placed trust and attention only in reason, but important as it is, it is only a part of man. A rediscovery of the complete man, not reduced to mere gray cerebral matter, the modern cultural currents reevaluate even man's instinctual nature, his natural spontaneity. Is there anything more instinctual and spontaneous than this certainty, witnessed throughout all history, of surviving death in some way?

Is this tension alone truly aimed toward nothingness? To perceive the truth of the lines I am about to propose one need not be a Christian, a Catholic, but simply must look within, without prejudices, at one's own human experience.

The Second Vatican Council says in *Gaudium et Spes*, the Constitution on the Church in the Modern World:

In the face of the modern development of the world, the number constantly swells of the people who raise the most basic questions or recognize them with a new sharpness: what is man? What is this sense of sorrow, of evil, of death, which continues to exist despite so much progress? What purpose have these victories purchased at so high a cost? What can man offer to society, what can he expect from it? What follows this earthly life?

JEERS AND FEAR

Quid post vitam hanc terrestrem?

Over the years I have received concrete and not just theoretical confirmation of how the question of the Council Fathers has been a termite that hiddenly gnaws at those who insist the most on security.

For a long time, the insistence of a journalist chasing after the clues left by a God in hiding has taken me around the world asking about the enigmatic, ambiguous adventure of life.

Among the acclaimed "masters of thought" who have granted me an audience, I had the impression that many regret having agreed to give an interview. I often perceived in them a discomfort, if not a bit of hatred. As a consciously rude person who does not accept the new social etiquette, I did not suggest brilliant, amusing, pleasant questions, because they are relevant to frivolous, irrelevant themes. Rather, I attempted to flush out those serious people with questions on final things, prohibited questions, excluded from their dogmatic decalogues.

Like a somewhat sadistic acupuncturist, with pen and notebook, I went searching for the sciatic nerve of these elegant thinkers. There was no need of great ability; little was needed to make nervous those wanting to hide even from themselves, those who had gone through life talking and writing about many things, taking seriously many things, except for the one thing that is behind everything and gives and takes meaning from everyone. People who want to hide the fact that at the bottom of every question lies (the more threatening the more one tries to escape it) a *question* one must decide to come to terms with sooner or later.

Too expert and clever now, I did not let myself be sidetracked by the attempts of these unfortunate victims to exorcise the problem, turning to politics or culture. The radical, vital questions raised by a certain Jesus Christ, by certain Gospels, are reduced to squalid, trivial problems of counting electoral votes: what they call the "Catholic question," as if a speech on the Christian Democratic Party might have some relevance to the absolute future of man. If not this, then every disturbing religious discourse is left to slide into "anthropological science."

It was impossible not to notice with what relief these people, despite their gluttonous desire for publicity and interviews, would accompany me to the door. It happened at times that I crossed Europe to listen to them, and yet, not once after the interview ended and my notebook shut, did someone suggest going for dinner.

Why not get rid of a pain in the neck as soon as possible, one who does not hide the suspicion that the Maginot Line, constructed against the anguish of death over the course of a life's labors, is not as solid as they might believe it to be?

These "strong spirits" (as they love to call themselves) are fragile and exposed in ways that are often pathetic. Oriana Fallaci, the journalist and writer known to readers around the world, loved parading her atheism by writing "god" with a lowercase *g* because, as she stated, "god is just a concept without content." A colleague who once went to interview her did not hide her perplexity: "I don't know," she told her, "how you can have the certainty that there is no God, to be so sure there's nothing after death." Fallaci yelled this answer verbatim: "This talk is profoundly illiberal, illiberal in an insulting way, fascistically illiberal!"

Pathetic, even more than foolish. To reply to an objective, irrefutable, serene observation ("How can you be so sure…"), she responds with hysterical convulsions. She exorcises the problem yelling with a choked voice, in falsetto, that her interlocutor is a fascist. This has been the usual manner for some time now to get rid of a question: everyone knows that it's no use responding to fascists.

Confirming the words of Cesare Musatti, another psychologist observed: "Those who delight in defining themselves men (or women) of doubt in every other matter, brandish certainties only in the face of these problems. But if they were really that certain they would not be so aggressive." They would not need to yell or hurl anathemas ("fascist!") against those who flush out of them a hidden yet omnipresent problem.

These revered cultural authorities who want to teach us how to live, and who actually know less what life and death are, often make me think of the "masterminds" of which Manzoni speaks telling of the sudden conversion of the unnamable. On the evening of the decisive day, this character convokes his personal army of good people, of the executors of his criminal plans. "Dear children," he harangues, "the road we have been travelling on so far leads to the depths of hell." This is the reflection of those "masterminds," as the author calls them:

> The things they heard from that mouth were odious to their ears, but neither false nor in the least extraneous to their intellects: if they had mocked them a thousand times, it was not because they did not believe them, but to ward off with mocking the fear that would have taken hold had they thought about it seriously.

Pascal, who was one of Manzoni's dearest masters, observed that many parade scorn because they are afraid it might be true, because they fear it is right.

THE MOST PERSONAL PROBLEM

The popular American writer Christopher Isherwood says, "There is no use believing that if we try to ignore something for long enough, it will end up disappearing on its own." Here, instead, the more one waits, the more the problem looms.

Reacting with the annoyance, panic, and hatred of my interviewees, or with the pathetic contumely in the manner of Fallaci, serves no purpose, nor does trying to ignore that: first, if the data is uncertain, death, our death, is not; second, this death is a mystery that neither science nor philosophy have dispelled nor ever will; third, this mystery involves our entire personal destiny, not only after but also before that final appointment; fourth, it is not only opportune, but indispensable that we try to create our own opinion about that mystery.

It is life itself that puts us against the wall, forcing us to make a wager, willingly or unwillingly. Because of the necessity of this wager, we need to see if there is some clue that, though without resolving it, at least orients our choice.

Each of us confronts death and its enigma alone, we must repeat; and so each of us is called to wager alone. "*You* die," admonished Martin Luther, "therefore *you* must choose." *You* must take a stance before the enigma; you cannot hope that someone else will do it for you.

This is a personal problem par excellence. It concerns everyone, but it consults each of us one by one. Whether you try to avoid it or not, each of us knows, or at least intuits, the inflexibly, mercilessly individual character of the only problem that cannot be delegated. It is the only problem that, to face it, others can offer solidarity and help, but can go only so far along that road, to the point when we have no choice but to proceed alone.

This is the reason for the torturous character that the "wager with death" assumes for those who put off day after day a choice that they nevertheless perceive as inevitable: it is so torturous because it is the personal problem par excellence.

In fact, it is precisely the personal problems, more than social problems, that assail man, that interrogate with greater urgency and with privileged force. Like it or not, the "private" always precedes the "public" in us.

I do not judge; I back up my arguments. I do not say it is good or bad; I merely ascertain that we are made in this way.

To be convinced that it is truly so, it suffices to look inward; there is no need to refer to the experience of Silvano Arieti, the famous Italian-American psychiatrist and psychoanalyst. "The evil of the century is depression," says Arieti, "now, in thirty years of work, I have never met a patient who at the origin of his depression had a concern for the energy crisis, for the public debt, for presidential elections or some other general problem. All of them, without exception, were depressed and came to me for therapy regarding personal issues." At any rate, as we have already seen in the classification of stresses, the sphere of the "public" or "political" dimension is totally irrelevant to their measurement.

A further confirmation comes from sociological investigations into the motivations of that extreme, desperate protest against one's fate that is suicide: it turns out that one never kills oneself because one's political party has lost the majority, but rather because one's personal affairs have gone wrong. One does not kill oneself because the local party leader dies of a heart attack, but perhaps because one has been diagnosed with cancer.

One does not kill oneself due to "social" disappointments, as long as they do not have direct consequences for our career, our finances, our personal future; one commits suicide because of a failure in love, because of a betrayal. The young man who leaps out of the window because a Kennedy or a Mao dies is not in the storyline: it's folklore.

This is the hard reality, if we want to face it without using any of the deforming lenses that society offers us today.

To be even more convinced that the interests of the private individual precede in every case those of society, we have the pathetic confession of one of the vibrant American political militants: "I was passionate about debates on

Latin America, I organized protest marches for every cause, I ended up in jail numerous times for having yelled protest slogans." But the woman continued in an outburst of liberating sincerity, "Now, though, I can admit it. My true interest, the authentic torment of all my days was something else: the excessive size of my hips. The political movement was important, sure; but more important for me would have been to be thinner, less chunky."

An extreme case, on the border of the grotesque? A case of "individualism" to be denounced indignantly? No, a case of sincerity and normality.

Moreover, try again to reason without systems and taboos: to find an acceptable solution for one's personal problems ("my hips" in this case), is this not the necessary condition for living fully one's humanity? Is this not the precondition, therefore, for taking seriously social problems too, which can be approached only after solving one's individual problems?

If you are not a balanced person (namely, a man or a woman who has found a livable compromise with his "id"), you cannot even be a good citizen, because you will only project externally, to the harm of all, your unresolved imbalance. This is what they have not understood, or have fully understood but feign ignorance about — the party bureaucrats, the vestals of the ideologies, all those who want to reduce us to mere social, collective, political reality.

POLITICS: IMPORTANT, BUT NOT EVERYTHING

Follow closely, here, for what I am about to say will be scandalous to some, but it is important for all, despite my ineffective way of saying it. Where I am lacking, may your attention compensate.

Follow me because hidden here is one of the most disastrous misunderstandings in which they try to keep us at all costs in the present. It is in the misunderstanding of a foolish, superstitious, illegitimate vision of politics. Politics in this sense is treated as something belonging to a sacred dimension, passed off as capable of explaining everything, the only nourishment worthy of man, a food that is supposed to satisfy us completely.

But it is not, and never will be.

Perhaps it is true that the churches made of religion an opium for the people in the past. But modern ideologies and their political parties have tried to make politics the new opium of the people. Not content with our vote (when they let us vote), not satisfied with our time, they want our soul as well — that is, in less spiritual terms, our entire person, our humanity.

Forced by pressure from below, the parties now hold conventions on "politics and happiness" to ask themselves why it is that politics alone has not made us happy. A renowned Italian Marxist intellectual, Alberto Asor Rosa, writes, "It is obvious that socialism has as its aim to give happiness through politics." But as he recognizes, "we have to recognize that politics does not give happiness."

He hastened to add, however, "It doesn't give it today."

Not self-criticism, therefore, but clarity regarding the misunderstanding; but still and always the putting off of an illusory future: what it does not give today, politics can give tomorrow.

Thus, the problem is not about changing or widening the perspective — no, the problem is in attempting the same thing once more, after so many disappointments, so many disasters.

You can sharpen as much as you want your old tools: the nineteenth-century political ideologies, in mortal crisis, and even nastier precisely because of this (Marxism is the most consequential, but all the others on the right or in the center keep them company), carrying on thanks to an ambiguous confusion of plans. They have only one item to sell; it is understandable that, like every good merchant, they overestimate its value, counting on the naïveté of the client.

But do not take as solid an opinion, but an evident truth: every policy, as sophisticated as it might be, can serve only on the plane from which it draws its name, the *polis*, or city. It can, that is, give answers and solutions, more or less reliable, on the mechanisms that regulate economic and social coexistence. But society is made up of people, of concrete and complete men, to whom politics can give something, but not everything.

This is not a question of demonizing it, although, truth be told, behind many noble words the objective and fixed essence is disturbing: its aim, in fact, is the acquisition and preservation of power over men by use of force.

By its very nature, no political system can allow itself the luxury of giving room for love, humility, meekness, sincerity, forgiveness, disinterested and defenseless ideals. If it were to do so, it would be a terrible political system, destined to be immediately overturned. One example: can the leader of the USSR or the USA "turn the other cheek" to the other power without betraying his duty to its own country?

If Niccolò Machiavelli, the great founder of modern political theory, scandalized many naïve moralists and upset many hypocrites (all those, that is, who in good or bad faith, fill their mouths with "power as service"), it is because he, the clear-headed, honest Florentine secretary, dared to be right. Or, at least, he risked being difficult to refute.

At any rate, is it licit to take one's hat off reverently to the word *people* (as all politicians do) and then want to hide the fact that one of the constants of history throughout times and places is the profound diffidence of that people toward them? Is it licit to forget that popular instinct feels that the virtues of the good politician rarely coincide with the virtues of the good man? What is more, perhaps the one set of virtues neither can nor should coincide with the other.

Am I wrong? Is history itself wrong when it confirms Machiavelli's raw but objective phrase, "States are not governed with the Our Father"? Do you want to go looking for a different political system where neither "foxes" nor "lions" are necessary? That's your concern. As for me, I did not warm the benches for the last four years in a university political science department classroom for nothing.

Based on that experience, I believe there is a reason if Giovanni Sartori,[17] one of the most important contemporary political scientists, did not tire repeating, "the more I study the sociological and psychological mechanisms that guide politics and politicians, the more I am afraid."

Agreed. We should not demonize politics, because that authentic "political" service, namely to the city of men to which the Christian is also and above all called, is not to be confused with politics understood in a narrow partisan sense, as happens in modern ideologies.

That we should not demonize it does not mean, however, that we can fail in our duty to demythologize it, remembering its objective and impassable limits.

Yes, man is, according to the ancient Aristotelian definition, a "political animal." But he is not only that. The politician can talk about man and to man when the latter is in the city square or the factory. Understandably, this is an essential dimension: we exist with others and for others. A truly isolated, solitary life is unthinkable.

Christianity, among other faiths, knows this well. I do not hear mean in its historical errors, which have led, along with ignoring or minimizing the social dimension, to a distance from the masses of the modern world. I am speaking

---

[17] Editor's Note: Giovanni Sartori (1924–2017) was an Italian political analyst and sociologist.

of Christianity in its authentic essence as faith that presents man with an eternal, individual destiny, which is nevertheless also inextricably connected to the eternal destiny of others, of every other person.

Acknowledging the essential importance of politics for the dimension about which it is concerned, about the only one it can and must concern itself, we need to remember resolutely, however, that that dimension is not everything. Man is not only the city square or the factory: man is also solitude with himself, in his private room, confronting his questions.

Man is also a mystery upon which the levers manipulated by the leaders of the nations, be they party secretaries or the prime ministers, have no say. Man is also his social relations, the most profound possible, loving relationships: this is a decisive social reality, but one that escapes the wizards of the political and the ideological, the politicians who peddle universal ideas for the masses. But they are mute and naked when an individual word is needed, when looking into the eyes of the other, and not from high upon a podium.

LENIN AND WOMEN

After the first exhilarating years of "fulfilled socialism," Bolshevik women realized to their dismay that political activism fulfilled some, but not all of them. Despite the promises, happiness did not come. Even without aspiring to much, it was difficult to be satisfied with the revolutionary catechisms that, under "marriage," recited the following (believe me, the quote is verbatim and I found it recently reproduced in the program of a group of Marxists, aging survivors of 1968): "The fundamental task of marriage is the reciprocal assistance of spouses in confronting the problems of the class struggle and in stimulating each other to increase their social and political conscience."

Someone dared to speak of their disappointment, with great caution, to Lenin himself. One can imagine him flying into a rage. "Comrades," he started yelling, "first we shall build the soviets and electrify the countryside. Afterward, we shall think about love."

More than a century has passed since that postponement and the solution is still not in sight. As the party bosses and union leaders know well, in their unrest and suspicion of women's movements within their own organizations, women's movements which for some time now have observed once more that lessons on surplus value are gladly placed beside speeches on the sentiments. Elections are important, but the affections are also important. A nice roundtable discussion on Southeast Asia is useful and appreciated, but it has little to say on daily relations with the husband and kids. In the end, their private, personal lives are inescapable and essential, too, which the party functionary, the boy with the blinders, insists on avoiding.

Now, is there anything more personal than the meaning of my life, my love and hatred, my pleasure and pain, my living and dying?

Lenin and his ilk (as for every other politician) cannot put it off forever: they are superficial but not always stupid. They know very well, then, that the possibility of responding to those questions, of giving meaning to what counts to us above every other matter, is not in their files swollen with documents, graphs, charts, and forecasts.

And so, rather than adapting themselves to man, they try to violate him adapting him to themselves and to the ideologies they promote, and which promote them. We have seen how they busy themselves hiding and denying the most important, the most radical issues. But they not only use the defensive strategy, they go on the offensive as well. Recognizing that the question about life and death is invincibly individual, that it escapes as such their instruments adapted only to the collective, that it threatens their power, they try to extirpate the problem from the roots.

In *Mein Kampf*, Adolf Hitler writes:

> The isolated individual is seized by a sense of uselessness, by the fear of death perhaps. But gathered in a group, in a political party, he has the sensation of a community bigger than himself: something with a reinforcing and encouraging effect.

Every totalitarian project (in the sense of wanting to reduce everything to politics) attempts this operation.

The right puts us in uniforms, a word that describes well the project aimed at suffocating our individuality, our uncomfortable personal world, rendering all of us "uniform" from our clothing. On the left, totalitarianism also uses uniforms (in Maoist China, were they not all dressed the same?), but employs above all a ferocious and methodical campaign against what it calls "individualism." According to Ho Chi Minh, the remote old man whose face took the place of the old portraits of the Virgin Mary on the living-room walls of petite-bourgeois students throughout the West: "Socialist society can be constructed only through the implacable suffocation of everything that is personal and individual."

All these good men love, *in theory*, the humanity that can adapt to their programs; they hate the concrete man who puts a wrench in their projects due to the fact that he lives and dies.

Their education of children and reeducation of adults consists in telling fairytales about the hypothetical "new man," who is satisfied with the food of politics alone and who returns without a fuss to the cage prepared for him.

If man is as we have seen (based on experience and not on preconceived notions), those who want to silence that within him that concerns him so intimately are greatly mistaken. Even less, that in which he is more personally implicated: "Who am I, where am I going, what will become of me? What is the meaning of living and dying? What is the mystery that I am approaching every day that passes?"

The National Institute of Mental Health is the government entity that concerns itself with the mental health of citizens in the United States. Every year, the institute carries out a survey among students from fifty universities in each of the states. With monotonous consistency, the results always retrace those of the preceding year. More than ninety percent of youth see but one means for attaining and preserving reasonable psychic equilibrium: "Finding meaning in my life."

But we repeat again: the "meaning in my life" is not in the least independent from the "meaning of my death"; in fact, it is the latter that is the prerequisite of the former.

Here, the drama explodes: though powerful and efficient, the National Institute of Mental Health is impotent in the face of the problem regarding "meaning." Both the Republican Party and the Democratic Party are impotent; all parties, agencies, centers for scientific research, specialists, experts all over the world, on the right or the left, in the West or the East, *all* are impotent.

Science does not know.

Philosophy cannot do it.

Politics is not enough.

And yet, *I* have to wager on the problem, on the mystery that concerns me most.

Can nothing and no one really help me to choose, to understand, to interpret myself and the world?

In this matter, could that anachronistic thing, so un-modern, that they call "religion" help me?

An Obligatory Exit Strategy

At this point, we see that the discussion necessarily opens onto a different dimension: the religious dimension. It cannot avoid doing so: it is an obligatory path.

Proceeding by process of elimination, as we have done, one realizes in the end that, in order to respond to our unavoidable questions, only one possibility remains.

We can only venture into, like it or not, the chaotic, at first sight scarcely credible or even downright repulsive religious bazaar, where each one sings the praises of his creed as the one best suited to resolve the problem that is most at heart.

These promises must all be verified. Is this really where the right answers are to be found? And if so, which of the scores of market stalls should we approach?

One fact is nonetheless undeniable: only religions (in the classical sense, not the current surrogates and political by-products) stare life and death in the face. Only religions (as opposed to science, politics, and even philosophy) have a proper eschatology, a proposal that concerns the "last things" and, for that matter, all of life. No small offer.

The prospect of such a search might not arouse our enthusiasm; in the end, we might find it was a waste of our time and effort. But we must make our reckoning with religion in some way. There is no other path to discover if there is a solution to the most personal of all personal problems.

By now we know it well: the path of hiding and negation is not only useless; it is also harmful. Anguish can be aggravated, certainly not dissolved, throwing oneself blindly into social causes as an end in themselves, or accumulating degrees and specializations: "I perceived that this also is but a striving after wind. For in much wisdom is much vexation, and he who increases knowledge increases sorrow" (Eccl. 1:17–18).

The biblical prophet speaking here is not some Lenten preacher; it is one of the most clear-headed and coherent witnesses of our time who reminds us to what end this world closed in on itself leads us. Albert Camus, the atheist writer of *The Rebel, The Plague, The Stranger,* and *The Myth of Sisyphus,* dug deep into the resources of a culture that is secular, but which, as we know, might better be called immature, amputated, one-dimensional. Camus's assessment was tragic: "In the end the only problem worthy of discussion is suicide."

In other words, discussion of awaiting the end assigned by destiny to this senseless adventure, to what Sartre called this "useless passion" that is thinking man.

One must discuss whether one should abbreviate his time here, resolve definitively the mystery of his destiny running toward him, taking in his own hand the death that, if it finds no room, threatens us, anguishes us, and deprives us of meaning even on our best days.

CHAPTER 8
A RISK, A SEARCH

NOT A HOBBY

I HAVE ACCUMULATED WORDS, put paragraphs and chapters into an order that I hope might be as convincing and logical as possible. Perhaps I have deceived myself; is there some error that escapes my line of reasoning? Have I not been persuasive? It is a real possibility.

Remember, then, that what I aim at is not to surprise your trust with the cleverness of dialectic: that would be propaganda. Nor do I intend to convince you that you need a product, using flattery of words and pleasant packaging: that would be advertising.

I shall reveal my game, show my cards: what I intend to do is to demonstrate that religion is not a hobby for slackers. Informing oneself on what religion has to say about the meaning of our life and death is not a pastime for the idle. Neither is it the extreme resource for the frustrated. It is rather the one last possibility allowed to those who do not want to suffer passively this journey which we have not chosen and which takes us to an unknown destination.

It is the one last possibility to make our lives full, to make our humanity complete: have we not seen the onerous effects of concealing death, of concealing our mortal reality?

In search of a possible crack where we can insert a crowbar, I have been groping along the wall of indifference, and because this obstacle is properly called "indifference" I am now pointing in the religious direction.

All polls in industrialized countries in the West report that thirty people out of a hundred say they are "believers" and say they accept (though with hesitation, contradiction, and varying degrees of intensity) an institution as well, a church wherein they can live their faith.

Non-belief, the explicit refusal of the religious dimension, is under twenty percent and, whatever one might say or think, the percentage has been stable for decades. "Atheism," reported Jean-Paul Sartre, who knew something about it, "is a long and arduous endeavor." For this reason it is, and always will be, a minority phenomenon.

The majority group, more than fifty percent of people, is that of the indifferent, the great mass of those who do not place their bets because they see no urgent reason for doing so. "Whether religions are right or wrong, or whether God exists or not, what could it possibly matter to us?" Hidden in this question is the cause of the death of God.

God, in other words, who dies not *in se* (and how could He?), but in us, as a value, as a reference point, as origin and goal. God agonizes and is extinguished in indifference, the premise of practical atheism that slides into a new idolatry of people, ideas, things, more than into aggressiveness in the cries of a theoretical atheism that is often a distorted and inverted affirmation of the reality one believes He is denying.

It is therefore in the grayness of indifference that I am looking for a point of leverage, convinced as I am that the reason for not wagering is a misunderstanding, a false perspective, and one with serious consequences.

The Error of Abstaining

Il faut chercher, "one needs to search, *you* must search," this is the appeal that arises from Pascal's *Pensées*. He was not only the penitent ascetic who wore a hairshirt. He was also the worldly one, the one who played poker or craps, the greatest mathematical genius of Europe during the Baroque period. And he went down in the history of science as the inventor of the calculation of probabilities, as the one who was able to reduce chance to a number.

It is the logic of the roulette wheel that Pascal extends to the game with the infinite that is the life and death of each and every man. It is possible, he warns, that the religious answers might not convince you. It is possible that, once this last path has been exhausted, you might have to resign yourself to the skeptic motto: *ignoramus et ignorabimus*, "we are ignorant and we shall always be ignorant." Before the capitulation, however, you must exhaust all the resources you have been given: you must know the game, understand the rules.

To dodge the search and thus the wager and risk has not been granted you. "To wager is necessary, it is not in the least optional, *aussi tu es embarqué*, you too are trapped." It is self-deception to absent oneself: whoever does not place his bet here has already made his choice for a solution, for the one that foresees an eternal nothing beyond the certain and inevitable end.

And what if, behind the threshold of the mystery, there was Something or Someone to encounter and perhaps give an account? What if this Something or Someone had left hints here and there to be interpreted, and which, superficial as we are, we have disregarded in our great distraction?

Do not deceive yourself with reassurances such as "nothing is visible behind the clouds," or "the heavens and the earth are silent." You are not allowed to be distracted by appearances, repeating that "if one of the many religions were right, it would be obvious to everyone."

On the contrary: there is at least one religion, Christianity, that bases its faith precisely on the concealment of God. One condition for Christian belief is recognizing and accepting ambiguity, the possible double reading of everything we see outside of us and everything we feel within us:

> Reality offers me nothing that is not a matter of doubt and apprehension. If I were to see nothing indicating a divinity, the denial would reassure me. If I saw the traces of a Creator everywhere, I could rest in the peace of faith. But I see too much to deny and too little to reassure me. Thus, there is sufficient light for the one who wants to believe, and there is sufficient darkness for the one who does not want to believe.

If that is how things are — and they are so — agnosticism and atheism are possible; but faith is possible as well. Here everything is possible, everything refers back to a character of risk and of daring: the roulette game of life and death is on.

The apparent silence that surrounds us, the freedom conceded to us, are not in the least reassuring, demonstrating that "if you see nothing it is because there is nothing." "Something" might exist not *despite* but precisely *because* of the silence, the freedom. "All things conceal a mystery. All things are veils that hide God." And if that were true?

Nothing and nobody can prevent you from chasing far away, like cumbersome, infantile wreckage, the possibility of a God beyond the silent film of the world, of a God hidden beyond life, of a continuation in some form of our adventure beyond the finish line of the tomb. But neither can they guarantee that your wager that "there is nothing" is the right one.

There is no insurance company here, not even Lloyd's of London, specializing in unlikely policies that can insure you against the possibility (or the risk) of an unexpected encounter, of an experience you had excluded without even looking into the problem.

It is not enough to wish that this encounter or continuation is impossible.

I would rather not be the first to use a word as ridiculed as it is feared, to use a term to be handled with infinite prudence, as with all words pregnant with mystery and meaning. We shall put it in the mouth of a secular agnostic, Leonardo Sciascia, the writer who (as if to reassure us) publicly records in his diary: "Hell exists if you believe in it."

Sorry, that's not how it is. As at the casino, the winnings and the losses are not linked to one's wishes and imploring; so too here, at the green, felt-topped table seated with the infinite, where eternity concerns us personally. A "Hell" (as obviously a "Paradise," or in any case some mysterious afterlife) could exist even if you do not believe in it. In the same way, it might not exist, although you believe it does.

Are believers and non-believers on an equal footing, then? Are the probabilities of winnings and earnings, of being wrong or right, thus the same for both?

It would seem so, although that killjoy Pascal does not agree here either; maybe he is not content merely to win but wants to win hands down. And I assign him full responsibility for a logic pushed to such extremes as to seem unbearable: "If the believer is wrong and beyond death there really is nothing but silence and darkness, he will never know. If instead it is the non-believer who is wrong, if there is something, he will verify for eternity the effects of his error."

"Nothing Changes." Nothing?

"I cannot imagine the day in which I will feel the need for religion. It is something extra. If it is true, things are in a certain manner; and, if it is not true, things are the same. Nothing changes: therefore, it is something extra."

Thus, the usual sybil, Moravia, has one of his protagonists say, autobiographically, in one of his novels. For Moravia, it is already a step forward, something better than the ridiculous affirmation that "eternity, obviously, does not exist." Here there is at least the intuition of a wager we have to make: "if religion is true," "if it is not true…"

But this intuition is not followed by coherent conclusions.

Once more, what seems to distinguish these miserable oracles of the age of reason is a disarming lack of logic.

It is in fact the logic of the problem, not faith, that marks how it is not at all true that "nothing changes" according to the different outcomes of the wager. We might admit that nothing changes if our circumstances were to remain the present ones, those of the living, for all eternity. True: Moravia and the like, if they could, would gladly kill death; but death does not seem phased by their threats. Death will come, then, and however it goes, it will change their circumstances forever.

How do we know, then, that that will not truly be "the day on which we will feel the need for religion"? That it will not be the day of discovering that what religion preached and announced was not at all "something extra"?

A God (and, with Him, the consequence of a continuation of life after death) who can seem frivolous, just an idle argument, for as long as our scraping by lasts, this "composite of forces that oppose death." But the "extra" of the present could transform into the most concrete reality (consoling? disturbing?) in another dimension that, we know well, to the shame of every "obviously" has in favor of its existence at least a fifty percent probability.

Like every true gamble, this one too carries a risk: a risk proportional to eternity, which is up for grabs.

"If I tell you that you must search it is not because I am urged by sacred zeal of some spiritual devotion," Pascal admonishes his interlocutor, one "who heard it said that the good manners of the world consist in playing distracted and haughty in the face of mystery."

In fact, Pascal understood that the most urgent problem, the most difficult task, is not confronting theoretical atheism, but rather awakening the average man from his stupor, from his indifference. To achieve this, he does not hesitate to grab by the collar the apathetic. As Albert Béguin[18] writes, "They accuse him of having furiously beaten man. In reality, he loved him too much to take him by violence when it was a matter of awakening him to the truth."

With the lucidity of the convert, he saw that the problem of God is in fact the problem of man. God, and all that this brief and immense word means for our eternal destiny, is not marginal to life, but is in the heart of its mystery. And

---

[18] Editor's Note: Albert Béguin (1901–1957) was a Swiss literary critic and writer.

the one who has not understood this has understood nothing about what it means to be alive.

If one loves mankind, then, one must set off an alarm (brutal if necessary) to induce man to search: are there not by chance some fireflies that faintly punctuate the darkness, helping us at the crossroads (the wager) to choose one path instead of the other?

Pascal repeats over and over:

> I say that one must search not out of spiritual devotion or as an optional curiosity, but out of one's own self-interest. I am amazed and frightened by the indifference over a question concerning our whole being; the eternity which death brings with it is something so relevant, so enveloping, that one must have lost all logic to remain indifferent before such a problem.

And again:

> Nothing is more important for man than his destiny; nothing is more disturbing than the infinite that nonetheless awaits him. Man behaves quite differently when it is a matter of anything else: he fears, hopes, foresees, consults. And yet, the man who spends so many days and nights in anger and desperation for a harm done to his career, is the same man who without thinking lurches toward his certain death, the death that is for sure the loss or gain of everything.

He then concludes: "To me it is monstrous to see in the same person so much sensibility for little though fleeting matters, and so much indifference for what is great and eternal."

He marvels at seeing a "mysterious blindness" in this circumstance that is incomprehensible according to reason: "God is demonstrated not only in the zeal of those who serve Him, but also in the indifference of those who do not seek Him."

A Duty

I proceed here amid hesitation and a fatigue greater than elsewhere. In fact, would it not be disconcerting if I tried to render myself worthy of attention by leveraging fear in some way?

I am looking for the crack in the wall of indifference, not the sinkhole that might be easy to open through recourse to fear.

It would be easy, but also unworthy of God, and of man and his freedom.

But then, would not every recourse to fear be harmful to "religion," to which we are trying to draw attention? If God is dead in the hearts of so many of our contemporaries, is it not also because He was portrayed more as one to fear than as one in whom to hope? Before all that is fearful, a mechanism goes off inside us, well known to psychologists by the term *repression*. One represses what is unpleasant, hides it in the depths and tries not to think about it; instead, one denies it, rejecting even its existence. This is the mechanism we have seen at work in cultures of recent centuries in the face of death.

For one with eyes to see, rendering these issues once again "interesting" or "important," the tactic of having recourse to the bogeyman of an irritated God, in whose omnipotent hands we might fall after He capriciously cuts the thread that ties us to life, is neither worthy nor opportune.

Interrogating oneself about one's absolute future and not merely about the relative future; asking questions about the meaning of one's existence, one's destiny; finding out what the religious proposal might have to say, the only one that faces these issues: this task is a duty for all, because everyone must take account of a real "risk."

But more than fear, this task should stem from a sense of one's dignity, from self-respect, a duty toward oneself and toward others, both personal and social. Because it is both personal and social, it is the failures of organized culture that have impeded those questions and blocked that search. Because, as we know and as Ernesto Balducci said, "without a faithful confrontation with death the entire universe of life's meaning suffers an inhumane deformation."

Interpret in Order to Change

Karl Marx said in a famous phrase, "Up to now the world has been interpreted. The time has now come to change it." The prophet of Trier was right in some ways; but that was then, in the now remote nineteenth century.

After so many disasters, we know today that the world does not change without first being interpreted — without interpreting, that is, the history of the world that is moving toward the end perhaps, without interpreting first of all *my* history that is moving toward its end for sure. Before attacking the world to change it, we need to see if by chance it is possible to dredge up some reason for my living and dying in this world.

For the very fact of being here, mysteriously and provisionally alive, each of us is responsible for reflecting, literally "for bending over oneself." Bending over to scrutinize, to listen, to interpret the universe that is in us, we find, in the words of Paul Tillich, that "without an attention toward the depths in each of us, that is, 'without religion,' individual and social history is no longer human history."

I know that the situation is much worse than in Pascal's time ("the good manners of the world consist in playing the distracted and haughty one"). I know that it is much more elegant and socially acceptable to concern oneself with the frivolous, the ephemeral (what do I know? With Guatemalan cinema, Bulgarian comics, Japanese music, Tahitian gastronomy?) rather than with problems considered unrefined, noisy, unresolvable, like religious questions. And I know by the direct experience of a man attracted to action and condemned to the fate of daily, solitary, often dramatic dialogue with the keyboard of a typewriter and a ream of white paper; I know that it is much less laborious to act ("change the world") than to reflect ("interpret it").

But it is not my fault nor that of anyone else if life and its laws are made this way. We must take courage and move forward.

It is not my nor anyone's fault if living is like being dragged onto that train we spoke of previously, hurtling toward the dark tunnel; or like driving through the night on a highway with your headlights off; or like walking around a city ignoring everything, except that every street ends in a wall that closes everything in a dead end.

If this is living (and it is, despite the impotent bonfire lit by the ideologues, politicians, scientists, and philosophers who are only capable of illuminating the inner side of the great wall), the time will come for everyone to take their turn on the other side of the road.

The time for examining within, and for examining the documents of certain exemplary companions on the journey. They say they have the train's schedule, a roadmap, a map of the walled city.

Illusions? Boasting? Speculation? Or a real possibility? An unexpected hope?

No one can say before undertaking a direct examination of the maps. Those travelers who style themselves informed assure us that the trains, the highways, the streets continue inexplicably after the tunnel, the toll booth, the city walls. And what if they convince us they are right? Would this not change matters, indeed change *everything*, despite the assurances of the foolish oracles of the age saying that "nothing changes"?

There is no confessable reason to refuse to look into the arguments of those companions on the journey who say they are so well informed. At any rate, their arguments are worth at least as much as those who assure us that there is no schedule, no roadmap, no street map, and who swear that the journey of life will not continue at all beyond the terminus, beyond the walls.

Il faut chercher, one must search, with earnestness, without preconceived notions. Whatever happens, it will not be a waste of time. Thomas Aquinas, one who understood the search for truth well, having dedicated every waking hour to it, said "The scarcest knowledge one can attain of the highest things is more desirable than the broadest knowledge attained about minor things." Is there something that is "higher" in our life, our death, than their meaning?

Examine before refuting. Search expecting neither *too much* nor *too little* of reason. Faith is the ultimate step, and it goes beyond what is reasonable. But it is thanks to reason that one can reach that point beyond which only the wager can decide.

Inquire, search, think: because, as has been said, "thinking can mean going beyond." Thinking can mean discovering that "the final step of reason is recognizing that there is an infinite number of things that exceed it."

PART III

CHOICES

Test everything; hold fast what is good.
1 Thessalonians 5:21

And Jesus said, "He who seeks does not stop seeking until he has found. When he has found he will be disturbed; and, if he is disturbed, he will be amazed and will be king over all."
Coptic Gospel of Thomas, Saying 2

CHAPTER 9
At the Bazaar of Religions

By Chance?

OUR JOURNEY INTO THE dimension, the profound dimension to which only religions have access, in which the meaning of life and death is hiding, will lead toward Christianity.

The proposal drawing our attention is that of Christian eschatology. Ours is a conscious choice that is not born of myopia.

Ambrogio Donini is among the few Italian Marxists to deal with the religious issue, although using the usual cursory methods, vitiated by prejudices and propagandistic reasoning, as always happens among the followers of an ideology where everything is at the service of politics, the end that justifies every means.

At Donini's villa overlooking Mt. Soratte, dear to the gods and the poets, we discussed for an entire day if one can be Christian by a free choice, or if one becomes a Christian by the mere fact of being born in one place rather than another.

"A Christian of any confession, had he been born elsewhere, would easily have been a Muslim or a Hindu or a Buddhist or a Confucianist."

This was the thesis of Ambrogio Donini.

Not a new thesis: already in the sixteenth century, Montaigne held that "we are Christians in the same way that we are Germans or inhabitants of the Perigord." This was no less scandalous, though we recognize the mechanisms that lead people to conformity more than to a free choice, to beliefs as a social inheritance rather than through an autonomous decision.

There is some truth then in the contemptuous certitude of the old communist professor. But is it the full truth?

I can reply only for myself; I can do no more than assure you that I am at least aware of a problem I must face every day. In the end, I find some comfort in rereading Pascal:

> It must be recognized that Christianity always surprises those who delve into it. "It is because you were born into it," one tells me. On the contrary: it is precisely because I was born that I grow tense against it, that I persist in my search. And, because I was born into it, I cannot *not* find it surprising.

As too often in the past, there are still people who would like to call periodic Crusades for their defense of Christian civilization. Pass over the fact that "Christian civilization," as they understand it, is usually more to be fought against than defended, and precisely in the name of Christ and of Christianity. Nor do we have to insist that behind certain ideals there are often very concrete material interests.

But even in the best of cases, Christian civilization would matter little to me if I were to be convinced that the gospel was not right about God, man, my destiny, and that of everyone in time and eternity. The fate of cathedrals would not move me any more than that of any other cultural patrimony site if in those admirable buildings I could not see the sign of a mysterious but true Presence.

If I had to choose between Christ and the truth, I would choose the truth. I would go without hesitation to the ranks of the Papua in New Guinea or the Toda in Tamil Nadu if I were to reach the conclusion that at least one word of salvation resounds in the world, and that that word is announced by one religion, however remote and obscure.

If the choice then must be a matter of one's culture, of ethnic roots, why not return to *my* religion, that of the people of my ancestors, which is not at all Christianity, but the worship of nature by the ancient pagans?

My surname, with its evident agricultural, Latin origins, (*messores*, harvesters), confirms that my ancestors were all laborers and peasant farmers of the Po Valley. The new Semitic faith that arrived toward the fourth century from the Middle East was imposed, often by force, at any rate quite late: even after the year 1000, the countryside of northern Italy remained pagan, as far as we know. Much of later Christianization remained superficial. The religion that the peasant masses, who had become the working class, had abandoned in those years was often not Christianity but ancient paganism with a thin veneer of Christian superstitions.

It is nevertheless certain that those unsung laborers in the Emilian countryside, my ancestors, remained pagan infinitely longer than they were Christian, and perhaps with greater spontaneity and conviction.

If Donini and those like him are right, I should start promoting the religion of my race, of my culture, of my ancestors. Above all, I would certainly not be alone in the defense of paganism, but in the good company of humanists, philosophers, artists, writers, and intellectuals from the fifteenth century to the eighteenth century and down to the present.

It seems clear, at any rate, that for a Latin descendant of the Po Valley (with Gallic, Ligurian, Celtic, and Etruscan mixtures), it would be more natural to place my trust in the ancient divinities of the earth, the forest, and the wellsprings, rather than to that complex Judeo-Greek system that is called Christianity.

Who says that for a European like me, I should spontaneously identify myself as a spiritual son of an obscure nomad from Ur of the Chaldees called Abraham? Who says that between the apparently irrational presumptions of an uneducated artisan from Galilee and the elegant Latin skepticism of the one who interrogated him, the Roman procurator Pontius Pilate, it would have been immediately clear for any of us which side was right?

Thus, if here we are examining with particular attention the Christian proposal on life and death, it is not out of myopia, nor Western patriotism, nor defense of our cultural roots, nor out of total ignorance of other religious messages.

On the contrary, it is precisely in discussion with others that the Christian wager seems to me the most complex, provocative, paradoxical, and in many ways the most contrary to common sense. But behind this apparent preposterousness it seems that reflection can discover what most satisfies the heart and reason, what most respects the terrible complexity of a drama with three protagonists: God, myself, and others.

If we are convinced that it is worth the effort to confront the religious issue, it is here that we must begin, and it is perhaps here that we must conclude. It was in fact Karl Marx, this unsuspecting witness, who wrote: "There is no way to move beyond Christianity in dialectical terms. It is the end point of religious thought. Beyond Christianity, nothing."

Neither Fanaticism nor Confusion

We do well to play it safe before venturing some reasons that might justify the privilege recognized in Christian eschatology.[19]

This choice, it must immediately be clarified, seeks neither to underestimate nor to esteem other religions less than is due.

We wrote in *Hypotheses about Jesus*:

> We all have due respect for the venerable messages of non-Christian religions. One looks with admiration at the intense longing for salvation in Buddhism and its abandonment to the eternal; at the struggle for union with the divine in the asceticism and meditation of Hinduism; at the immersion in the incomprehensible and disinterested love of Taoism; at the values of Islam's faith.

We have certainly not changed our opinion since then. We are also even more convinced of the Christian duty to draw as much nourishment as possible from Judaism, the venerable root of the tree of the gospel. "Separated from Israel, Christ is not Christian": we recently repeated this truth in Jerusalem, called to the responsibility of reopening (in dialogue with a Jew and before a Jewish audience) a serene, objective debate on Jesus of Nazareth, this son of Israel whose name, usurped by unworthy Christians, has become a nightmare for his brothers circumcised in the flesh.

---

[19] In conformity with common usage, in this book we speak of "Christianity," although we are aware that it is an imprecise and ambivalent term that leads one to think of but one "ism" among many, of one ideology among the many. Authentic Christianity ought to be, if anything, the contrary: not an idea, but a Person; not "something," but Someone; not a theory, but the life, death, and miracles of a man in whom the faith detects God Himself; neither a wisdom nor a philosophy, but a history of salvation; not a book, but a new life.

For this reason, many people today prefer to speak of the Christian message, of the gospel (in its etymological sense of "good news"), of a biblical proposal of salvation, rather than of *Christianity*.

There are also Christians who ask themselves if Christianity is a religion or rather a faith, a revelation, a Word of God living and true that announces the transcendence of one's own religion constructed by man himself. Having warned of this problem, it is for convenience that the term Christianity and Christian religion will be used here.

And yet, we see no contrast between respecting and loving every religion and its adherents and yielding to the words of the pious Jew Simon Peter who, called to respond to his faith in Jesus, confessed, "There is salvation in no one else, for there is no other name under heaven given among men by which we must be saved" (Acts 4:12).

The Second Vatican Council says in its declaration on non-Christian religions: "The Church rejects nothing in them that is good and holy." But immediately afterward, the Council Fathers clarify, "the Church announces and is bound to announce Christ who is 'the way, the truth, and the life,' in whom men find the fullness of religious life and in whom God has reconciled all things to Himself."

Fanaticism is not only a certain sign of mental disturbance, but also the warning light of insecurity in one's own motives. Although a decisive refusal of fanaticism does not mean taking refuge in an irenic indifference ("one religion is as good as another") or in universalism ("there is only one religion in various forms according to times and peoples"). Nor does the horror of fanaticism mean finding oneself in the snide but justifiable characterization that has been given today's Christian: "One who believes in all religions, except for his own."

AMID LIGHT AND SHADOWS

The problem of this chapter has not yet been touched: why look to Christian eschatology and not to other types of eschatology? The attempt to answer such a question is among the most difficult and insidious things in the world.

Let it be clear: one cannot (nor do we want to) sketch a treatise on "the comparative history of religions." Mircea Eliade, the renowned Romanian scholar, has dedicated his entire life to this discipline. He has established two points in his assessment: 1. Even if one were content to study just one religion, a man's whole existence would barely suffice for bringing it to completion. 2. If one were to propose the comparative study of all religions, many lifetimes would not suffice.

Aware of this, I proceed rashly forward, delineating a first attempt at a response, making every effort to keep precision from falling into simplicity, or worse, injustice. I am convinced that the law of this mysterious topic is the impossibility of being convincing to everyone. But I am also convinced of the necessity of stimulating to overcome laziness, conformism, resistance to penetrating the religious forest. The effort is required of each one of us personally and cannot be substituted. Better this way, at any rate, because, in Pascal's words, "much more persuasive are the reasons we find ourselves than those found by others."

As for me, I do not limit myself to recognizing a duty of respect, esteem, and love toward non-Christians. I go further: I refuse to believe that God has given the news of Himself only during the Judeo-Christian timeframe that spans all history, from its confused beginnings down to our days. For the Christian, humanity has the same origin. The remembrance of an initial truth, a primordial revelation, could persist in some way among all peoples, even if disfigured and amputated of the privileged revelation that, through Israel (according to the Christian), reaches its fullness in the New Testament and lives in the Church.

The more one looks into religious traditions, the more one finds significant coincidences on the big themes that concern God and man. I believe there is in the world no religious person who cannot pray saying "Hallowed be thy name, thy kingdom come, thy will be done on earth as it is in heaven. Give us this day our daily bread, and forgive us our trespasses, as we forgive those who trespass against us. And lead us not into temptation, but deliver us from evil."

This is the prayer Jesus taught his followers as the distinctive sign of the Christian.

Problems arise, however, over the opening to the prayer: "Our Father." The disagreement over this way of addressing God (God is not a "Father" for everyone) is a warning light that marks essential differences. But it is nevertheless meaningful that the adherents of all religions could unite around all the other words that follow. Teilhard de Chardin said, "All that rises must converge" — converge not only above, but also below, in the depths of man and of history.

It is increasingly difficult to be convinced by the line of Protestant theology that sees only darkness, deceit, illusion, and diabolical malice beyond the confines of Christianity.

I had long been fascinated by the exclusivist theology that in our century culminates in Karl Barth, though it began with Martin Luther who, as has been said, "hurled at ancient paganism and every other religion besides Christianity, hatred, disdain, and insult." According to him, every virtue that does not have as its origin man justified by Christ is only "disgrace, corruption, and lies." The missionary cards of Protestants were colored black, "the color of the devil," the non-Christian countries; and often, even Catholic countries were considered "slaves of the pope-antichrist."

I now believe another Protestant is right, an Anglican priest who was also a famous scholar of comparative religion, Alan Coates Bouquet: "No religious experience is due solely to a simple inclination. On the contrary, the active agent of the situation is not man as such but, in one way or another, God. Divine action sustains all religions, from the most primitive all the way to their apogee reached in Christianity."

If in the future only Christianity should remain, it will not be because it will have "destroyed the competition," but because it will have fulfilled and surpassed other religions.

For those who receive it in faith, the Gospel is the Truth in the uppercase, without adjectives or limitations. But, according to Vatican II, "a ray of that truth that enlightens all men is not infrequently reflected in other religions." Nor should we believe that this recognition began only with the last council. "All that is true, by whomever it has been said, comes from the Holy Spirit," taught St. Thomas Aquinas in the heart of the Middle Ages, though it is taken to be the age of the blindest intolerance.

The German theologian Karl Rahner wrote, "As Christians we must remain firm in the truth we know we possess; but we can and must realize that all men are on a journey toward the truth." And he added, "If we want to be Christians, we must hold to the dogma of the universal and effective saving will of God toward all men, whatever their religious profession."

In a more subdued manner, yet no less firmly, I believe that, after passing the threshold of death, it will be Christ who comes to meet us. I believe that when it shall be granted to us to see beyond the curtain of life, the Christian will find confirmation of his faith and its eschatology.

But I believe with equal firmness that on that day none of those who in good faith in any form have believed in a reality transcending terrestrial reality will be humiliated.

It is not for me to know the way in which this will come about; but I am certain that the God of Jesus Christ (the image of God that most fully respects the freedom and dignity of man) will give confirmation to His own: but He will not humiliate the others. They too, as men, are His children, His creatures. God will not say to a just man who followed any other religion, striving to love: "You were a fool, you got it all wrong."

If anyone is to be humiliated or confused, it will be those Christians who did not take care to make of their faith a gift for others, though they said they were living the fullness, the highest expression of religion. Conversely, many non-Christians will be accompanied to the throne of the God of the Bible by their founders, prophets, saints, and brothers.

It is also necessary to admit that the rays of light, the venerable values that can be found everywhere, are mixed with thick darkness, with dross and debris where wisdom cohabitates with superstition, benevolence with cruelty. There is another face of the religious world, a face where the devil and sin seem to be truly at work: from human sacrifice to ritual cannibalism, from sadistic initiation rites to the bloody governance of priests (Islamic Iran in these years has been the most eloquent recent example of this), from the oppression of freedom through merciless hierarchies and caste systems that have produced petrified societies, to racism and the harm of women, foreigners, and the non-believer.

In this respect, one must dispel the widespread myth of a tolerance of non-Christian religions compared to the intolerance, the sectarianism, the dogmatism which would characterize only Christians. In reality, a religion without dogmas, rites, and churches has never existed: therefore, there has never existed a religion exempt from the temptation to fanaticism and intolerance.

The "meek" Hindu, the "seraphic" Buddhist, the "wise" Shintoist, the "innocent" animist have shown throughout history (and often still show) that they do not disdain the gallows or instruments of torture to be applied to those who do not think like they do. Heretics, schismatics, and infidels of every sort have often found the same deplorable end among these religions as those falling into the hands of certain Spanish Dominicans, Swiss Calvinists, or English Anglicans.

While Christian intolerance belongs by now to the past (for Catholics, Vatican II put to flight the last temptations to this), it is not so in other religions which, when they hold the levers of power, still today mete out the death penalty to those who convert to a different belief from that of the majority.

Those "beautiful souls" of modern ideologies say they are indignant in the face of every form of religious fanaticism. They would do well to contemplate first the mountain of dead bodies produced in recent centuries as a ritual offering to their goddess reason and to her cortège of idols, from the revolution of progress.

But beyond the disdain of hypocritical secularists, does this not move us to reflect on the universality of religious intolerance? Men, all men, react with violence in the face of whatever might endanger their faith. Does this defense mechanism not confirm the importance that religion has for mankind? Does it not indicate by chance how rooted the need to protect a dimension perceived as essential and inalienable really is?

TRUTHS, THE TRUTH

Against the chaotic backdrop of the religious world, where greatness and misery are intertwined, the Bible is not *a* revelation for Christians, but is *the* Revelation. That is to say, it is the apex, the fullness of that truth whose shreds survive in other religions, perhaps underground and disfigured.

The Christian has not been invited to accept a conviction that appears especially in Asia: "Many are the paths, but the truth is one. Behind the various beliefs there is a super-dogma that unites them all." Although this has not prevented it from bloody fits of intolerance, for Asia, every religion is a path toward the divine.

The Christian cannot accept such a general *embrassons-nous*, just as he cannot accept the skepticism of Pilate (*Quid est veritas?* What is truth?) that triumphs in today's society: Trying once again to attenuate their anguish in the face of the mystery, contemporary culture seeks to convince us that there is no one truth that is "truer" than the others.

One attempts to dissolve everything in debate, in a round table, in discussion with many voices, ennobling a fierce pluralism that is simply a pretext for avoiding the search for truth, which can be consoling as well as disturbing.

Those who write for the newspapers of neo-capitalism, the periodicals of the bourgeois radicals, know that there is a rule that must be respected in writing an article: when anyone affirms something, it has to be accompanied by someone else who states the contrary. The day after I was interviewed by an editor of one of these widely read and powerful newspapers, he called me up to ask me "a favor from one colleague to another": "Could you indicate someone who would be willing to argue the opposite of some of your Jesus hypotheses? You know how it works here; you can't publish an article that isn't dialectical."

Authentic dialectic demands that from the clash between thesis and antithesis a synthesis emerges, however provisional it might be. But every synthesis is forbidden by the masters of thought who find more appeasing the farce that every decision is possible, that everything is only inconclusive debate because truth does not exist — or better, there is no truth but theirs when they state that truth does not exist.

This is not the case for Christians who find here another aspect that opposes them to the dominant culture. Christianity would dissolve if it were not convinced that there are many partial truths, but only one higher, fuller Truth that surpasses all others, while containing all that is positive in them.

Thus, in dialogue with secularism, Christianity has always opposed and obviously opposes those who affirm that *all religions are false*. But, in dialogue with those religions, Christianity also opposes (and with no less energy) those who affirm that *all religions are true*.

The French journalist André Frossard, a convert to Christianity during a sudden, mysterious experience, asks, "What can I do about it if Christianity is true? What can I do about it if the Truth exists, and this Truth is a Person?"

Far from any presumptuousness (if anything, following the example of St. Paul, "with fear and trembling"), the Christian confesses that Jesus is not one of many "illuminati" or "initiates," that He is not even the greatest of prophets, or teachers of salvation. For those who believe in Him, Jesus is salvation in Himself, in His words, but also in His person. In Him, says the faith, God did not limit Himself just to speaking, as He did through many prophets, perhaps even outside the biblical tradition: but in Him, God Himself appeared among men by becoming man. In Christ, the salvation that men have sought through many often disappointing paths is definitive and conclusive. "What therefore you worship as unknown, this I proclaim to you," (Acts 17:23) says St. Paul to the Athenians, proclaiming the Resurrection of the Nazarene. If Christianity were a "wisdom," a set of exhortations and prohibitions, a series of old books, one could find a compromise with other religions. But the fact is that Christianity is neither a thing nor an idea but a man; and one can either accept or reject men, they are not interchangeable.

Jesus, that man, did not give good advice to help people overcome the anguish of death. For those who accept Him, Jesus has triumphed over death through His Resurrection, pledge, and downpayment of the resurrection of all.

For this reason, Christians see in the gospel an apex that cannot be exceeded, because nothing can be imagined that goes beyond the Incarnation of God Himself; nothing can be imagined that goes beyond the resurrection of the dead; nothing can be imagined that goes beyond a God "able to raise men even from the dead" (Heb. 11:19), in such a radical and unheard of manner, in body and soul, in the unity of the whole person; not (as in other religions) as simple survival, but as truly immortal, participating in divine life.

SIN AND SALVATION

The contact between the great religions (whether in hyper-developed areas such as California or in underdeveloped areas such as Brazil) is certainly beneficial to Christianity. Every point of contact allows one to learn; every point of competition stimulates and fights against ossification. The more one draws near with respect to different traditions, the more every Christian can discover treasures that help him to know and live his own faith. The Second Vatican Council pointed this out: "By means of dialogue with religions, we understand better the mystery of Christ."

But we must always remember that dialogue (a word both conflated and betrayed) is a point of arrival and not of departure. How can one "understand better the mystery of Christ" who ignores it or wants to compare it with other "mysteries"? And yet, this is exactly what happens among many enthusiasts in the East who know little or nothing about Christianity. They are among the many who ignore the invitation of a wise Hindu: "If you are not satisfied with the water of your well, before digging another one, try to dig your own deeper."

This is more than ever urgent when, for the first time in history, the current seems to be reversing: the East is sending its missionaries into the West, who not infrequently find an open ear among the young.

This phenomenon, which frightens the cowardly, at times depends on contingent causes, like the invasion of Tibet, which pushed thousands of Buddhist lamas out of the country, bringing their ancient wisdom westward. Certainly, however, this can also be read as a judgment on the churches that, either due to indolence or errors, have caused people who were part of their flock to look elsewhere for spiritual bread.[20]

[20] In Japan, as the official religion Shinto was declining, the impressive phenomenon of Shin-Shukyo took hold, the "new religions" or churches and sects with spectacular growth and mostly of Christian inspiration. Then from Korea, the most aggressive of these recent Eastern sects spread throughout the world (now present in over one hundred twenty-seven countries), that of Sun Myung Moon, who presented himself as a new messiah, not intending to reject Christianity but to fulfill it. The official name of the sect is the Holy Spirit Association for the Unification of World Christianity. It is significant that in Korea, as in Japan and throughout that part of Asia, where the Christian mission reached, whatever is new, or vital, or autochthonous in the religious field is now inspired by or at least draws from Christianity. Then there is the case of China, in which some see (paradoxically, but with good reason) the most amazing case of mass

But Christianity can clearly learn from such experiences. It learns, for example, to recover the richness of the symbol, so present in the liturgy of the primitive Church and then forgotten under the influence of Greek rationalism first, and the Enlightenment later. It learns to rediscover the sense of mystery, of the sacred, undermined by the coarse positivism of the secular world. It learns, above all, techniques developed by Eastern traditions: techniques of prayer, asceticism, self-control, introspection, meditation, finding balance between body and spirit.

Christian mysticism and spirituality certainly do not lack a wealth in this field (consider, for example, the treasures of patristics of the Eastern Orthodox traditions), although at times these are forgotten or even rejected. Among the many misunderstandings is the conviction that Christian hierarchies foster superstition and irrationality. On the contrary: the temptation of the churches

> conversion to Judeo-Christianity. Accepting the theories of Karl Marx, the German Jew whose father became a Protestant, China has abandoned its millenary tradition to accept the "Judeo-Christian byproduct," the "secularized Bible" that is Marxism. Through this, a fourth of humanity has come to consider as its own the Jewish-Christian theology translated according to Marxist mythology. The Chinese have thus learned to recognize the categories of messiah (the proletariat), chosen people (the working classes), devil (the bourgeoisie), sin (exploitation of the worker), Original Sin (surplus value, the capitalist means of production), Paradise or Kingdom of God (the socialist society of the future), church (the party), prophet (the revolutionary leader), redemption (revolution), heresy (revisionism), asceticism (political militancy), brotherhood (proletarian internationalism), sacred scripture (the writings of Marx, Mao, and their followers), dogma (the party line), confession of sin (self-criticism), penitence (political re-education) — the list could continue: there is no Judeo-Christian concept that does not find its mythological equivalent (disguised as political) in Marxism, and embracing this, China (as well as Vietnam and other countries, not only in Asia but also in Africa) "converted" to realities previously unknown to its culture. Through communism, born in nineteenth-century Europe from the Holy Alliance, the deepest regions of Asia have come to know and make their own the biblical conceptions of family, person, marriage, woman, and so forth. Many even see in the case of China the most resounding case of "pre-evangelization" and foresee that the work of Christian missionaries, once they return to those areas, will be greatly facilitated by the massive work done by those who believed they were doing the opposite. Could it be one of those "clever twists of reason" mentioned by Hegel, Marx's predecessor? Or is Pascal right once again when he discerned the hidden work of Providence in the apparently chaotic river of history, "Beautiful to see with the eyes of faith the history of Herod, of Caesar"?

if anything is to rationalism, a soft alignment with Western enlightened positivism. The charismatics, miracle workers, visionaries, and others with extrarational gifts, or even just mystics, those who pray with their whole being and not just their minds and their lips, have never been welcomed with open arms by the churches.

This justified prudence finds traces in some letters in the New Testament. But this is a prudence that, while preventing official Christianity from mingling with the ungovernable chaos of so many sects, has also precluded paths that might have been fruitful. Now, some of these paths have been reopening in the encounter and clash with other religious traditions not impeded by Western rationalism.

But in those non-Christian religions, the greatest development of the techniques we mentioned (and which seems to be the aspect Christians most want to learn) is not a sign of superiority, but if anything of a dramatic impotence.

Every religious person, in fact, recognizes the distressing presence and power of evil, sin, and death, but not always the redemption and salvation in which Christianity believes. In the paschal mystery of Jesus (His Passion, death, Resurrection, and Ascension into Heaven), the Christian sees evil, sin, and death confronted and defeated once and for all. Not by animal sacrifice, nor by the immolation of a hero or a demigod, but confronted and defeated by God Himself, by the true God who is also true man: died on the Cross and risen from the tomb *for us*.

He is a God, then, whom one can reach without effort because He has gone looking for man. Unlike every other, the God who manifested Himself in Jesus is not the impassible one into whom man must pour his vital energies until they are exhausted, estranging himself, hoping in this way to ingratiate Him and so to reach salvation. But the Christian God is the only one who *alienates Himself*, manifesting Himself in the form of a suffering servant and finally triumphing over death.

All this is unknown to non-Christian religions: to them, life is a daily struggle to reach the divine, to be worthy of the divine, to gain the hope of salvation, to implore liberation, to restrain sin, to confront death hoping to take part in some form of survival. To them, life is even seen as resignation to an invincible power of evil and is transformed then into a painful effort to attain nothingness.

Everything, one's very existence, is only pain without hope of redemption in anything besides annihilation and oblivion.

It is into this extenuating struggle to attain salvation that the non-Christian pours out his energies, effort, and genius, developing those "techniques." In their refined wisdom, they are often merely exertions to attain redemption with human strength alone. They are the pitiable baggage of the poor man more than the overflowing treasure of the rich man. This is the man who had to be an acrobat to scale the heights of Heaven.

The Christian has merely settled lazily into his wealth, relying on his faith in redemption, in the Resurrection, in the paternity of God that goes as far as the unprecedented *abbà*, "papa," as Jesus calls His Father, unique in all religious traditions, shining a revelatory light on the eternal destiny of man. Even if we did not know the precise content of Christian eschatology, should we not presume it to be a priori consoling and loving in the light of this precondition? Namely, from the fact that the believer (and only the Christian believer, for as much as you might search everywhere, even in the Old Testament) is exhorted to turn to the Most High, to the Eternal, to the Lord of Heaven and Earth, addressing Him not only as "Father," which is already amazing, but even daring to call Him "papa," like a trusting child.

Contact with other traditions can awaken the Christian from his torpor, can offer him richer means to externalize the faith. But the comparison, in the end, is not capable of disturbing the certainty that one alone is "the way, and the truth, and the life" (John 14:6).

As with every reality based on faith, the Christian solution to man's destiny after death is open to acceptance or rejection. There are no theorems to demonstrate, just mysterious truths to accept with trust.

And yet, up to a certain point, it is possible to remain on the level of an objective comparison of religions, which makes it less difficult to observe the concrete superiority (though unpleasant, this word must be used) of Christian eschatology.

In the light of what we have already seen, we shall proceed to several further previews, several incursions into the destiny of man as understood by the vast non-Christian world.

FROM INDIA TO THE INDIES

There is a preliminary difficulty confronting anyone who wants to explore eschatology: one proceeds from the chaotic, superabundant luxuriance that characterizes many religions, to the reticent silence of many others that go so far as to ask if they believe at all in a destiny for man after death. This is the case, for example, of Chinese Confucianism, which lacks an eschatology almost entirely.

But moving just a little westward, one encounters the opposite case in Hinduism, which seems to exert great fascination among modern Westerners. But which Hinduism, seeing that this religion has a different appearance in each of India's two million villages? It seems a sort of virgin forest where everything and its opposite can be found together, where more than three thousand divinities cohabitate, and each believer can freely choose according to his preferences. Regarding the last things, Hinduism is usually identified with belief in the successive transmigration of souls, with reincarnation and metempsychosis, which we shall consider below. In reality, the chaos of Hinduism considers not only reincarnation, and it is not clear at all what actually awaits the believer after death.

For example, in the case of a particularly evil person, the cycle of reincarnation is interrupted by sojourns of greater or lesser duration in a type of Hell.

As with Hinduism, Buddhism as well (another enthusiastic discovery for many Europeans and Americans in our day) escapes the Asian doctrinal anarchy. In a luxurious complex of myths and legends accepted by some and rejected by others, Buddhism, like every religion of the Far East, speaks of successive reincarnations, and by means of these, promises a final dissolution into nothingness. But some Buddhists hold that there are souls that escape reincarnation (which is both a condemnation and a liberation) to be reborn just once, under the form of lotus blossoms that open with infinite slowness until they are completely open in the eternal vision of the Buddha. According to others (perhaps those most faithful to the intentions of their founder), there is no survival after death because there is no God: the original form of Buddhism, in fact, is not a religion, but a philosophy tending toward atheism. According to still other Buddhists, the soul of the deceased passes through a series of heavens characterized by greater and greater satisfactions, especially culinary and sexual.

Here we touch upon the typical phenomenon of the projection into life after death of concrete terrestrial needs and desires which we shall see in full force when we consider Islam. In fact, according to the Buddhist schools that support this journey through a series of heavens, at a certain stage the soul is hosted in a castle with one thousand seven hundred rooms. In every room, the fortunate deceased is awaited by seven goddesses and seven servants ready to satisfy him in every way, beginning with (clearly) exactly what you are thinking.

Furthermore, for many religions, class distinctions and racism, to which they contributed and maintained on earth, continue in the afterlife as well. An exemplary case is Valhalla, the Paradise of the ancient Germanic tribes resuscitated in the crazed cults of the Nazi SS. It is envisioned as a room with just a few places reserved for the warrior kings, tribal chiefs, and those warriors who die in combat. All others do not count.

Another typical example of the classist afterlife is that of the pre-Columbian Aztecs, according to whom the common man descended forever into a dark, inhospitable kingdom, while only the nobles and priests flew into a rich, comfortable "Palace of the Sun." Could such a blatantly classist vision of the afterlife have contributed to the sudden fall of the powerful Aztec empire? Although the brutal Spanish conquistadors were not the most credible heralds of the gospel, the masses converted to Christianity because they were struck by its "democratic" afterlife, by its Paradise promised to the lowly and the poor, and its Hell that threatened the rich and powerful — precisely the opposite, that is, of what their leaders had wanted them to believe.

The Hindu afterlife is also radically classist, confused and uncertain on every other point, but not about the fact that there were to be separate sectors according to their caste. The same happens (as I pick through many possible examples) in Polynesian cults where the eternal destiny of the soul corresponds to the social rank in life of the deceased: the worst places in the world of the dead are reserved not only for the poor and the plebians, but also for women.

At any rate, what are the proud Egyptian pyramids if not tombs for kings, the pharaohs, the only ones with the right to a comfortable immortality, while the bones of the slaves who built those mountains of stone are darkly interspersed, like their souls, with the sands of the desert?

What happens throughout history (including social injustice) is destined to prolong into eternity: this is the despairing message of many eschatologies. The afterlife is simply the mechanical repetition of this life, with the naïve elimination of the negative aspects of life and the exaltation of the positive.

An example that has become famous, thanks to the myths of Westerns, is the image of the afterlife of the Sioux Indians: an immense prairie covered with easily hunted bison. For those Indians there was another disturbing element that is found in innumerable religious traditions, namely that one did not win access to the Eternal Pastures of the Great Spirit thanks to a virtuous life, but rather thanks to the capacity of bearing stoically the cruel and bloody initiation rites, during which (as happens in many African tribes as well) the young man to be initiated often ends up losing his life.

These are tragic examples of what I sought to point out above: beyond Christian redemption, the need for salvation is so great and man's means to attain it are so inadequate that one does not hesitate to risk death among the torments of this life to be "initiated," namely to have access to the hope of escaping death in the next life.

THE AFTERLIFE FOR THE MUSLIM

Among the "alienated" eschatologies (namely, those that project beyond death their earthly dreams), the most famous and striking case is that of Islam. According to Islam, Paradise is simply the apex, almost a caricature, of what a poor Arab of the seventh century might imagine in his wildest dreams: shady gardens, fruit trees, ponds, streams flowing with milk, perfumes, beautifully clad horses, interminable banquets, and especially slaves — for Islam, social equality has not even been established in Paradise.

Nor has equality between the sexes been established there: this materialist, classist, exclusivist (it is reserved solely to the followers of Muhammad, the true prophet) afterlife is also famously misogynistic. Before the backdrop of a luxurious heavenly oasis, the deceased Bedouin is promised some four thousand virgins, eight thousand married women, and more than five hundred "Houri," a true specialty of the Muslim Paradise: maidens "with large black eyes, similar to pearls hidden in their shell" whose perspiration "smells of musk" and whose flesh "is transparent to the marrow of their bones." Thus, the Qur'an describes these creatures whose prodigious trait is the renewal of their physical virginity.

In some Muslim schools, thanks to Christian influence, the expectancy of such a concrete Paradise has been mitigated to some extent. Nonetheless, the general framework does not change, nor can it, founded as it is on the Qur'an itself, which does not tolerate readings that are not literal: streams of milk and honey, black slaves in the role of masseur, and renewable virgins will always remain the principal attractions.

Clearly, such conceptions of the afterlife end up troubling the whole Islamic system. In fact, in the face of such blatant materialism, Marxism goes on the offensive with its theory of religion as an illusory alienation in the heavens, as the "sigh of the poor man" that projects his frustrations and impotent desires onto an imaginary world.

Furthermore, what happens to the worldly ambitions of a religion that (as the crowning of its every promise) has nothing else to offer in Paradise than the image of an oasis as it was imagined by a desert nomad? Perhaps this is one of the reasons why the Muslim faith (despite its amazing initial expansive force and the current revival on the heels of oil money), in contrast with Christianity, has never been able to expand beyond the torrid zones around the tropics. Burning, scorching heat and the lack of water are needed to arouse the desire for the eternal prize of a Paradise like the one promised by Muhammad, the man of the desert.

On the other hand, all of these versions of the afterlife imagined like a photograph of this life bear witness to a fundamental need in man: namely, not only to save for eternity his own soul, but all that pertains to him, body and soul. Furthermore, there is a need to save, with his undivided individuality, his world, his environment, his life, his entire history. This is the aspiration that will find fulfillment in the Christian concept of the afterlife, where everything is saved, everything continues, but where everything is also transfigured.

No less naïve and materialistic is Islam's concept of Hell: just as Paradise is the best face of the only world known to the Muhammad, so too is Hell simply the worst face of that same world. The deceased are immersed in real tar, they are boiled over a low flame in a pot of real copper. The commentators of the Qur'an are certain of many things: they know that the infernal flame is seventy times hotter than earthly flames. They know that this extraordinary fire took a thousand years to reach a red color, which after another thousand years turns white, and after another thousand years takes on its definitive color: "Black that burns but does not emit light." In that fire, the damned eat poisoned fruit that has the form of a demon's head. We note in passing that the Buddhist Hell is similar to the Islamic version, a true university of torture with two hundred seventy-two departments, each specialized in a particular torment.

Just as Paradise is reserved for Muhammad and his followers, so too Hell will receive the infidels. The Qur'an says that this place is "for those who do not profess the true religion and who call our witness lies." Muslims, on the other hand, as long as they continue to believe in the prophet, can be sure of reaching the appetizing eternal oasis, except in cases of homicide, idolatry, cowardice in battle, and adultery; but even in these extreme cases, the condemnation of the faithful is only temporary. Eternal torment is reserved only for infidels or those who, born Muslim, have renounced the "true religion."

Thus, as for nearly all religions (though in Islam with particular virulence), the threat of terrible punishments in the afterlife seeks to reinforce the religion, aiming at frightening the faithful to avoid recanting and passing to another belief. We see here the exact opposite of the gospel that calls to participation in the heavenly Kingdom everyone who has loved in deeds, whether Christian or non-Christian, whether they have heard the name of Christ proclaimed in this life or not.

Some Questions

It is worth dedicating to Islam more abundant attention than to other religions — first, because the followers of the Qur'an are the most numerous religious community in the world after Christianity. Nor should we forget that the particular importance of Islam is derived from it being the third monotheism (with Judaism and Christianity), the third and last world religion that worships one God. That God is, according to Muhammad, the same God of Moses and of Jesus, the God of the Bible, of the Old and New Testaments. For a Christian, it is of particular interest to see how, from the same premises, the Qur'an makes such different use of its faith, elaborating an eschatology so distant from that of the gospel.

Should we now turn to other religions, create inventories and classifications, proceeding in a parallel manner? Perhaps it is possible to avoid this, with the obvious exception of that entirely anomalous case that is Israel, and of which we shall speak separately at the end of the chapter. Filling more pages with picturesque details, anecdotes, and curiosities would not suit our purposes; it would only confirm certain basic characteristics that have already emerged. We shall stop here, then. From the few things said, one can intuit clearly enough certain fundamental ideas of non-Christian eschatologies.

Among these fundamental ideas is the fact that, for many religions, what little or much they imagine after this life is not only the naïve projection of earthly desires and fears. This projection in fact mirrors the cultures of certain peoples and times. How can one get excited about their afterlife to the point of sacrificing one's life to attain it unless one is a Native American, or an Indian of Tamil Nadu, or an Arab nomad in the desert, or a member of a particular African or Australian tribe?

Almost always, a certain economy (of hunters or shepherds, of nomads or farmers) is projected into the afterlife. And therefore, what would a peasant farmer do in the eternity of prodigious fishermen on a lake or on the high seas?

Or a fisherman in fabulous hunting grounds? Or what would the descendant of Native Americans, now perhaps a factory worker at General Motors in Detroit or a lawyer in Los Angeles, do on the Eternal Prairies amid herds of domesticated bison, the hope and longing of his ancestors?

Again, how can those who are not of the nobility, or rich, or priests accept one of the many futures of the many religions that promise happiness and eternal life, but only for the nobles, for the rich, and for priests? And what woman would accept to be one of the ecstatic maidens that constitute the main dish of so many versions of the afterlife, not only of Muslims? Provided, that is, that those systems foresee a form of survival after death for women as well, even if in a minor tone with respect to that of men. That even the Catholic Church, which venerates a woman, Mary, as Mother and model of the Church, could have debated whether women have an immortal soul is simply a foolish, old calumny.

But recognizing that, in so many non-Christian eschatologies, Heaven is entirely prohibited to the other half of humanity is not at all a misrepresentation; it is an objective truth.

How can one accept, then, the innumerable versions of the afterlife open only to believers of those religions, while for all others (the great majority of humanity) there is only an eternal torment awaiting them? Or, in the most fortunate cases, annihilation, a definitive disappearance?

The lack of universality in its various forms is therefore a characteristic of most eschatologies.

Julius Evola[21] was the Italian scholar who sought confirmation for the Aryan delirium of Nazism in the ancient Indo-European religious traditions, from India to Germany, Scandinavia, and Rome. The predicament is that, on the level of facts, Evola was right: racism, elitism, the cult of blood and earth, militarism, the whole baggage of Nazi hatred, truly find their roots in certain religions. Exalting these, Evola rages against another tradition: Judeo-Christianity, which he characterizes as "degenerate and subversive," "extraneous to the true Aryan spirit" because it announces "a salvation open to all, regardless of every concept of race and caste." Thus, he implored Nazis and Fascists to fight Judeo-Christianity because, as Evola says, its Paradise is "universal, cosmopolitan." A fine confirmation, it seems, of the singularity of biblical eschatology.

---

[21] Editor's Note: Julius Evola (1898–1974) was an Italian philosopher, poet, painter, and writer, particularly influential in far right circles.

The lack of justice seems to be another trait of most of those versions of the afterlife.

It is an injustice at work in many ways: either in the case of the many types of "class Paradise," or when the judgment that decides the eternal fate is not based on the merits or demerits of the deceased but on the performance of rituals and formalism; or when that judgment depends on the proper performance on the part of the survivors of particular funerary norms. For Christianity, on the other hand, it is not some chance circumstance that is not imputable to the deceased which decides his eternal destiny: the only criterion of judgment is the law of love and obedience to personal conscience. This is another novel, liberating aspect of the gospel message.

"Human, all too human!" Friedrich Nietzsche's complaint seems justified before the many versions of the afterlife imagined by the religious universe.

There is an unbelievable historical confirmation, all too often forgotten, of the superiority of Christian eschatology above every other. It was this that brought about the mass conversions in late antiquity to the new faith. Historians recall how Roman enthusiasm was shot through by an anxiety about salvation, one's eternal personal salvation, no longer placated by paganism at its twilight nor by the new religions from the East. As happened for the Aztec empire, so too in the Roman Empire it was especially the ultimate concerns of Christianity that irresistibly attracted religious men.

SOME FACTS

Up to now, we have mentioned just one eschatology, but there are at least two possible eschatologies, as discussed in a footnote in the first chapter.

There is *individual* eschatology, which concerns the fate of each individual. But there is also *general* or *collective* eschatology, which proposes to describe the final destiny of all humanity, which speaks of the end of the world.

Most religions elaborate an even more confused collective eschatology, swollen with even more details than their individual eschatology.

In many cases, a collective eschatology is entirely lacking: attempts were made to give answers to the questions about the fate of individuals, not to the final destiny of humanity. This is not a secondary omission: in this way, they have truncated the indispensable link between the part and the whole, between the individual and society, between the history of each person and that of all.

On the contrary, in other religions there is an imbalance on the side of collective eschatology: they provide answers for the fate of the world, but not about the destiny of the individual.

It seems that in no case is a balance reached between the ultimate concerns of individuals and the collective concern that characterizes Christianity, and which is among the most ignored and yet most convincing aspects of its credibility.

Among the decisive criteria of truth is that called the "maximum of coherence." The truth of a vision of man, of history, or of the world (and that is what concerns religions and ideologies) is measured by its capacity to give a coherent and complete meaning to each and all of its elements.

This is precisely what is not found among contemporary doctrines that appreciate one aspect of man but do not know what to do with the others. And so, Marxists emphasize the social while ignoring the personal; the bourgeoisie rely on an individual that does not know how to coordinate with the collective. Both are impotent, then, in giving an answer to total meaning of life and death: an omission like a hole in a jar one is pouring wine into.

For religions as well, the ability to coordinate all aspects is decisive, an ability that finds its infallible proving ground in eschatology. A convincing conception of the afterlife must be capable of saving and harmonizing the three dimensions in man: bodily, spiritual, and social. Now, contrary to many other religious messages, Christianity announces the salvation of man in his totality, body and soul, through the Resurrection, incorporating individual salvation into general salvation. In Christianity, everyone is connected to one another: one goes to Heaven not despite others but thanks to them and with them. And perfect joy is not attained by the blessed for their own part, but by the entire glorified humanity. The more we have made others happy, the more we shall be happy with them for all eternity.

Along these same lines, it can be demonstrated that no religion has anything that can be approximated to the entirely Chrisitan concept of the communion of saints, where "saint" includes all of us, sinners sanctified through Baptism and integrated into the Church, which is not "saintly" in its exterior appearance but is so by its faith, in its profound essence.

All men, thanks to the Spirit, are united in Christ; all are members of His Body, which is the Church. This solidarity exceeds not only the barrier between the sexes, races, and nations, but exceeds and nullifies even the barriers of time, of life and death. In this way, we the living, the pilgrim Church, are united among ourselves and united in the same life that is stronger than mere biological life to those who have preceded us beyond the threshold of death: those still being purified and those who already enjoy God in the Church Triumphant.

Within this one Body of Christ the very same life flows, which allows all to pray, intercede, and assist one another; it allows the living and the deceased to be united in a reciprocal exchange that death has not interrupted but if anything has exalted. Through faith it is certain that our beloved, all the just who are now in God, are much closer than they were on earth.

The communion of saints not only signifies a profound union among the members on earth and in Heaven, of the Body of Christ, but also the complete communion of "holy things." It derives from this that all good done by one member overflows to the good of all, living or dead.

Carnal men unite among themselves in political parties, in societies that are called "anonymous" in clubs, associations, and lobbies: all unions based on interests that nonetheless remain on the surface and which terminate at the threshold of death. Religious men unite in communities more or less structured, and in any case (not merely silly Christian boasts but a documentable reality) all oblivious to the depth of relations between rich and poor, men and women, white and black, just and sinner, living and dead, which only the Church professes, proclaiming in the Creed the "communion of saints."

Decisive problems all, which it is not possible to address here in the breadth they merit lest we test your patience more than has already been done. Here, as elsewhere in this book, I can only indicate a direction, stimulate research, shoot the flare I spoke about earlier.

A scanty recollection is also necessary regarding another decisive aspect that characterizes Christian eschatology.

Once more, it concerns a question of balance: in this case between this life and the afterlife, between time and eternity. In the current ideologies, time hides in the eternal; in too many religions the eternal erases time. Thus, the secular world loses its balance to the advantage of action, the religious world to that of contemplation. Yet it is the balance between action and contemplation that characterizes Christianity. The afterlife is not irrelevant, but neither is it detached from life, because the afterlife is constructed *in* the here and now.

For the gospel, human life is a demanding journey toward a personal encounter that one already begins to realize here, and yet which is not entirely realized.

Christian eschatology cannot really be called such, then, if we read this term in its etymological sense as "last things." In fact, here we are not talking about "things" but, as we know, about a Person, a man par excellence. For the Christian, eternal destiny is not a package of things to await and hope for: his eternal destiny is Christ Himself. Christ is the *Heaven* we are to attain; Christ is Hell for those who lose Him; Christ is *Purgatory* for the one maturing in Him, being purified by Him, and being urged to the full expression of His possibilities.

If these are not "things," they are also not "ultimate." That encounter is not at the end of life but at its center; the "end times" are not at the end of history but are already here, because the risen Christ is the *Eschaton*, the Last. He is here, tangibly, in that eucharistic "sign" of which we shall speak: "I am with you always, until the close of the age" (Matt. 28:20). And His Kingdom must still manifest itself to the senses of all, but the eyes of faith already discern it and live it: "The kingdom of God is in the midst of you!" (Luke 17:21).

Metempsychosis, Reincarnation

Not the least of the reasons for the superiority of Christian eschatology is also its decisive rejection of every form of reincarnation, namely the belief in the passage of the human soul after death into another human body.

Christianity says no to metempsychosis as well, which is a form of reincarnation not only in humans but also in animals, plants, and, in some cases, even in minerals.

Some might be surprised or even irritated to read that we consider it a Christian superiority to reject the transmigration of souls. For them, this rejection is rather a deficiency, a sign of inferiority.

An impressive phenomenon is happening among us: every investigation into people's beliefs in the afterlife demonstrates that a quarter of the baptized in Western countries is convinced of the possibility of some form of reincarnation. In the so-called advanced nations, the number reaches more than half of the baptized, if one adds the "I-don't-knows" to the number of believers in the transmigrations of souls.

If we add to these Christians the followers of Eastern and African religions as well (for all of whom the hypothesis of reincarnation is essential), we arrive at a disturbing conclusion: the reincarnation of souls is the expectation shared by the majority of religious people around the world, and not the biblical resurrection of the dead. Contributing to the recent, continual expansion in the West of this belief is not only direct importation from the East, but also post-Christian products born in Europe and America such as spiritualism, Theosophy, and Anthroposophy, all forms of syncretism.

As with many other aspects, it seems that here too the situation of nascent Christianity is returning, when practically only the Church and the Synagogue were opposed to metempsychosis, taught even by some of the most prestigious currents of Greek philosophy. Christianity has been besieged from within by cyclical infiltrations of this belief, sustained in the early centuries by isolated thinkers, in the Middle Ages by heretical groups like the Albigenses, and today by certain post-Protestant sects, as well as by the enormous masses revealed in surveys of the faithful in churches that officially reject it.

In reality, belief in reincarnation is not only among the most constant temptations of the human spirit, but is also among the most dangerous. It is one of the scourges of the soul that the gospel came to heal. Just as its millenary persistence in the East does not exalt it, so too its reemergence in the West as a mass phenomenon does not seem to be a sign of progress but of regression. At the bottom of every reincarnationist conception there is a type of spiritualism, a belief of having to save in man only his soul, an attitude that corresponds fatally to indifference, if not to contempt for the body.

For Christianity, man (every man: beautiful or ugly, noble or plebian, genius or dullard) is an inseparable and unrepeatable unity of elements both spiritual and material. Our body is not a garment that can be changed, nor a temporary wrapping to leave to its fate when we are wrapped in another. We do not *have* a body; we *are* a body—so asserts a healthy Christian materialism. The object of God's love in creating us, in redeeming us and finally in allowing us to enjoy Him eternally, is not a soul but a human person in its entirety.

As St. Thomas Aquinas taught in his medieval language, "this soul of *mine* is a 'substantial form' of this *my* body"; it therefore cannot transmigrate elsewhere, in the distressing itinerary of metempsychotic cycles.

For the gospel, the whole man, not just one part of him, is immortal: Christ, in His Kingdom, is not "King of souls" purified through pitiful reincarnations; He is the "King of men," saved, joyfully resurrected forever in their inalienable individuality.

Those who think it would be "more modern" to take metempsychosis seriously rather than Christian eschatology do not realize that it represents a terrifying leap backward. It is a return to the Greek idea of the body as the soul's prison, uniting oneself to the Asiatic disdain toward, at times even horror at and hatred for, matter (beginning with the matter that allows us to live in the world bodily), and so fighting it, ignoring it, overcoming it, humiliating it, defeating it, and annihilating it.

These people do not realize that the millenary Christian struggle against belief in reincarnation is also defended by the concept of the person as a unique reality, unrepeatable and thus precious more than anything else. They do not realize that the Christian's rejection is also a reaffirmation of the absolute dignity and preeminence of man: if in the horrid fly that's buzzing around the room there is the soul of my great-great-grandfather, if in that plant out on the balcony one of your ancestors is languishing, how can we distinguish human nature, its nobility, from animal or vegetable nature? It too is praiseworthy, created by the same God, certainly, but it is qualitatively different from us.

Which justice, then, would oblige me to live a "dog's life" (perhaps literally) for sins committed by another and whom I have never met?

In the fortunes and misfortunes of this ancient belief, there lies the real fear of all that is definitive, irrevocable.

Significantly, in Italy two popular referendums have been called to erase the definitive, irrevocable character of the only two realities that have remained such: marriage and the death penalty. Seeking refuge in the transmigration of the soul is, for many of our contemporaries, the substitution of an impossible referendum that would take the definitive character away from life and death.

Today we are frightened by the fact that one lives and dies just once, with all the gravity that this entails. Frivolous cultures, allergic to commitments like ours, search for mitigations and appeals. One rebels against Christian seriousness, which warns of the need to spend every last one of our talents in the life we have been given, because "night comes, when no one can work" (John 9:4).

Just one life, one death, one eternal destiny gambled once and for all: in this "Christian inexorability" there is without a doubt one of the most powerful stimuli to the morality of service to others, which is visibly lacking in many Eastern religions. Knowing that "we shall be judged on love" and that the time granted to us for loving is limited, those who believe in the gospel are not tempted to act like students who take it easy, knowing they can take a make-up exam. One must give his all, because there are no remedial classes ("if it doesn't go well, I can always expiate reincarnating with some serious illness or in a rat, in a tree..."). In this life there is only a passing or a failing grade, once and for all.

It is probable that the fascination worked by reincarnation on the typical Westerner is also rooted in the evolutionary mentality that permeates modern culture. If we see it as a cycle that progresses toward superior forms of life, metempsychosis is in fact the application to eschatology of the pseudo-scientific naïveté of infallible progress, of evolution always and everywhere toward what is better. In this sense as well, this belief is not part of an alternative culture but seems if anything to be the banality of a dominant scientism.

Behind this belief in metempsychosis and reincarnation, which is a common bond to many religions and unites many moderns with the ancients, there is another reason, the most grievous among all the reasons: the tragic, unsatisfied need for redemption and salvation, which one tries to satisfy in life with those techniques we mentioned previously. In death, one imagines that this salvation can be the fruit of a ponderous cycle of redeeming reincarnation.

Beyond the gospel (by which Christ saved the world once and for all, which He definitively liberated from sin by assuming the Cross, freely thrusting open by His Resurrection and Ascension the doors of the Kingdom), outside of this "good news," we can only daydream about a salvation not outside but within the world, through a process of metempsychosis whose aim is either rendering us finally worthy of God or consuming ourselves until we finally dissolve into nothing our need to live happily forever, to be saved.

Throughout all Asia the swastika is a recognized symbol, the same one that Nazism unfortunately flew on their flags above Europe. The four arms of that hooked cross symbolize, for Eastern religions, the four degrees of existence in which a soul can reincarnate: the human, animal, vegetable, and mineral worlds. Distinct from the Christian cross, the hooked cross is not a sign of liberation, but of oppression; not of victory over death, but of death victorious once more.

WHO CANNOT JUDGE

Forced to make haste, I have done so reluctantly and with difficulty. For one who knows and respects the complexity of these problems, it is challenging to give the impression of proceeding by summary execution.

In any case, as long as one tries to safeguard truth and justice, the right to take a stand regarding other religions must be granted to the Christian who bears in himself a vision of man that, whether it convinces or not, is nevertheless comprehensive and organic. This right to judge is not to be granted, however, to intellectuals who deny death; Marxists or the bourgeoisie cannot make a judgment. To them, all access to this courtroom has been denied.

The answers given by many religions to the enigma of human destiny seem (and often are) unacceptable, naïve, maybe even cruel. They are born nevertheless from the effort to face and resolve the unavoidable problem of giving meaning to life and death. Without that endeavor, every solution to every problem, whether personal or social, is merely illusory.

Religions, all of them, look in the right direction, even though Christian faith suggests that the others stop at an insufficient level of profundity. For the believer in the Gospel, one must go in the same direction, but much more deeply: lower and lower, down to the heart of the abyss where this mystery finds a solution in the encounter with Christ.

On the other hand, there is no effort to go in search among the inhumane atheisms practiced in the West and in the theoretical atheisms in the East.

On the contrary, atheists look with superiority upon the savages and underdeveloped and on all those whom they sneeringly define as "developing." Developing toward what? Toward what type of progress? Maybe toward that which has allowed us to be no longer savages but barbarians?

Some only know how to offer the savages (for their "development," of course) arms and the old nineteenth-century European superstitions ("revolution!," "class struggle"); others offer more arms as well as capital to create deadly artificial needs. In both cases, they export disaster, toppling millenary equilibriums between man and nature, between the visible and the invisible, between living and dying.

In exchange for venerable beliefs that sought to placate the need for salvation and for meaning in life, in exchange for ancient words that tried to penetrate the mysteries of man and the cosmos, they offer *Capital*, the old book of some German professor; they offer *The Wonderful Seller*, an American bible for the perfect travelling salesman.

No, these types cannot offer any judgment on any aspect of religion, not even about the most primitive ones, these new, verbose teachers to whom one can apply a word from Elias Canetti, a Nobel laurate for literature, "Nothing is closer to a blind man than the one who sees everything;" and the words of Someone else, "if a blind man leads a blind man, both will fall into a pit" (Matt. 15:14).

You can reject all, including Christian eschatology. But, in this case as well, do not waste time with those who want to lock you into a glass case at a museum of natural science with a reassuring sign around your neck: "*Kingdom*: Animal. *Phylum*: Vertebrate. *Class*: Mammal. *Order*: Hominids. *Family*: Homo. *Genus*: Homo sapiens."

There is much more between Heaven and earth than they would have you believe with their strategies for combatting anguish, trapping mystery in a cage. There is something much greater that has been recognized and confronted by religions, by all religions, that have sought to teach us to accept our mortality. Today's teachers want, if anything, to teach us to accept the death of our neighbor.

THE CASE OF ISRAEL

Israel is a case apart, wherein one moves in an atmosphere that is quite different from the others and quite familiar to the Christian who has not forgotten his fathers.

First, one of the many mysteries of Israel is that it breaks the obsessive circle in which all ancient cultures (and still today some Eastern and African cultures) represent their history, including the eternal history of man and the world. It was the Jew, and only the Jew, who broke the desperate bondage of a chain of centuries that led nowhere, but only wound around itself.

Thinking of the human series of events as a hill climb, a march, or an arrow that aims at a target (the messianic "Kingdom of God"), the Hebrew Bible literally invents history with the idea of progress and of the future, which lies at the foundation of the modern world. If there is progress, there can be a future, and thus hope: for the world, for society, for man no longer captured without hope of escape in the circle of reincarnations.

Israel came to the idea that the definitive destiny of man is one of both continuity and novelty: the afterlife is a continuation of this life but, at the same time, is also a totally other dimension.

It is not merely one part of man that is to be called to this eternal dimension, but his whole person. On this path, the Jew, and only the Jew, arrives at the expectation of a resurrection from the dead that Christianity will specify, deepen, and take to its extreme consequence, placing it at the center of its hope. This eternal destiny, this resurrection, is universal, promised to all people, whatever their race, sex, or social condition. Here too, Israel opens the path (though with uncertainties, contrasts, and exclusivist temptations) that will be trod to the very end by Christianity.

What's more, in another unique case, the eschatology of the Old Testament avoids the explosion of fantasy production. In the Hebrew Bible, there are no descriptions of a picturesque Hell or Paradise. There is only a haggard sobriety regarding these themes that usually unleash the fantasies of other peoples.

This line will be pursued in the New Testament and the official teaching of the Church will espouse it faithfully, marked by a constant refusal of wanting to appear to know too much. "The ideas on the afterlife that only arouse curiosity and superstition, are prohibited as scandalous and dangerous for the faithful." Are we citing a demythologizing theologian of the twentieth century? No, this was the admonition to bishops by the Council of Trent in the sixteenth century.

The Jew is the prototype of the man of faith in the one God, eternal and omnipotent, the man of transcendence, of the vertical dimension. But at the same time, no people has been as bound to the earth and to life and to the concreteness of the here and now as the Jews. Every temptation to "seek refuge in the heavens" is far from Israel. Its eschatological vision is one of the secrets to its inextinguishable vitality, even when life has filled them with brambles and thorns and threats.

Even when the earth has become his enemy, the Jew does not allow his realism and earthly pragmatism to be stolen from him. In the confines of the ghetto, he has prayed with unspeakable intensity, respecting with obstinate scrupulosity the many rules of the law; but he also works, does business, procreates. His fidelity to God is accompanied by his fidelity to the earth. He knows the Old Testament and the faith of his people could be turned to the advantage of those coarse doctrines whose tactics place the biblical tradition among the types of "religious transference into the afterlife," without recognizing the radical difference.

In certain of the oldest books in the Bible, it is difficult to establish whether the Judaism of the Patriarchs believes in the survival of man after death. Some scholars have spoken of a sort of "religious materialism" in that period. As one biblical scholar noted, "For many centuries the gaze of Israel was fixed on mere human possibilities in this life, without taking an interest in what might await man in the afterlife. Even a purely terrestrial existence was seen as an authentic religious possibility." The sinner is threatened not by Hell but by illness, misery, or a precocious death. The instinct of avoiding death is placated by having numerous descendants, such that the worst anathema was biological sterility. What is interesting is not the future of the individual but that of the nation, the messianic destiny of Israel.

It is significant to observe that this tendency of Judaism will reemerge in Marx, who, forgetting the "private," will count on the "collective."

At any rate, this afterlife of primitive Israel is shrouded in a constant half-light; it is neither the place where the powerless are consoled, nor the place where earthly frustrations are projected. Quite the contrary: the dead descend into a desolate abode, *Sheol*, where there are no distinctions. "One fate comes to all" (Eccl. 9:3), and it is a very sad fate, a wretched existence without joy. *Sheol* is the kingdom of distance from God, an insurmountable distance that separates Him even from the most venerable of the just. After so much familiarity with Him in life (in worship, in prophecy, in Providence), the harshness of death seems to interrupt every relation.

The meditations of Israel, however, are not resigned to this fate, buoyed as it is on the progress of revelation. Thus, with the passage of centuries, the road is opened to faith in personal retribution, in an eternal, differentiated destiny: a happy one for the just, a miserable one for the wicked.

Proceeding still further, faith in the resurrection of the dead is finally reached. But the first explicit mention of the resurrection of a whole man one finds only in the prophet Daniel, written, so it seems, just a century and a half before Jesus. The Nazarene (as witnessed in many controversies in the Gospels) had to confront many who were opposed to the idea of resurrection. The most well-known case is that of the Sadducees, staunch conservatives who stopped at the Pentateuch, the first five books of Scripture.

The debate among Jews of various schools had gone on for centuries, as the Talmud (this complex work that collects the teachings and commentaries on the Scriptures of the most venerable rabbis) bears witness to. The discussion took place as well within the schools that professed resurrection: would it be limited to Israel or would it extend to the non-circumcised, the gentiles, as well? Or, with an even more selective vision: will the Jews who are not buried in Israel rise, too?

Christianity, it is known, welcomed the Jewish faith in the resurrection in its most radical, most universal meaning. By doing so, it did not create a rift: it inserted here too (and perhaps above all here) into an evolutionary line, which ascends from Genesis, the first book of the Old Testament, and ends up in Revelation, the last book of the New Testament, passing through the Gospels.

Examining this progression, this deepening of faith in final things within the Bible, the Christian finds confirmation in the words of Jesus: "Think not that I have come to abolish the law and the prophets; I have come not to abolish them but to fulfill them" (Matt. 5:17).

Using biblical eschatology as our standard, in its ascendant dynamism, book after book, prophet after prophet, the Christian understands Paul who throws his life into witnessing to Jesus risen from the dead not despite, but thanks to the fact of being, as he says of himself, "circumcised on the eighth day, of the people of Israel, of the tribe of Benjamin, a Hebrew born of Hebrews; as to the law a Pharisee" (Phil. 3:5).

It is Paul who establishes between Judaism and Christianity a mother–daughter relationship, or a root–tree relationship: development, therefore, but in the same spirit, blood, flesh, sap. It is a continuous movement toward a fuller and more complete revelation.

> Take your share of suffering for the gospel in the power of God, who saved us and called us with a holy calling, not in virtue of our works but in virtue of his own purpose and the grace which he gave us in Christ Jesus ages ago, and now has manifested through the appearing of our Savior Christ Jesus, who abolished death and brought life and immortality to light through the gospel. For this gospel I was appointed a preacher and apostle and teacher (2 Tim. 1:8–11).

The proclamation of the New Testament on the final things, and the reading the Church makes thereof, are not for the Christian novelties to be feared, but natural outcomes of an uninterrupted history that began with Abraham and Moses.[22]

---

[22] Often in dialogue between Jews and Christians, it is not sufficiently emphasized that the latter did not forge an unlawful faith based on a biblical text that was foreign to them. Christians are who they are because they believed in the interpretation of the Hebrew Scriptures as it was made by Jews. Jesus the Jew was recognized as the Messiah, as the Christ of Israel by other Jews.

In the Bible, many teachings grow from book to book toward a higher truth, toward a fuller comprehension of the plan of God. But this growth, this deepening, is often subterranean, not infrequently subject to falls and regressions. The revelation about the final things, the eschatological message, is in fact that theme which seems to progress most securely and explicitly throughout all the Scriptures: from near silence, and the chiaroscuro on man's destiny in the ancient books; to the sad survival in *Sheol* that awaits good and bad; to the discovery of personal retribution; to the proclamation (though uncertain, opposed, and limited) of a resurrection of the dead, reaching, in the end, the Resurrection of Easter that testifies that Jesus is the Christ, placed at the center of the preaching of the good news. This is a destiny of salvation proclaimed to every man, that definitively breaks the temptation that runs through all the history of Israel, to restrict divine benevolence.

Placing his hope in the New Testament, the Christian must reject nothing of the Old; on the contrary, he is convinced he is legitimately carrying the faith forward, taking it to its ultimate consequences. He believes he possesses the second volume of a book in two parts: the first volume is indispensable for understanding the second, which is also indispensable.

The gospel believer considers himself a natural heir to a venerable message in the company of men like Henri Bergson, one of the great philosophers of the twentieth century, a Jew who wrote in his spiritual testament, "The meditation of an entire life has drawn me ever closer to Catholicism, in which I discern the final perfection of Judaism."

Bergson does not say "Christianity"; he wants to specify *which* Christian tradition he now identifies with: "Catholicism."

This pushes us to take one more step, and introduces the following chapter.

All of the Apostles and disciples were Jews, at least three of the evangelists were Jews, all the authors of the New Testament were Jews (perhaps with the sole exception of Luke and the Acts of the Apostles), the pillars of the ancient Church were Jews, the Church herself and her upper management for decades were all Jews. We gentiles, we the non-circumcised, we wild olive trees grafted into the trunk of the olive tree that is Israel (Rom. 11:17) did not invent our faith, but have believed in what has been proclaimed by the sons of Israel precisely as a natural development of the faith of their Fathers.

CHAPTER 10

THE DIVIDED CHRIST

A DIFFICULT ROAD

CHOOSING IS PAINFUL, BUT life is choosing. And our choices never come to an end. Therefore, in our search for meaning and hope, we leave in the background the other religions and stoop to examine the Christian proposal. But which Christian proposal? This is the immediate question. Which one should one choose among the many confessions, churches, sects? Each swears to be the custodian authorized from above of the true interpretation of the gospel. Which one should we take seriously among the many communities that claim authentic fidelity to Christ?

We would like to clarify the matter immediately, removing every suspicion of ambiguity. It is the Catholic message and practice that we shall examine, while admitting our awareness of and respect for the other Christian traditions.

As when dealing with the choice among religions, here too (where it is a question of confessions within the same religion, or at any rate, the same faith), we hope that our choice is not tied to the random place of our birth.

Among them all, Catholic eschatology is without a doubt the most well-structured, the most radical, perhaps the most insolent in the face of the wise of this world. Roman doctrine on the last things was clarified and defined through an impressive theological effort that began nearly two thousand years ago and the development of which has not yet terminated; nor will it ever, for, if as the faith teaches, God is infinite, then His Word must be inexhaustible as well. Catholic eschatology is defended by a doctrinal authority that so jealously guards its "stash of faith" (the *depositum fidei*) that it seems intolerant, or at least dour and suspicious.

This is the hope of the oldest and numerically largest Christian community. It is the most numerous religious group in the world, in fact, which is recognized in one well-defined Creed: Catholicism's doctrinal uniformity, ensured by a hierarchy culminating in just one head, is, however one might judge it, a unique fact in all religious history. The truth demands we observe that this continuous deepening of the continuity of Catholic teaching contrasts strongly with the stasis, if not paralysis, of the Orthodox churches, which in the millennium since their separation from Rome have not yet succeeded in convoking an ecumenical council. And yet, according to their theology, this is the only way of deciding controversial issues or open questions. In the West, this corresponds to the irrepressible, ever-growing fragmentation of the Protestant world: nearly a thousand denominations of different churches, all so-called "Evangelical," counted in the United States alone, and separated not only in name.

The unity of Roman doctrine guides the Church to a "catholicity," a universality that is geographic as well, though it is one: there is no country where the Catholic Mass is not celebrated every day, perhaps even in a hidden basement. This catholicity is unknown to other religious traditions, almost always confined in their place of origin, however vast.

Clearly, this is not enough to confer on Catholicism greater doctrinal credibility. It can serve, however, to lead us to a particularly attentive examination of its message, if only to combat it with greater determination if it seems unacceptable. Among all the alienations, Catholic alienation would be the worst, if it is just an illicit projection into the heavens of frustrated desires. Among the many religious vampires, Catholicism would be the one that for the longest and with the most abundance has sucked men's blood, robbing them of the earth to disperse them in an illusory heaven.

Not by accident, in the USSR, where Catholicism was but an infinitesimal minority, there has always been greater concern about Catholic popes than Orthodox patriarchs. In all the propaganda pamphlets printed by the Institute for Scientific Atheism of Leningrad, the Soviet militant was warned that the true enemy, the most fearful of opium pushers, was neither the autocephalous churches of the East, nor the Protestant churches of the West, but the Church par excellence: that of Rome.

Due to this, a "privileged" persecution was unleashed, based on the awareness of a force that even Lenin knew well. Though already quite ill, the protagonist of the October Revolution received Fr. Viktor Bede, a Hungarian priest. "Within a century," said Lenin, "there will be just one form of government, socialism. And just one religion, Catholicism."

As with many "infallible" Marxist predictions, this one too was refuted by history. But it remains as an unsuspecting witness to the stature of the Roman Church.

There Is the church and the Church

Perhaps more than the comparison of religions, the comparison of Christian confessions is serious and complex. It is also more painful for the believer, forced to recognize the divisions that lacerate gospel faith. But this is the reality, and if we have been given freedom, it is to be exercised with all the risks incumbent upon our choices.

Obviously, this theme deserves much more space and attention than we can give it here.

Will it suffice to assure you that I know and admire the theological and spiritual wealth of Eastern Christianity, Greek and Slavic? And that I know and admire the energy of Protestant faith and its love of Scripture, the radical Christ-centeredness of the churches born from the trunk of the Reformation?

I also know and admire the complex world of the "free churches," of the sects, of the old and new heretical movements that attempt to answer questions that are often forgotten by the "official" churches, and which prod them not to rest on the satisfactions of their long history or on their liturgical and doctrinal treasures.

While I examine the Catholic Church, I do not in the least hide the dark side that cohabitates with the light that I recognize in it.

Faith is needed to go beyond what is seen, to overcome the often-unpleasant appearances of the visible institutional church, to discern the invisible behind it: the mysterious Church, the Church that continues the Incarnation of God in history and makes Christ present again in the sacraments; the Church that, in the words of the Second Vatican Council, "is already, here among us, the seed and beginning of the Kingdom of God."

One must always be aware of the distinction, without which misunderstanding lies always in ambush; never should one lose the awareness of the inescapable ambiguity of the Church. There is, in fact, the *church*, and there is the Church. The former is the church that everyone can see, and often it is not a pleasant sight.

But "as hidden from our bodily eyes as it might be, behind the necessary episcopal curacy and the codes of cannon law" (to use the words of Jacques Maritain), there is the Church, which not everyone sees, which only the faith can distinguish from the heavy façade. The Church in its entirety, said St. Augustine, is like the new moon: the side facing us is dark, but, though without seeing it, you believe there is another side illuminated by the sun.

Many of the attacks and the accusations against the Church are justified, but at the same time miss their mark because they do not recognize its double nature. The Catholic knows well that his Church, according to the medieval definition, is *casta meretrix*: chaste, like Christ in its essence; a prostitute, like many of its members and in its structure. Believers certainly did not wait for the controversy over who is outside of the Church to notice the flaws of the institution. Giovanni Papini[23] said, "One could put together an anticlerical anthology of the Christian Middle Ages compiling only pages written by saints: and it would be terrible."

Yet, those men lived and died in a Church they loved and which in the end vindicated them by glorifying them on its altars. Those saints did not confuse the plans: they knew the Church is holy, but that it includes sinners in its ranks; they knew that the Church's members sin, but doing so they betray its essence, which is Christ. Therefore, the Church is never without sinners, but is always without sin.

Because of this unresolved and unresolvable ambiguity, Hans Küng was able to write, "The Church is often more of an obstacle than an aid to becoming Christians." Nor can we deny the truth of what Jean Delumeau says: "Every discourse that would claim to be Christian must first of all understand why so many of our contemporaries feel repulsion, diffidence, and rancor toward the Church." "The Church appears to many as an institution that divides rather than reconciling men. It appears not as a gift given to us, but as a price that is requested of us." Is this last quote from a pamphlet of the usual, evil ex-Catholic, ex-priest? No, the preceding lines were taken from an official text, from the catechism for youth of the Italian Episcopal Conference. It all rests on whether one is speaking about the Church or the *church*.

The faith helps me to discern more light, truth and life in Catholicism than anywhere else. It is a sharpness of sight that is certainly a strange gift, but

---

[23] Editor's Note: Giovanni Papini (1881–1956) was an Italian writer and poet.

one in which I am trying to allow to participate that other gift which is reason, insofar as it is possible. It is a certainty that seems to me more valid the more I get to the bottom of the analysis of authentic Catholic dogma. But it is, at the same time, a conviction that I do not proclaim with triumphant haughtiness, but rather confess with humility.

I love the impassioned shout of Martin Luther, which is now inscribed on the base of his monument in a park in Worms: "Here I stand, I can do no other! Help me, O God! Amen." So yelled the monk with the Bible in his hands at the famous trial in the presence of Charles V (the Holy Roman Emperor), the archbishop of Trier, the legates and theologians of the pope. If it is licit for us dwarves to stand in the company of such a giant, the poor journalist who writes these lines with such difficulty can do "no other" than to unite himself to that shout: but despite it all, not against, but rather in favor of the Church of Rome, the "Babylon" upon which the Reformer invoked the divine wrath.

Do not think that I do not have my problems. I am incapable of feeling moved in the very heart of Catholicism, among the columns of Bernini, in St. Peter's Basilica, in that mountain of marble, the construction of which brought misery upon the miserable through financial speculation on their piety toward their faithful departed (the sale of indulgences), thus setting fire to the powder keg of Northern Europe. "They say this basilica is a true work of art," grumbled a Catholic acquaintance crossing the famous square hurriedly and hardly taking a suspecting glance at the gigantic hulk at the far end of it, "a true work of art. Too bad it cost only the equivalent of eleven wagons of gold coins, as well as the loss of unity in the Church, the wars of religion, and the detachment of half of Europe."

Sure, the construction of St. Peter's is not the only factor responsible for this, even though historically it was the drop that caused the flood. But that construction site is the sign of a certain type of Catholicism, of a certain Church that, while it proclaims the gospel to others, seems to forget to preach it to itself. Yet, if I reflect on it, I am not scandalized to the point of refusing to seek inside it, amid the luxuriant marble, the hope that saves.

The Church has the duty to witness what is humanly irreconcilable: on one side the glory of the One, Most High, Eternal God; and on the other side the humiliation, the Cross, the concealment of the same God, whom the faith recognizes under the rags of Jesus of Nazareth.

The Church must remain faithful to the Old Testament and the splendor of its symbol, the Temple of Jerusalem, this wonder of the world. At the same time, it must stay faithful to the New Testament that begins in the squalor of the grotto in Bethlehem, a disgrace according to the world. St. Peter's, the Vatican with its treasures of art, the exterior triumph of the Baroque Church, all the way down to Vatican II, is an accent placed (in a nearly unilateral way) on the glory of God. But those churches that seem too triumphalist to our modern tastes are not the most important matter. What is truly important, decisive even, is the humble sign within those buildings.

It is the red lamp which, in Catholic churches, marks the presence in the tabernacle of the greatest of mysteries, the Eucharist. What matters is that presence that faith perceives behind the mundane appearance of bread and wine. What matters is that altar, that table on which that food is prepared and distributed, food thanks to which the believer is united with St. Paul in asking, "O death, where is thy victory? O death, where is thy sting?" (1 Cor 15:55).

A Disappointed Love

But, as I said, I have my problems. I did not surrender easily (and, deep inside, something fights on) to the fact that the truth of man can be safeguarded by a Church that is also an institution ("the biggest non-public bureaucracy in the world after General Motors," according to the definition of one sociologist), one which in many respects is foreign to me. Everything — family traditions, studies, friendship, intellectual tastes — not infrequently makes my cohabitation with certain aspects of the so-called "Catholic world" embarrassing for me. It is not the Church, to be sure, but rather so much of its visible façade.

In the face of that world (beginning with those ambivalent "Catholic political parties" which dare to raise a cross on their coat of arms, whose primary function seems to be to honor Christianity with words and to defame it in their actions), the sense of irrelevance can mutate into allergy, into a reaction of rejection. At any rate, I am in good company. For example, the deeply Catholic François Mauriac, a great writer, said:

> In truth, I cannot say I love the Church for herself. If I were not to believe that she had received the word of eternal life, I would have no admiration for her structures or her methods. And I would detest many chapters of her history. I am at the antipodes of those who do not believe she teaches the truth but admire her for her organization. What interests me is that the Church has preserved

intact the deposit she has received, that she has saved it and therefore, thanks to her, a Word has reached us; not as a memory, not as a simple re-evocation; but as a Word living and efficacious: "Your sins are forgiven," "This is my body given up for you."

I shall immediately preempt anyone wanting to psychoanalyze me. That would be too easy: I am well aware that in the controversy against secular culture, in the denunciation of the hidden worm gnawing away at their shiny apple, there is also in me the resentment of a disappointed lover.

Ignorant of the gospel (nor did I consider this ignorance a great loss), in university libraries I devoured books in which God was not even considered, in which the Church was merely a folkloristic wreck of a world in agony. Why should I deny that I was much more at ease among those authors than I had found myself among many devout, edifying, spiritual writers? Those who (I understood later) had the privilege of witnessing to me the true "alternative culture," the only authentic "counterculture," that all this was reduced to subculture, to what Bruce Marshall, a Catholic writer, calls "pious Catholic trash."

I am a defeated Voltairean, a humiliated rationalist, neither a *naturaliter christianus*, nor a *naturaliter catholicus*. I had to surrender, doing violence to myself (*plier la machine*, says Pascal): first, before the mysterious interior evidence, the sudden burst of an immense wonder; then in the face of confirmations that reflection and experience were giving me about this clarity that, surprisingly, had ignited within me.

The normal route, the usual path, is contact with the gospel within the Church. But it can happen (and this was true in my case) that one clashes with the gospel outside of any ecclesial mediation; that one is deceived in thinking he can do without it, perhaps; and then that he discovers, like it or not, that the gospel comes down to him by means of a Church, and only through her can he attempt to live that gospel. It can happen that he realizes that the Church is not something merely optional, an accessory to Christianity, but instead, it is indispensable because it is the life that keeps the Incarnation of Christ alive. One might even be forced to concede the truth of that famous line (that left me perplexed, however) of St. Cyprian, bishop of Carthage in the third century: "One cannot have God as his Father, who does not have the Church for his Mother."

Belonging to a church (in my case to the Catholic Church) is more than a spontaneous impulse of the heart; it is rather (at the beginning, at least, to overcome reluctance) an act of will guided by faith, which discerns the pearl under the gray covering of the shell.

The Apostle Peter once seemed to remain attached to the Master for a lack of options, almost out of desperation: "Jesus said to the twelve, 'Will you also go away?' Simon Peter answered him, 'Lord, to whom shall we go? You have the words of eternal life; and we have believed, and have come to know, that you are the Holy One of God'" (John 6:67–69).

Thus spoke Simon Peter, whom Catholics call "the first pope." Something similar can happen to many before the pope and what he represents: namely to be forced to recognize, despite everything, that the Church continues to be throughout history "the Holy One of God." This Church, inside the opaque external crust, safeguards the only "words of eternal life" that resound in the world.

There is another word, not Peter's, but of Jesus, directed to Peter, in which I hear familiar echoes. It is one of the last sentences narrated by John: "Truly, truly, I say to you, when you were young, you girded yourself and walked where you would; but when you are old, you will stretch out your hands, and another will gird you and carry you where you do not wish to go" (John 21:18).

In my lowliness, I too have felt myself dragged "where I would not": it has happened to me even in the long preparation and writing of this book. Do not think that I set out with the intention of arriving all the way to that praise of the Church that you will find especially in the last part. No, that was not my design. What I wanted to do was indeed to point out its assets, but with good measure. I amazed myself, I have resisted and fought against certain conclusions to which my research and reflection led me.

I, too, like Peter and who knows how many others after him, would have preferred "to go where I pleased." Thus, I would have liked to save something more of the ideologies of the world, this my ungrateful homeland; I would have liked to maintain greater detachment from the Church, not from its faith, certainly, but at least from its praxis. But the further I proceeded, the more I realized that, like the God to whom it must give witness, the Church too is jealous: having set off on her path and accepted the logic that presides over her life and teaching, one discovers that that sort of partial identification which I had had in mind at the start, when, as a younger man, I "girded myself," is no longer permitted.

I too had to accept the death to which the words of Christ to Peter allude: in my case, a death to my prejudices, my prior intentions, my reticence, and my scruples.

Yet, despite it all, I repeat what I said when I chose Christianity: along with Mauriac, I would not hesitate to leave to its fate the complex dogmatic pyramid elaborated over twenty centuries by Rome's theologians if I were convinced that it is nothing but a luxurious fraud, a giant blunder, a dangerous and superstitious misunderstanding.

I have not yet been able to convince myself. On the contrary, examined in its bare authenticity (stripped of illicit encrustations), that pyramid constructed piece by piece, with framing blocks taken from Scripture, does not cease to amaze me.

The more one studies it, the more one realizes that *tout se tient*: "everything sustains everything else"; each of the many stones seems to fit perfectly with the other.

Over the past years, I have understood the experience of Joseph Ratzinger. As a university professor of Catholic eschatology, he had long been fascinated and tempted by other Christian doctrines regarding the last things. "But," he later confessed, "the more I considered the various issues, the more I immersed myself in the sources, the more I interrogated mind and heart, all the more did those other hypotheses, as evocative as they were, disintegrate in my hands. And all the more did the interior logic of Catholic eschatology reveal itself to me."

THE HERETIC: A BURDENSOME TRADE

After impatience, furor, contestation, anticipating the times (even for me, that mythical 1968 did not come in vain!), I believe I have made at least one discovery. I hope it is not merely due to a question of birthplace: "One is born a pyromaniac; one dies a fireman."

It seems I have understood that the more one penetrates the biblical message aware of its terrible complexity, the more one discovers how difficult is the trade of the heretic, but also of the innovator, the objector. I am speaking, one understands, of matters of faith, not of problems concerning the ecclesiastical institution and some of its socio-political choices, "tempests" where criticism is not only possible but obligatory: *ecclesia semper reformanda*. Precisely *ecclesia* with the lowercase, because this famous Latin slogan refers to that aspect.

I will try to explain. There can be no Christian faith that is not based on the Bible: this is not only true for Protestants, whose program is *sola scriptura*, with their refusal of Tradition; it is also true for Catholics, whose dogma insists that there can be no legitimate Tradition that does not find its support, at least implicitly, in the Bible.

But the Bible is a long, laborious book, at times prolix and incomplete, often obscure and perhaps contradictory. The Bible is entirely integrated with the logic of the Incarnation, following the style of a God who enters into history and accepts its laws completely. Thus, the "inspiration" the believer attributes to those pages does not rob them of their character as a collection of ancient writings of various periods, authors, and languages.

It required centuries and the greatest minds throughout the innumerable lands of the Roman Empire to construct a systematic theology, a synthesis of faith that respects all the data of the great cauldron, of the potpourri formed by the Old and New Testaments. I have studied, and will continue studying, the history of those offshoots from the Catholic trunk, straining to abandon prejudice as much as possible: the history of schisms and heresies, the history of those who presumed to see the errors of the Catholic Church.

I observe those "schismatics," those "heretics" attentively, fascinated by the psychological mechanisms, and I reconstruct their motivations (perhaps tempted to follow them).

Like everyone, I am very indebted to them for the emphasis they gave to some aspects of the faith that the great Catholic tree seemed to have forgotten, like branches and leaves that risked withering for a lack of sap.

But it is only *partial* aspects, if any, of their theologies that are capable of convincing me; never the *whole*, the *synthesis* they offer.

Every heretic ends up reminding me of the mechanic in the anecdote, who was great at taking a motor apart, but not in putting it back together: a piece or two were always left over. "And this?" he would ask his assistant, showing him a piston that had not fit into the reassembly of the motor. "Well," was the embarrassed reply, "it just shows that it was extra, not needed."

The same seems to hold for the many Christian theologies outside of the Catholic Church, the authentic one, I repeat again, the defined nucleus that the believer is obliged to accept, and not its many caricatures.

In too many Christian traditions something is left out — a verse, a book, an entire part of the amazing mass of biblical data that must be coordinated into a whole.

The beautiful Tower of Pisa is a splendid witness of architectural genius. But something was missing in the calculations of the foundations regarding the resistance of the terrain with respect to its weight. Therefore, the tower leans to one side, incurably askew. That inclination can be an additional reason for its originality, its fascination; not only picturesque, it can turn out to be useful. Did not Galileo use it to demonstrate from its summit the laws of gravity? Yet that incline is the visible sign of some sort of failure on the part of the architect, who did not coordinate all the necessary data.

This seems to happen for every theological architect who has detached himself (schism) or opposed (heresy) the theology of the Catholic Church, which navigates heavily, slowly but surely, keeping a center tack, and thus favoring the mutiny of the impatient, the extremists, or the drastic. After having tried to take hold of the helm of the great, overloaded freighter, they end up setting off to sea in their own boat. But the detour, though fast and more exhilarating, suffers desertions and deviations. The helmsmen are forced to throw overboard some of the cargo, calling it useless ballast; but it really is not.

This has happened ever since the very first heretics saw their theses confirmed by one Gospel but then denied by another. Thus, they were obliged to throw overboard, say, the Gospel of John; or vice versa, the three synoptics, Matthew, Mark, and Luke. If they were not obliged, for the sake of saving their rafts, to choose between the Old and New Testaments even. Does not the word *heresy* derive from the Greek verb for "to choose"? This way of proceeding reached its apex in Martin Luther, that same impatient Luther who, whenever a text of Scripture contradicted his theories (the famous case of the Letter of James comes to mind, though it is not the only one), he rushed to expel it, slandering it as a "book of straw," and then placed it in the apocrypha. He who proclaimed he obeyed *only* Scripture rebelled against it when it contradicted him. He reached the point of saying that "the Lord must be censured in his words" before passages such as chapter 16 of the Gospel of Luke, which did not confirm his theses.

This method has continued down to our day: one can simply characterize as "late," "interpolated," "unreliable," or "non-essential" those passages of the Bible that (like the piston in the tale of the mechanic) one cannot fit into the reconstruction.

"The faith embraces many truths which seem contradictory," noted Pascal, "the cause of all heresies is not having been able to conceive of the agreement of two opposed truths." Though quite attentive to the motivations of ecumenical dialogue, Jean Guitton says, "While every heretic develops certain aspects of

Christianity and atrophies or hides others, the true Catholic is the one who tries to remain faithful to the name: *katholikòs*, that is, universal; therefore, those who try to save everything and to harmonize into a higher synthesis."

Thus, to restate the matter in Ratzinger's words, it can happen that the deeper one goes, the more one discovers the "interior logic of the Catholic Tradition," the *tout se tient*, the "all which sustains everything," forgetting nothing and coordinating everything.

One discovers in the end that this synthesis is not only an admirable house of cards, a feat of daring, a demonstration of ability in the reconstruction of a puzzle with many disparate pieces. Theory, yes; but with profound resonances within the concrete man. It is not intellectual fireworks, but a key made to fit effortlessly the complicated lock of our heart. The Catholic vision is one of life and death (as I intuit and feel it) that establishes a profound correspondence between life and dogma, need and response, practice and theory. It is a proposal that can satisfy one who interrogates both mind and heart.

DIALOGUES AND NOT

In the encounter among religions, we reject every fanaticism and every form of syncretism, the dishonest *embrassons nous* that denies and minimizes contrasts. We also reject the superficial ecumenism that denies or minimizes dissent. Honesty and clarity in the various positions are the indispensable presupposition of dialogue among Christians that is without tricks and truly fruitful in the future.

The Vatican II decree on relations with other Christian confessions invites Catholics to "recognize with joy the truly Christian values promoted in our common patrimony, to be found among our separated brethren." The Council Fathers observe that "recognizing the riches of Christ, and the virtuous works in the lives of others that give testimony to Christ to the point of shedding blood, is something just and salutary." But the Council also admonishes Catholics to abstain "from any levity or imprudent zeal" that, while seeming to hasten unity, "can instead harm its true progress."

The ultimate task of ecumenical dialogue is not to compare the various churches, but for each and all of them to compare themselves to Christ: the reunification of the scattered Christian members will not occur primarily through theological academies but through the cross of more complete conversion to Christ.

As always, it will be the saints, the just, the men of God, and not professors to say and do the decisive things. In this perspective, no church is truly Christian because no one is without sin; in all churches too many are sinners.

This does not exempt each Christian from the duty to ask, at least once in his life: where is the Church of Jesus Christ, according to my conscience?

The Church is not the Jesus Club, nor an association of readers of the same book. The Church is indispensable to the faith. Even if Christianity is divided, the Church must exist and must be one: the schismatics of the East believed this, as did the Reformers of the West, as do the sects of today. All, Catholic, Orthodox and Protestant, recite the Nicene-Constantinopolitan Creed that says, "I believe in one, holy, catholic, and apostolic Church."

What else is the ecumenical movement if not the rejection of division, the refusal of ecclesial relativism which says one church is worth another? Unity among Christians is what Jesus asked the Father in the solemn prayer before His Passion; it is the condition "that the world may believe" (John 17:21).

Now, among many Catholics of the post-conciliar period, even in ecumenical dialogue there has occurred the phenomenon of an imbalanced reaction, which we shall examine in the following chapter in regard to relations between Christianity and secular ideologies, where we have passed from closure to everything to an uncritical openness to everything. In inter-Christian relations it has meant going from a type of Catholic triumphalism, perhaps arrogant, to a sort of shame to call oneself Catholic.

The dutiful recognition of the faults of the institutional Church cannot involve the faith of the Church in her essence. On this level, there is nothing to confess with bowed head, "Catholic and repentant." There is no need to abandon the Catholic vision of the future of man as if it were preposterous compared to others. There is no need to slap our separated brethren on the back, declaring that, "in the end, we all agree; what divided us were only verbal misunderstandings, questions of form and not of substance."

No, unfortunately that is not the case. As always, death and eternal destiny is the revelatory litmus test that shows what something is worth and what it is not, what unites and what divides. The various Christian theologies are divided by quite different conceptions of God, of man and of their relationship: different points of view that have repercussions especially in eschatology.

Take Protestants, for instance: to them human nature has been entirely corrupted by Original Sin, that of Adam, such that we his descendants are nothing but "naked sin without grace." Thus, God is seen as the "totally Other," without any analogy to us.

This is a God whose grace, whose salvation, is granted to us with a judiciary decree: *actus forensic*, a court order. This is exactly how Luther expresses justification. The Eternal, in other words, declares man "just," but he remains internally a sinner: his guilt has not been canceled by Baptism, only *covered*, not imputed.

According to Protestant pessimism, everything descends from above, from the divine holiness and majesty of God; nothing can rise from man's good will. An undisputed principle of the Reformation says, "Before God, man is always and only an object, never a *subject*." Thus, the relationship between God and man is transformed into a monologue.

Catholicism, on the other hand, seeks to preserve the possibility of a dialogue, which is possible only between two subjects. For the Roman Church, man is not crushed, even though anticipated by the absolutely free initiative of God: the relationship of the creature with the Creator is not that of the maser to the slave but that of father to son, or even of friend to friend. "You are my friends if you do what I command you. No longer do I call you servants, for the servant does not know what his master is doing, but I have called you friends" (John 15:14–15).

Catholicism has fought over two millennia against every type of heretical temptation so as to save that which characterizes the relationship between the biblical God and man: namely, the previously unheard of, shocking, unique concept of covenant — a true pact, with reciprocal rights and duties, between Creator and creature. The Christian Bible divides into two parts called the Old and New *Testament*. Now, this word *testament* reproduces the Hebrew term *berith*, which means "alliance" or "covenant."[24]

---

[24] From the awareness of the reality of covenant derives everything Catholicism says about Mary and which Protestantism, despite the good intentions of the fathers of the Reformation, has been obliged to reject, following its own internal logic.

In fact, for the Catholic Church, Mary is the model of the associate, the ally, the friend, the collaborator of God. Thus, she is the figure, the type, the example of the Church and of every believer, because in her, the humble Galilean girl, the Creator's respect for His creatures has been guaranteed. He who could carry out His entire will alone wanted to do nothing without the free collaboration of man. Thus, even the loftiest decision, the Incarnation of the Word, passes through the yes of the Virgin.

Predestined?

From the Protestant conception according to which God does everything and man nothing in the work of salvation, there derives a disturbing consequence: it is the black cloud of the doctrine of predestination that weighs unavoidably above every eschatology born of the Reformation.

Luther in Germany, Zwingli in Switzerland, the theologians of Henry VIII, all advised their preachers to proceed with caution, not to insist too much on the inevitable consequences of predestination in order not to frighten or demoralize the faithful. The Reformer of Geneva, John Calvin, however, had the courage to place it in the foreground, to admit and even highlight that this was one of the fundamental cornerstones of the Reformation. "We call predestination," he wrote, "the eternal decree of God by which he has established what must come of every single man. Indeed, not all are created equal, but for some eternal life is predestined, while for others eternal damnation."

"A terrible, mysterious decree," as the same Reformer called it, upon which the good or evil will of man has no effect: man goes to Paradise or to Hell, and his eventual "merits" or certain faults cannot influence in the least this eternal fate.

Calvin reminds us of the natural conclusions of this concept which we already know, and which are shared by all Protestants, "we are only a mass of corruption without the right to say anything." Indeed, our eventual protests

---

Karl Barth, the greatest Protestant theologian of the twentieth century, saw the problem clearly. He comments, "In Marian doctrine and veneration by Catholics there is Heresy, in the uppercase, that from which all the others derive."

For the Catholic, on the contrary, Protestantism reveals itself heretical above all in the rejection of this "Mariology," which is the sign and defense of the friend-to-friend relationship between God and man. The Catholic response to Barth's declaration, the intuition of the mystics (confirmed by theological reflection) of "Mary enemy of every heresy": the truths that concern her (and which Catholicism has rendered secure by formulating them in dogmas, not accidentally) reiterate, reinforce, and defend the central truths of Christianity. These are fascinating arguments, so often misrecognized, and to which the dedication of a little book might be useful. In fact, too many Catholics today (reacting to the excesses of saccharine, though not erroneous, preaching) consider the Virgin Mary an embarrassing, unwarranted appendage to be suffered with difficulty in old devotions.

In this case, however, we find ourselves before a rock that cannot be moved without endangering the solidity of all the Church's faith.

are only "the grunts of pigs," and what counts is only that "God be glorified." Man, do not forget it, is only an object to him.

In fact, it was not long before the Reformed theologians, immediately following the first Reformers, began to sound the "grunts of pigs"; not capable of eliminating predestination without reconsidering the foundations of the edifice, unleashing war and death throughout Europe, one attempted at least to attenuate the brutality of its name. Thus they preferred to speak of "divine prescience" or "election."

But if this seemed harsh to the men of the sixteenth century, predestination became increasingly intolerable to the mentality of modern man, as he gradually became aware of his dignity, his freedom, his equality ("Why am I damned for eternity and my brother, my neighbor is eternally saved?").

Trying to reassure himself, to placate his anguish, he went in search of "signs of predestination" in social, political, and commercial success, in that "good conscience of one's well-executed economic management of commercial and industrial enterprises," of which Max Weber speaks in his famous work that brought to light the disquieting link between Protestant theology and the spirit of capitalism.

In the end, the difficulty of proposing to modern man the theory of predestination and the attention transferred to this life in the search for success through which the decree of divine benevolence shines, have caused eschatological themes, the proclamation of life after this life, and the tension of Christian hope to have practically disappeared from Protestant preaching. We shall see one of many examples of this in the following chapter, remarking upon the otherwise inexplicable silence in the "catechism" of Italian Protestants.

Let us speak clearly with fraternal candor: Is it possible to insist on an afterlife subject to the "terrible decree" according to which some are created to rejoice eternally, while others to suffer eternally and that clashes with all that modern man believes and hopes? This could be possible, seeing how we would be naïve if the contents of the faith were to depend on approval ratings.

Here one must add the difficulty of proclaiming this from within the typical Protestant creation which is the state church. Is it credible today that, as is still theoretically possible in Anglican England, questions on Heaven, Hell, and other issues of the faith are decided upon in Parliament by a vote? Is it possible that the church that announces predestination to me has as it "supreme governor" Queen Elizabeth II? What sort of "alternative space for hope" can churches like those of Northern Europe and Scandinavia represent when they are so intimately dependent upon and financed by the state?

Two Temptations, One Solution

As we know, Catholicism refuses the Protestant concept of predestination, while admitting the serious problem of reconciling divine foreknowledge and grace with our freedom.

I cannot venture into the steep pathways of a theological chapter on which generations of thinkers have struggled. Suffice it here to discuss the conclusions, contained in a series of affirmations which the Church has declared *de fide*, that must be believed as defined truths: thanks to the concept of covenant between God and man, of movement not only from high to low but also from low to high, with respect for the mystery the Catholic affirms that the damnation of man is due to his own sin, and that his salvation (though anticipated and sustained by divine grace) comes *also* from his "merit."

Delving more deeply into the problem, Catholic theology denounces a serious misunderstanding at the root of Protestant theology on predestination: a misunderstanding that comes from a very partial reading of St. Paul's letters made by St. Augustine and received by the Reformers. Predestination is understood as the mystery of a choice that God would make in the humanity (rendered a mass of damnation by Original Sin) of some few who would be infallibly brought to salvation, while the others would remain in their condition of sin that would lead them ineluctably to Hell.

"In reality," writes the Catholic theologian Giorgio Gozzelino:[25]

> Predestination is something quite different. It is not a mystery of fright and torment, as it would be if the Protestant reading were correct; but a mystery of joy and confidence without limits. Indeed, as the word itself indicates, it is the prior destination of man: the destination to salvation, namely, that the Father gives His children and which he, God, draws them on the chance he receives their response. This destination is absolutely universal, that is, addressed not to some but to all men; and naturally all men as they are, that is, as sinners. It is a gratuitous destination,

---

[25] Editor's Note: Giorgio Gozzelino (1930–2010) was an Italian priest, theologian, and writer.

surely: but not in the sense of being reserved to few, as the Reformers thought, but in the sense of bringing man to a haven far beyond any of their expectations or needs. And it is, we repeat, an infallible destination in whoever responds to the Father.

Thus, according to the theology of the Church of Rome, predestination is revealed not as a nightmare, but as a consoling hope, a synonym for the "universal offer of salvation." It is our joyful destiny, not the condemnation to a morbid maceration, in the nightmare of being called into life only to end up in the eternal night of Hell.

Judaism liberated men from the prison of the cycle of reincarnation; Christianity freed them from the slavery to the law of the Old Covenant; but Catholic Christianity continues to liberate them from the nightmare of predestination of Protestant Christianity.

We have seen that, according to the logic of the system and in contrast to the expectations of the Reformers, the Protestant temptation is that of a history without eschatology: thus, for the believer, the world ends up assuming too much importance.

It has been shown that the "Reformation spirit" is not only at the bottom of the capitalist scourge (not by chance is the United States the country most impregnated by this spirit), but is equally certain that on Protestant terrain the seeds of those other weeds developed, namely rationalism and the Enlightenment. And these opened the path to modern atheism, both theoretical and practical, which is precisely *history without eschatology*.

But if we turn toward the East, toward the Orthodox world, we find the opposite temptation: *eschatology without history*. Here too, on the basis of a precise vision of God and man, the theology of the Eastern Churches separated from Rome tends inexorably to diminish the value of the world.

Here, a precise sign has been given. Protestants reject the figure of the "religious," namely, the person who commits himself freely to live in poverty, chastity, and obedience in order to bear witness with his very life that "the form of this world is passing away" (1 Cor. 7:31), that history is not everything, that the eternal is already here. The Reformation began with Friar Martin, an Augustinian religious, who threw his habit away, married a nun, and went to live with his children in a convent emptied by his preaching.

The Orthodox, on the other hand, not only know the figure of the religious, but hold it up as an insurmountable example of Christian life. The friar, the monk (or the hermit, the most radical version, the most detached from the world) is for the Christian East the ideal to which everyone aspires, even married lay people.

How does Catholicism handle the matter? On one side, it rejects the Protestant condemnation of religious life; but on the other side, it also rejects the Orthodox pretense of making consecrated religious life the only possible model of radically Christian life. In this way, marriage and chastity "for the Kingdom of Heaven" are seen as two distinct vocations, two equally legitimate paths to sanctity. Heaven is equally open to those who make profession of religious vows as well as those who pursue lay professions, as long as they bear witness to the same Gospel in their calling.

Despite concrete lapses, the Catholic proposal is as usual one that unites opposites in a synthesis: in this case, history and eschatology. The authentic Catholic project, its theological tendency, is to keep far from the horizontal temptation of Protestants as well as the vertical temptation of the Orthodox.

CHAPTER 11

WITH WHICH CHURCH?

IF THE THEOLOGIAN IS INTELLIGENT

UP TO THIS POINT we have decided in favor of the following: among the many religions, Christianity; among the Chrisitan confessions, Catholicism; at least as an initial path of enquiry, a privileged direction in which we are setting out in search. Does this suffice? Unfortunately, it does not; it is not enough. We still need to ask: Which Catholicism? The question is justified.

The panorama of the post-conciliar Church appears chaotic not only to the outside observer, but also (and perhaps more so) to the believer at the base, to the average Catholic, the simple practitioner who knows little or nothing about theology. It is he for whom the clergy is least concerned (or whom they mock, identifying him as a conformist, the petty bourgeois, the Pharisee), the clergy busily fighting each other with obscure, encoded language, or words that are all too clear. I know of priests (a great many north of the Alps, but also not a few here in Italy) who scold as superstitious the faithful who insist on having requiem Masses celebrated, or who keep candles lit at the tombs of their deceased loved ones.

I know of preachers who (not at theological conferences but during Sunday Mass in their parishes), in the name of reversing the "Hellenization of Christianity," of which their listeners know nothing, call them pagans if they insist on believing in the soul and its immortality.

This also can happen in the Church: the priests of old chastise you for not believing in certain things; while the priests of today (perhaps the same ones as the former, but now having become "adult," as they say) chastise you for believing in the very same things. As the ironic lay observer and director of the Parisian *École de Hautes Études*, Alain Besançon says (with reference to the situation in France):

Thus, the limit of clericalism has been reached, for the dominion of priests, patriarchal and paternalistic as they were, has become cynical and a bit sadistic. Many distressing anecdotes have been circulating about the faithful being chased out of the sacristies, about old ladies being ejected from confessionals, about the violent destruction of altars dedicated to the souls in Purgatory, about the debasing of some as second-class parishioners insulted weekly and placed under accusation, of those Catholics who insist on wanting to stay faithful to the catechism of their youth.

Behind this situation in ferment, often grotesque, there is a precise theology that must be commented upon. We can do so, though we are neither theologians nor particularly intellectual. Indeed, "with the Cross and sin and sanctity, the other world is already among the things of which an intelligent theologian should never speak." This was the bitterly ironic comment of Jacques Maritain, the Catholic philosopher who was among the most courageous proponents of conciliar renewal and, as often happens, was sent to the ghetto of "fascists" because he wanted to remain faithful to Vatican II without distorting it. Clearly, this is also the fate that I am risking by presuming to write these things. Patience. Maritain gave us that ironic comment shortly before his death in 1973. Since then, the situation has certainly not changed: it would seem that in the Church, these "intelligent theologians" are increasingly numerous.

IN THE PROTESTANT CAMP

Among Catholics, the refusal to talk about the so-called "other world" comes from individual scholars (though they might hold chairs in prestigious faculties at Catholic universities) or from precise theological schools or currents.

The hierarchy of the Church opposes and at times scowls at those measures condemned by journalists and op-ed pages, the more indignant the less informed they are on the issues under discussion or the less concerned they are with faith and the Church, desirous, if anything, to express their gratitude to those who, even among the faithful, might help them to minimize or hide that fearful mystery of the afterlife that fills them with anguish. Believe me, for I have worked for years inside the "independent," "secular" mass media, which gluttonously devours theological disputes and the most reckless novelties. The media has always carried out this effort either of elimination or of assimilation of the Church and its faith; if that disturbing message cannot be destroyed, they must at least attempt to capture it, normalize it, and reduce it to the horizontal, socio-political dimension.

Among Protestants, the liquidation of traditional eschatology seems to have been nearly completed, officialized at the highest levels of various churches. We have already mentioned this, proposing some explanations for the phenomenon. I have in front of me the most recent edition of the catechism or little manual for the instruction in the faith of youth, edited by the Federation of Evangelical Churches in Italy. Every discussion of ultimate things has been handled with great haste, almost with embarrassment.

Hell and the devil are removed, naturally, as being myths unacceptable to today's man, though they were once constant, almost obsessive themes for the sixteenth-century Reformers. A German university subjected Luther's collected works to digitization. It was found that under the pen of the ex-Augustinian monk, the word *Teufel* (devil) appears only slightly less frequently than the name Jesus Christ or *Gott*, God.

Excessive, no doubt. But is it not also excessive the haste with which the current descendants of Luther, Calvin, and the others have relegated with particular zeal *der Teufel* to the old junk in the attic? What was the modern scientific discovery that has proved that the men of the sixteenth century were wrong about this, that they followed unacceptable myths? And if they were wrong about this, why should they be right about anything else? Is a choice legitimate, according to current tastes, among the contents of faith, without threatening the whole edifice of the faith?

Reading again in that catechism for Evangelicals, we find: "When the Bible speaks of the afterlife, it is not so much to describe future life, as to speak to us of the present." There is truth in that, but that is not all: the problem is much more complex, even if one rejects the Tradition of Catholicism and clings to the Protestant *sola scriptura*. And resurrection from the dead? Keeping with St. Paul, the Paul so dear to the Reformation (a particular reading of Paul is at the basis of the great wildfire of the sixteenth century), precisely on this point Christianity stands or falls:

> For if the dead are not raised, then Christ has not been raised. If Christ has not been raised, your faith is futile and you are still in your sins. Then those also who have fallen asleep in Christ have

perished. If for this life only we have hoped in Christ, we are of all men most to be pitied (1 Cor. 15:16–19).

This warning by the apostle, so clear and determined, does not seem to suffice, given that this book for the formation of young Christians did not dedicate the central place to the resurrection of the dead that according to the New Testament is its due; it is given only three lines in all.

Yet not many years had passed since Karl Barth[26] had admonished his Reformed brothers: "If we want to be Christians, we must in some way have seen and heard the angels at the tomb of Jesus, open and empty."

From Individual Death to Eschatology

But it would be wrong to want to teach a lesson in the house of others. Let us return then to Catholicism, which we have chosen as our subject. We notice immediately that here too they don't mess around, at least not some theologians. Many eggheads in cassocks, habits, or clerical collars throughout these confusing years have buried us in discussions on every aspect of the faith re-examined in the light of Scripture, but almost never have they spoken with clarity on the other world to which the New Testament gives so much space.

This is grievous, very grievous. As a recent official document of the Church warns, "if the Christian is no longer capable of giving a sure content to the expression 'eternal life' the Gospel promises, the sense of Creation and Redemption disappear and this present life itself is deprived of every hope."

Among the pre-conciliar manuals of theology there was a chapter titled in Latin *De novissimis*, "on the last things," those very things that now one prefers to indicate with the Greek term "eschatology."

This *De novissimis* had an air of being placed there as an appendage and not as the fulcrum around which everything ought to turn. In the pre-conciliar Church (according to what I know from books and conversations, given that in those years I was occupied in quite different matters) it seems hope was the most forgotten of the virtues: it was abandoned, if anything, to the accountants of the afterlife who calculated the debits to be paid in Purgatory in "venial sins" and the assets of the corresponding days of indulgence.

---

[26] Editor's Note: Karl Barth (1886–1968) was one of the most important Protestant theologians.

But what has happened now to this *De novissimis* chapter, so decisive and so forgotten? According to the Swiss theologian Hans Urs von Balthasar, access to it is now barred by a sign that reads, "Closed for work in progress." The usual experts have mounted the barricades, confabulating, arguing, and distinguishing in their erudite manner. The information desk remains closed, however, to the profane.

There is a suspicion that someone does not intend to reopen that information desk, and would even prefer to see it closed definitively. Many would not be dismayed to keep the old *De novissimis* on the shelf, at least the disturbing individual sequence: death-Judgment-Heaven-Purgatory-Hell. Better that these superstitions go to their ruin than alienate. They are so poorly aligned with our biblical rereading today! Enough with these medieval myths that disturb the purely political image of Jesus (a social agitator, a "Palestinian political leader") or purely cultural: a teacher of wisdom, a guru, a charismatic intellectual!

It even happens that in many books and articles, the flower of theologians maintains the necessity of not speaking about death and anything that faith awaits beyond the threshold because it would hinder dialogue with non-believers; it would be a form of blackmail (exactly what they say) toward the dominant culture. Instead of taking up the faith to denounce and disrupt the cruel silence about death that keeps us imprisoned, they recommend silence so as not to disturb the dominant ideologies in their efforts to avoid the discussion that most upsets their dominance.

Silence, silence, please! One must respect the taboos, the neuroses, the vileness, the dogmas of Marxist hierarchies and of the powerful neo-capitalists, of the masters of the political scene and of production and consumption, of the intellectuals who are their lackies and courtiers. One must not judge the world in the light of the Bible, but on the contrary, one must judge the Bible in the light of the world, or if necessary, censure it!

WITH SUCH TEACHERS

Hans Küng,[27] perhaps the most well-known contemporary theologian, in his *Being Christians*, offers a tremendous witness to the Western theology of our

---

[27] Editor's Note: Hans Küng (1928–2021) was one of the most famous theologians in the field of Catholic progressives. The word "contemporary" here naturally refers to the moment the book was written.

time. In this great work, erudition and faith attempt to render Christianity credible once again. This is one of the more praiseworthy intentions; on many of its nearly thousand pages I found light and nourishment, as have many readers. But I constantly asked myself if certain silences, if certain astute dialectics were not by chance inspired by the desire to gain for the faith a spot among the goods on display in the opulent shopwindows of West Germany. From the desire, that is, not to blackmail the man of today, who is often nothing more than the petty bourgeois wanting to continue to enjoy his well-being while adding to his many consumer goods a little bit of religion.

The man of the West today does not want to be disturbed by discussions that might deviate from his crude rationalism, from his ridiculous and anachronistic trust in science. He does not want to abandon his good sense, not even for his faith, that will satisfy perhaps the mediocre, the secular humanists, the party militants, those who believe in the "ideals of the United Nations" or in their political hopefuls; but which certainly does not appease the Christian who sees in the gospel the killer of every superficial triviality, the radical upsetting of values, the intrusion upon history of a distressing surprise, "a scandal and a folly" (1 Cor. 1:23).

How can one explain, if not with this desire to avoid disturbing the middle class of the industrial West, that in this celebrated book by Küng, written with the ambition of representing all of Christianity, there is but one, brief mention of the *novissima hominis,* the last things toward which every man is heading, according to the faith? A brief and gratuitous mention, as well, added at the end of a paragraph that, significantly, has as its title "Legends"?

In these few lines, the theologian (student and teacher of many others today) does not confront the topic because, as he declares, he does not speak of arguments that concern "death, Hell, devil, Purgatory, Paradise." He writes with a bit of annoyance: "It is not our intention to furnish here a dogmatics in miniature with a solution to every theological problem."

This is surprising: those "theological problems" over which he so hastily passes, in the economy of faith, are not in the least minor questions among the many. Furthermore, *Being Christians* does truly seek to be "a dogmatics in miniature."[28] It seeks to be that in every other part, except where it might

---

[28] Page 14 of the original German version states, "This book is presented in fact as a little summa of the Christian faith."

disturb dialogue among the distracted and suspect German bourgeois and the theologian who wants to explain to them Christianity diluted and spiked with a modern schnapps so as not to hinder its strenuous digestion.

Are we unfair? If so, we shall make amends immediately. Not without remarking, however, that Hans Küng followed up his monumental *Being Christians*, with the equally massive *Does God Exist?* This book was also extraordinary for a number of reasons, not the least for the fact that of its 952 pages, only three were dedicated to responding to the most demanding of questions, in a short paragraph to which he gave the title, "Death, and Then?". With such teachers, what can the mislead infantry of the Church do, or the poor priest, the unfortunate catechists called to proclaim a message that not even they know well what it is? From Küng's countryman Alois Müller,[29] another a "progressive" theologian and, as chair of pastoral theology, scholar of "common" preaching, came similar desperate confirmations.

"In parishes," wrote Müller, "priests have by now habituated themselves to the orders of secular culture and also of much Chrisitan theology: hide, remove. One hides, one removes the topic of death and the afterlife, to the point of cleverly avoiding every mention of those realities even in homilies on All Souls' Day."

Yet how can you proclaim Resurrection without talking about the Cross, about the death that precedes it? And if you do not talk about Resurrection, you can accumulate all the beautiful words you want, but you are not talking about the gospel, you are not announcing Christ and His good news.

Impressed by the mutilated Judeo-Christianity called Marxism, impressed by neo-Enlightenment culture with their thought systems (these, too, of a distantly Christian origin, but out of context and therefore gone haywire) a certain theological school has attempted to enter into competition with it. Having thus set aside individual eschatology (considered alienating), if they speak of eschatology at all, they focus entirely on collective eschatology, that of the future of society and of the world, suspecting however some unacceptable vertical emphasis in every attempt to project beyond history the "new heavens and new earth" promised by the biblical prophets.

In reality, there is no Christianity, not the least possibility of Christian hope, if one remains within the tight confines of history. And there is no Christian hope if not in the synthesis between individual and social, between I and we.

[29] Editor's Note: Alois Müller (1924–1991) was a Swiss theologian.

QUESTIONS ABOUT THE COUNCIL

So much silence among so many churchmen on death and what follows it is certainly an understandable reaction after too many centuries of "funerary" preaching. Was it an accident that the color chosen for priestly garb was black, as if to identify him with specialists in funerals, as jinxed heralds of death and of possible chastisement, rather than as joyful announcers of Resurrection?

In their ordinary preaching (also in much theology, though not official), the insistence on the afterlife was the sign of a superficial vision, oversimplified, or perhaps not Christian at all. One needed to diminish the importance of the world to give space to heaven, ignoring the *already* and investing in the *not yet*. This is where the revolt began, first an attack on the Church and then on Christianity itself. One believed it was necessary to attempt its elimination to reconsider the world, history, this life. This is all well known, and we have already mentioned this briefly and shall consider it again later, seen in its proper context.

Here, it suffices to note how the movement that gave rise to Vatican II and then in the authentic analysis in the documents of that historical council allowed Catholicism to rediscover the indispensable equilibrium between Heaven and earth, the necessary synthesis between the already and the not yet.

But that providential council is one matter; certain commentators (on the left and the right) that stretch out its documents are another. There are those who want to return to the Council of Trent and others who already think about life after Vatican III.

And so, the poor average Catholic we spoke of, that true Cyrene of today's Church who, perhaps mocked and scorned, drags the cross of confusion, often not knowing what to say about Vatican II. Was it the beginning of his liberation? Or was it rather the start of his mortification, showing him that he got it all wrong?

There are not only problems for those on the "inside." There are also those on the "outside" who hesitate on the doorstep of the Church but go no further, unable to understand what the common creed is or what the differences might be between that creed and the many secular creeds, and why it might be worth it to leave them.

In the 1970s, the phenomenon of the return to the Church came to a halt, the conversions (from other Christian confessions, from agnosticism, from atheism) that up to that moment had assumed almost mass proportions in countries like the United States, Great Britain, and Germany. The end of the conversions excited certain theologians who, in the name of their idea of *aggiornamento*, preached the need "not to uproot oneself from one's own cultural tradition," even if that happened to be atheism.

We are retrograde, on the other hand, and therefore we prefer to continue to reflect seriously on the last, imperious order Jesus gave to his own: "Go into all the world and preach the gospel to the whole creation. He who believes and is baptized will be saved; but he who does not believe will be condemned" (Mark 16:15–16).

Not heading this *aggiornamento*, therefore, we continue to believe that the Church renounces herself if she attenuates the missionary tension, if she renounces running with open arms to assist those who have fallen along the way, if she does not send clear and distinguishable signals to those searching for hope. "It is not to debate that one converts, but to learn," said a convert in the nineteenth century, John Henry Newman. What would he say today when there are so many who present the gospel not as a faith that moves mountains but as something that moves doubts, problems, and endless reinterpretations?

Let it be clear once and for all: Vatican II did not change (nor could it have) the Catholic faith as it was defined by the millenary Tradition, based on the even more ancient Scriptures.

The council left the substance intact, although the work of deepening and analysis continues to render more precise the authentic content of that substance, closed as it is in formulas often tied to particular languages and exigencies.

This work of continual deepening and clarification, which began with the beginning of Christianity itself, is a service to the community ensured by theologians within the Church throughout the centuries. Theologians can err, working more on the basis of their prejudices and their personal psychological problems than with the actual data, but their role does not cease for this reason to be indispensable to the Church, whose duty it is to draw conclusions and decide solemnly upon what one may and may not believe.

Returning to the last council, one can say that it reached a point of arrival and opened new paths as well, without damaging the "inner core" of the faith.

If anything, it indicated the principles for a change in method, of mentality, of perspective. Its primary intention was pastoral more than dogmatic: not an unacceptable change of the message but an *aggiornamento* of the way of proposing it and presenting it to the men of this moment in time. In this way it removed unnecessary encrustations, it reorganized the hierarchies of truth, returning to the place of honor what is essential and putting aspects that were believed to be essential (but in reality were not) in their proper place.

The great decision of Vatican II was to abandon an a priori negative attitude to the world and its values. This means neither uncritical acceptance of those values, nor renouncing one's own. *Dialogue* does not in the least mean *resignation*.

The Council Fathers worked as gardeners in an old but fruitful orchard: giving breathing space to the trees, liberating them by pruning the branches and trenching the roots, removing parasites, brush, and weeds left to grow wild among the rows. Some plants were moved to a different spot, transplanted from the shade to another place in the sun, or *vice versa*.

The old taste for overabundance was substituted with the current preference for the essential; the choice focused more on the fine quality rather than on abundance.

But those trees were not cut down to give space to a meadow or to replant the orchard entirely with new saplings. The bishops worked as expert gardeners, not as bulldozer drivers. They were artisans of restoration, not laborers in a demolition crew. For the believer they are "teachers and custodians" of the faith of our fathers, not mercenaries in a band of saboteurs.

But Hope Has Not Changed

With the conciliar texts in hand, it is possible to reassure the faithful: the Catholic hope in the afterlife has not changed; the ancient promise of eternal life has been neither abrogated nor attenuated. Paradise for Catholics has not suffered the fate that the Marxist or liberal utopias have suffered, hidden from embarrassment or proclaimed wearily, with a wink of the eye, by people who have long since stopped believing in them.

Those who instill in Christians an excruciating suspicion do not respect the council; their deceased, and they themselves, have believed and hoped for certain things that were entirely or partially erroneous.

This too can seem an act of charity today: turn to the people, the non-theologians whom the scribes and clerics of every age have always looked down upon from on high ("This crowd who does not know the law," the Pharisees say contemptuously, John 7:49), turn to the dismayed people of God to reassure them: "Our deceased have not been deceived, the more than hundred generations of Christians have not been deceived who have fallen asleep in the faith. We are still called to share that very same faith."

The billions of baptized who have crossed the threshold of death before us were sustained by a faith that (accepted or not) has not been changed. This has not been renounced by the Church, called to proclaim today as it preached yesterday and will continue to preach until the end of time. One can be sure: it cannot do otherwise without renouncing itself and thus disappearing.

The contents in the travel bag of hope that the Church entrusts to its dead to confront the eternal journey have not changed. Nothing essential has changed.

What has changed is the language we use to recite it, but in the passage from Latin to the vulgate nothing has changed in the Creed that one repeats every Sunday at Mass, which will be repeated in every future Mass, and which for at least seventeen centuries resounds in the Church as the symbol of our common faith:

> On the third day He rose again, in accordance with the Scriptures. He ascended into Heaven, and is seated at the right hand of the Father, from whence He shall come again in glory to judge the living and the dead, and His Kingdom shall have no end... I await the resurrection of the dead and life of the world to come.

The Catholic faith in the final things, both for man and for humanity, was reconfirmed in every aspect by the council in its documents. Since the council, it has been repeated over and over by Paul VI and his successors. St. John Paul II wanted and approved just a few months into his pontificate a letter to the Congregation for the Doctrine of the Faith that firmly and lucidly reaffirmed the part that is most contested or forgotten today, the individual part (Judgment-Paradise-Hell-resurrection of the dead) of Christian hope. The letter denounces "the slow degradation and progressive extinction" of the certainty of many Catholics in the afterlife. This situation "places in danger the faith and the salvation of believers" and states that "it is a repercussion, undesired, in the spirits of the theological controversies widely diffused in public opinion, of which the majority of the faithful are capable of understanding neither the precise object nor the scope."

Many theologians today, while saying they profess constant, complete obedience and fidelity to the Scriptures, often seem to forget the harsh warning of Paul to his ancient colleagues, "And so by your knowledge this weak man is destroyed, the brother for whom Christ died" (1 Cor. 8:11).

THEFT

I open one of the many "new introductions to Christianity" edited by restless religious, *An American Catholic Catechism*, printed in New York and reprinted numerous times and translated into foreign languages. As in the Protestant catechism, in this "Catholic" book as well the appropriate struggle against an alienating presentation of eschatology is understood as the liquidation of hope.

In just a few hasty pages dedicated to death and what comes after, they seem to strain above all to minimize the problem. Just like Soviet propagandists or Western intellectuals, the objective of these American religious is (as they declare explicitly) "to remove the preoccupation with death from the people" because, they say, "this would be the sign of unacceptable individualism." According to the counsel of these new friars, every problem vanishes in the face of the unavoidable end if, quoting verbatim, "the consideration of an individual about his future is dominated by the thought of his family, of his children and grandchildren, and if he imagines the great destiny that is reserved for his people and for the great conquests to be carried out in the unstoppable evolution of history to which he belongs."

Are we dreaming? For a Christian, for one who still "hopes against every hope," this resembles more a nightmare than a dream.

So: wait until after death, when the stars and stripes will fly in the wind bigger and stronger than ever ("the great destiny that is reserved for his people"); is this the hope offered us by those who proclaim the gospel? Or must we find comfort in the hope, if we take seriously the other catechisms ("Christians for Socialism"), of powerful red flags emblazoned with the hammer and sickle?

As for me, I would not repeat every Sunday, "I await the resurrection of the dead and the life of the world to come" if I really meant, "I await the technological and economic marvels of the capitalist society of the future" or "I await the dictatorship of the proletariat and the socialist society of tomorrow." I will not stand for any demonstration that the Christian afterlife is only alienating, unacceptable mythology and then substitute it with the myths of the age (which are on their way to putrefaction), whether neo-capitalist or Marxist.

Rather than heralds of hope, certain Christians, certain Catholics today seem to be *thieves of hope*.

While the unfortunate children of today's culture seek in drugs an illusory artificial Paradise, many theologians busily hide their own Paradise, the original of which so many miserable facsimiles have been made. From contempt for history, they have passed to its overestimation. From a *farsighted* theology that only saw what was beyond history, they have passed to the many *nearsighted* theologies that see only what is in history. But the mystery of faith needs healthy sight to see both near and far at the same time.

Concrete results are not lacking to this type of preaching. A recent survey, commissioned by the Churches of West Germany, gave dismal results: only two percent of Protestants and ten percent of Catholics state they have a clear idea of what awaits Christian hope after death. Everyone else confesses they know nothing. And certainly not because it does not matter to them. But, as they say, no one talks about it, if not to ridicule the age-old hope.

To understand what is happening, it helps to refer not to the Italian experience, still (but for how long?) partially preserved from the liquidation of Catholic eschatology that is already in an advanced stage in Northern Europe and in the Americas. To judge what is happening and its gravity, the true theft of hope, do not consider the homilies of the average Italian parish priest, but the books and articles of the many specialized magazines translated into Italian.

At any rate, as the document desired by Pope John Paul II says quoted above, "even when the Christian has not arrived at positive doubt regarding eternal life, often he renounces the thought of what comes after death, because he begins to feel that questions arise within him for which he is afraid to find answers."

FROM SADISM TO MASOCHISM

A strange fate, that of so many theologians and Catholic intellectuals who have passed in just a few years from *sadism* to *masochism* with respect to secular culture.

They have gone from persecution and rejection of everything that was not Catholic, even of what might have been commendable, to the uncritical and enthusiastic acceptance of the good and the bad, "in complete openness to any idea, especially to anti-Christian ideas," as someone has said.

From a superiority complex they have assumed an inferiority complex, incapable of finding a point of equilibrium.

Christians and Catholics, perhaps intelligent and surely generous, have exchanged in good faith an industrious construction site loaded with potential for a desolate field covered with the ruins of contemporary ideologies. They have liquidated and sold off so much of Christian hope, thinking they were in "dialogue" with the future, while instead they were only entertaining the vestiges of a society and a culture already condemned.

Paying its debt once more chronically overdue, part of the Catholic world amputated as much as it could of the dimension of hope from Christianity precisely at the moment the world was looking confusedly for hope, for an oxygen mask as it suffocated.

Too many Christians in this period have believed naïvely that the oft proclaimed "new man" had arrived but was not to be seen. It was merely a myth invented by illuminists to cover their incapacity to give answers to the old man, the one who will always investigate into the meaning of life, love, and death, who will always need hope, charity, and faith. In other words, this man will always need the *New* that precedes the word *Testament*, whose words have always warmed his heart and will continue to do so.

Closed within the halls of convents and seminaries, those many pathetic theologians engage in dialogue with imaginary interlocutors who exist only in their bookish programs. They sow the seeds of refined "re-readings" of the Gospels on paths now desolate because laypeople (the authentic ones, those whom these clerics do not know, or have come to know only too late) now trod other paths. Right as Marxism has begun to show signs of an irreversible crisis, excited priests and sacristans discover it and try to adapt Christianity to it, even at the price of mutilating Christianity. Precisely at the time when wrinkles start to appear announcing old age on the made-up face of affluent society, of Western neo-capitalism, other priests emerging from their cells raise a hymn to the "secular technopolis," the new Promised Land of the man of the Gospel. Right when psychoanalysis, despite its many merits, begins to show its limits, behold other clerics welcoming enthusiastically what secular culture has begun to shun.

And on it goes: examples are possible for each of the fashions of dominant culture of the past decades. One will always find theologians asking Christians to conform themselves to any trend, as long as it's on its way out. Jean

Guitton[30] snidely foresaw that "parish priests of the Vendée and of the Bergamo hillsides will be the last, enthusiastic preachers of bourgeois progressivism and Marxist dialectical materialism when both are dead and buried in the consciences of the laity."

WHEN SECTS SHALL PROSPER

"From their fruits," says the Gospel, "you will recognize them" (Matt. 7:16). Now, the many surgical operations performed on Christianity to normalize it within the confines of history, with the goal of rendering it "acceptable to the world of today," seem not to have born the desired fruit.

We have already mentioned, for example, how practicing Catholics in the United States are now fewer than practicing Christians in the Soviet Union. In the US, religious attendance has fallen from seventy-two percent in the 1970s to about twenty percent at the start of the 1980s. Similar results have been recorded around the world.

Yes, I am aware that quantity, success, numbers on the rise are not categories used in the gospel, the story of a stunning failure according to the world's standards. But it must be noticed that the few who continue to attend church in the United States and Europe are what is left of those who were practicing their faith before. They are not agnostics or atheists who have been convinced by the new merely horizontal Christianity that, to some theologians, should be so well-adapted to the modern mentality.

Furthermore, if Christianity seems headed toward statistical extinction in many areas, this is not because the religious demand has decreased, which is in fact not the case.

Corresponding to this crisis of the "historical" churches is a significant phenomenon in the same countries, namely the boom of new sects. These sects develop precisely what the historical churches tend to compress, hide, and stigmatize: the laceration of history, the need for transcendence, the hunger and thirst for a clear word about eternal and personal life. Those that are prospering in the United States and throughout the West are Adventist, millenarian, eschatological, apocalyptic sects, united by their emphasis on the themes that our churches have soft-pedalled.

---

[30] Editor's Note: Jean Guitton (1901–1999) was a French philosopher and was considered by Vittorio Messori as a leading figure for his personal spiritual journey.

Naturally, by pulling the cord far in the opposite direction, these new movements also fall into another excess: while the churches (or some of their theologies) have concentrated all their attention on this history, the sects concentrate their attention on another history. While the former considers the gospel to be a message only of liberation *for* the world, the latter reads it only as liberation *from* the world. It seems that it is precisely this reading that gives them so much success with the people.

It is cause for reflection that one of these apocalyptic sects, the Jehovah's Witnesses, is the confession with the highest growth rate in the world. Its followers are now everywhere among the most numerous religious groups (in Italy, they are the second most numerous religious community after Catholicism, exceeding by far both Protestants and Jews), and are perhaps the first in fervor, zeal, activism, and ability to make proselytes.

Nor is their increasingly accentuated presence limited to traditionally Christian lands, but extends throughout the entire world where, in the name of Jehovah, they have reached in the least amount of time results often superior to those attained in centuries of work by Catholic, Protestant, and Orthodox missions.

This amazing expansionistic force is incomprehensible only to one who refuses to admit that, as improbable as it might be, the Jehovah's Witnesses' reading of the Bible corresponds to an authentic need that other theologies no longer satisfy.

It is not fair to dismiss the problem by insinuating that Jehovah's Witnesses prosper by using fear as leverage. If anything, it is the opposite: unlike the "official" churches, they deny the existence of Hell, preaching that what awaits the wicked and the unbeliever is annihilation, definitive disappearance after death. An unpleasant prospect, perhaps, but certainly less terrifying than the threat of an eternity in wretched punishment.

It seems that the throngs of former Catholics, former Protestants, and former agnostics are attracted to the new banner of Jehovah (where, moreover, they must face sacrifices and harsh commitments, to the point of incarceration and perhaps even death), precisely by that which many Christian theologians consider "no longer appropriate to the mentality of today's man," and therefore to be minimized or even hidden.

The disciples of Charles Taze Russell (the founder of the movement) proclaim that history is not everything, and in fact this world is entirely unsatisfying and destined to end soon. They offer at the same time answers that might be naïve but are clear and concise on the questions regarding the death of the individual and his destiny; they point to a rupture on the horizon of history; and propose the hope of eternal life for the individual, though stylized according to the idea of happiness of the average American.

The new world to be established by the imminent Kingdom of Jehovah is indeed a classic example of projection into the afterlife of cultural models proper to one time and place. It is a sort of Muslim Paradise reinvented by Americans. The promised Kingdom of the Jehovah's Witnesses is a universe of single-family homes set in pleasant neighborhoods surrounded by yards with swimming pools. Radiant married couples live there with their two children, a boy and a girl, just like in a TV commercial, picking flowers and fruit effortlessly in perfect harmony with their neighbors, singing merry hymns together. All these blessed (as portrayed in the images on their pamphlets disseminated by the millions around the world), wearing colorful casual clothing for an eternal weekend. All while a lion frolics with a lamb, a tiger with an antelope in meadows under a splendid blue sky.

The Catholic or Protestant immediately recognizes in this naïveté a simple, literal reading of the Bible and its promises, an eternal life where Semitic prophecy is re-read by the Anglo-Saxon Yankee. But this does not stop the *Homo religiosus* from joining them, for he must placate a need and respond to a question that, according to his pastor or his priest, he should no longer ask, or should at least chase away as the temptation of a Christian who is not in step with today's mentality.

WHAT GOOD IS THE GOSPEL?

I believe Christianity has been unacceptably betrayed by certain theologians who have defamed it, as if one were to see life as a dark tunnel, full of dangers and filth, to pass through as quickly as possible, one hand over one's eyes and the other closing one's nostrils, toward an exit that gives access to Life, to the World, the only true one because eternal, without any communication with what preceded them except for the bureaucratic counting carried out on the threshold of one's merits and demerits accumulated in the valley of tears.

But in the same manner, it seems Christianity would become useless and insignificant if, after having recognized that the tunnel of life is not as it was presented, seek to absolutize it to the point of making it the only place worthy of attention. In this way, one closes and hides the exit through which the only air, light, and meaning available arrive.

Christianity has something important to say if it is a remedy to this claustrophobia provoked by this closed space, by windowless rooms with no way out. "Without the risen Christ," said Pierre Teilhard de Chardin, "I would have suffered from suffocation in this world."

Let us ask ourselves the simplest of questions, which are also the most radical and therefore the most clarifying. The questions that propagandists, demagogues, and the scatterbrained detest because they risk being unmasked by them. Let us then ask: Is being Christian worthwhile? What good is the gospel? What does faith in Christ give us? Is Christianity something more or just an extra? Is it a luxury, folklore, a form of alienation, a superstructure, a complex of old traditions?

Answering these questions in a positive sense for the faith is not as easy as believers once thought; or as those still clinging nostalgically to a presumed *societas christiana* insist on thinking as they climb the barricades over the ruins of their world now devastated by the modern hurricane.

Over the last few centuries, Christians have had to abandon a lot of baggage along the path. The implacable trials of history have constrained them to the poverty preached by others who tried to elude its grasp, even in the social and cultural spheres. They were obliged to discover that they were not allowed to plant their crusaders' flags everywhere, that the Christian stamp could not be placed on all the merchandise.

From politics to economics, from science to art, to culture in general, everything that counts most in the world has been emancipated from the Christian embrace and seems to be doing quite well on its own, without needing a baptism quite often compulsory and almost always exterior. The council took stock of the situation, recognized the legitimate autonomy of "earthly realities" which move on a *distinct* plane (though not *separate*) from the religious, and have their own laws that do not depend on ecclesiastical ones.

So, to respond to the questions we have asked, it is no longer possible to show the many trunks that one believed were part of the essential baggage of Christianity, of Catholicism. Who can say today that there is a "Catholic" politics, art, or culture?

Those who accept with realism the lesson of facts has no doubt: much of what one believed Catholicism could ensure, that it had as extra, has been revealed to be illegitimate, or has become uncertain, undefinable or contested. Many rafts and much ballast have been thrown overboard the bark of Peter. Furthermore, much of what the helmsmen decided not to throw overboard and abandon, has been blown away by the winds of an ocean in tempest.

Like it or not, the ancient, impressive galleon of the Church has been increasingly assuming the traits of a bare lifeboat. Not bad; in fact it is best this way, if one considers this transformation under the light of the gospel. And we know that, compared to the proud freighters, a poor raft is uncomfortable but does not sink.

A HOLE, NOT A DOOR

All is well, especially because, on those boards, thrown about in the raging storm, reduced to their bare essences, Christian survivors can perhaps discern what their faith gives as "extra" with respect to the world that is very well-stocked in all other things.

This "something extra" is the ability to discern the light breaking on the horizon, to see the hiatus, a hole in the suffocating dome of history, an opening from which light breaks out, guiding the navigators and giving a destination, a meaning, from which a breeze blows out filling the sails, giving breath to those lungs poisoned with foul air.

Perhaps this is the only superiority of the Christian and his faith over worldly ideologies which appear much wealthier and more powerful. It seems so little; and it can be everything. In the book of Revelation, Christ says, "I have set before you an open door, which no one is able to shut" (Rev. 3:8).

It is not misfortune, then, but his good fortune and that of others who do not share his faith, that the Christian is returned to the condition of Peter before the crippled beggar, "I have no silver and gold, but I give you what I have; in the name of Jesus Christ of Nazareth, walk" (Acts 3:6).

The gold and silver and all the impediments, the wagonloads and bundles that the churches and Christians believed necessary to drag along, they have had to abandon along the road. The true, invisible wealth has remained, that "extra" that the world is not able to give: a hope, a direction giving the strength to "get up and walk."

The oldest Christian document, the first written text of the New Testament, is not one of the Gospels, but a letter, the first letter that Paul wrote to the inhabitants of Thessalonica, today the city of Salonika, at the beginning of the year 51, not even twenty years after the death of Jesus.

From the very first lines of this ancient text, the apostle gives his definition of the Christian. He is the one who has "turned to God from idols, to serve a living and true God, and to wait for his Son from heaven, whom he raised from the dead, Jesus who delivers us from the wrath to come" (1 Thess. 1:9–10).

In our times, which could very well be the last, history takes Christians back to the bareness of their origins: believing means turning to God, abandoning every idol (both those of reactionary Catholicism, which confuses the Church for the dusty shop of the junk dealer, as well as the progressive Catholic, with his obsessions and myths no longer so fashionable), waiting to rise with the Risen One who is to come again.

The hole, the door, the hiatus: is this the "Christian specificity," the phoenix they have been looking for in their erudite theological dissertations for years? Committing oneself in the world but in the perspective of its eventual passage; living history to the last drop, yet in the spacious certainty of its definitive emergence upon the eternal.

This tension regarding the absolute future, toward life without end, toward the resurrection of the dead, is the strength that animated martyrs, saints (those few known to men and the infinite number known only by God), the energy that has propelled the Church through the seas of history, saving it not only from its enemies but also from its many "friends."

True Christian charity, service toward those who do not share the faith but are no less brethren for this reason, is not teaching what the world knows better than the Christian does, not doing what others know how to do better.

Charity, the only kind possible to the Christian, the only kind the Christian can perform, is to proclaim from that raft to whomever will listen, that the horizon is not closed as it seems. That there is a tear in the heavens, similar to that discovered by astronomers: the black holes. Therein lies a mysterious world that continues this one while being completely other.

> The people who walked in darkness have seen a great light; those who dwelt in a land of deep darkness, on them has light shined. Thou hast multiplied the nation, thou hast increased its joy... For to us a child is born, to us a son is given (Isaiah 9:2, 5).

Is this not the great promise of the prophets of Israel? Are these not the words with which Matthew has Jesus begin His preaching? Is this not the passage in Scripture that the Church proclaims in the Christmas Mass because of its exultance? It is certainly indispensable that the believer commits with goodwill to social action in an effort to give bread to those without. But at the same time, the Christian must not forget that "man shall not live by bread alone, but by every word that proceeds from the mouth of God" (Matt. 4:4).

Only the Christian has heard these words, and he has the social obligation to propose them to the world unceasingly. They are the proclamation that enlightens everything: "Remember that you shall not die." Believing means trying to love, now, and in the words of Gabriel Marcel,[31] "loving someone means telling them: you shall not die."

FLAVORLESS SALT

André Frossard,[32] one of the most well-known French journalists, was a young Jewish atheist, or as he wrote of himself: "more than an atheist, indifferent and concerned with things quite different from a God whom he didn't even think of denying." Suddenly becoming a Christian and a Catholic meant for him nothing other than *"becoming aware of an immense laceration in the canvas of the world."*

This was, as he later wrote in a famous book, "the moment of discovery of meaning in life." I spent a winter afternoon with him in his house in Neuilly-sur-Seine. "I decided immediately to educate myself about that strange Catholic religion that had crashed into me," he said. "I knew nothing about the catechism, but the priest who explained it to me told me nothing I did not already know: all Catholicism was already contained in that 'other dimension' which for a moment I had seen through the laceration of history."

Frossard is therefore a convert. And converts are, today more than ever, a hindrance, embarrassing.

There have been many studies on the phenomenon of Christian conversion which, as we have seen, has become so rare today. Yet, those who examine these studies immediately realize that one never converts because of the aspects that are considered the most presentable to the current re-reading of the

---

[31] Editor's Note: Gabriel Marcel (1889–1973) was a French writer and philosopher.
[32] Editor's Note: André Frossard (1915–1995) was a French writer and essayist and a famous convert to Catholicism.

Gospels. Conversion is a lightning bolt that burns up the accessory, that blows up the formal structures to reveal what is essential to the faith.

When his priest friends began to chomp at the bit to become his psychologist, sociologist, manager, cultural guide, political lobbyist, anything if only not to remain a sign (both disturbing and consoling) that the new world is already here, François Mauriac admonished them:

> I confess that I am entirely indifferent to knowing what a friar or a monk thinks about the European Economic Community, the technological revolution, or the crisis of French cinema. They are the last ones whose opinions on these issues interest me: I know more about them than they do, or I know of experts more qualified to whom I can turn. It is to something quite different that you religious must continue to bear witness; something quite different, at any rate, is required of every Christian, of each according to the measure of his gift.

This "something quite different" is what Roger Garaudy[33] speaks about, the French Marxist, former director of the Communist Party. To bear witness, says Garaudy, "that Jesus Christ, and he alone, has opened the arms of man's horizon, proclaiming that all human limits have been defeated, including the supreme limit: death."

It is, in fact, the men of the world (at least the most honest among them) who feel cheated by a Christianity that passes from alienation (according to which the only true believer was the cloistered monk) to claustrophobia (according to which the only true Christian is the man entirely immersed in action, political or union action preferably) without any reference anymore to Paul's attitude we have already quoted:

> Brethren, I do not consider that I have made it on my own; but one thing I do, forgetting what lies behind and straining forward to what lies ahead, I press on toward the goal for the prize of the upward call of God in Christ Jesus (Phil. 3:13–14).

---

[33] Editor's Notes: Roger Garaudy (1913–2012) was a French writer and political activist in the Communist party.

Leonard Sciascia[34] is a writer who loves to define himself as an agnostic, a Voltairean, who sees himself in no religion, in no church, while confessing that, "like the Christian who has doubts about his faith, I often have doubts about my incredulity." In his diary, Sciascia narrates how, as a skeptical, disenchanted observer, he found himself one day at a convention of Catholics whose theme was "Hope."

"It seemed I was dreaming," he notes:

> But slowly as it continued, wonder gave way to doubt: was I witnessing the onset of tolerance or of confusion? Behold, the end of the world? Not at all. Behold, death? But in two days I never once heard this word pronounced, not even by accident, in the talks that had to do with theology, doctrine and exegesis. But maybe precisely because of this. But maybe my death, from without, is a "reactionary" question: what is left of Christianity without the thought of death and the end of the world? There remains only an ideology of pauperism confused and quite contradictory — so confused and so contradictory that Catholics who profess their faith, forgetting about death and the end of the world, anxiously tend to fuse it with another more precise ideology, more consequential, more "scientific."

Marxism, in other words. The writer continues:

> The fact that a Catholic assembly did not react to the affirmation that "the Church is against hope, it has always been against hope," made me apprehensive and added fears and doubts to those I already had.

This testimony of the Sicilian writer seems as precious and disturbing as the intricate investigations of sociologists of religion.

"What remains of Christianity?" In this question of the agnostic Sciascia there seems to be a confirmation of what we have tried to explicate in this chapter.

Without the dimension of hope, without "the thought of death and of the end of the world" (to use the imprecise but clear language of the non-Catholic), without explicit and continual witness that "Jesus Christ and He alone has

---

[34] Editor's Note: Leonardo Sciascia (1921–1989) was an Italian writer, poet, and politician.

opened a crack on man's horizon;" without this, then, the faith becomes what Jesus Himself foresaw: "salt that has lost its savor," "leaven that does not rise," "a lamp hidden under a basket." All things, the Gospels add, that are to be thrown out without regret. They are of no use to anyone, anyway.

A Cross, Two Poles

Except for the legitimate, precious, but particular contemplative vocations, perhaps no one today can be nostalgic of an entirely "vertical" Christianity.

The problem, if anything, is examining (in a spirit of service toward others) what contribution, what assistance the one who recognizes his Lord and Savior in Christ can give to the world. This service, this help is to indicate a cross to his companions on the journey of life's adventure. Now, a cross is not formed only by a *staticulum*, the vertical pole; nor only by a *patibulum*, the horizontal pole. A cross is a sign that points our gaze in two directions at once, and it is "emptied" (the expression is Paul's) if it is reduced to just one dimension.

The continual synthesis required of Christians between "horizontal" and "vertical" is certainly not easy. But who has ever said that Christianity was easy or simple?

Man and history are complex; the message that presumes to give answers and meaning to man and to all of history must be complex as well. There are those who left (and rightly so) a Christianity whose cross had been reduced to a *staticulum*, a sign that pointed only vertically. They protested against the heavens that they might be able to rediscover earth.

But then there are those who leave (equally justified) a Christianity in which the cross is only a *patibulum*, in other words a sign indicating the earthly horizon. Among them was Ignazio Silone, the writer, politician, and communist who was persecuted by Fascists first and then by his ex-comrades later, who said one day while explaining his defection from the Church, "I could not remain among people who say they are awaiting eternal life, the return of Christ in glory, the New World, with the same indifference with which they await a tram."

Recently, an entire issue of one of the most prestigious international journals of Catholic theology (at least it defines itself thus) was dedicated to deriding the ancient dialogue of the baptismal liturgy.

The one baptizing asks of the one receiving Baptism if he is certain he wants to "die to the old man and be reborn in the new man": "What do you ask of the Church?" "Faith," respond the catechumen or the godparents, if the protagonist is a child. The one baptizing replies, "What is the fruit of faith?" "Eternal life," is the response.

This journal for priests and by priests was mocking and at the same time rejecting the extraordinary concision of the dialogue. In the name of "a re-understanding of Christianity," of the "dialogue with contemporary culture," one asked for the usual "investigations," "completions." But those wanting to attenuate, almost ashamedly, that "the fruit of faith is eternal life" (and all the rest is only commentary) belongs to that fauna of the sacristy with lungs burned from incense, who considers the expectations and needs of others from the standpoint of its intoxication by too many rosaries and ejaculatory prayers mumbled by force ever since childhood. Those dawdling, out-of-sync clerics are no longer able to intuit the vivifying breath emitted from the baptismal dialogue for those not intoxicated like them, for those not inured like them to the mystery and to the incredible promise.

Those who drag themselves from the university classroom to the party precinct, from a town hall gathering to an environmental protest, from a mindfulness group to the couch of a psychoanalyst, from a yoga class to a cultural conference, are hopeless beggars for a response to the truest and most urgent questions, seeking fruitlessly a lifestyle, a meaning, a door in history, both his own and that of the world. Those who have been reduced to this can understand the extraordinary uniqueness of a dialogue that, in all the world, resounds only at the baptismal font.

"For forty years," says André Frossard:

> Since the time I was made a Catholic, without having asked to be and without even desiring it, I have sought to convince my brothers in the faith (and especially priests, theologians, and bishops) of an elementary truth so often forgotten: when we know there is another world, that life continues into eternity, *we need to say so*. When we know that there isn't, and there shall never be on the earth any other hope for men beyond the Christian hope, *we need to say as much*.

"If you do not know this, what are you preaching?" the indignant cardinal in *Promessi Sposi* asks the lazy priest, "What are you teaching? What is the good news you announce to the poor?"

Not to Die Like This

There is another ancient dialogue, equally forgotten if not mocked by the socio-theologians, and equally extraordinary for those who hunger and thirst for life.

"Why did God create us?" "He created us," one responded, "to know Him, to love Him and to serve Him and then to rejoice with Him forever in Paradise." This is the old catechism, today (rightly so) revised, lengthened, rewritten in narrative form, although the question and response structure is used in the more recent *Compendium*. But the substance remains the same, always announcing that incredible hope that definitively tears the veil of history: "and then, rejoice forever with Him in Paradise."

It is an objective fact that only the Church can present herself as a bank of hope, of life, of eternal life! Surely, the question whether her credit is just a boast or if her vaults really do have in them what they promise. But it is a concrete reality that, in a world ever more devastated by a famine of hope, those tellers' windows are the only ones making this sort of promise.

Among the many, far too many professors who want to teach us how to live, only the Church, pointing to Christ, promises to teach us how to die; or rather, how not to die. She alone proclaims that man is not the segment of a line soon to be brutally interrupted, but a straight line that starts at one point and runs to infinity.

Giorgio Gozzelino, a theologian quoted above, remarks with the simplicity of truth, "The gospel is good news because it announces Paradise." Gozzelino is a Salesian, a son of Don Bosco, who proposed to the wayward youth he gathered from the streets of nineteenth-century Turin "bread and work."

This promise made by many during his time and which today many Salesians continue to make, but with the little warning that St. Giovanni Bosco preferred facts to populist declamations and "manifestos": the first work contracts in Italy (from 1851) bear his name as the guarantor of the worker, complete with working hours, holiday rest, vacation, and protection for apprentices, which nascent socialism did not yet dare to demand. At any rate, only Don Bosco, only a Christian like him, could complete the promise: "Bread, work, and Paradise."

Let those speak who, unlike those giants, are afraid of words and would rather distinguish, nuance to attenuate the Christian scandal. That perspective on "Paradise," that promise that what does not merit to die in us will never die, must be stated clearly, because if it is true everything changes for us. Outside of that promise, there is only condemnation, without the prospect of liberation, to exchange for something big what is often just small and base. There is only the suffocation of one who, for lack of anything better, is forced to bow down over his books and study, taking seriously the results of administrative elections of towns with fewer than five thousand inhabitants. Of one who is condemned to doing exegesis, as though it were important, of the bad prose of a provincial secretary of some party during a Sunday assembly. Or of one who is condemned to having always more; to consuming always more. And so, to illude himself with being more.

Guido Ceronetti,[35] perhaps not a Christian writer, but certainly sensible to religious matters, says that man reduced to just one dimension, the horizontal, "is damned to the atrocious expiation of never being able to leave the trap of history, to spin around in it like a top gone berserk, without rest or fresh air."

The Christian God has taken history seriously to the point of incarnating himself in it, of becoming a citizen of it. He is within history, and only in it does the Christian play out his eternal destiny. History is the only dimension where man can find fulfillment. But history is also a life sentence if there is not someone somewhere who (as Vatican II says speaking about the believer's indispensable social commitment) does not proclaim in the same breath the possibility that man "is not limited only to the temporal horizon but, living in human history, but preserves intact his eternal vocation."

USELESS AND DANGEROUS

A Christianity that nuances or hides or even denies its specific identity is not only useless, but dangerous for everyone: opening to an Absolute Future, the hope of a complement to history beyond history, an open door on the line of the horizon. Not by accident is world terrorism crowded with former Catholics. The more devout and clerical their past, the bloodier the present of these brigands and guerrillas.

Indeed, if one occludes the opening that gives a way out of history, the insuppressible Christian tension toward the future that fulfills the possibility of man crumples upon itself and is unleashed within the mere confines of

---

[35] Editor's Note: Guido Ceronetti (1927–2018) was an Italian writer and poet.

history. Here, the ex-Christian (though not for this reason an ex-believer) sows his need for the absolute.

But history is the kingdom of all that is relative. This is the root of the bloody fury born of delusion, the "religious" need to kill, because there is no religion that does not have sacrificial victims. "Many disasters today are born of the broken tension in many believers with the complicity of certain theologies," writes Alberto Ronchey,[36] an agnostic journalist. "The world goes to pieces if the need for the absolute is not attenuated by pointing to an afterlife, and if instead the confines of the historical world are sacralized."

This creates a predicament for everyone when "religious" people lend a hand to politicians in making history the only legitimate dimension of mankind. When this happens, horrors lurk just around the corner: Fascism, Nazism, Marxist-Leninism, Maoism, totalitarianism, and terrorism of every sort. At this point, there is only History with a capital *H*, which man is obliged to transform into an idolatrous absolute. There is only Politics, elevated to an obsession that demands that man sacrifice everything: his very life, and before that, the life of others.

A DIVINE SMILE

We have seen how it would suffice if everyone were to rediscover their own mortality, to love each other with irony, that invincible means against powers that hold sway only if taken seriously. This possibility of subversion, of liberation, is open to all, believers and non-believers alike.

But if one adds Christian hope to this awareness of the death that awaits us all, then irony can be transformed into a still loftier gift: humor. But even this treasure is threatened by Christians trying to fog up the skylight through which others might catch a glimpse of the beyond, busily trying to close the windows that bring in fresh air. This theft would be among the most serious consequences, because, as the moral theologian Bernard Häring[37] suggests, "humor ought to be included among the greatest of Christian virtues." It is a gift that derives only from faith in the gospel, if it is accepted in its entirety, in its intertwining of action and contemplation.

---

[36] Editor's Note: Alberto Ronchey (1926–2010) was an Italian journalist and politician.

[37] Editor's Note: Bernard Häring (1912–1998) was a German Redemptorist priest and a well-known moral theologian.

The one who possesses humor has the following:

> A positive, healthy relationship with reality and, therefore, can laugh gracefully at human folly, beginning with himself. The one who possesses humor can smile always, despite everything. He can smile because he knows that in life and in history everything is serious, but nothing is truly tragic, everything is important but nothing is irreparable; because he knows that drama is always mixed with comedy.

Thus, Häring suggests that "humor is a visible sign of redemption": only the Christian who has found balance regarding life and the afterlife can possess it; one must live in history with earnestness and passion but also with detachment and a pinch of irony, aware that the part he is playing at this moment is important, though never ultimate, but rather penultimate.

The man equipped with authentic humor is the authentic disciple of Jesus who has come to know the truth, and the truth has set him free (see John 8:32). Humor born of the gospel is the opposite of the sullenness of the politician, the dark fanaticism of the terrorist, or the anxiety to climb higher of the career-driven businessman, or the myopic cynicism and smug cleverness of the wheeler-dealer. It is the opposite of the attitude of all those who, as St. Paul says, "have no hope" (1 Thess. 4:13).

Thus, instead of transmitting distress or even just sadness, the consciousness of death united with faith in the final opening of my history and that of the world provokes a serene smile that has something of the divine in it. It is born, in fact, of the fall of idols: what seems to be *everything* to one who sees nothing beyond the horizon is only *almost everything* for the one who sees further.

If I have understood this, I will no longer have idols to adore or masters to adulate: I can accept simply to kneel *next to* someone else, but never *before* them, or worse before something, like the world closed in around itself necessarily pushes one to do.

The stone rolled away from the tomb so many centuries ago, in the distant city of Jerusalem, has caused that mysterious hiatus to open unto a hope and therefore to the benevolent smile of humor. The professors, theologians, demagogues trying to demythologize Christianity would like to take this away from the faithful, but they end up mythologizing the principalities, powers, and authorities of this world, those whom Christ will reduce to nothing (cf. 1 Cor. 15:24).

THE EVERLASTING FAITH

I would hope that the preceding words might justify the choice being made here. That they might explain why the words and praxis we have placed under examination in our study of Christian hope are not simply working hypotheses confused with certainties, passing fashions presented as dogma.

It is Catholic eschatology, without other adjectives (neither "of the right" nor "of the left," neither "traditionalist" nor "progressive"), that we are emphasizing in this book. We place before the Church's faith in the ultimate things as it has been reiterated by the Second Vatican Council, in the light of all the preceding faith.

The conscientious fidelity to the council, therefore, which takes seriously even the complaints of the final years of the pontificate of Paul VI, this man whom we have not loved in life, and at times perhaps not even respected, but whose tormented greatness we have discovered only after his death. "We must desist from using Vatican II as a marble quarry from which we extract only the blocks that are useful to us, while ignoring others."

We must desist from making appeals to an "imaginary council" that each of us molds according to his own expectations; we must desist from peremptorily referring to a presumed "spirit of the council" in the light of which the letter of its decrees would become irrelevant.

Whoever harkens back to orthodoxy, even post-conciliar orthodoxy, risks being suspected of various crimes: conformity, close-mindedness, superficiality, lack of creativity, seeking one's personal gain, even. In reality, we are witnessing the curious misunderstanding according to which what today is called "courageous" is simply conformity to what is fashionable at the moment; those who band together with those Christians whom Maritain called "chronolatrous" are adorers of the times with their passing idols. In fact, today one needs much more courage to resist the fashions, to remain clinging to the everlasting faith.

Rest assured: I have nothing to defend on the personal level, not even the prospect of some honor bestowed or some psychological gratification. I am just an isolated man: behind me there is no one, only my struggle to live, my anxieties, my long studies and interminable reflections, the observations of a curious journalist, a need to communicate to others what I have discovered: *comtemplata aliis tradere*. This is the best of mottos for a journalist. "Free thinkers" freely choose Christianity, Catholicism.

In my worst nightmares, I see myself transformed into a "notable Catholic," suspected of officialness and therefore of pompous hypocrisy. Fortunately, that danger has been distanced from me by many churchmen of the Catholic world who are wary of me, as they are of any layman they cannot directly control and, if necessary, silence.

Circulating in Catholicism today is what a German theologian has called the "anti-Roman complex." I would prefer to think with my own head, with analysis and reflection and not based on complexes.

Let it be clear: if I am examining Catholic orthodoxy here (as that which I believe most worthy of analysis and consideration), I do not intend by this to play the minstrel to certain monsignors, strumming serenades under their balconies. On the contrary: in my moments of bad humor the Catholic faith seems convincing not thanks to them but despite them.

For some time now, however, I have learned to distinguish between the Church, its faith, its mystery, and those who are called to administer these treasures: the often nearsighted, cowardly, mediocre men of the cloth. People like me: am I not also part of the Church? Neither am I perfect. And it might be true that you, too, are imperfect; it happens to many along this journey through life.

"We always ask if the Church meets all of our expectations," wrote Balthasar. "We never ask: do I satisfy the expectations of the Church?" We always say, "The Church should"; we rarely admit that the correct phrase should read: "I should."

Not being the spokesman for any Curia, not even the Vatican Curia, I have no vocation to become the pit bull of some reconstituted Inquisition. I do not intend to run for the office of grand inquisitor of those "advanced," "new," "open" theologians, whose words and whose silence we have mentioned at length, without hiding the criticism.

I do not agree with them, but I respect their labors, which seem in good faith, stimulated by important and generous questions: How can we speak to our contemporaries about Jesus Christ? How can we render the gospel credible once more?

If I remain clinging to a faith almost two millennia old, the faith of the Church, it is also because I know from experience the ephemeral value of all fashions and trends. The wager we are forced to make has as its bet the eternal, and fashions, by definition, are contrary to the eternal. If it is always dangerous to take fashion too seriously, it is particularly inadvisable to be guided by them here, in front of the infinite.

Just as war is a matter too serious to leave to generals, so too death and what comes after it, eternal life, are issues too serious to leave to the hypotheses of some theologian who has just discovered the world and its fascination. Better to stay close to the faith of the Church, whose law is most reassuring: *quod semper, quod ubique, quod ab omnibus* — what has been believed always, everywhere, and by everyone.

PART IV

REALITY

The disciples of John told him of all these things. And John, calling to him two of his disciples, sent them to the Lord, saying, "Are you he who is to come, or shall we look for another?" And when the men had come to him, they said, "John the Baptist has sent us to you, saying, 'Are you he who is to come, or shall we look for another?'" In that hour he cured many of diseases and plagues and evil spirits, and on many that were blind he bestowed sight. And he answered them, "Go and tell John what you have seen and heard: the blind receive their sight, the lame walk, lepers are cleansed, and the deaf hear, the dead are raised up, the poor have the good news preached to them. And blessed is he who takes no offense at me.

Luke 7:18–23

Lo, I am with you always, to the close of the age.

Matthew 28:20

CHAPTER 12

Words and Things

Between Hell and Paradise

BY NOW WE KNOW: everything has two sides, nothing is univocal, nothing is simple except to the simpletons. This is a cumbersome rule but an unassailable one from which, according to the logic of the Incarnation, not even the Church can escape: the Christian attitude in the face of death, the Catholic word and practice, the proclamation and expectancy of an afterlife that are said to derive from the gospel.

On one side, those who do not renounce objectivity, those who know history and the heart of man, recognize as an asset the massively long presence of the Church, its way of sustaining and guiding man in a life that is realistically always perceived as an uninterrupted march toward death.

On the other side, and not all in bad faith, there are many who reproach the Church with a "loss." The simple and terrible adjective and noun suffice: "eternal Hell."

First of all, the Church has announced good news, "Paradise." But this too has been written down as a loss, as an intolerable incentive to our "alienation in Heaven."

Thus, much of modern history, whether right or left, bourgeois or proletariat, appears as controversy, struggle, liberation from this alienation.

Paradise is the enemy of man, it has been said. But what shall we say, then, about Hell? A priest and contemporary theologian, Gianni Baget Bozzo,[38] saw Western history as "the history of the gradual exit from the nightmare of damnation," as a "violent liberation from the hell-hypothesis." Could this be the

---

[38] Editor's Note: Gianni Baget Bozzo (1925–2009) was an Italian priest, theologian, and politician.

secret, unconfessed reason behind the aggression first against the ecclesiastical institution, and then against Christianity in general? And if those who pretend to be the noble objectors of an "alienating Paradise" in the name of man's freedom and social commitment were actually seeking reassurances against a Hell whose possibility terrorizes them?

It is difficult to forget how a man of Bertrand Russell's stature reduced all the reasons for refuting Christianity to just one: the Gospels, and therefore the Church, promise not only eternal joy, but speak also about eternal damnation.

It is difficult to forget the echo, immense and fierce, of Paul VI, guilty only of having pronounced the words so mocked because so feared: Hell, devil.

It is difficult to forget that the dominant ideologies are all united by a common fundamental dogma: the hysterical negation of sin, precisely the reality that Christianity links to Hell.

When I still hoped to be able to concentrate in this one book an analysis of the contents of Christian eschatology, I wrote tens of pages not only on a part of verse 46 of Matthew chapter 25 ("the just shall go to everlasting life"), but also on the other, terrible part: "The others shall go to eternal punishment."

The file with those reflections rests on a shelf with the drafts of other books in need of settling like fermenting wine, to be given energetic treatment later. Naturally, my hope is that this rest will not be eternal, and that I shall be granted time to attempt at least to demonstrate that even Hell is *not like that*, as with so many other matters of the faith. Namely, how so many wholesale preachers have depicted it, as too many believers imagine it to be (or better, how we no longer imagine it to be, after millenary indigestion); how many people deform it in attempting to discredit the gospel. What I would like to see is that if one must reject Hell, one at least does so in light of what it is and not reject what one ignores.

Among the things many ignore is that Christianity is not at all a "doctrine of the two ways," that it does not place on the same level Paradise and Hell as the two possible outcomes in the same manner. To be more precise: Hell (and everything behind this name undoubtedly quite dated and in need of rereading) in a certain sense is not part of Christian eschatology. For this reason, individual history and the history of humanity do not have two destinations but one alone: salvation, Paradise, "a new Heaven and a new earth," Incarnation, Passion, death, the Resurrection of Christ, all signify that, taken altogether, history has already been redeemed, already been saved.

This is the certainty of the believer, a certainty that does not erase for the individual, for each man, for me, the terrible and concrete possibility of total failure.

Perhaps there is no one in Hell, other than demons (the Church has a canon or list of the blessed, but not one for the damned). This does not remove the possibility that *I* might be the first to experience it. In any case, if this were to happen (*et Deus avertat!*), it will not be due to the judgment of a cantankerous, vindictive God, but if anything, a "self-judgment": one does not *go* to Hell, one remains there as the radical choice of one's entire life.

It is of this *possibility* that I would like to speak one day, demonstrating that it is this, paradoxically, that defends the decisive values always threatened not by those who affirm it but precisely by those who deny it, values such as liberty, dignity, the greatness of man. I would like to show that the goodness of God ("How can you reconcile a God whom you define as love with eternal damnation?") is placed in doubt not by the possibility of Hell but by the negation of that possibility. I wish to show, then, that this aspect so apparently negative can in the end be classified not as a loss but as an asset of Christianity.

Let us be clear: here, as elsewhere, the contents of the faith do not depend on indicators of their momentary appeal. That Hell exists is not in the least tied to the answers to the questions: "Do you like it?" or "Do you think it is fair?" Market surveys have no relevance whatsoever to the content of the Creed, which, in this sense, has nothing to do with the presumed democracy promised by politicians. Christianity is a revelation, not a human construction made to please the ever-changing tastes of the masses. The Church does not have clients to satisfy or electors to flatter. For the Church, what is true is not what a particular majority likes, in a certain age, in certain countries. For her, what is true is only what is found in the Scriptures explicitly or implicitly.

A referendum among the apostles and disciples of Jesus could have decided by a great majority that the history of the Messiah should have been quite different, that it should have ended not in the shameful checkmate of Calvary but with the happy ending of taking power and distributing offices and benefices among the old guard.

Thus, despite every reassurance or explanation, it is certain that a referendum on Hell would decide for its abrogation. If the faith is correct, its content is objective, not tied to subjective approval. Our task is only to try to indicate and explain it as well as possible.

One also needs to explain what the faith means when it says "Paradise," this word that refers to images that are no longer our own.

The term derives, in fact, from a defunct Iranian language and means "garden, park": in other words, the highest blessedness for a Middle Easterner tormented by the implacable desert sun. The Bible (which always makes itself sensible in the language into which it is translated) also calls it "Heaven." Here too, we are outside of our vision of the world: we return not to Copernicus, but to Ptolemy, with a three-tiered universe: if one must descend into Hell, one must likewise ascend into Heaven.

Another image of which Scripture makes use is the "banquet," the "nuptial feast," referring to a society in which the one invited to a wedding had the rare opportunity to satiate his hunger! Today, with problems of obesity and diets in Western society, this type of invitation runs the risk of causing more problems than it gives cause for rejoicing.

As occurs in all aspects of the Christian afterlife, if we stop at words we risk running astray; or worse, we risk running into the images of Gustav Doré, the illustrator of Dante's *Divine Comedy*.

We need, first of all, to show that the Christian vision of Paradise is not the projection into the heavens of our impotence, our frustrated desires. Ludwig Feuerbach got stuck on ill-advised preaching and did not know the authentic content of the faith when he wrote the famous sentences that Marx took from him in an uncritical manner: "Life on earth loses its value for one who believes in heavenly life. To believe in eternal life means believing in the nothingness and insignificance of this life."

These are the misunderstandings of the superficiality of one who was uninformed and could not get past the bad example of certain practices, but who had and continues to have an enormous influence on those who have only theoretical knowledge of faith and do not know what it means to live it. Concerning this, Vatican II removed all residual doubt, recalling in the document on relations with the modern world, "Eschatological hope does not diminish the importance of earthly commitments, but rather gives them new reasons in support of their fulfillment." In the same document, it addressed those who might still live Christianity as a form of alienation:

> They are mistaken who, knowing that here we have no stable citizenship but seek a future homeland, think that for this reason

they can neglect their earthly duties, and who do not consider that it is precisely faith that obliges them even more to fulfill those duties, according to the vocation of each person.

We note here, that to the contrary of its many verbose men, for whom the mystery seemed to hold no secrets, the eschatological faith of the Church has always been characterized by admirable sobriety, far from any suspicion of mythologizing. Here more than ever, dogma has been limited to establishing the bedrock, respecting the *mysterium tremendum*. And yet, among the few matters defined *de fide*, there is from 1493 the following affirmation: "In Paradise, the degree of heavenly beatitude is different in each of the blessed according to the degree of their merits." Some decades later, the Council of Trent explained: "The just see God clearly one and three, as He is; but more or less perfectly according to the diversity of merits acquired on earth."

Now: merits, for a Catholic, go in the direction of the social commitment, which a certain individualistic, spiritualistic devotion had forgotten, provoking the accusation of "alienation." Therefore, the more beautiful Paradise will be (and not only for the individual but for everyone, thanks to their common efforts) the more this work, this commitment to others will be intense. There is, in Catholicism, an unbreakable bond between history and eternity, this life and the afterlife, which many Christians might have forgotten, but it is not for this reason any less essential. Not seeing it, they contradicted once more the fundamental law of Catholicism: *et–et*, and not *aut–aut*.

The Catholic Paradise is not a hotel room prepared from all eternity in God's heavenly Disneyland. Paradise is the city of God and of man, which comes after the earth, but comes from the earth. It is the fruit of our work as well. This is an immense problem, nonetheless, which I can only mention in this primitive synthesis, postponing to the hope of a future development, when it will be possible to demonstrate the failures of an approximative presentation which aroused in many even a fear of "ending up in heaven." Thomas Mann, the great German writer, reflected, "Paradise? Oh please, we hope to avoid it. It must be fatally boring." And Jorge Luis Borges, the Argentine, wrote, "I confide that Christians are wrong. The only thing that truly terrorizes me is their threat of making us live forever." One must point out here the naïveté of projecting our categories of time (and space) into a dimension where these coordinates have already been radically surpassed. Let it be quite clear: the blessed are not stupid.

We need to set right much spiritualism that bears only the name of Christian and has indeed emphasized (as Catholic dogma teaches) that Paradise is "the heavenly blessedness that perdures for all eternity." But it has also too often forgotten to emphasize that in this "blessedness" not only our souls will be immersed, but we will live in wholeness: "body and spirit"; that our person in its totality will enjoy forever, transformed and glorified in the image of the body of Christ (2 Cor. 3:18).

Travel agencies sell their presumed "tourist Paradises." Christians and theologians do not take out ads or make publicity (or have done so in the wrong way) for their Paradise, which is nevertheless the prototype. Yes, "Heaven" needs an ad campaign. The most effective advertising is the simple explanation of what the true content is of this immense hope, of an incredible promise of joy without end, although it has become so unappetizing to the common man.

A Wise System

We must therefore postpone for another time (if there will be one) this exposition of the authentic content of the so-called Catholic *et–et*. In this book, we want above all to consider the here and now, to remain on earth before we travel to Heaven or Hell. Let me explain: what does the Christian proclamation on life and death mean for the life and death of a concrete man? What attitudes and outcomes has the acceptance of gospel hope brought to the here and now?

Philippe Ariès, though a secularist, concludes his unwieldy research on death with the affirmation, "Catholicism has created the most comprehensive, articulated, and sapiential system for domesticating death, rendering it bearable and humane. In this way, it has also rendered life more bearable and humane." What could have motivated such a demanding analysis? This is what interests us here.

Beyond the chemical analysis of the Christian "medicine" one must note, empirically, how it has acted and acts concretely, *for us*. We must see why an atheist like Michel Foucault was able to make the bitter (to him) observation: "Christianity has succeeded in teaching us to accept our own death. Those who came later, if anything, have taught us to accept the killing of others."

We will be attentive, here, to the objective facts: we shall speak of faith, but especially to verify its effects. As the title of the chapter indicates, we will be examining the *words* to see if and in what way they have influenced *things* that concern us up close. We must begin, then, with historians, scholars, whose trade leads to dealing with the facts.

We add a third historian to the two we have already quoted, Jean Delumeau, professor at the Collège de France, one of the oldest, most prestigious universities in the world. Delumeau not only knew Christian history better than most, he was among those modern historians who, leaving behind popes, emperors, kings, and battles (superficial qualitative history), strike out on the new quantitative paths of history from below, trying to penetrate the mystery of the hidden, anonymous masses, those whose names only God knows and who are ignored by history books because they neither massacred nor oppressed nor used others as cannon fodder or material for the construction of pyramids to their own glory and that of their bloody ideologies, all deeds invariably presented as done "at the service of the people."

Concerning these obscure and suffering ones in their anonymity, this truly silent majority, the "quantitative" historian reconstructs their lives, their mentality, their sufferings, and their joys. Looking into the stuff of history, Delumeau, a Catholic open to the new and critical toward every form of nostalgia for the past, writes:

> The historian has no doubts: for many centuries and with ruthless economic taxation, the Catholic Church was able to render the material life of men even harsher and more difficult. But for the historian there is also no doubt that the same Church that seems to have failed in helping men live, did help them to die. It sustained them in accepting with courage and realism the human condition, in making room for death in one's life, in giving meaning to both. And when the moment came, it helped them to face it with dignity and hope. This analysis is undeniable and is unique and extraordinary. It was one of the most arduous endeavors in all the human adventure, and one of the most successful. Thus, the historian will have to conclude that the Church, despite errors and even horrors, improving death was able to improve life. Helping men to die helped them to live.

Past, Present, Future

What do we desire, then? Do we dream of imposing once again the "Catholic system" upon everyone, like it or not, to suppress death in the hope of improving the quality of life? Do we yearn for a return to the Middle Ages, to the *ancien régime*, to the Papal States, to government by the clergy, to a Christianity of the masses?

While avoiding deplorable misunderstandings, it is urgent that we clarify that among all possible forms of nostalgia, those are the most extraneous. "You cannot cry over everything, you have to choose," says Jean Anouilh,[39] the French playwright. As for me, I gladly withhold my tears over the end of so-called "Christendom" and its dubious protagonists: the pope-kings, the Christian kings and their holy alliances, the cardinal-ministers, the Jesuits-counsellors-of-princes.

No, I do not cry over the definitive end of every "Christian society" or those presuming to be one: from the medieval kingdoms to absolutist realms, to the grotesque extreme caricature of Franco's Spain or even Italy under the Christian Democrats in the 1950s. Here too, I agree with Pascal: "Beautiful the Church's condition when she is supported only by God" and not by dubious potentates, even (and especially) if they define themselves as "friends of God." As historians remind us, regarding Christendom, "God was perhaps much less alive in those times than we think and is much less dead today than is said."

Denouncing forcefully what is negative in the present does not mean being nostalgic for the past. Authentic Catholicism loves Tradition, in the uppercase singular; not its historical incarnations, traditions, which have often been questionable and always destined to change with the times.

On the other hand, pay attention: it would be unacceptable to turn from nostalgia for the past to condemning it as a whole and without appeal. The demonization of the past is one of the disastrous traits of Enlightenment superficiality, to which the present and the future are the happy periods of light, while behind us there is only darkness. One of its clichés (passed into popular prejudice) is that of the "Dark Ages," which certainly was not a golden age (was any age?), but certainly was no worse than recent centuries.

They say the people were left in ignorance. Certainly: literacy was not diffused enough to read the ads for detergents; nor did they speak the official languages well enough to understand the sullen facetiousness of a TV show.

---

[39] Editor's Note: Jean Anouilh (1910–1987) was a French dramatist and playwright.

Precisely this is the aim (according to an unlikely witness, the communist Pier Paolo Pasolini) of that wretched vulgate to which public schools have been reduced. The schools are now specialized in new slaughters of the innocent, uprooting children from their culture without giving them a new one. "When a new school opens, a prison closes," reassured the nineteenth-century apostles, perhaps generously, of a progress that some still insist on taking seriously. Despite what abundant experience teaches, namely that every opening of this type of school, a new wing must be added to a prison (*statistica docet*: rates of criminality rise parallel to the rate of instruction) as well as another drug rehabilitation center.

Let us leave this matter alone. What matters is that, among the many things that the Middle Ages ignored, there was not that which really counts: a hypothesis (which was a certain consolation for many) about the meaning of our life and death. And this was sufficient for the "intellectual elite" among us, armed with a match to do battle with the darkness of the night.

The Middle Ages, perhaps because one believed in the devil, was in many respects much less diabolical than the last two centuries. As even a neo-Marxist historian, Fernand Braudel,[40] recently admitted, "if one really wants to speak in these terms, it is the twentieth century that has truly been demonic: with its concentration camps, gulags, and other niceties, the sum of suffering inflicted on humanity in recent decades probably exceeds the sum from all preceding centuries."

The Christian should not join today's crude ideologies, whether bourgeois or Marxist, confusing what's new for what's true. For some time now, a few too many priests and friars have been going around spreading their conviction that every change is per se a sign of progress.

Among the traits that should characterize a Catholic is his equitable attention to the past, present, and future, living these dimensions with the same intensity, because his faith comes from *yesterday*, he lives it *today*, and it will come to full fruition *tomorrow*. Poignantly, the heart and summit of Christianity is the Eucharist, which is at once the memorial of the *past* and an announcement of the *future* made in and for the *present*.

As happens in the present and will continue to happen in the future, in the past as well not everything is to be saved. In fact, there is much that is useful to the believer as a warning that what has been should often not be repeated.

---

[40] Editor's Note: Fernand Braudel (1902–1985) was a French historian.

Among the infinite possible examples of what must not be repeated, there is the provision emanated in 1566 by Pius V, the pope of the Battle of Lepanto, where the military power of Islam was checked. This order stated, recalling a similar decree decided by Fourth Lateran Council in 1215, exemplary of a mentality that dominated for centuries: "doctors, under penalty of perpetual infamy, the privation of their title, the expulsion from the guild, and proportionate fines, must not visit a patient more than three times if the latter has not proven with a written document to have confessed his sins." Whoever refused the physician of souls had no right to the doctor of the body. This ordinance of Pius V was reiterated nearly two centuries later, in 1725, by Pope Benedict XII, who hastened to exacerbate it, adding the excommunication of doctors who transgressed it. Nor was this an isolated decree: they simply repeated the regulations of many hospitals where the sick, upon admittance, were subjected to Confession. No sacraments, no treatment. Giacomo Martina,[41] a Jesuit historian, comments, "Fortunately, there was never a lack of Catholics of good sense and authentic sanctity, like St. Camillo de Lellis, who would override the letter of the law, unable to suppress it."

To Understand

These are aspects of a system that the Christian certainly cannot allow himself to regret, although he always remembers that, as Delumeau admonishes, "the conviction of having become adults does not give us permission to spit on our parents."

Those believers who have preceded us are the ones who, though perhaps mistaken about the Gospel (or so it seems to our mentality), have allowed it to reach us, permitting us, therefore, to interpret and live better (so it seems and if we are able) the faith that *they* have handed down to us. According to many enraged innovators, their theology was shoddy, they followed an alienating spirituality, they prayed with an obfuscated liturgy: yet they nourished an explosion of sanctity that we tend to forget today or even to slander, perhaps because it frightens us, and because, though without confessing it, we ask ourselves what the fruits of sanctity will be that come from the tree of our form of Christianity, so proud to be "adult."

---

[41] Editor's Note: Giacomo Martina (1924–2012) was an Italian Jesuit priest and historian.

The great agnostic historian, Benedetto Croce, reminds everyone, whether a believer or not, that "history must never be an executor, but always an exonerator."

The decrees of those popes, of those hospital directors, of those Christians, are to be judges not from the outside, but from within their system of values, in the light of the intentions which inspired them. Under the light of faith, measures that today seem cruel appear instead to be animated by a "humanitarian logic" that helps us to understand them, though not to justify them. When one is convinced that the greatest fortune for man is to be saved for eternity and that the greatest misfortune is to be lost forever, then the sincere friend is not the one who is indifferent to your true good, who abandons you to your own will, which is weak and erroneous, but the sincere friend is the one who urges (perhaps even forces) you to frequent the sacraments, the means held to be indispensable for facing illness, death, the encounter with God, and His judgment.

This is the same dynamic at work in some "pedagogies of fear" practiced extensively by those churchmen who leveraged the risk of Hell: what seems deplorable to us moderns, in those centuries, on the contrary, was the laudable example of active charity.

Thus, the defense of Christendom to the bitter end by the popes (and by the Protestant and Orthodox churches as well) with the inevitable throne-and-altar alliances and repressive laws for the non-practicing, was inspired not only by political calculations, by the desire to preserve the ancient privileges of men of various churches. There was this, too.

But to the contrary of what approximative readings by materialists would have one believe, the history of man and of Christianity cannot be explained only in terms of the economy and politics. Certainly, a motive force for the world is also the pursuit of money, power, and glory; *also*, but not *only*.

The history of the Church has been made *also* by the powerful, who have brandished the crucifix like a cudgel; *also* by the rich, who have accumulated and defended their fortunes in the name of the poor man par excellence. But it has also been made by a multitude of priests, bishops, lay people, popes (why not?), and believers throughout the centuries who drew inspiration from their faith. In the defense of Christendom, therefore, together with other spurious motivations, there were also concerns that were not ignoble, concerns of a sincerely religious nature.

When the faith was considered the supreme good, it follows:

> One was able to fight in the defense of the Christian structures of society convinced that these enabled the faithful to fulfill their religious duties. The Church is not the little flock of Jansenist memory, but the immense people to which even the weak belong, incapable of staying coherent with their own ideals by the force of their intimate convictions, perhaps fighting against the surrounding environment. Experience shows the need these people have to feel the support offered them by a society with Christian structures.

Giacomo Martina again reminds us that "the Church has always refused to be a chosen group always wanting to be the instrument of salvation for all humanity, above all for the most abandoned, for the underdeveloped, for the nonintellectuals, for the weakest."

Behind all the clerical coercion of consciences stands the great evangelical conviction that the destiny of man, even the most miserable or ignoble man, is more precious than all the kingdoms of the earth.

> For what will it profit a man, if he gains the whole world and forfeits his life? Or what shall a man give in return for his life? For the Son of man is to come with his angels in the glory of his Father, and then he will repay every man for what he has done (Matt. 16:26–27).

Nothing, then, is omitted in the effort to save him, even at the cost (for his own good) of violating his freedom.

This was the reasoning of all Christian confessions for centuries, people for whom the gospel was evidence enough. To them, Paradise and Hell were not "wagers," but concrete realities they sought or fled with all their strength.

Paradoxically, in those aspects of Christian history denounced as ignoble by the wise of today there can be found a nobility they did not suspect. To these wise ones, the masses are only crude matter from which history is constructed according to their outline. Instead, for Christianity, there are no "masses" but only persons, each with a unique, eternal destiny; brothers to accompany with trepidation, and if needed, with severity; always "in fear and trembling."

We must not forget that if you want to find some trace of the chain of anonymous men who have preceded us, you must look in parish archives. There, and only there, is the sign of the passing among us (at least the name, birth, marriage, and death) of those to whom we owe our existence, both I who write and you who read — those whom the state is interested in only insofar as it can tax them or enlist them in its armies to go and die. To the Church, on the other hand, they were children of God: the salient stages of their lives merited to be blessed and registered, and who now, according to its faith, live in eternity.

A No to Hypocrisy

One can and must, therefore, understand and avoid being scandalized, and know how to discern the goodness of the intentions behind the masks of Christendom that seem intolerable.

Yet, it is one thing to understand, another to want to return to those paths, and not only because history does not go backward. Those paths are precluded to the Christian by the logic of his faith.

Christian faith tends to be *totalizing*: it invests everything in man. Whatever he says or does, the Christian never has a day off: there are no neutral spaces for him, free zones immune of the gospel that animates and judges every moment.

But *totalizing* is quite different from *totalitarian*, absolutist: alone among religious beliefs, Christianity can only be proposed and never imposed.

Among the central truths of Christianity is in fact the *Deus absconditus*, the concealment of God who speaks to the heart of man, who solicits his reason to look for him, but who does not impose the recognition of his existence, nor his essence.

Hans Küng observes, at the end of his long study on the search for God, "It is possible to say no to God. Atheism cannot rationally be eliminated: it is *unassailable*. But it is also possible to say yes to God. Atheism cannot be established rationally: it is *indemonstrable*." Contrary to every other faith, biblical faith takes seriously this objective situation.

It is thus a Christian paradox that faith is possible only when one can decide freely to believe or to refuse belief. Those who wish to impose Christianity destroy it because they reject the very plan of God. This happened in all the "Christian regimes," where even the non-believer was forced to feign belief.

Now, that the faith is not an obvious fact to everyone means those societies are necessarily kingdoms of hypocrisy. And hypocrisy is precisely the fault condemned with greatest vehemence in the gospels where Jesus stamps it with words of fire, as the contrary to faith, as a sort of "devil's virtue."

In "Christian societies," many clergymen, in good faith perhaps yet nearsightedly, fell into an error until recent times: they imposed Christian morality independently of Christian faith. This lies at the root of the revolt of the modern world, from the libertines of the eighteenth century to the mass uprisings in the face of recent attempts by some episcopates to maintain as a crime in civil codes what for the faith is sin. "The law," said Dietrich Bonhoeffer, a Christian murdered by the Nazis, "cannot be preached before or outside of the gospel." If this happens there is rebellion against the Church. And if rebellion is not possible, the worst of evils occurs: hypocrisy.

Thus, Christian societies, the "Kingdom of God on earth," risk becoming "kingdoms of the devil," despite all their good intentions.

It is not a tactical or opportunistic maneuver: one must be cautious of dreams of Catholic restoration, which, if they were to come true, instead of bettering life would render it a nightmare for many, disfiguring the gospel, because there must be the freedom to accept or refuse it in order for it to be revealed.

YES TO A PROPOSAL

Naturally, refusing every imposition of the Christian project upon man, his life, his death, his eternal destiny, does not mean refusing or attenuating that project. The error of the past was not in proposing it with courage and clarity; the error was in the intolerable, sacrilegious slide from the proposal to presumption.

I do not want any form of a state church. But I do not want its "state" precisely because I want *the* Church.

I wish for it to become an increasingly poor servant; to lose, whether some of her churchmen like it or not, as much of its worldly, political, economic power as possible. And I wish this because I wish neither for myself nor for anyone, whether believer or non-believer, that its word on life and death might weaken, that its actions freely proposed to man might cease.

I would like to see a Church that renounces the old, disastrous illusion of directly controlling the sociopolitical structures. But I would like this so that it continues to do everything it can to convert the human person, walking by their side to the goal announced by faith. Woe to all if that reserve of hope that remains were to be further clouded; if the Church, after having hidden for centuries its expectation of the Kingdom of God grabbing at the kingdom of Caesar, were to be transformed now into a sort of sacred labor union, a movement of supporters of other Caesars, as long as they are on the left. Not only those with political-economic power, but also those who fight to inherit that power, have little to do with the gospel and should have little to do with the Church. And woe to all if, after having blessed so many cannons, the Church were to become a dispenser of blessings to those wanting to construct Paradise on earth and only on earth.

Ecclesiastic hierarchies have, for too many centuries, made a "class choice": first in favor of emperors and kings, then of the aristocracy, and then of the bourgeois, the landowners, the greedy landlords, the miserly conformists. By these class choices, the one true patrimony of the Church risked becoming classist: the proclamation of forgiveness, of hope, of salvation, of eternal life *for all*, not only for those belonging to a particular social class. Placing hope in a ghetto in this way cannot be remedied by moving the Church (as many would like to do today) toward new class choices, even though this time not to the right but to the left. The gospel is neither right-wing nor left-wing: it is *beyond*, it is always *ahead*, it is *elsewhere* with respect to those trying to capture it for their own material advantage.

Vatican II takes into consideration the facts and finally renounces the desire for Christendom that brings together all and everything at the cost of freedom: "The messianic people," says the Constitution on the Church, does not include "effectively the universality of men" and appears "at times like a little flock." Of this "little remnant," which is the community of believers, the same document indicates service to all humanity: being, remaining, proposing itself as "a seed strong in unity, hope, salvation."

This is meant for all humanity, without any exclusion. Few or many, it matters little: believers are asked to sow the seed, not to harvest. What matters is that this Church, for as small as it might be statistically, is the leaven, salt, light; with its very presence it signals the reality which she alone knows, that which has been witnessed by the One who "likewise partook of the same nature, that through death he might destroy him who has the power of death, that is, the devil, and deliver all those who through fear of death were subject to lifelong bondage," according to the incisive expression of the Letter to the Hebrews (2:14–15).

Returning to the Second Vatican Council, namely its document most open to the future, *Gaudium et spes*, the community of believers must "safeguard its universality" against the recurring temptation to impoverish itself in the particulars that mark and fix in time every human institution. The Church must always remember that "empowered by its mission and its nature, it is not tied to any particular form of human culture or political, economic or social system."

What reality, if not the Catholic Church, can continue to go beyond the firewall of hate erected by a world wherein the life and death of a man have different value according to the color of their shirt or their party membership? For a Fascist, the cadaver of a communist is nothing but roadkill for wild animals, and vice versa. For the shareholder of a multinational, the cadaver of a black man or a campesino in a goldmine or on a banana plantation is a statistic or, in the best of cases, an insurance policy; while for a guerrilla, the massacred body of a boss, a bourgeois, a servant of the system is only a motive of scorn, if not of exultant satisfaction. And so on, in the odious discrimination of lives and deaths that is not the least horrible of today's horrors.

A quote by Mao, the Chinese leader who inflamed with hope the hearts of so many Western youths, whose hearts bled when he was renounced by his successors: "All men are mortal, but not all deaths have the same value." Another communist, attentive and sensitive to what the gospel and Church have signified for believers and non-believers, said, "For me, a non-Christian, the eternal merit of Christianity is the absolute and absolutely equal value recognized to every human life" (Lucio Lombardo Radice[42]).

"The faith of the Church," confirms Karl Rahner, "knows no human life that is not worthy of becoming definitively valid." This is a truth to be defended at all costs.

Love and Death

It was indispensable and urgent to clarify that restoring today the ancient Catholic wisdom does not mean pining away dreaming of a *coup d'etat* to return to some form of throne-and-altar politics.

Having clarified this, we can take up again with greater freedom the discourse from earlier paragraphs, that of the undeniable "asset" of the presence

---

[42] Editor's Note: Lucio Lombardo Radice (1916–1982) was an Italian mathematician and Communist politician.

of the Church. In concrete terms, what urges historians beyond suspicion to pin on their chest a medal of merit, despite what can and must be said about many aspects of her past as well as her visible face today?

Scholar like Delumeau and Ariès are just two examples among many. Among Italians, the first who comes to mind is Benedetto Croce, who wrote the famous essay *Why We Cannot Call Ourselves Christians*.

Many are they who, though neither accepting the Church nor loving her, know how to recognize the wisdom and efficacy of her words and of her actions on behalf of mortals. Many are they who, though not sharing her faith and her hope, nevertheless recognize her coherence and uniqueness.

We shall now anticipate some of the load-bearing ideas that run through the following pages. We shall see something of the strategy in the battle against death in which the Church is engaged. This strategy moves in three main directions.

The first is the fight against *fear*, exhorting the faithful to overcome it in the only way possible: not fearing the truth, but facing it. One must face it in order not to fear everything that reminds us of the truth about ourselves: the dying person, the elderly, the sick, the crazy, silence, cadavers, cemeteries, tears, mourning.

A fight against *solitude*, grasping Heaven and earth to fill the desert of death, to break the anguish of that mysterious isolation with the sympathetic presence of a community and its compassion: in its public prayer, the liturgy, the Church never says *I* or *you*, but always *we*.

A fight, in the end, against *desperation* that always threatens to grip the one who faces his own death and sees it approaching at every turn, proposing meaning to life which slip away and soon ends without an apparent purpose. "Every hour wounds, the last one kills," says a motto inscribed on ancient sundials. Why is this the case, and not otherwise? Why "Upon creating our fate / was it granted only to die"? Why "this dying, this supreme / discoloring of every resemblance, / and perishing of earth, and the diminishing / upon every use, of loving company," as that other implacable witness of our anguish Giacomo Leopardi inquires?

The Church exists precisely to confirm the fact that, without eternity, time is desperate, absurd; it exists to indicate a possible path out of the looming disintegration; it exists to announce the possibility of the victory of life, despite it all. And it exists to give a concrete pledge to that expectation with signs, gestures and words.

Reflecting on its message and examining the behaviors it inspires in the liminal circumstances of death, I have found confirmation of a conviction: Christianity is for children and adults who accept to return to being children. The post-Christian surrogates foisted upon us in this century appeal to adolescents (something quite different from "children"), to the immature who want to remain such. We have found examples of these here and there.

It is significant that in their nascent state (when they have not yet become institutions by means of power or theft) all ideologies and the "movements" to which they give rise attract adolescents in particular: whether Fascists or Marxists or liberal bourgeois radicals; yes, even they, with their various labels: radical, nationalist, patriotic. During the Years of Lead in Italy, the militancy in groups and gangs, probably armed, to the right or the left, became a sort of epidemic that becomes virulent in the age of acne and peach-fuzz beards. All the immature were involved, until leaving the movements upon reaching their thirties. The explosion in 1968 of so many movements that ended in a backwash of drugs, terrorist homicides, or even "merely" in burning delusion was the prime example of this.

Christianity, on the other hand, is for the children to whom Jesus points as an example for their innocence, simple, humble, and far from the mental chaos and failed education of the adolescent (I was once an adolescent, too; I speak from experience) who, as soon as he sees something, thinks he has seen it all. Christianity is for the mature, because before it is words, the gospel is life: to understand and love it, one must have known life and its joys and dramas. One arrives at the gospel either through the instinctive simplicity of the pure heart of children, or through the conscious experience of the adult, whatever his age. Therefore, even youth can come to know the gospel as long as they have gained experience from the tragicomedy of life.

True maturity seems to foster this adhesion to Christianity as it is proposed by Catholic orthodoxy, by the Church that youth must necessarily contest, but whose wisdom they can rediscover over the years. Catholicism, as we have seen, is about circular vision, good eyesight, 360 degrees (*katholicòs*) and about equilibrium (*et–et*). The nearsighted, the imbalanced, the sectarian can neither understand nor appreciate it, nor can the semi-erudite: namely, the one who has not yet understood that true culture is about grasping the meaning of the complexity of matters, fleeing simplifications, respecting the mystery hidden behind every appearance. Nor, again, can it be grasped by the one who is still subjugated by "Culture," in the uppercase, who has not frequented it enough to embrace the liberating Pauline paradoxes: "For it is written, 'I will destroy the wisdom of the wise, and the cleverness of the clever I will thwart.' Where is the wise man? Where is the scribe? Where is the debater of this age? Has not God made foolish the wisdom of the world?" (1 Cor. 1:19–20).

The more one advances in the desert of life, the more one notices the inglorious end every expectation meets (Goethe said, "Fear whatever you like in the first part of life, because in the second you will have it," and you will say now, "That's all?"), the more our relatives and friends abandon us and are lost to death creating a void around us, the more the darkness thickens even around our future; the more all this occurs, the more it is possible to rediscover and love a community that perhaps once irritated us.

Arriving at a certain point along the road it is easier to understand the wisdom of the mysterious plan recalled by Vatican II in its document on the Church: "God wanted to sanctify and save men not individually and without any bond among them, but to constitute a people out of them, and to recognize this people in the truth that they would faithfully serve."

Maturity (psychological, not merely in number of years) is what makes it known that true poets and philosophers, as well as the people with its instinctive wisdom, do not err when identifying two fundamental realities among many, two mysteries around which all the others turn: love and death.

Since its beginning, the Church has concerned herself precisely with these two realities, to the point of creating irritation and rejection. It has given the impression of not only wanting to sanctify, to give a transcendent as well as social meaning to the love between a man and a woman, but almost of wanting to peek through the keyhole into the bedroom at what happens in bed, to the point of having us believe they are here for the purpose of terrorizing people, conjuring up the bogeyman of death more than proclaiming the victory of life.

But the excesses (which, at any rate, she has humbly recognized and promised not to repeat) do not erase the value of its attention and effort to understand and to help, fair and beneficial.

It is precisely about love and death that the semi-intellectuals do not and cannot speak, these half-wise "experts" trying to help us with their impotent culture when our need is so much deeper. The Marxists, we know, dismantle the problem of death by defining it as a matter for the petty bourgeois; as for love, they promise to talk about it after reaching the "realized communism" stage. Never. The bourgeois (we know this, too) compete in their ability to hide death; and as for love, what they are really interested in is making the most profit possible and avoiding unpleasant consequences.

Yet these are the people who tried to show us that faith and Christianity were condemned, expelled from history. They believed they had found confirmation in the statistics that show how belief is spontaneous in children, falls in adolescence and early adulthood, and then rises gradually but constantly as one grows older. Would Christ and His Church be, therefore, a refuge for the old and their impotence? And what if they were, on the other hand, a harbor for those open to growing in maturity through life's lessons, of those who have left adolescence behind them, along with acne, naïveté, misunderstandings, and imbalance?

"The man worthy of this name," writes Jean Guitton:

> The one who does not resign himself passive and blindfolded before the passage of time, arrives sooner or later at the dramatic situation in which he believes that everything is allowed and possible and discovers instead from the lesson of facts that, left to his own powers, he can only destroy himself or go desperately toward his inevitable destruction. After which, there is the abyss or the return from the abyss. Now then, belief in God, faith in Christ, adherence to the Church, instead of proceeding from above, from revelation alone or from reason alone, can arise from the depths of one's experience and tears.

From life, that is, and not from the arid distinctions of philosophies incapable of satiating and saving.

A Certain "Prodigal Son"

Let it be clear: here I am considering not what I want to be true, but what is. Now, what is the reality? The reality is that of a society marked by the arrogance of ideologies that are substantially non-Christian. Those entering life, those without any experience and therefore defenseless, can resist only with great difficulty that violence because it is so often hidden behind shiny, attractive appearances. Only after tearing the layers of decorative wrapping paper off the package can we discover the snake it contains — all so well packaged that even the snake is mistaken for a treasure, or at least the best one could attain.

Certainly, the gospel project arouses enthusiasm and informs one's life from the very start, the first and final hope of one who has learned that all the paths that seemed so wide were in fact dead ends. This often happened when everything around the young person favored channeling in the Christian direction his generosity, his need to give, to love, and to live.

But now? Now, for most youth, the fragile young shoot of faith, even when it takes root, is often suffocated by the incessant bombardment of contrary signals and attractions.

Churchmen during these confused years have directed all the residual resources of proclamation and pastoral effort toward youth. Yet the results often remind us of the parable of the sower in Matthew 13:1–9, "A sower went out to sow. And as he sowed, some seeds fell along the path.... Other seeds fell on rocky ground, where they had not much soil.... Other seeds fell upon thorns, and the thorns grew up and choked them." The seed that fell "on good soil," giving abundant fruit, is often disproportionate to the effort put forth.

Those Catholics who live sheltered among the surviving tatters of Christendom, in their oratories, their elite groups, do not even do what politicians do, those blind guides, who, seeing a crowd in the town square in front of them, think that everyone is with them. Any serious investigation, even those carried out by sociologists at pontifical universities, confirm that those youth for whom the gospel is a totalizing life project represent only a fringe, and one on its way to further decline, no less. Giancarlo Milanesi,[43] the Salesian who coordinated the most recent and broadest survey of youth, observed:

> The most reliable forecast is that in our society the reduction of the importance of religion is destined to continue. The number of youths who turn to the Catholic faith as an element capable of giving sense to their lives will diminish. Christian life is destined in the coming decades to become a minority behavior, dispersed amid a majority moving toward a type of life that is profoundly secular.

---

[43] Editor's Note: Giancarlo Milanesi (1933–1993) was a Salesian priest and a scholar of youth phenomenology.

If the quantity diminishes, the quality (in human terms) is also disturbing. Can we not see every day, among the residual of believers, hybrids of the gospel and ideologies, mixtures of faith and politics of every kind, between Christianity and other religions, cults, and Eastern sects? Can we not observe the widening gap (even among those practicing the faith) between their faith and the Church, above all in the hierarchical aspect and in its ethical teachings, in particular sexual ethics?

If this is the situation, perhaps the attempt to proclaim the Gospel almost *exclusively* to youth is really not at all as modern as one believes (because one is not attentive to the signs of the times), as has been done by many in the Church, to the point of risking discrimination of certain age groups.

Christians and Catholics who are truly attentive to reality, who have left behind the illusion that structures and cultures still exist that are capable of helping (from First Communion to Viaticum) even the weak, the immature, will perhaps accompany this necessary, indispensable, urgent evangelization of youth with the rediscovery of the most upsetting of Jesus' parables, the one called the "Prodigal Son."

We do well to reread the central part of this story, which is not only, in the common opinion, one of the most beautiful in world literature, but also at the heart of the message and work of Christ:

> Not many days later, the younger son gathered all he had and took his journey into a far country, and there he squandered his property in loose living. And when he had spent everything, a great famine arose in that country, and he began to be in want. So he went and joined himself to one of the citizens of that country, who sent him into his fields to feed his swine. And he would gladly have fed on the pods that the swine ate; and no one gave him anything. But when he came to himself he said, "How many of my father's hired servants have bread enough and to spare, but I perish here with hunger! I will arise and go to my father" (Luke 15:13–18).

Who could ever know how many hearts were touched and set on the path homeward by these words? These eternal words are more relevant today than ever, when so many "feed the swine" and "suffer hunger" without even knowing they have a Father. One must continue to offer the gospel as a project of life to those who are not yet so fortunate. But we must never forget those who have been *deformed, disfigured* by a life as a spiritual orphan.

Today more than ever, one who knows the comfort of the gospel and the circumstances of most of his peers is ready to imitate one of the protagonists of the parable: "while he was yet at a distance, his father saw him and had compassion, and ran and embraced him and kissed him." These are the moments when, with the Father, we rediscover the community: this Church which, like it or not, is not an accessory to the faith but an indispensable condition for living it. These are the moments when the word of John Paul II can resound within one: "No one is deprived of a home and of a family in this world, because the Church is home and family for everyone, especially to those who are weary, oppressed, and desperate."

In search of objective confirmation of all this, we finally descend into the message and the practice of the Catholic Church, with a few insights which illuminate a much broader reality.

ON OPPOSITE EXTREMES OF LIFE

In the so-called "civilized world," only the Church can allow itself the rarest of luxuries, namely, to speak the truth about death and to say it on both extremes of human life, both when it is most distant, in children, and when it is nearest, in the old and those in agony.

A document put out by the French bishops says, "It is essential to know how to live with death, and because this is a very difficult wisdom, believers must educate their children from infancy."

Many denounce today, and for good reason, the pedagogy that sought to create around the child an oxygen tent that would preserve him from the harshness of reality. Sex, violence, injustice, war? The little darling was to know nothing of these, fed only on saccharine readings full of good people and animals, prize-winning literature, wherein the bad guys were invariably punished.

Now the tendency has been overturned. It is not only considered a duty to give precocious sexual education; even the primers and early-readers with their unreal rhymes have disappeared, and instead newspapers have appeared on desks whose necessary, essential function is to refer to the dark side of life. This is the obscure logic of information: bad news is "more" news than good news, a little Hell interests a lot more than every imaginable Paradise.

This new pedagogy suits us quite well, for it allows the little ones to get to know immediately the reality which shall be theirs in the future. Less agreeable is the fact that the courage of these new pedagogues goes only as far as their ideology allows it to go. It is the usual, miserable mechanism of repression, of hiding that we have seen so often at work.

"Let the children come to me," warbled the master, "secular and democratic," but that they come only to speak about socio-economic-political problems. In other words, only about what one hopes to resolve with "commitment," by means of "struggle" and "reform," with "a certain type of approach," as they say with their strange new-speak. In a word, with the only resources at the disposal of a *Weltanschauung* that reduces everything to party, labor union, and therefore to politics.

In order that politics might not serve to confront the questions that are upstream, namely, our human condition (mortality in a word), everything is blabbed in an infantile manner. Everything but *that*, please! We hammer him over the head with theses, theories, slogans for everything; just not for that. He remains then, although filled with all kinds of penultimate information, in the usual perspective of fairytales: "And he lived happily ever after, committed to his party and untiring in his obedience to the united labor union." Or, if one prefers, "and they lived happily ever after, in their luxury home with a tennis court, three cars, a yacht, and a shopping mall around the corner."

The one who has spoken clearly, saying everything and hiding nothing, has always been the Church that is accused of telling consoling legends, of raising us in the alienating mists of mythology.

The French bishops continue in that document: "Death should not be hidden from the little ones, but rather they should be habituated from their infancy to visiting the sick and agonizing, and in knowing how to speak about their own death."

"Sadism, the usual, morose clerical sadism!" We can almost hear the educators who, while yelling about this regurgitation of obscurantism, restlessly try to keep this smoke screen from dispersing over what frightens them much more than it does children.

Elisabeth Kübler-Ross says, "One of the most urgent tasks is to remove from our hospitals and from homes for the elderly the signs that say 'Minors under fourteen years of age are prohibited.'" But in this society, the experts are heard only when they confirm our prejudices.

It is not the fault of a presumed conspiracy that today's children will infallibly become the ill, the old, the agonizing, the deceased of tomorrow. Honestly, it does not seem sadistic to educate them in the truth, the *full* truth.

In the same way, would it not be sadistic, then, to reveal to the little ones all the social problems in the world, class divisions and the resulting class struggle, the existence of exploiters and the exploited, the tragedies of the Third World, and so many other realities all true, none of which are pleasant, but which many now are so anxious to tell children?

From start to finish, the Church has never been afraid of reality, nor has she hidden it, but rather exhorts her faithful to repeat fifty times a day in the Rosary, "pray for us sinners, now and *at the hour of our death.*"

According to Catholic moral teaching, it has always been a serious duty of conscience to help the sick (with charity and compassion, of course) come to full awareness of their condition. In other periods, if the relatives had not already taken care of it, a representative of the community of believers would do so. This was the *nuncius mortis*, the one who announces death: usually a doctor, a religious, or a friend conscious of the duties of friendship. He alone was considered a true friend, a "spiritual friend" as opposed to the false "carnal friend."

Here, too, is this morbidity, sadism? It was in fact not Catholic moralizers, but once again a team of secular researchers in America who discovered that only the one who stares reality in the face can attain a humane death. Only the one who knows how to look death in the face can hope to reach the final phase of acceptance, the only one that allows the dying person to grasp his own death, to dominate it without being dominated by it.

This extreme step is not the time for comedy, for an operetta: dying is the highest of dramas, and therefore the moment of authenticity, when one needs sincere friends, not improvised actors who recite their simulating lines. How can you truly count on a relative or a friend whom you know will lie to you in death? Are sincere relations possible when they are destined to end in such a grotesque charade?

Certainly, we need to understand that a *nuncius mortis* today would have the terrible task of announcing death, and only death, with all that it means: the end of everything, precipitating into a black mystery. For the *nuncius* of a past age, imminent death was only the destination of the message. The whole announcement was the perspective of life through dying.

A Policeman for the Hospital

The Church and her faith, not fearing the truth, know the secret for passing from words to facts. They show concretely what it means not to be afraid of the sick and the old, the two categories that most terrorize us today.

It has been proven historically that no community like the Catholic Church has dedicated so much attention to the sick, on the basis of the very word of Jesus who identifies Himself with them: "I was sick and you visited me" (Matt. 25:36). One of the characteristics of His activity is physical healing: in the Gospels, He is always surrounded by crowds of suffering people who implore Him and thank Him for what He does for them.

Christianity did not just develop hospitals. It did much more: it literally invented this institution that was unknown to the Greco-Roman world as well as in the East. From a certain time onward, as we have seen, the sick had to undergo the blackmail of the sacraments: but it remains the case that without Christians, there would not have been hospitals.

The *domus hospitalis*, or "hospitable house" (hence the modern name), was born around convents and monasteries. In the Middle Ages it was also called the *Hôtel Dieu*, the hostel of God, the God of Jesus Christ that the faith recognizes in the suffering brother. This commitment was taken so seriously by the clergy and the laity, united in confraternities, that in his journey to Rome as a young man, Martin Luther was so scandalized by everything that he began to suspect that it was not the Vicar of Christ who lived there but rather the antichrist.

Everything seemed betrayal and shame to him: everything except the hospitals of the religious, which he was still praising as an old man, though still in mortal battle with the Catholic Church. "They are constructed out of regal edifices, there is excellent food and drink that everyone can afford, the servers are diligent, the doctors quite learned, the linens and clothing perfectly clean, the beds painted," he affirmed in one of those "table discourses" that his disciples annotated piously.[44]

---

[44] The work in those institutions was ensured by the religious and laity of the confraternities (Luther: "honest maidens flock here, all veiled; for some days, almost anonymously, they serve the poor and then return home"). The great expenses incurred were covered by the donations of wills: in some dioceses, they even prohibited religious funerals to those who did not donate at least half of their goods to works of charity. These latter were quite varied: not only hospitals, but also orphanages (Luther: "Also the homes for abandoned children are amazing, where the children are housed, nourished, and educated in an excellent manner, paternally cared for in everything"), leprosaria, cloistered convents, hostels for unwed young ladies, even the construction and restoration of bridges and roads for pilgrims. For many centuries, until the French Revolution, the Christian vision of death, preaching the necessity of helping the poor to facilitate one's entrance into Paradise (the poor = doormen of

Not by chance did the lay organization for the assistance of the suffering founded in Geneva in 1864 take the cross as their symbol. It was the same red cross that St. Camillo de Lellis had placed on the habit of his "ministers (servants) of the infirm," giving them just one rule: "Serve the sick with the affection of a mother for her only child."

With the victory of the Enlightenment, the state took over from the Church in the management of hospitals. And it was right that a social service par excellence was assumed by the entire society, made up of believers and non-believers.

> Heaven, said a slogan dear to preachers) determined an enormous, constant transfer of income from the wealthiest to the neediest.
>
> Now, all of this causes indignation, one speaks with derision of a "welfare mentality," yelling that this is not the way to solve social problems. And it might be true. But what we have today in exchange are the poor humiliated and waiting in lines in bureaucracies manned by other spiteful and exasperated people because they are filled with hate being continually instigated to want more and more. What we see today is people abandoned in the chaos and filth of public hospital corridors, at the mercy of absenteeism and strikes that curse the bosses, even when the boss that pays their wages and fills the deficit in the budget is society, all of us. Certainly, the union boss prays he never has to run up against the moment of need in a staff that is too unionized: for good reason they leave the hospitals to outsourced workers, and they make use of private clinics when they need them, usually run by religious.
>
> What we see are disastrous reforms that swallow enormous quantities of everyone's money for miserable or even harmful results: all the statistics throughout the world attest that when hospital admittances are blocked by strikes, mortality diminishes quite suddenly. Unfortunately, this is no joke.
>
> One admits that, whatever their effectiveness, Christian hospitals that were at least paid for by the rich and their money truly reached the needy; it was not sucked up by parasitic bureaucracies and avid head physicians.
>
> They also say, ironically, that it is "comfortable" charity to leave to the poor the money one cannot carry to the tomb. This is also true. But here it must also be said that when the Enlightenment had swept away the ancient Christian *ars moriendi*, the rich, merciless, secular bourgeois of the nineteenth century entirely forgot others in its testaments and left everything to their relatives — so much so, that the bourgeois state had to close many institutions for a lack of funds; the others were subsidized with indirect taxation (from the monopoly on salt and quinine for the malarial patients and even taxes on milled goods) extorted above all from the indigent. According to the cynical saying of a politician: "Money is to be sought where it can be had. Namely, from the poor."
>
> Thus, as always, everything is much more complicated than the shouting of demagogues and the dominant mythological mentality want us to believe, incapable as they are of seeing the chiaroscuro, good only at dividing the world into angels and demons.

But it was not at all right that the state should transfer the responsibility from religious to the police. This is no typographical error: the police. "The hospitals, once laicized, lost their *charitable* identity only to take on that of *detention.*" Thus commented the *Grand Larousse.*

This was not right, but it was inevitable when one considers the presuppositions of the new culture: we have seen that what interests this culture is not the physical health of the sick but the psychic equilibrium of the healthy, who must not be disturbed by a spectacle that could shatter the entire system into pieces. Society must be protected from the infirm, from the dying killjoy. The gendarmerie must guard against the diffusion of news that might disturb public order: namely, that our condition is such that, sooner or later, sickness and death will reach us all.

From a *locus religiosus*, a religious place inviolable to the state police (they had been granted the right to asylum on a par with the churches), the hospital was transformed into a police concentration camp. It would then evolve into the land of conquest for politicians who fight over the control of their enormous budgets, and then into the power bases of those macabre barons of the kingdom of suffering.

Thus, it does not surprise at all that the management and supervision of other institutions that resemble death up close are entrusted to the police as well. The secular nineteenth century would then impose a uniform on these latter, as well as their paramilitary discipline.

Retirement homes, however, to the contrary of hospitals, were not an invention of the Church, but are a typical provision of societies subjected to the treatments of the new barbarism. For Christianity, this phenomenon of old people being kicked out by relatives who no longer wanted them in their hair was inconceivable. Retirement homes were born precisely with the rise of the new culture of individualism, terrorized by death and by whoever reminds one of it, even one's own parents, grandfathers, or in-laws. This mentality reaches its extreme in the multitudes of prosperous and well-educated citizens in America who want nothing to do with their old mothers and fathers.

Obviously, the old, merciless military hand is employed by the new obscurantism against other infirm people, namely the mentally ill, for whom the insane asylums were created, which were unknown in previous "Christian" centuries. The Catholic Middle Ages recognized a space for the "idiot"; it could not do otherwise. In fact, Jesus, in His preaching, overturned all the values of that good sense that the bourgeois was to present as a *non plus ultra* of wisdom. The Beatitudes and the "Woe to you" of the Gospels turn the world upside-down.

According to the mentality of the world, the gospel is folly, as St. Paul would shout. Jesus barely escapes the grasp of His relatives who want to bind Him as a dangerous madman: "And when his friends heard it, they went out to seize him, for they said, 'He is beside himself'" (Mark 3:21). With these Christian premises (though they had now been comfortably installed in power and had become the gatekeepers after having been labelled insurrectionists), how could they have set hands upon the madman?

It was the Enlightenment that imposed by force the new dogma of reason as they defined it, which was to demonize and persecute anyone who might distance himself from it. Anyone who dared to use categories other than those which had been declared "rational" by the bourgeois intellectuals of the eighteenth century was declared crazy, and therefore, a criminal because he sabotages the dominant framework and with it, the social system.

And so, this is how the new age (which had already created prison hospitals and the barracks-like rest homes for the elderly) constructed that other even more merciless prison that is the modern insane asylum.

These caused a terrifying amount of injustice and suffering that ideological blindness thinks it can solve (at least in Italy and in a few other adventuresome Western countries) with the usual attempt to destroy and deny reality. It is the mechanism (more pathetic and more perverse) that we have already seen in action on other occasions. When pain, sin, and death (psychic illness and madness are part of these) raise questions to which the masters of thought have no answers, they decree that those questions are insignificant, that the problem does not exist.

This is the logic behind the Italian law that suppressed psychiatric hospitals: based on political prejudices and not objective, scientific facts (science is brought to the discussion table only when it confirms one's ideological superstitions), a parliamentary majority decreed that madness no longer exists, that it never existed, that it was finally discovered that it was only social disempowerment, that all will be well with a few nice promises of reform. In this manner, the gates were opened and the unfortunate who had been locked up in the name of the old bourgeois Enlightenment disappeared from sight in the name of the new Enlightenment, composed of Marxist frameworks and brutal, radical egoism.

Any problems? They would soon be resolved, ensured politicians and intellectuals, by dumping the former patients into the open arms of a society that, as we all know, is filled with love and openness, crowded with saints and heroes who seek nothing else than to sacrifice themselves for the good of the suffering.

An Italian writer and doctor, his whole life the director of a mental hospital, Mario Tobino,[45] commented, "I would believe the words of those who wanted such laws with obstinate ideological insistence if at least some of them had welcomed into their own homes someone who had been discharged from an asylum. Up to now, I have not seen one such case."

The old doctor and writer will have to wait a while. It is all too easy to recite slogans proclaiming love for humanity; it is much less easy to love an actual person. It is one thing to speak, another to act; the Church knows this well: before she proclaims one of her members a doctor, a teacher recognized as such for all believers, she first demands recognition of their personal sanctity. One who has not lived out what they say does not have the right to teach others. This principle has been somewhat forgotten, observing the teachers of today, those authoritative opinion leaders of post-industrial society, people who are ready to fight to the last drop of ink and to the last TV roundtable on our behalf.

The abolition in Italy of psychiatric hospitals is nevertheless an incredible example of the scourges today's culture can inflict on the backs of the weakest, saying all the while that they do this for their good. What we saw in the neurotic laws, always insufficient, to hide cemeteries from view, happened again in insane asylums. It is a logical progression, as psychoanalysis teaches: the anxiety of death and the anxiety of madness are twins; they are the two, terrible fundamental anxieties, unbearable for men and for defenseless societies.

In the madness of a law that decrees that madness does not exist, the persecution rages no longer against corpses but against the living bodies of the sick and their relatives. "I am counting the dead," says Tobino, alluding to the mound of suicides and homicides provoked by a provision that is part of a system that threatens us "in order to improve the quality of life." And be careful! All of this is called "progress," "victory over medieval darkness": for those who doubt, other prisons are ready, other asylums, other ghettoes, where the new obscurantism locks up the ones who threaten its insecurity, its need not to see, not to know anything about evil, sin, and death.

---

[45] Editor's Note: Mario Tobino (1910–1991) was an Italian physician, writer, and poet.

Autopsies, Catacombs, and Anguish

Faith cannot even fear the cadaver that unleashes the hysterical reactions mentioned above.

In just one case does modern culture accept that the corpse be exposed to view and handled: behind the closed doors of the halls of anatomy classrooms. The diktat of culture regarding cemeteries and its propaganda pushing cremation to hide the corpses were the same that exalted the dissection of cadavers as a symbol of victory against Catholic anti-humanism.

We know that the Church was for centuries contrary to the generalized practice of desecration of the dead by whomever, whether physician or not. I say generalized because, even at the height of the Middle Ages, a limited number of dissections was permitted at the universities every year, at the end of their studies. Those autopsies were preceded by religious ceremonies that bore witness to the true nature of the hostility of the Church: to avoid debasing the corpse as just one object among many other objects, to avoid confusing it with a mere mixture of minerals, liquids, gases available to first comers who might want to satisfy their curiosity, but rather to honor the remains that were destined to resurrection. The defense of the cadaver thus became the defense of man, of every man.

When "religious obscurantism" fell away, one saw only meat to be sliced up (and then thrown in the trash) at universities, hospitals, and the labs of necrophiles of all sorts. The corpses to be studied were invariably of people condemned to death, of the wretched, of those locked up in ghettoes for the old and alienated, of prostitutes: with the loss of faith in the equal dignity of every deceased person, whatever their social class, even death became classist. It was inevitable that distinctions would be made between the "honored remains" of the notables and the roadkill of the pariahs of society, destined to supply material for the instruction of the sons of the bourgeois who set off on their study of medicine.

But there was another motive, perhaps even more important, behind the religious resistance to indiscriminate autopsies and behind the corresponding Enlightenment controversy that took that "liberation" as a symbol. Michel Foucault intuited this reason, too:

> Modern pathological anatomy not only had scientific aims but also exorcistic aims against death and its mystery. Endeavoring to identify the causes of death, the autopsy gives the illusion of

being able to explain death itself, of being able to desacralize and therefore to unveil the enigma.

We see here the usual, obsessive fear of death and the mystery that accompanies it: in this case, they tried to deceive themselves that identifying the cause of death would mean solving the problem. Not incidentally, autopsy literally means "to see with one's own eyes": but after having seen that death was due to blood clots or a heart attack, one is no closer to dissipating the mystery. But one knows that these big Greek and Latin words with a mysteriously scientific ring, used by physicians, have a soothing power on our superstitious society.

Once more, we have only attempted to ennoble the neurosis by giving it the name of "science," just like one used the word *hygiene* when they sought to make cemeteries disappear from sight.

Cemetery is a Christian word that in its very name refers to a comforting hope: it means "dormitory." Early Christians replaced the term that had been in use in the pagan world: *necropolis*, city of the dead. Furthermore, to indicate inhumation they introduced a term used only by Christians: *deposition* (substituting *to bury, burial*). After death (which they called *dormitio*, falling asleep, a word which speaks volumes) the body is given "as a deposit" to the earth, but at the command of Christ, it shall be given back. Thus, for the believer in the Gospel, the cadaver is not a reason for horror and terror as it was for the ancients and as it is for us moderns, but of respect, veneration, affectionate care, of washing understood as memorial liturgies in remembrance of dying and rising, symbolized in Baptism.

The first places of Christian worship, of gathering, and of art were precisely their underground cemeteries, the catacombs. These were not, as the story retold by Hollywood would have it, as places for escaping persecution. Above all, they went there to be close to the bodies of brothers who had passed to eternal life, leaving here their remains like a seed awaiting springtime. Those tunnels where the dead awaited resurrection were so important that the diggers of the tunnels and tombs, the *fossores*, were not mere laborers, but members of a minor order of the ecclesiastical hierarchy.

As soon as Christian worship was recognized, the cemeteries were brought into the center of the city: around and inside the churches themselves. Macabre tastes? No. As already in the catacombs, we see a sense of solidarity between the living and the dead who are not forgotten and, in faith, help each other; a lived awareness of the mystery of the communion of saints.

An old Christian custom in medieval Europe required young couples to go to the tombs of their deceased elders and ask their consent. In other countries, the newlyweds, upon leaving the church, went to the tombs of their parents promising them they would continue their bloodline and their virtues.

Serene solidarity, but also appropriate realism, a tangible memento ("What I am, you too shall be," reads one of the most common tombstone inscriptions) that does not seem to take away the spice of life, nor to diminish the importance of history.

The medieval city, with the cemetery in its center, amazes historians by its vitality. In the midst of famine, pestilence, and the scourges of nature and of man, medieval society ignored anguish, perhaps because it knew how to make room for death. The same culture, in a fit of communitarian fervor, constructed cathedrals and, under its floors, laid their dead to rest wrapped in white tunics, symbol of the resurrection, with hands crossed over the chest to remind that one enters life accepting the cross without a coffin, that they might be mixed with the earth from which they came and from which they rise transformed; with their feet directed eastward, that they might rise quickly to receive Christ at His return in glory.

Angst is the product of societies born of modern cultures, which deceive themselves thinking they can escape death by chasing the dead far away from the living. Unknown in the Middle Ages, at least as a social phenomenon, anguish reemerges in the West, after the French Revolution and the Napoleonic massacres, with Romanticism, worsening gradually until our time, with existentialism, nihilism, the drug culture, and so on.

In front of me lie the results of an investigation carried out by the city of Milan, Italy's most "European," most "progressive," most "enlightened" city, as they say. The investigation was quite significant, therefore, and the results show that nearly all inhabitants suffer from one or more of the following ailments: depression, insomnia, and digestive disturbances. In other words, from "syndromes of anxiety and anguish." It is an eloquent set of symptoms, which the city administrators promise to fight by "strengthening social services," "increasing green spaces," "working for a cultural renewal."

Let us be honest: what more can a poor politician do? He certainly cannot presume to get to the bottom of problems! Something else is needed here than "decentralizing" the city offices, than opening another "family counseling" clinic, than hiring some child of a wayward society with the gratifying qualification of "social worker."

If, as psychoanalysis teaches, the anguish of death is a "fundamental angst," ignoring it and repressing it means unleashing an infinite number of other problems that will devastate the life one is trying to defend. It is not the only cause, certainly; but neither is it among the least important. It is a lesson that Christianity had already learned from its very beginning.

THEY CALL IT "CULTURAL FERVOR"

At the bottom of it, one discovers that the undeniable superiority of the religious, Christian, Catholic vision over the tragic infantilism of a world that is afraid of the truth can be summarized in a strongpoint that concentrates everything: *do not fear silence*. This leads us to solitude, reflection, meditation — everything that terrorizes the world. The world, as we have seen, needs entertainment and distraction, it needs to travel and to be always together, making noise that will cover over the disturbing questions. To do this, it needs words that prolong into interminable chatter.

Talk, talk, talk... Because talking is natural, it is an instinctive remedy for getting rid of angst. What else does the psychoanalyst do with his clients, if not talk for a hundred dollars per hour? It lightens the wallet, certainly, but allowing him that expensive "storytelling" alleviates the patient of something else: his anguish, his sickness of living.

Thus, among the most characteristic, visible signs of our time are the conference, convention, meeting, seminar, roundtable, stage, debate, course, encounter. And the more, the better. Organizing these chatter binges is a very lucrative affair: millions of dollars circulate around each of them. In many cities, the congress hall is the most impressive, state-of-the-art building: a real monument to verbiage, which bloats with pride the chests of local administrators and the hopes of hotel and shop owners.

Here too, I risk the accusation of being obscurantist, an enemy of culture, which, together with politics, has an embellished altar, resplendent with candles in the temple of this century's obsessions.

To each his own cult.

Here, I limit myself to observing that in the same scientific settings (those most interested in congresses as an instrument of work) it is thought that only ten percent of the meetings of this type throughout the world are justified. All the others are merely expensive, vain kermises, showcases for intellectuals to show off, as once the soubrettes of old did.

The same sources recall that professional conferences began in the 1800s to allow for the periodic exchange of information among the cultivators of the same discipline. Now, in the age of instantaneous information, they ought to have become a less frequent event; instead, they grow in number from year to year. This increase has little to do with logic, but rather with a psychological reality: not reason, but rather the subconscious and its problems.

Thus, the conference hall carries out an important therapeutic function: the escape from oneself, liberation and stupefaction by means of words. Not by accident do politicians allot a growing slice of their budgets for this type of activity. To the plebians, *circenses*; to the cultural elite, *conferences*. Nor does the object of the conference matter, the aim will always be reached: keep the people from thinking about what the fervent organizers of these cultural occasions cannot resolve.

You are not yet convinced? That's your right. For what it is worth, here is a modest yet concrete and unsuspecting testimony. It comes from an Italian secular intellectual, Claudio Magris,[46] a sort of "repentant convention-goer." In the most widely read Italian newspaper, he wrote:

> This so-called "cultural fervor" is a fashion for hiding the void. It was born of a *horror vacui*, of a horror of emptiness that must be filled at all costs. It does not stem from a cultural need, but from the incapacity to sit still with oneself even just five minutes.

Exactly what we suspected. But conferences and the like will prosper more and more. Their fourfold preciousness lies in the following: first, they allow one not to think while feigning to be thoughtful; second, because the flight from real problems is ennobled and transfigured by the sacral aura of culture; third, the conference is united to travel with its consoling values which we have already discussed.

Finally, this "fervor" responds to another necessity we have mentioned elsewhere. Raising an impenetrable verbal curtain between man and truth,

---

[46] Editor's Note: Claudio Magris (1939) is an Italian writer.

confounding ideas instead of clarifying them, giving the impression that truth does not exist; or that, if it does, it cannot be reached in the swamp of the blah-blah-blah, in the labyrinth of pluralism, of different options and values and issues. Tranquilizing, therefore, by blowing up the bridges offering access to the one possible truth, frightening as every truth is, through debates and dialectical interventions, interdisciplinary contributions, in which everyone goes his own way, talking non-stop, concerned mainly with hearing oneself; far from every concern for real confrontation with the other to see if a synthesis, a point of convergence, a shred of a conclusion might be possible.

Not only for these dark reasons, perhaps; but it is certainly also for these that the chair, the stage, the table, the bottle of water, the microphone of the moderator and participant have all become symbols of our time. Perhaps for this reason the more sensible youth (and adults) look to Eastern meditation and silence, exhausted by these fake dialogues, encounters, and debates.

Hermits and Cathedrals

The symbols of traditional Christianity are quite different. There are two in particular, and as usual, they are opposites according to the old Catholic logic, balanced between two poles, to be united in an arduous and for this reason precious synthesis.

One symbol is the church, the cathedral, the place of communal encounter, of moments of being together with all the living and the dead.

The other symbol is the hermitage, the monastic cell, the bare and silent room, a reminder of solitude, of reflection.

The town square and the desert: the two poles of Christian tension. From the earliest times, believers constructed churches for the assembly as well as hermitages for the solitary.

The history of the Church is inconceivable without its places of solitude and silence: hermitages, monasteries of contemplative life, grottoes and huts of the anchorites, houses for "spiritual exercises." The Church has recommended this latter practice for centuries to the faithful, clergy, or laity. It has been made obligatory at least once a year for priests and consecrated religious of every type. With the renewal and restructuring of the spiritual exercises, the Church confronted the most serious crisis of her history, the Protestant conflagration of the sixteenth century. Ignatius of Loyola imposed an entire month of silence on his Jesuit confreres, praying and meditating as the indispensable basis of action. He organized these spiritual exercises for the laity as well. The great, drawn-out debate of the Council of Trent was able to bear fruit (of a true Catholic Reform, more than a simple "Counter-Reformation") only because it was rooted in silence.

The success of a conference is measured by the quantity of words pronounced; their content matters much less. The validity of the spiritual exercises, on the contrary, is measured by the ability to say as few words as possible, because the less one talks, the more one can reflect on the world, on the ultimate questions, on life and death: "Enter into yourself," exhorts St. Augustine, "It is there that truth abides." *There* is the truth that is so painstakingly covered by the gasping clamor of our times.

If there is something one might mistrust about churchmen who disturb the appropriate Christian balance between praying and doing, between contemplation and action, who want to transform the faith into the *management of the sacred*, there is much more to mistrust in churchmen who have inflicted their words appropriate to conferences on the faithful to the harm of the silence of retreats. "These you ought to have done, without neglecting the others," admonishes the Gospel here and in many other places (Matt. 23:23).

Someone once asked (perhaps in jest) if it were not a disturbing sign that the Italian bishops, with unusual submissiveness, had accepted to bow down to the motivations of industrial leaders, allowing the ancient feast of St. Joseph to be erased from the civil calendar, thus downgrading the liturgical feast, March 19 that had been so dear to Christians. On that occasion, they scrapped the obligation of rest and Mass participation.

Now, that demotion seems doubly unsettling: according to the ancient, consoling tradition that dates from the Judeo-Christian community, Joseph, having died in the embrace of his two extraordinary relatives, Jesus and Mary, is the patron of a peaceful death.

This is not all: he is the great taciturn, the radical protester against every chatterbox through his silence. In the Bible, everyone speaks, even Balaam's ass. Only Joseph keeps obstinate silence, the one who would have so much to tell us.

Better to demote him, then: he could not have coexisted with so many Catholics overwhelmed by "cultural fervor." These Catholics, who have so much to say and to debate that they have forgotten the ancient Church practice of praying for "the dissipated," who are dispersed amid chatter and busyness, it is these he could have helped find their interior quiet. With so many believers who do not even remember that the highest expression of the faith is the mystic: the one who no longer speaks because he listens, contemplates, who no longer has words to say because the Word has invaded him. With many readers of the Bible who forget that all the prophets begin in solitude and in the silence of the desert: from Moses to Elijah, to John the Baptist, to Jesus *himself*. In the logic of the Scriptures, only the one who has learned to speak one to one with God can speak fruitfully with men.

Only the true *Homo religiosus* can allow himself to retreat into silence, to frequent "spiritual exercises," whose final goal is to reflect on one's life and thus on one's death. Every course of this type has always been understood as a progressive itinerary toward meditation on ultimate matters.

The world laughs here, as well. It speaks of "alienating practices." Let it vent: they seem to mock, but in reality, they are protesting what they do not have and which, without even confessing it to themselves, would like so much to possess. What would their solitude feed upon if they were to stop and reflect? What could they bring to a retreat, if they were to detach themselves from the murmur of the debate? New annotated editions of old socialist utopians of the nineteenth century now mocked by history? Political propaganda pamphlets or advertising? The classics of economy? Corporate balance sheets? The collection of the speeches of their favorite politician? Essays on sociology and journalists who are in fashion, aged before their time between the printing press and the bookshelf? Novels? Mysteries? Spy novels? Science fiction? Monthlies for men only? Radical-chic weeklies with their standard three sections: politics, culture, economy?

Interesting reading, perhaps, I don't deny it. But good for making one reflect on problems that are always superficial, always penultimate. Completely impotent to confront the issues which Fyodor Dostoevsky called *the cursed questions*, because they are the most radical, the ultimate.

Modern absolutist and totalitarian regimes, not by chance, have often tolerated the secular priest, the parish priest, in whom they recognize one of their own, one who did his work, as despisable as it was: a reassuring "man of action." But those powerful men did not tolerate the man of contemplation, the monk, the solitary, the hermit.

The Enlightenment brought forth the "enlightened despots" who, as their first reform, suppressed the monasteries under the pretext of extinguishing idleness and social parasitism. In reality, what seemed to have exasperated them most was the root *monos*, "alone," which for them was intolerable. Their fury to blot out this scandal never stopped: it invaded the Jacobins of the French Revolution, it tormented Napoleon; the constitutional regimes of the nineteenth century and the totalitarian ones of the twentieth were all dedicated to suppression and dispersion of religious communities.

Those monks and hermits (persecuted so thoroughly that the once vibrant presence of Christian hermits up to the eighteenth century was completely eradicated in the West), all those defenseless Christians, were the true enemy according to the philosophy of their persecutors. Demonstrating with their lives the possibility of remaining alone, in silence, reflecting on a message that is evidently capable of filling the solitude, they were the true subversives to those working to eliminate through their frenetic action the danger of thinking seriously and profoundly.

"Give me faithful parish priests who can help me keep my subjects submissive, but remove from my sight the religious," repeated Napoleon between an order to massacre and the dictation of his delirious "Catechism of the Empire," in which he assigned himself a place in the Holy Trinity.

When they finally had him in their hands, his enemies did not shoot him. They did not dare to touch a hair on his head. They did more: with ironic British cruelty they inflicted upon him the greatest punishment for one like him, isolating him in the heart of the Atlantic Ocean. It was too much for one who had displayed his genius on the battlefield, taking on all of Europe. But he was defenseless in the face of solitude, alone with himself. There in his coerced hermitage, in fact, his prodigious energy wilted, and he died after just a few years of an illness affecting parts most sensitive to psychosomatic stress. He would have lived one hundred years if he could have continued his quest to find new victims to immolate to his own glory. Even killing is a valid *divertissement*.

Silence enriches the religious man, the Christian, or anyone who knows how to give a response to fill it. But it can also bring death to one who perceives it as a threat to avoid at all costs. Who can cite an example of politicians, businessmen, managers, who have spontaneously retired to their private affairs? It would be a rare case in a non-existent category of the public figure who voluntarily retired.

Modern ideologies have all copied Catholicism insofar as they could: parishes (becoming local sections of the party); dioceses (provincial and regional federations); processions in which each confraternity bears its standard, sings its hymns and prays its prayers (the marches with songs, flags, slogans repeated mechanically); relics (Lenin's mummy, the Unknown Soldier of liberal democracies); the symbols (how many stars, ancient religious symbols, are there in the political firmament, from America to the Soviet Union to the Red Brigade? How many crosses, from the hooked cross of Nazism to the various crosses in the Scandinavian flags?); fasting; the liturgical year with its sacred feasts (May 1, April 25, September 20, June 2, to cite just the secular holidays in the Italian calendar). As Albert Camus reminds us, "the dream of every secularist is to kill God in order to construct a church." Everyone, then, has copied the Church; every aspect of it except the hermit, the monastery, the retreat house, which they loathed.

CHAPTER 13
Not to Die

One Can and Must Cry

NOT TO FEAR THE truth, but to respect it, means giving to pain and tears their due.

Neither here nor elsewhere has Christianity ever minimized or hidden reality: in the face of death, our own or others', one can and must cry. Crying flows freely. When needed, it bursts out and gives vent to suffering that involves our being to the most profound fibers.

There exists a "psychiatric service for the assistance of the incurables," a private, lay organization that arose in the United States to try to offer help to the victims of the cruel way of death in America. In their courses for future nurses, they teach their students to repeat to the dying: "relax, take it easy, it's nothing." Nothing? I am not completely convinced of this psychiatric service: they say, "We encourage patients and their relatives to cry. We encourage them to overcome social conventions which say that those who cry and lament are cowards, or, if they are men, not manly." Usually, what one discovers late and timidly, the Church has always taught: Christian authors of spirituality have always considered tears a "gift," a "grace" of truth and humanity. The Church points, tirelessly, to its hope in the resurrection; but it does not forget that this passes through the cross, it does not ignore that in this matter, all that one hopes for is veiled under the opaque screen of flesh and tears.

Two brutal, illusory attitudes have always been foreign to Christianity, and into these philosophy and the wise have fallen: the modern *fuga a morte*, "flight from death" and from what it recalls, as well as the ancient *contemptus mortis*, "the despising of death," as if it were irrelevant.

Faith proposes a choice between a senseless grief and grief with meaning; the choice between desperation and a hope conquered through suffering. "Clement God," prays the new liturgy for funerals, "dispose our hearts to listen to your Word that, finding light in the midst of darkness and faith in the midst of doubt, we might console one another."

In one of their documents, the German bishops warmly invited parish priests and hospital chaplains to what they called "an often difficult but essential task." To help the relatives of the deceased to express and externalize their pain because, as they said, "it is important that they be able to manifest their reactions, even the liveliest, provoked by the bitterness of the moment and the brutality of death." "Accepting those reactions, fostering them even," they continued, "is to give valuable support to the survivors." They end by recommending encouragement for the relatives "to give their loved ones a goodbye that is in some way bodily, suggesting, for example, tracing the sign of the cross on the forehead of the corpse."

In her judgment that mourning is necessary and beneficial, despite being demonized by our "adult" culture, the Church once again finds herself in agreement with the painstaking and always partial discoveries of modern psychology.

She does not share our mutilating modesty; in fact, she condemns it. But she also condemns the morbid wallowing in memory and regret: without forgetting the past, there is a need to stretch toward the future in which our deceased have already entered.

As the German priest Albert Mauder, a man of great pastoral experience, said:

> Following the most ancient wisdom, mourning must not extend for more than forty days. Afterward, life must be taken up again as normal once the path of death has been walked to the end. Any feigned indifference, any protraction is a sign of worldliness: we Christians have nothing to do with such things.

The renewed post-conciliar *Ordo exsequiarum*, the funeral "ritual," recommends that funerals be preceded by a vigil, to relieve the pain and as a sign of participation in a drama that, by striking an individual and his family, strikes all society through them. The same ritual clarifies that the Catholic liturgy for funerals, which has its center in the Mass proper to it, is a remembrance of Christ died and risen "offered for the deceased," but also "offered for the consolation and hope of those mourning his passing." "All this," said St. Augustine, "the Church does for the relief of the living as well as for the help of the dead." Along this line, the *Ordo exsequiarum* recommends avoiding, in the homily of the priest presiding over the rite, "the literary genre of the funeral eulogy."

Christians must therefore distance themselves from secular custom, from civil funerals which have as their high point the discourse given at the open tomb. The "world" can do no more than remember, arouse melancholy and regret, recalling the merits of the deceased (often hypocritically). The world looks to the past; the gospel looks to the future: the deceased brother is entrusted to God and His mercy; it is not our task to play the defense attorney. Our task is to read the Word that uproots us from the shadows of history and replants us in the afterlife, in the light that knows no dusk. Our task is to arouse hope among the survivors, not desperation by embellishing this "irreparable loss."

In its rituals, Christianity comes to meet humanity still on its journey, not in superstitions. It knows that the rituals of death are an efficacious help in confronting and sustaining death in all its reality. But never has the Church suspected that the forced omission of these funerary honors (due to war, shipwreck, or calamity) might damage the eternal salvation of the dead or the physical or psychological health of the living, threatened by the return of the unburied dead. Christianity rejected the ritual lamentations of paganism made by paid wailers. It is not the dead who need this hired shouting. His living relatives and friends, if anyone, need such manifestations of suffering.

This rejection of funerary superstitions is among the most original and liberating aspects of Christianity. There are very few religions that do not torment the dying and his surviving relatives by threats of punishment and even eternal unhappiness if certain postmortem rules are not observed. These might range from foods being placed at the tomb of Egyptians or Etruscans, or the Hindu belief in the soul's imprisonment in the skull. If the latter does not explode during cremation, those standing by must smash it with a bludgeon. And woe to the deceased who has no one to perform this service for him. Woe to the Chinese (Confucian, but also Taoist or Buddhist) who dies without a male heir: those without try desperately to adopt one who will perform the "cult of ancestors" on his behalf, without which there is no survival.

The Gospel stands alone (nearly) in holding the good news that the deceased proceed to divine judgment, responding "for himself," evaluating what he, and not others, has done. The latter can help him with prayers, which are efficacious only insofar as they are an act of love in the communion of saints, neither a legalistic prescription, nor indispensable for salvation.

A Catastrophe

Those who have been struck by death can and must cry, and others must do all they can to console them, because for the Christian, death is more than a drama, it is a catastrophe.

While our desperate ideologies attempt to free themselves from it, to convince themselves that it is insignificant, the faith takes it seriously in a radical way. Compared to every other religious message, Christianity denounces the tragedy of death more forcefully than all of them. Christianity does not accept compromises: far from proclaiming *resignation,* as many believe, it proclaims *rebellion.* It neither ignores nor underestimates death; it does not deceive itself, thinking it can suppress it with its own strength: it wants to conquer it by means of God's gratuitous, omnipotent help.

Not by chance does it call death *agonia,* a "combat," the "struggle" of the dramatic final confrontation. According to faith, dying is not at all something natural: man was born for life, not for death. The new Italian catechism for adults says that "the repugnance of suffering is human. The Bible pities suffering, it does not love pain, not even for the sake of asceticism, as some other religions affirm."

Although the "ignorant educated" might think the opposite, Christianity is not masochistic: pain and suffering are not sought out, but only accepted in the name of the One who can overcome them. Even less so is death sought out. From the earliest centuries, Christianity has substituted the typically pagan saying "Die young if you love heaven!" with its salutation *"Ad multos annos!"* (May you have many more years of life!).

It is a curious fact that those who are accusing the gospel and the Church of being enemies of life are precisely the cultures of the last two centuries. These latter are not only *necrophorus,* bearers of death through the unprecedented disasters they have caused; they are also *necrophiles,* lovers of death in so many ways. From the most trivial, like the passion for so-called extreme sports (the race-car driver is the hero, the ideal life for many; the car itself, an obsession of contemporary man, the apple of his eye, is the greatest cause of his death), to the cult of death of all the far-right cultures (¡*Viva la muerte!* was the battle cry of every expression of Nazism and Fascism, privileging the color black for its clothing, its fez, its flags, and not incidentally pulling out all the stops in its funeral rites for the fallen comrade; Soviet Marxism did not mess around either, whose decrepit autocrats, often semi-cadavers kept on their feet by medical technology, followed the most solemn of ceremonies standing upright at the tomb in Red Square), to the preaching in the West of egoistic pleasure and hedonism as life's supreme goal, hastening our end and provoking that of others. Does not the unceasing advertising blaring in the West deal with instruments of death for the most part? Cars, as we said, and thousands of other contraptions with a motor, on two or four wheels; alcohol, tobacco, sweets, medicines quite often more poisonous than beneficial, contraceptives of every type — all take aim against life.

The Christian, though ready at any moment to leave life, never forgets that death is an integral part of it, and with realism keeps his baggage always ready, aware of the words of Jesus, though mentioned in apocryphal gospels, but which nevertheless seem authentic: "You are in transit," and "The world is a bridge, cross it but do not build your home there." But the believer is not tempted to love death, but rather life, wanting to protect and prolong it, grateful for it as a gift to be jealously guarded.

Every wise doctor can agree without hesitation with the behavior the Church proposes to its own. These are man's authentic "instructions for use": as such, they are the most well adapted for fostering health and life, on a psychological level as on the physical level, in the unity of the person. These rules and instructions can be summarized in two cornerstones: serenity of spirit, temperance of body — golden rules for the Catholic moralist as for the atheist physician.

The misunderstood word *mortification* (as the masters of spirituality teach) refers to the struggle to put to death in us sin, the very cause of death, both spiritual and corporal: one "mortifies" himself to live here and in the afterlife. Thus, it happens that the most "mortified" Christian lives, like the monks of strict observance, have the greatest longevity: gerontologists have long studied and admired the statistics on the extraordinary longevity attained by Carthusians, Trappists, and cloistered monks and nuns in general. The religious who has chosen to bear witness in this life to the reality of the next, shows in the fact of his long life that he is not called to despise or attempt to shorten this life.

For One Sin

Vatican II reminds us, reiterating the Christian teaching of all times, that "man would have been exempted from death had he not sinned."

This affirmation echoes what St. Paul synthesized efficaciously, "sin came into the world through one man and death through sin, and so death spread to all men because all men sinned" (Rom. 5:12). In this way, "the wages of sin is death" (Rom. 6:23).

The "one man" to whom Paul alludes is Adam; the "sin" is what Christian theology has traditionally indicated as "original." This term, *Original Sin*, dates to St. Augustine, and one might consider altering it. But the mysterious reality that lies behind those two words needs no revision and should be repeated with insistence. This reality is essential to the faith and is evidenced by the sequence: Adam–Jesus; man's sin–Christ's redemption.

Few aspects of Christianity have been as thoroughly rejected by modern culture as "Original Sin" (or however one wishes to call it), all based on the presumption of man's innocence, all convinced that the one true evil is to talk about evil. This denial is so violently hysterical that it raises suspicions about what lies hidden behind it.

Running to the aid of the many who claim innocence (it goes without saying) are the usual carefree theologians, those superficial, soft-hearted clerics whom we have already met, convinced that, between modern humanism with its tragic consequences and the Christian vision of man, the differences are only in the details, the fruit of trivial misunderstanding easily unmasked with an appropriate "revision".

But precisely here, on sin, the "great chasm" (Luke 16:26) that separates faith in Jesus from faith in the various modern myths opens wide. It will be worthwhile to return to this issue with adequate attention on a later occasion, if time and strength permit. I shall not attempt today, however, to analyze a matter such as this, so imprudently forgotten, yet so decisive. Here more than ever, it is better to be informed than to ridicule oneself *("ils rient de ce qu'ils ignorant")*, careful not to exchange belief in Original Sin for the usual, naïve Christian fairytale, adapted for children, illiterate peasants, and the mentally ill.

> Adam's sin is folly in the eyes of men, but we present it precisely for that reason. You must not reproach me, therefore, the defect in reason of this doctrine, because I consider it precisely for this

reason. Yet, this folly is wiser that all the wisdom of men. Nothing is more incomprehensible than Original Sin; but everything becomes incomprehensible if one denies it.

Thus reasoned Blaise Pascal in the seventeenth century, one who could not yet imagine how the following century would render much less absurd this aspect of the faith by unleashing the infernal disasters that distinguish modernity.

It is certainly possible to lampoon the "old myth of the apple and the serpent," especially if one ignores that what really matters to faith (and therefore what the Christian must believe) is not necessarily the historical existence of a man named Adam and a woman named Eve. What matters to the faith is what those "symbols," those "myths" (symbols and myths are false only to the crude modern rationalist in the West, while for every other culture they are truth of a higher order) signify: a mysterious fracture, a deviation, a rebellion against God's plan from the beginning of history.

Those who are aware of what the faith has to tell us in the first pages of Scripture, who know man and his heart and his history, can in the end discover that the real dupes are those who boast of being free of the "repressive taboo of sin," as they say with disarming superficiality confused for intellectual profundity.

One who seeks and reflects can discover that Original Sin is not only essential to the faith (and this holds for too many Christians today who deny or ignore it) but that without it, Christ the Redeemer and Savior is reduced to a random "Mr. Jesus," a wiseman, a moralist, a protester like all the others, so bland as to risk a Nobel Peace Prize or an award from the UN, or any other costly hypocrisy of the sort.

But one who seeks and reflects can discover that to take into account the hypothesis of Original Sin can be essential beyond the faith as well for anyone who wants to understand the tragedy of every man and of all history.

> The doctrine of Original Sin and of man's sin in general is perhaps the only Christian belief that can be verified empirically, almost scientifically, by anyone who looks with impartiality inside and around himself; by anyone who looks at malice which, kneaded into good, is at the bottom of his heart, and at the wickedness, mixed with heroism, he observes in history.

Thus, Reinhold Niebuhr,[47] the American theologian and exponent of one of the most optimistic and self-righteous cultures in history.

According to the faith, death is therefore a catastrophe of such proportions that God Himself would have to suffer and die to vanquish it with His Resurrection.

Original Sin, this mysterious reality from the beginning of history, and the innumerable sins that have followed that first one, separate man from God. It is precisely this separation that constitutes death: spiritual death, first of all, of which physical death is only the sign. According to faith, many who seem to be alive are actually dead, even when they do not realize this; and many of the dead are more alive than the living.

I say "many of the dead" because, if for some the terrible possibility called Hell has become a reality, then they are truly and radically dead, though alive enough in some mysterious way to suffer eternally their definitive no to Love: it is the damned, in fact, that sin (and therefore death) has vanquished in a total and definitive manner.

Sin = death: in this link identified with such clarity by the biblical tradition, and only in this, there are truths that elude only those not wanting to see them.

It has always been evident that sin (personal and social) has not only a vertical dimension visible to the believer, but also a horizontal dimension quite evident to all: it generates death under the form of homicides, wars, exploitation, injustice, and violence of every type, among which we count today even the poisoning and polluting of the earth and of men.

But, in the link between sin and death pointed out by faith, there are also less evident depths that only now we have begun to discern with amazement. "He who does not love, remains in death," observed the Apostle John (1 John 3:14). Today we know "scientifically" that it is the failure to love (which is hatred, and therefore sin) that hides behind so many of our predicaments, so many illnesses and so much death. Today we know, "scientifically," that to love and therefore to oppose sin, heals, brings life. George Vickers, the great English psychologist, says what in thousands of forms is confirmed by a crowd of his colleagues: "The most significant discovery of modern science is perhaps the power of love to protect psychophysical health and to re-establish it."

---

[47] Editor's Note: Reinold Niebuhr (1892–1971) was an American reformed theologian.

The rosy future of psychosomatic medicine unmasks the arrogant blindness of Enlightenment medicine that beholds man as a mere complex of chemical reactions and laws of physics, to be cured just like one might fix a car. Psychosomatic medicine teaches instead by concrete experiences that though illness manifests itself in the body, it is born in the spirit.

The new physicians know that love gives life, and that sin (always a form of not-loving) gives death. It is the lack of harmony in the spirit that breaks the equilibrium of the body and its functions.

It seems that even cancer, this scourge of our century that does not believe in sin, is often nothing but sin: the rebellion of cells, gone crazy because of the violence that man commits against his profound vocation when he orients himself (or is forced to orient himself through the pressures of a merciless society) toward hatred of self and others. We speak not in a moralistic sense, clearly, but of an unconscious "fault," an erroneous attitude toward the appeal to love hidden in the very structure of our being.

While the white coats of the pharmaceutical multinationals (pathetic alchemists without the secret wisdom of alchemy) hasten in search of the miraculous pill or injection capable of destroying the tumor, an oncologist was forced to notice:

> We shall never know how many evils, even physical ones, Christianity helped man to avoid, exhorting him to love, to pray, to forgive offenses, to find peace with himself and with others. It is nevertheless a fact that the curve of cancer and heart attacks continues to grow more and more, especially in the countries where the curve of the religious vision of life has diminished to the point of disappearance.

Chance? Who knows. We do know, however, that in its profound logic, every language has always used the same term — corruption — to indicate the effects of both sin and death: moral corruption leads to the corruption of the body and death.

According to faith, it is not death as a biological fact that is linked to sin. It is certain that in the unfathomable plan of God, even without the Fall of Adam, there would have been for man some sort of death, a passage to some form of life that is different and superior.

Sin does not lead, therefore, to death as a serene, natural, biological end to a cycle, a sort of transformation. Sin leads to death as a tragedy, a painful rupture, as an experience of loss and anguish. Sin imprints on dying the sneer we recognize: from a natural fact, it transforms it into a punishment, binds it to solitude, because guilt breaks communion with God and, through Him, with all creatures.

Death, *this* death, is unbecoming of man; it does not fit into the original plan of Creation. It is the greatest of catastrophes, in the etymological sense: an overturning, an upheaval.

For this reason, the Church reacts against all those who, though they might call themselves believers, trivialize death, making of it a false problem. The Church condemns *materialism*, which reduces this drama to something obvious and natural, but also condemns so-called Christian spiritualism, which considers death an easy, peaceful passage from an "inferior" life to a "superior" one, as if it were simply a matter of opening a door, relieving oneself of the burden of the body.

Such a vision is not Christian because it is not biblical. According to faith, the end of the body's physiological activity is not in the least, as Plato wanted us to believe on the heels of Socrates, the joyful liberation of the soul imprisoned in the flesh: *soma–sema*, the body is a tomb, according to the ancient Greek play on words. It is, rather, the end of man, who only by means of that "flesh," so despised by the spiritualists of every sort, but not by the Bible, can live with himself and with others. Thus, for Paul, the body is not a tomb but, if anything, a temple (1 Cor. 6:19).

Only the divine omnipotence, the mysterious and irresistible force that emanates from the Resurrection of Christ, can remedy that radical disaster. To trivialize death is to trivialize the promised resurrection as well, which is not only the crowning of our expectations but also a stunning reversal. Resurrection was not obvious or normal, but rather an unforeseen twist of divine creativity.

Thus, in the face of my own death and that of my loved ones, the exhortations "do not remain in doubt," "be renewed in your faith," "be fully convinced that what he has promised he is also capable of bringing to fulfillment," in other words, exhortations to believe in the final, general resurrection of the body, are not (forcefully emphasized by Paul as we see in these expressions) an easy surrender, a cheap confidence. It is, rather, the incredible *spes contra spem*, hope against all hope (Rom. 4:18).

ON THE MOUNTAIN

The believer looks to the behavior of Jesus as his only model. "I have given you an example, that you should also do as I have done to you" (John 13:15).

Now, confirming that the end is catastrophic, Jesus' attitude in the face of His death is the opposite of the Stoic master. Fortunately, Jesus is not Socrates, who calmly drinks hemlock, strolling with his disciples speaking in elegant phrases all the while, awaiting the poison to take effect. Neither is Jesus the hero of patriotic rhetoric or a political martyr who faces his agony and death in a mixture of temerity and fanaticism.

Remember to be wary of every gold medal hero: behind them there always lies something unspeakable, a dark neurosis. This is not my opinion, but is stated in psychological studies of the "brave," the volunteer in war, the political "martyr," the one who (as generals and parliamentarians say in posthumous commemorations) "in the name of the ideal, despised danger and death." In reality, according to reliable psychologists, the poor man was just as terrorized of death as the others but resolved his problem by running toward and seeking out death in company, in the exhilaration of an assault (no drug is stronger than risk and danger) rather than in the much more difficult solitude and normalcy of his bed. At any rate, even before modern "experts" gave their verdict, already in the seventeenth century La Rochefoucauld, the French moralist, suspected that "whoever despises death is afraid to look it in the face."

No, Jesus is not like that. Before the tomb of His friend Lazarus, before the suffering of His relatives, John says, "he was profoundly moved," "he was upset," "he broke out in tears."

He was moved, He was upset, He cried in front of the two whom He called back to life, according to the Gospel: the son of the poor widow of Naim and the twelve-year-old daughter of Jairus, the head of the synagogue. Three people reanimated, all three young: the scandal of dying is to Him even more intolerable when it strikes those who have only just begun to live.

But Jesus is at the extreme opposite of the apathy and the temerity of one suspected of heroism, not only in the face of the death of others.

He is deeply troubled in the face of His own death, insofar as He is a man (and the faith declares Him to be fully man, as well as "true God") He wanted to live, not to die. And as a man, He cried out in desperation on the Cross, "My God, my God, why have you forsaken me?" In the first three Gospels, He alludes to the prospect of His violent end a full nineteen times. "I have a baptism to be baptized with; and how I am constrained until it is accomplished!" (Luke 12:50).

When the end is near, the night on the Mount of Olives in Gethsemani, He "prays in anguish"; "his sweat becomes like drops of blood that fell to the ground"; He addresses the Father as *Abba* (papa), reminding Him that "all is possible to him," imploring Him to "take from me this chalice." He even rebukes the disciples who were not able to stay awake even in the hour of His anguish. Death is the enemy, and He wants to be surrounded by life.

"In the days of his flesh," comments another New Testament text, the Letter to the Hebrews, "Jesus offered up prayers and supplications, with loud cries and tears, to him who was able to save him from death" (5:7).

Domine humanissime! So shouted the medieval mystic, meditating on this extreme mystery.

Of the many unprecedented parts of the Gospels, that of Gethsemani seems truly the most extraordinary. Here we get a taste of true history that goes in search of signs of credibility in the Gospels. How could one invent a God like this one? It is already quite improbable that God would become man only to suffer for men and thus to liberate them from death! But would He become man to such an extent as to be anguished and stunned by the prospect of His death as a criminal condemned to die? On the night before their execution, the anarchists and communists in *The Wall* (the celebrated tale by Jean-Paul Sartre), awaiting the dawn and with it their death by firing squad, tremble, rave, urinate, and vomit, similar in some ways to the night on the Mount of Olives near Jerusalem.

"I believe Jesus never complained if not in Gethsemani," noted Pascal. "He sought company and comfort from men. It seems to me the only time in all His life."

Unique, as well, we might add, in the history of all religions: no one would have lowered his God to the point of risking to confuse Him with a coward. In his last hour, Socrates continued to pose as a master of wisdom to his followers; Jesus, on the other hand, asks for solidarity, trembling and imploring, from those uncouth commoners who follow Him and who soon would betray, renounce, and abandon Him. Above all for this humanity of His, He is "the true

God for men," as another phrase of Pascal insists. In the words of the contemporary exegete Oscar Cullmann:[48]

> Jesus is not afraid of those who will come to kill Him, nor the pain and suffering that precede death. He fears death as such, because it is the great power of evil. To Him, death is the rupture of the divine plan: for this reason it is so horrible.

If death is a friend according to the Greeks, the schools of wisdom and religions, to Jesus and for Christianity it is instead the "ultimate enemy" (1 Cor. 15:26). Like sin whose cause is something contrary to nature, opposed to God's project, death is a curse due to a fault. Here, there runs a dividing line between the Gospel and other messages: you must decide which one is closer to the truth.

The words of Professor Perrin from the Union of Atheists merit attention. He speaks of the "cowardice of Christians in the face of death, following the bad example of Jesus." We who feel a bond with mankind and not with superheroes find this cowardice to be just fine; we would have no other protagonist in the Gospels. "In fact," it is written:

> Because he himself has suffered and been tempted, he is able to help those who are tempted.... For we have not a high priest who is unable to sympathize with our weaknesses, but one who in every respect has been tempted as we are, yet without sinning. Let us then with confidence draw near to the throne of grace, that we may receive mercy and find grace to help in time of need (Heb. 2:18, 4:15–16).

CHRISTIAN-CRETIN

There are those in the Church who would like to hide this. There are those who admit it under their breath. Yet, it is a fact: the word *cretin* is directly derived from *Christian*. This derivation is even more evident in French where the difference in pronunciation between *chrétien* and *crétin* is made only by an *i*.

All agree that *cretin* in English, *kretin* in German, *cretino* in Spanish, and so forth, are part of a significant phenomenon that involves the Slavic and Eastern languages as well.

---

[48] Editor's Note: Oscar Cullmann (1902–1999) was a French Lutheran theologian.

But why, according to the infallible warning light of language, is the Christian a cretin? Why, from the very beginning, did they believe as much as can be read in the Letters of Paul? Paul, in fact, instead of becoming indignant, admits that it is true: yes, one becomes a Christian because he entrusts himself to "nonsense."

The fact is that we have become obtuse through habit: we are no longer aware of the shocking uniqueness of the gospel. To take this book seriously is not only to believe that God manifested Himself in a man; it is not only believing that that man was a subject in the most despised province of a proud, pagan empire; it is not only believing that that subject was moreover an uneducated, poor manual worker who popped out of an obscure, reviled village ("Can anything good come out of Nazareth?" John 1:46).

Beyond all this, believing in the gospel is also believing that this story, so improbable, did not have a happy ending; in fact, it had the worst of all possible outcomes. It came to an end on the *taeterrima crux*, as the classics called it with horror, on the most infamous torture instrument invented by human sadism, on the cross that so repulsed the ancients that it took Christians centuries before they dared to draw it. Their adversaries drew it, however, as a sign of derision, portraying a donkey nailed to the cross.

Is it not perhaps the act of a "cretin" or an "ass" to kneel before that disgraced man degraded officially by the cross (sanctioned by Roman law) from a person to an animal, a thing? This debased, demoralizing image of God is in fact a *scandal*, intolerable for the other monotheisms: for Islam with its inaccessible Allah, but also for Judaism with its Yahweh, so near to Israel and yet so far that not even His name could be pronounced.

It is a pathetic *illusion* for all the Asiatic religions, beginning with India: just as the poor cannot help the poor, so too the suffering cannot help the suffering.

It is unrefined *foolishness* to the religions of the philosophers, those deisms which Pascal could not forgive because they envisioned a God who limited Himself to giving "a push" to the world to set it turning and then left it to dedicate Himself to His own business. Each for his own, and God for no one.

It is a vulgar *barbarity* to historians of religions who classify Christianity among the very lowest types of worship, inferior even to the mediocre level of the late Roman Empire, which at least, wanting to adore a man, chose the emperor, not one of his dishonored slaves.

True, all true: to recognize God in Jesus, a Galilean carpenter, is a scandal, an illusion, foolishness, a barbarity. It is true. Or perhaps, considering the matter, it *would* be true, if we lived in a world without the cross. God nailed to a beam seems scandalous, illusory, foolish, and barbarous to us, but only until we too find ourselves nailed to sin, suffering, evil, and death.

When this discovery occurs, and sooner or later it happens to us all, then we can agree with St. Paul: faith in that man condemned to death is *stultitia*, the foolishness of cretins. It is absurd that "while Jews ask for miracles and Greeks seek wisdom," we preach "Christ crucified," which is nothing but "scandal for the Jews and foolishness for the pagans." Yet "to those who are called, both Jews and Greeks, Christ the power of God and the wisdom of God." Because in the suffering one, Paul observes that "the foolishness of God is wiser than men, and the weakness of God is stronger than men" (1 Cor. 1:22).

All the Christian *artes moriendi* insist: the sick must be able to see a crucifix from his bed. It is an indispensable condition, suggested by the direct experience of those authors, nor can one find fault in this.

Beyond this death, is there any other worldview that can say as much to one who is dying? "Only the God who suffers can come to our aid," repeated Dietrich Bonhoeffer from the depths of his cell, quoting it seems the Letter to the Hebrews: "For because he himself has suffered and been tempted, he is able to help those who are tempted" (Heb. 2:18).

Hans Küng comments this as well:

> The love of the God of Jesus Christ does not protect me from every suffering. It protects me in every suffering. I can and must rebel against a God who sits enthroned in undisturbed beatitude or in apathetic transcendence. But I cannot rebel against the God who in the suffering of Jesus has revealed to me all His compassion.

The Gospel replies to the mystery of suffering and death that follows it everywhere, by proposing the greatest of mysteries: *Deus patiens*, the suffering God. This is not an explanation of the enigma of evil. It is, however, an example; it is the presence of a God who did not choose to destroy our cross but laid Himself upon it — a God who therefore has the right to say the efficacious words, "Come to me, all who labor and are heavy laden, and I will give you rest" (Matt. 11:28).

We must not forget: Christianity is not mere words, but facts. Now, death is a fact, the most concrete and terrible of facts. You can search anywhere, but you will find only the Christian response which opposes that fact with another. Not ideas, not vague worldviews, not astute dialectic, not even refined techniques, but the concreteness of the paschal mystery, of the Passion, death, and Resurrection of a man. The one who, as the Creed says, "suffered under Pontius Pilate," "died and was buried," and who, "on the third day rose again."

Suffering and dying, when they are emptied of meaning and hope, neither elevate nor ennoble. They simply demean, throwing a shadow of absurdity over the happiest of lives.

Suffering and dying in this way are neither beautiful nor good.

Suffering and death will never become "beautiful," but can mysteriously become "good" if lived with a Person (no other has been given) who suffered, died like us, with us, to point to an empty tomb beyond the catastrophe, to indicate a light beyond the "darkness over all the land" (Matt. 27:45) that sooner or later will fall on us all.

"And In His Will"

Behold the crucifix: Christian art of good suffering and of good dying, it is full of wisdom, hidden or obvious. We shall seek to shed light on some of it here.

Keeping one's eyes fixed on the suffering Jesus means imitating Him when He ended up prostrate with His face to the ground, praying: "'My Father, if it be possible, let this cup pass from me; nevertheless, not as I will, but as thou wilt.' ... Again, for the second time, he went away and prayed, 'My Father, if this cannot pass unless I drink it, thy will be done.'" (Matt. 26:39–42).

These are the same words ("Thy will be done") as in the prayer He once taught His followers: the Our Father. In fact, the cause of the unbearable face of death is sin, but this is non-obedience, rebellion against the will of God: "The reason why sins are sins is solely this, that they are contrary to what God desires" (Pascal). But death can become bearable, or even hiddenly fruitful only in the contrary of sin, namely in obedience, in free submission to the plan of the Creator for His creatures.

These same conclusions were reached by Paul, writing to the Romans: "For as by one man's disobedience [Adam] many were made sinners, so by one man's obedience [Christ] many will be made righteous" (5:19). Jesus is the Christ, the Savior of men, because, as He reveals to His disciples, He accepts to eat a food that we so often refuse: "My food is to do the will of him who sent me" (John 4:34). If the Father exalted Him and gave Him the name that is above every other name, it is because "he humbled himself and became obedient unto death, even death on a cross." So says the ancient hymn that Paul found in the primitive liturgy and hands down to us in the Letter to the Philippians (2:9).

There is then a mysterious bond: between the free assent to the defeat represented by death and the final victory of life; between the obedience to the Father and overcoming the Cross.

These are not the usual academic discussions; these are not merely theological theories, innocuous as they are useless. As always, there is here a truth that only faith can penetrate entirely, but something transpires from everyone's personal experience.

We return to the investigations into the experience of the dying: it emerges that the greatest desperation (unfortunately almost always not overcome until the very end) explodes in those who always presumed they could do whatever they wanted, follow their own will; in those who deluded themselves in thinking they held their lives in their own hands (and perhaps the lives of others); those who granted obedience only to themselves.

Are not sickness and death, by definition, out of our control, escaping our domination? Do they not always demand obedience? Is not "to die" the passive verb par excellence? For this reason, the death of the powerful has always been terrible and desperate: habituated to being in charge and to being obeyed, they discover for the first time, when it is already too late, that there is something stronger than them.

It happens, however, that the dominant mentality has now succeeded in rendering everyone's death despairing, even for the anonymous, as it once was only for those unfortunates called "VIPs."

Indeed, Marxism encourages its own to see all life as a struggle, at least until they take power (then they become conservative and repressive). This ideology proposes as the unsurpassable model the rebellious, the "global protestor." "Continual struggle" is not only the name of a movement of Italian communists, but also a code word that identifies an entire mentality. Unfortunately, life is a struggle that we wind up losing, always. There are no resistance movements that can hope to prevail here.

On the other side, the "spirit of capitalism" also preaches a continuous struggle, of course, but a struggle to be the masters of one another. Life here is a battle of all against all to reach the success that has become an absolute value: success is always in the right. Yet death is failure in ambush, even at the end of a long string of uninterrupted successes. Capitalism, in its current radical form, exalts personal autonomy above every other thing, the independence of everyone from everyone (liberating one from every trace of duty), always saying yes to oneself and always no to others, while death requires a yes, nevertheless.

The technocratic mentality, as common in the West as it is in the East, is causing a worsening of this situation, giving the illusion that, if we cannot control something, it can at least be suppressed by technical and scientific omnipotence. This might be true for many other matters, but it remains an illusion in the face of death, which no technocrat can control, let alone vanquish.

If there is so little peace today in the heart of man (and therefore among men, as John XXIII loved to repeat, "there will never be peace on earth until there is peace in each one of us"), it is also because so much violence has been committed we can no longer make sense of the truth expressed in Dante Alighieri's famous verse: "*E 'n la sua volutade è nostra pace*" (And in His will is our peace).

The constant defamation of every form of obedience (not only, as is fair, to the unwarranted will of others, but also to reality itself) has extended to all the cruel death once the exclusive fate of the powerful. Could this also be one of the fruits of democratic societies?

The Church, nevertheless, in her genuine faith, remains firm in the exhortation of the obedient one par excellence; of abandoning oneself like Him to the will not of *any* other but of *the* Other; to trust the Father; to say yes to a plan that often seems impenetrable, but which the faith ensures is for our good. In good and bad, in joy and pain, in life and death, the Church seeks to catch sight of what is called "Providence."

The saints, even the most penitent, have always taught that the highest virtue does not consist in extraordinary sacrifices and holocausts but rather in obeying the will of God as it manifests itself in the little quotidian things. This includes that Last Day, which will be human only for one who will live it with the yes spoken every day preceding it.

A Lesson in Realism

Only here, in the mysteriously reassuring circle of Providence, does obeying the inevitable not mean crushing oneself, but rather rising to walk toward the true realization of oneself.

From the cross, from that symbol of our faith, comes the liberating lesson of the healthy, adult realism that marks Christianity. To the contrary of ideologies, the gospel asks us to make room for reality *as it is*, not *as we would like it* to be.

From left to right, the preaching of the secularized world orders us to try to be happy, always and everywhere. In this way, it creates a mass of unhappy people, because one is always slamming into the limits of the human condition.

The problem today is how to avoid evil, suffering, and death at any cost. Given the fact that there is no possible answer to this question, suffering only increases. Nothing renders live into something harsh like trying to flee life's inherent harshness.

Psychoanalysis confirms this, speaking of "existential frustration" as one of the scourges of our time. It is the suffering that takes hold in one who has not resigned himself to the discrepancy between the dream of life and concrete life.

Different is the question of the believer who, accepting reality without ever losing sight of it, asks himself, "Why are suffering, pain, and death a necessary part of our experience, and how can I make them more bearable and human? Is there a way to face and transform into a positive value the negative that cannot be eliminated from life?"

Thus, to the contrary of the world, faith knows that anyone wanting to flee the cross will find only the cross barren and raw, in its unbearable hardness; that only those who accept it to its bitter end can hope to find consolation and life. Among Christianity's many paradoxes, there is the union between the maximum of realism and the maximum of utopia: awareness of reality without illusions and, at the same time, hope against every hope.

An anonymous prayer recites: "Lord, grant me the serenity to accept the things I cannot change, the courage to change the things I can, and the wisdom to know the difference." This prayer nicely summarizes Christian realism, which, at any rate, is the only practicable way not to render life despairing. Regardless of any faith, is it better to accept freely the inevitable, or better to fear it in anxiety and then, when it strikes, to suffer it by rebelling and cursing? Yet it is precisely to such an agonizing attitude that the infantile refusal of reality (reality that is always a tangle of good and evil), which marks our world today, leads without fail.

If it is evident that there is in the human condition a blind spot that is inevitable, it is equally clear that the continual effort to erode its borders is the duty of every man, beginning with the Christian. Christianity was remiss in this duty for too many centuries, not distinguishing what it could from what it could not change.

Who can ignore how (especially in economic and social issues) what was alterable was often taken for inevitable? Who can ignore that in the face of injustice, oppression, and violence, the Church too often preached resignation, when action was called for? Who can ignore that the sacrosanct Christian realism has been lived by too many believers as a paralyzing pessimism about the possibility of changing anything, especially when things not only could have been but ought to have been changed? It is for having wrongfully extended the blind spot of the inevitable that the Church has merited the accusation of preaching only resignation, of being bound to those who had an interest in keeping the social situation unaltered.

In reality, the Christian is called to fight without ceasing to limit the evil that is within us and in the world. This obligatory task is always sustained by the equally necessary realism of which we have spoken. If certain churchmen have abusively widened the confines of what for human reality cannot be modified, it is not licit for this reason to pass to the opposite extreme, deceiving oneself that all can be changed, that every evil can be expelled from the world. If by chance we were tempted in this way, sickness and death would arrive to disabuse us of such a temptation.

A truly evangelical response to life and its commitments is not only a "yes," it is a "yes, but..."

Faith knows that the necessary work in history will never end until history itself ends, and even then, will still have much to do. Only the Parousia, the final manifestation of Christ, the end and the overcoming of history, will overwhelm every limit.

Only on that day will injustice, pain, and dying cease to be, but not solely by *our* strength. It will be by the power of God, if only based on what we will have constructed.

"Yes, but..." But only at the end, in other words, "every tear will be wiped away," as the prophets of Israel foresaw, and as the New Testament promised in its valediction, the book of Revelation. Until that time, it is useless to deceive oneself: the crucifix is there to admonish that the substance of sin renders laborious and painful our path toward unlimited and definitive happiness.

TESTAMENTS ON THE COMPUTER

In every preceding page we have made soundings which, though insufficient and incomplete, confirm the suspicion provoking us: *Is the truly Christian also the truly human?*

A positive response would be no light matter, given that the new intellectual elite, who present themselves as ambassadors of true "humanism," see as necessary the dissolution of inhumanity, Christian anti-humanism, and Catholic anti-humanism in particular. Theirs is a humanism, according to the elite, that is truly worthy of moderns. But this button of "modernity" requires great prudence.

Is there anything more modern than computers and digital technology? And yet how strange that, precisely from the use of those instruments applied to the human sciences, there seems to come a warning to modernity that, instead of attempting a fruitful but difficult synthesis with the past, has escaped from it as if from an inhospitable desert. Conversely, from those very modern apparatuses there seems to come a confirmation, not theoretical but practical, of the efficacy of the Christian proclamation.

What is happening, then? Treading the new "quantitative" paths, historians have begun to use the computer to collate documents that otherwise would remain beyond the possibility of investigation for the scholar armed with eyes and pen alone.

One of the richest and hitherto least explored historical sources has been digitalized: the collections of wills and testaments that, in some countries, are preserved by law for centuries in notary archives. It is this enormous mass of documents that, more than anything else, allows contemporary historians to reconstruct the attitudes of men in the face of death through the ages.

One of these quantitative historians, Michel Vovelle,[49] has uploaded tens of thousands of testaments from the French region of Provence, all from the eighteenth century. In this period, very few, even among the poor, died without putting down on paper their last dispositions (and often with great anticipation, even as soon as they began their own families). Among the eloquent signs of our day, there is also the demise of the practice of writing wills. Who would ever think of his own death beforehand? Who in this society of ostriches has sufficient strength to consider his own funeral?

---

[49] Editor's Note: Michel Vovelle (1933–2018) was a French historian.

This strength was not lacking in the peripheries of eighteenth-century Provence, where, while in the cities the enlightened were already raging, the *societas christiana* survived intact, with its good and its bad, with its profits and its losses.

In the profits column, without a doubt, is the conclusion of the historian Vovelle. "These testaments," he writes:

> Give the extraordinary witness of a society that had made peace with life and death as perhaps never before and certainly never since. They testify to a realistic, adult society where no one, whatever social class he belonged to, seemed to give in to the temptation of hiding what cannot be erased.

Our scholar continues:

> All testaments begin with a phrase written in one's own hand (if learned) or by a notary (if illiterate). It is a phrase that (after the invocation to the Trinity: *In nomine Patris et Filii et Spiritus Sancti*) invariably says something like: "Considering that nothing is more certain than death, nothing more uncertain than its hour; I, the undersigned, dispose here my last will and testament…" Everything is regulated beforehand, in simplicity and peace, without fear and without morbidity. And everything is pervaded not by desperation and not even by apprehension or fear, but rather by hope, indeed often by restrained joy.

That was a society of men who died surrounded by their loved ones and who could say to each of them a simple, incredible word: "*Goodbye!*" It was a society in which the deathbed did not represent an object of repulsion to be hidden, but a tenured chair. The dying, after having asked and given forgiveness to those present, gave his blessing. "He could be an old wretch or a young person," observed Philippe Ariès, "yet everyone in those moments was clothed in sovereign authority by the power of the nearness to the mystery of death and therefore to truth itself."

That last eighteenth-century glimpse of Christendom, continues Vovelle, is also displayed in the testaments, as "dying was truly a collective, social reality before the following century, the nineteenth, displaced it from the great framework of the entire community to the enclosed circle of the family." Social solidarity was pushed to the point of creating orders, congregations, and confraternities whose primary task was praying without end for the dying.

Thus (the computer speaks), after so many centuries of Christianity proposed and at times imposed, at least they had arrived at this: reconciling man with his life and death, uniting him in profound and total solidarity with others, participants in his same destiny.

Bertrand Russell[50] said, "I believe that in the entire calendar there is not one saint whose sanctity was due to some socially useful work." Forget any other consideration that might distract us from our reflections. One must ask of Russell, was this vision of life, which urged not only the few saints but also the mass of normal faithful to feel liberated "from anxiety and fear," to find themselves pervaded by hope, and perhaps "restrained joy," truly a vision without social utility?

Was the message truly useless and harmful, this vision that, despite everything, had created "a realistic and adult society," according to the documents?

According to Ariès, the Church in its preaching and its liturgy was able to give to death a "style." This truth has been historically documented, and not only from archival records.

Decades have passed, but those who lived back then still remember the days of the first "public death" of a pope, John XXIII. Although seen through the deforming lens of mass media, that agonizing though mysteriously peaceful death gave millions of people, believers and non-believers, more comfort than anguish, to the point of disturbing (according to what he said) the brutal and crass despot in the Kremlin, Nikita Khrushchev.

But giving death a style is not everything. Socrates had said that "the task of philosophy is to die." Jesus and His Church, in accordance with His word, go far beyond every philosophy: they tend toward not merely the art of dying, but the art of dying in order to live. What they teach is a style for rising again.

What remains to be said here is situated in the scenario of eternal life.

---

[50] Editor's Note: Bertrand Russell (1872–1970) was a British philosopher and mathematician.

DEMOCRACIES

"During the life of her children," it has been said, "the Church can show herself strict and harsh. But on the deathbed she reveals her motherly countenance, affectionate and inspiring trust."

This is precisely the opposite of the world, where so often friends disappear when misfortune strikes, or if they remain faithful, must flee from a sight that cannot be tolerated. It is not a question of goodwill, but of psychological impossibility.

I once spoke with a hospital chaplain. He was one of those churchmen who can perhaps reconcile you with an institution whose shadows you see all too clearly, and who, above all, can lead even those far off to enquire into the mysterious force that is behind the institution.

That elderly priest confided to me that, thanks to a lifetime's experience, he had learned to read in the eyes of the dying, in those hours when cognizance is spasmodic and weakness impedes speech:

> I can often understand what is in their eyes: whether anguish or trust, or something else. Because only by distinguishing one inner state from another can one find the words that help: the person who is afraid needs consolation, the desperate person hope, the one who already feels secure must be confirmed in his feeling. Just as no single life is the same as another, so too death is different for all. And so, to help the dying, it is not enough to be a psychologist; one must allow one's heart to lead him.

Perhaps more frightened than admiring, I listened to his magnificent words, spoken with a simple, subdued air. Thanks to that tone of normalcy, he bore witness to an abnormal strength. Who among us (beginning with the author of this book), seeing the splinter in our neighbor's eye and not the beam in our own, would dare to look at death, literally, in the eyes? Who among us would have the courage, buoyed only by the desire to help a stranger from whom we expect nothing in return, not even a word of gratitude?

And yet, that help, so impossible for man but so indispensable, the Church has placed at the disposition of all; she has rendered it "institutional." She has not only entrusted it to charity, to the heroism (which could be lacking) of her children, but has entrusted it to a liturgical system hinged on facts called "sacraments."

Here, much more than elsewhere, is one of their claims to glory, if glory is allowed to Christians.

It is undeniable that, in her millenary history, the Church has offered everyone the strength that passes through her, but which does not come from her, but which infinitely exceeds her. The Church has helped not only the rich and privileged to face death — in fact, the gospel was meant to disturb them. The Church manned the courts of princes with her astute counsellors, she sent her chaplains to serve the most ferocious of despots. But true history was made by the billions of people who lived in obscurity and died in obscurity. It is the history of poor parish priests in poor parishes. The Church has been made above all by unknown pastors for anonymous flocks of illiterate Christians — with many like Don Abbondio, certainly, but also with not a few temperaments like Friar Cristoforo.

Beyond the few royal palaces (beginning with the Vatican), where worldly clerics intrigue and plot, the reality of the last twenty Christian centuries is that of poor men at the service of other poor men.

There were also cardinals, the lavish princes of the Church, unapproachable in their palaces and whose wardrobes were worth unimaginable sums. But there were above all (though they never made the news) those missionaries spoken of in the old reports, who crossed the Europe of the *ancien régime* on foot, dragging on their shoulders like a cross a confessional to bring the forgiveness of Christ to the peasants who were ashamed of revealing their sins to the village priest.

For the last two centuries there has been no easier target more aimed at than the Catholic Church. To defame it costs nothing; if anything, attacking it procures advantages and prestige from presumed anti-conformists. But matters are always more complex than certain controversies would make them seem: people have been extorted by churchmen, people have been refused help or helped very little, perhaps discouraged from changing their social conditions. But contrary to what modern ideologies think today, there exists not only economic poverty. There exists poverty and wealth of another order, as well.

Jesus was moved in the face of the hungry and multiplied loaves of bread and fish to feed them. But the same Jesus was said to have felt "compassion" for those who are "like sheep without a shepherd," and He "began to teach them many things" (Mark 6:34). Following His example and the order repeated three times to Peter (John 21:15), at least this task of teaching, of "feeding the sheep," has not been forgotten by the Church. Only the unrefined can ignore that it does no good to multiply *things*, forgetting to attach the instruction manual for their proper use. In the end, we might discover that the open arms of those praying were at the service of their brothers just as much as the closed fists of the revolutionaries.

Luigi Firpo, one of the most prestigious Italian neo-illuminists, narrates how he (not a believer) found himself in a church where Mass was being celebrated. According to the efficacious prose of the scholar, the assembly consisted of the following:

> A group of men and women, modest, elderly, with marked faces, bags under their eyes, poorly shaven, grey women with hair hidden by formless caps, threadbare coats turned inside out, traits marked by years of hard living, by nastiness and malignities washed away by the flow of an impotent existence.

A sort of human waste, therefore, that, having received the Eucharist, dared to sing a hymn that stated, "I believe I shall rise again, my body shall behold the Savior." Firpo,[51] this combative believer in "enlightened democracy," comments:

> The contrast could not have been more excruciating between that poor humanity of the vanquished and wretched, marked by obtuseness, by lack of culture, by secret vices, and that hope of immortalizing forever their obscure souls, and the glimpses of a conscience bound for all their existence to the banality and instincts of the quotidian.

Can even such worms, therefore, dare to hope of being taken seriously by God? Dare they hope of not having lived by chance, though they are the opposite of "sublime souls, teachers of wisdom, oceans of culture, treasures of goodness"?

Yes, those worms hope as well, and there are those who have been nourishing that hope of theirs. In fact, the Church teaches that above all for them, for those contemptable masses of rags, for those tangles of "mediocre" sin, not

---

[51] Editor's Note: Luigi Firpo (1915–1989) was an Italian historian and politician.

the least "noble," that even *for them* God died and rose again. The same Church teaches that it is not in the least certain that the many "teachers of wisdom," or the "oceans of culture," will be able in the end to find a spot in the very last gallery of the Kingdom.

Never as in these past two centuries have democracy and equality been so discussed. But only in a shameless time such as ours could one call quintessentially democratic precisely those regimes where the *demos* counts for nothing and, every time it asserts its rights, is massacred without hesitation by those who transformed the dream of the dictatorship *of* the proletariat into the nightmare of the dictatorship *over* the proletariat.

Only in shameless times could one boast of the equality of the so-called "free world" (free, that is, to choose between various labels of merchandise, if one has the money; free to imprison oneself with the greatest number of superficial goods possible), when it is quite difficult to see where the equality lies among the unemployed or wage laborers and the omnipotent Brahmins of the new "master race" in the West.

Concretely, after so many centuries of social struggles, authentic democracy and equality end up being realized only in death, as has been the case since the dawn of history. It is disappointing, I won't deny it, but objectively that's how it is. This is a reality that the Church has understood, practicing democracy in what matters, in the end: giving the same sacraments to all; indicating to everyone the hope of a world finally free and equal — not around the next bend of history, however, but *beyond* history.

Signs, but also Facts

The Church did not stop at merely speaking about hope to everyone, beginning with the "vanquished, the wretched, the obtuse, the uneducated."

A law of Christianity is that of facts. The believer's entire life, in its decisive stages, is accompanied by objective, concrete facts ("signs" that are "perceivable and efficacious," as the *Catechism* says), which are the sacraments, which draw their strength from the fact par excellence: the Incarnation, Passion, death, and Resurrection of Jesus Christ, the Son of God made man.

Baptism at birth; Confirmation as an adolescent; Matrimony at the time of psychosexual maturity. Grace flows by means of these signs, for which the liturgical formula is essential, as well as the material reality (*res*), namely gratuity, the mysterious but concrete divine life that instills supernatural energy, the power one must lean on to live — and to die. Here, in the decisive crisis, Catholicism deploys all of its power of compassion, of instilling hope, of saving by transmitting sacramental grace. It seeks, in other words, to render human even this act so prone to sliding into inhuman cruelty.

For those who have lived under the sign of the primordial sacrament (Baptism), the Church comes to their assistance with its sacraments of Reconciliation (Confession) and Anointing of the Sick (Extreme Unction, as it was once inappropriately called).

The "efficacious signs" placed at the disposition of those who are approaching their end are not two, but three: there is also the Eucharist (Communion), under the form of Viaticum (literally, "the provisions the wayfarer needs to face his journey"). But the Eucharist is not a sacrament like the others: all the others derive from it.

The Eucharist, Vatican II reminds us, is the "source and summit" of the Church herself. And because the Church is (according to the Council's *Lumen Gentium*) nothing less than "the Kingdom of Christ already present in mystery," the Eucharist is, according to faith, the summit of all the universe discerned by that great mystic confused for a scientist, Pierre Teilhard de Chardin.[52]

Thus, the Eucharist is a reality that projects a light that changes every perspective on living and dying, that explodes our poor projects, our temporal distinctions, our geographical coordinates, even our biological principles that distinguish life from death.

On this extraordinary "secret weapon" of Christianity (a weapon that does not bring death but sanctions death's end, the definitive victory of life, beginning now), on this bread, on this wine full of the greatest mystery of the cosmos — on *this* it will be necessary to speak separately, and at greater length. We shall do so in the following chapter, the penultimate.

Here we shall only mention Confession and the Anointing of the Sick, set in the framework of the Church's strategy for life. The liturgy and sacraments were prepared for a human world, but today we neither live nor die in a human world. Today one either dies suddenly (in traffic accidents, by heart attack) or too slowly (devoured bit by bit by cancer, or kept artificially in life for as long as something to devour remains).

---

[52] Editor's Note: Pierre Teilhard de Chardin (1881–1955) was a French Jesuit and paleonthologist.

The disaffection of some priests and their fatigue in liturgical practice come not only from the pressure on believers by a world that censures death, but also from the fact that one appeals to the Church and its assistance in the sacraments (if at all) when it is too late; or better, when the agonizing person has already lost consciousness: "so as not to upset him," one understands, "to keep him from further suffering," as the complicit humanitarian hypocrite murmurs.

In this way, the man who ought to testify with "efficacious signs" the life-giving power of Christ and the brotherly presence of the community of believers is demoted to the bird of death, or a jackal that arrives furtively. It is expected that he trace some magic symbol on the dying, and then return quickly to that anachronistic world from whence he briefly escaped. They think that recourse to the Church is a sort of bureaucratic duty to be discharged "when all hope is gone," as they say. And they do not notice (also the fault of Christians, certainly) that this can be the only way to open wide Hope when all hope has gone.

BE RECONCILED

During his entire life, the believer is encouraged to frequent the confessional to have his sins forgiven. When death approaches, the Church proposes and practices a "general confession" — not the review of a segment of life from one confession to the next, but an examination of one's entire life, one's profound orientation.

Here we mention only the mystery through which, by means of the voice and the hands of a man (perhaps unworthy, always a sinner, yet invested by the divine omnipotence: "Who can forgive sins but God alone?" Mark 2:7) the voice and the hands of Christ Himself reach the penitent, caress him, and assure him he is forgiven.

As happens in every sacrament, this is one of the moments in which the Church acts in a dimension that is not only incomprehensible, but also entirely inaccessible by any other human community, as powerful and proud as it might be. It is in the sacraments that one observes how the often-clumsy ecclesiastical institution is only the façade that covers the mystery of grace.

There is a meaning that only faith can see in Confession: dying to sin and, therefore, dying to death, rising with Christ. To faith, every Confession (every time we ask forgiveness, granted by God and witnessed by a man) is a new start, a rebirth unto life, the freshness of a new day. Every Confession renews the Christian paradox of death and resurrection inaugurated by Baptism: descending naked into the depths of the night to find the light.

Only faith can discern this reality, which only the experience of the believer can confirm. And we know that what interests us here is what can be seen by everyone.

As for what can be seen, we must turn again to the few but rich psychological investigations into the dying.

It has been verified that, when the end draws near, every person, without exception, feels the pressing need to give an account for his life. Everyone feels the need to be understood, accepted, forgiven. And this one cannot do alone: a silent, solitary accounting of one's life is not liberating. Although death is solitary, it also has a social dimension, just like sin.

In those days, in those hours, believers and non-believers need to *forgive* and to be *forgiven*. As psychology is discovering, this is necessary because enmity, resentment, and hatred destroy what mysteriously binds people together.

For this reason, the scales that are both personal and social, giving and receiving, can be weighed only before a man — a representative, that is, of the whole human community.

"In this confessing to ourselves and to others through one similar to us," says a psychologist commenting merely on the human dynamics of Catholic Confession:

> we are welcomed in our situation, just as we are. Entrusting someone with our past, with its good and its bad, we insert our personal matters into a common history, and we are encouraged to accept ourselves with our concrete life. Thus, we can be liberated from the anguished sensation of absurdity, of failure, that always threatens one who sees his end approaching.

This is why the Church calls Confession the "Sacrament of Reconciliation," confirming its character of response to a profound need. Reconciliation with God means reconciling oneself with all His creatures, and with our brothers; Reconciliation means grafting oneself profoundly back into the social body, reconciling oneself with it.

And then, to the desperation that clutches one who is aware of not having done what he could have or should have and knows that his time is up, faith reassures those who, in humility, offer God their empty hands, and admonishes the satisfied, the proud, and the reckless, who believe they can present a balance sheet full of gains. But what in our past deserves to remain will not be forgotten.

A convert, the "obedient protester" Don Lorenzo Milani, said, "Confession is that marvelous institution that erases evil with a wipe of the sponge; the good it does not erase, but rather accumulates it."

The Americans at the Psychiatric Service for the Assistance of the Incurables still hold to a reformist mentality. They are sons of a culture that deceives itself that every human problem can be resolved with the creation of laws, better organization, more financing. And therefore, having perceived from experience that in every seriously ill person there arises the need for Reconciliation, this group has encouraged the creation of a group of "lay confessors." These functionaries, at public expense, and exclusive of any religious dimension, perform the task once entrusted to the priest.

A generous idea. But what will come of those in need when those innovative government employees go on strike for a better contract? And how do they solve the problem of overtime and holidays? Not easy questions, though mostly provocative. There is an authentic drama here: one seeks outside the Church what only the Church can give.

It is impossible, as we have repeated in many ways, to ensure an effective presence at the bedside of a dying person if the one assisting is lacking the essential traits, which are antithetical to a non-religious mentality. "Lay confessors" are inconceivable, as are other naïve monstrosities of that type, in a dimension that by its nature can only be mercenary, subject to the logic of labor unions.

What is needed here is not just anyone, but, as John Henry Newman wrote, a person who, "empowered by his faith, is strong enough to bear us and humble enough not to despise us." What is needed here is that courage, that love that goes beyond us, that gratuitous availability, that faith in another reality to which the words of the hospital chaplain quoted above gave witness. But courage and, above all, faith and love are not foreseen even in the most sophisticated and generous work contracts.

It is always that liminal situation called death that reveals the true depths of things. In this case, it is a matter of the importance of what exists outside of the worldly logic of giving and taking. The tree will give its fruit, and the fruit of the dominant culture is what it is. It is useless, desperate even, to discover men's needs, if men themselves are impotent to give them a satisfactory response.

Perhaps it is better that the insolence of the usual sociologists stays far away from ghettoes of the dying. Here, the usual greetings yelled from blowhorns and the reform programs at party congresses are all out of place. Here there is only one reform possible, which the gospel calls "conversion." And the Church offers it precisely by means of this Sacrament of Reconciliation.

AN ANOINTING

We read in the Letter of James:

> Is anyone among you suffering? Let him pray. Is any cheerful? Let him sing praise. Is any among you sick? Let him call for the elders of the church, and let them pray over him, anointing him with oil in the name of the Lord; and the prayer of faith will save the sick man, and the Lord will raise him up; and if he has committed sins, he will be forgiven (5:13–15).

The Roman Church bases on this exhortation, attributed to the Lord's brother and head of the church in Jerusalem, the sacrament that came to be called by the imprecise name of Extreme Unction, and which Vatican II returned to its biblical denomination of "Anointing of the Sick."

This "efficacious sign" is not reserved to the dying alone, as is the last Eucharist, the viaticum, which is the essential baggage for one departing on the eternal voyage, never to return. In case of life-threatening danger, the renewed liturgy of the council prescribes, in a return to the ancient usage, that the order be: Reconciliation, Anointing of the Sick and finally, as the climax, the Eucharist.

The Anointing of the Sick was thus restored to the scriptural identity it had in the primitive Church: the sacrament for the sick. Every person who is ill is intrinsically linked to death, oriented toward it. St. Thérèse of Lisieux called the death rattle "the murmur that disturbs the sinner and consoles the just and which announces the arrival of the Groom." Infirmity and death depend on the same reality of sin, such that the anointing remains one of the foundations of the Catholic system for accompanying man toward his final destiny.

James assures us that "the prayer of faith will save the sick man," and that the Lord, having forgiven his sins, "will raise him up." For too long now, this has lost its literal veracity in the physical sense in which the apostle doubtless conceived it. Some, with good reason, think that this is no longer the case because we ask too little of God, because we do not dare to ask enough of Him.

The New Testament describes the nascent Church as bristling with miracles; believers healed the sick, and according to Jesus Himself, this charism, the gift of healing, was to be a distinctive trait of His followers. Among the signs accompanying those who believe, the Risen One solemnly assures, they will "lay hands on the sick, and they will recover" (Mark 16:18). The Gospel of Luke narrates that when Christ sent His disciples out on mission, He gave them "power and authority over all demons and to cure diseases," then "he sent them out to preach the kingdom of God and to heal the sick" (Luke 9:1–2).

With the passage of time, those extraordinary words were forgotten by all, except for a few saints, by those who take the gospel literally, *sine glossa* (and precisely for this reason are saints). The saints took it seriously and experienced its truth. There is not one beatification or canonization dossier that does not overflow with miraculous healings. Be careful not to laugh: sarcasm is acceptable only from those who have first done thorough research. Irony is appropriate only after having looked into the matter.

We mediocre people, who at best know how to stutter "if you can do anything, have pity on us and help us," in whom faith and incredulity cohabitate, we are resigned (Mark 9:22–24).

We try to justify our hesitation in believing by saying that the time of miracles has passed, that the plan of God for today has changed. Others will say that it is not God who has changed but we the faithful who have changed, because we have allowed ourselves to be saturated by dark rationalism, convinced of the immutability of the "laws of nature," as they are called by those who naïvely attribute to nature all the powers that only the naïve attribute to God, according to them.

The unprecedented surprise, the fantasy, the color, and the hope of the gospel have been chased behind the suffocating, superstitious fate of the ancients, rebaptized by moderns as "scientific thought." It is the despairing Greek trap (Zeus himself is a prisoner of the immutable laws of the cosmos, he cries impotent without being able to do anything against destiny); it is the trap from which the gospel liberated us, and into which many Christians are now falling again, and for this are called "moderns."

Nothing is less modern than this adoption of ancient superstitions. These allegedly modern Christians are the ones who breathlessly toil to "demythologize," to seek to demonstrate that every "miracle" is only a vague symbol because (as a presumed avant-garde theologian tried to teach me) "the scientific laws that support the universe cannot be contradicted by a few impossible prodigies."

Do you see the folly that, in the mouths of Christians, lies behind this term ("scientific"), so often used to intimidate, to terminate every debate? So, we would like to establish God's limits (the great Unpredictable, who is the God of the Bible!), limits that are those of our own ignorance, which we call science? Would we imprison God behind "laws" that only now, after great toil, we have just begun to discern, while under every structure that we erect an even greater mystery opens wide?

"God is the first to subject himself to the physical laws of the world," that priest of Jupiter and fate more than of Jesus Christ and his good news of liberation continues to recite; so, too, is the diktat of the modern theologian, convinced that the true problem with rendering the gospel credible was to purge it of every suspicion of the "extraordinary" — beginning with, let it be understood, the Resurrection of Jesus.

And while the strange but unfortunately not isolated "expert" warmed up in his role as ambassador to what he called "modern science," I thought of the Old and New Testaments, Isaiah in particular, "behold [says the Lord], I will again do marvelous things with this people, wonderful and marvelous," (29:14); and of Paul, who takes up and elaborates the words of the extraordinary Hebrew prayer that says, "I thank you, O God, because you will what you have prohibited." Prohibited, that is, by the scarcity, the misery of our good sense.

Allowing ourselves to be blackmailed by the decrepit and allegedly modern mentality, "we no longer have the courage to believe in Christ living and acting in us. We no longer dare to believe in the effectiveness of prayer, including the possibility of a miracle." This is the disheartened observation of the theologian and cardinal Léo J. Suenens, one of the leaders of the Charismatic Renewal movement, those groups of Christians who rediscovered in the faith the unprecedented explosion that is the triune God, rediscovering the "charisms," the gifts promised to every believer, beginning with the healing of the sick.

Returning to the Anointing of the Sick, although today the "salvation of the infirm" does not seem to find an expression on the physical plane, it is found however always on the spiritual plane. The prayer, and the consecrated olive oil (*res*, the material of the sacrament), are for faith the sign of definitive healing of the entire person in the promised Kingdom.

But then, in the dynamics of this sacrament, is there not perhaps the usual psychological wisdom, a knowledge of man and his needs? Notice, to begin with, how Scripture demands that it be the infirm person who "calls for the elders." Personal initiative is demanded, which helps the one who is suffering, so often closed in on himself and on his pain, to leave his inertia and isolation. In calling the elders, then, there is a realistic acknowledgment of the gravity of the situation, its possibilities, and its risks.

This is the exact opposite of what lies at the base of the modern paths of death: hypocrisy, silence, the theft of responsibility, the diminishing of the patient to a vassal whose duty is to keep silent and obey whatever the specialists command, those masters of liberty, life, and death.

This is the exact opposite, we repeat, from what Christianity proposes: one cannot arrive at the request for the anointing except by passing through truth, through becoming aware of one's own state of soul, nor can one reach that request without a renewed sense of individual responsibility.

To highlight these aspects, the post-conciliar liturgy insists on the necessity of a free initiative of faith: the anointing should not be administered to a person who is already unconscious. In fact, relatives, friends, and doctors fall into grave sin if, through their hypocrisy, they cause the sacrament to be delayed to the point that the agonizing person is no longer in control of his mental faculties. What is desired is precisely to reawaken and to defend around that bed what is most in danger and at the same time most precious: freedom, truth, responsibility.

The new ritual for the Anointing of the Sick forcefully reiterates what the Church has always foreseen but had rarely practiced for many centuries: the sacrament is not only reserved to the dying, and not only to the sick. It is to be administered even to the elderly who desire it — *senectus ipsa morbus*, old age is itself an illness, admonished ancient wisdom.

This wisdom has been abundantly denied, for sure. But who could doubt that the old Christian who, as the new liturgy allows, goes to church with a group of peers to be "oiled" with a double anointing (on the forehead and on the hands, according to the renewed norms) fortunately stands far from the model of "old person" imposed by our times?

That unhappy modern elderly person who does not want to face the death that approaches every day, who, if anything, sees death desperately as the fault of medicine, which has not yet found a remedy for the illness that sooner or later will strike him and will be fatal. That old man setting off toward death, not realistically aware that the Easter morning is always preceded by Good Friday, but blindly angry at the world and its science that is incapable of healing him. Perhaps this old man is jealous of those will come after him, when (don't the futurologists tell us this?) every illness will have been cured.

The old Christian who asks prematurely for "Extreme Unction" (which it is not, because it can be renewed when the moment arrives) is the one who shows that he has not lost the ancient sage awareness of the link between his decline and the sin of the world. He does not connect senility, and its painful aspects, only with the idea of a pharmacological cure to be invented or with a surgical intervention to be tried; he connects it to evil, even moral evil, to be vanquished with the omnipotent power being offered him.

He is a fortunate man: in requesting the sacrament, which the faith suggests, his trust in the support of the infused virtues of the Spirit is implicit. He holds on to that which the world tries in every way to slander, incapable of bestowing them: patience, temperance, courage, perseverance — everything, namely, that forms the secret of knowing how to grow old, how to suffer, and how to rejoice, the secret of dying in order to live.

In his decline, in the pain and in the end that await him, he knows he can count on not only the analgesics and anesthetics offered by the persuasive salesman of the pharmaceutical multinational. He does not place all his hope in the attractive ads of the health clubs, the "gyms for the always fit," which promise that seniors can be happy simply by attaching their signature to a fat membership check.

Above all, that old man is fortunate because he knows what John the Baptist meant when, to those sent by the Pharisees, he responded, "among you stands one whom you do not know" (John 1:26). He knows the significance of Jesus' exclamation to the Samaritan woman by the well: "If you knew the gift of God" (Johnn 4:10).

Faith has opened his eyes to penetrate the sign of bread and wine, to discern behind those trivial appearances the truth of the mysterious and shocking words, "he who eats my flesh and drinks my blood has eternal life, and I will raise him up at the last day" (John 6:54).

That man is fortunate because he knows what is behind the ancient Greek word used to describe the reality of the Eucharist.

Of this we shall now speak.

CHAPTER 14

LIFE AMONG US?

ANCIENT WORDS

WHAT THEN IS BEHIND that sign which is called *eucharistia*? What is behind that thing that the Church offers the believer from the age at which he is able to recognize it, and which she proposes to him every day, until his very last day when it is offered to him as "Viaticum," as provision for the journey without end? What is behind this sacrament from which the others are derived, and which is so relevant that it merits a separate discussion?

Eucharistia comes from the Greek and is a word that is full of significance. Its literal meaning and original usage indicate the thanksgiving of one who has received a precious gift. There is a good reason for saying "thank you": if our faith is correct, herein lies a most unexpected surprise, the most incredible reality.

Let us proceed in order. If you have followed thus far, follow me just a little further. Here your time and attention will be richly rewarded. We shall seek to find life behind the word of a dead language. We shall attempt to clarify the meaning that faith gives to that "ceremony" called (with a term taken from another dead language, Latin) Mass, namely "take leave," from the final words of the celebrant to those assembled: "*Ite, missa est!*"

The Mass is therefore the assembly during which the Eucharistic mystery is celebrated. And unfortunately, it has now become "a less than transparent sign," as was recognized by an Italian catechism.

Here we shall try to wipe off the dust and grime from the stained-glass window to help us understand what the faith intends by that complex structure of gestures and words which are so essential that the Catholic is often defined *tout court* as "one who goes to Mass."

Around the year 150, in an attempt to explain to Roman pagans who Christians were and to rebut their calumnies, St. Justin Martyr could find no better way than to describe the Sunday liturgy. It is extraordinary that what he describes is substantially identical to our Mass, eighteen hundred years later:

> On the day named for the sun, everyone, in the city and in the countryside, gathers in the same place and reads the memories of the apostles and the writings of the prophets. When the reader has finished, the presider delivers a discourse to exhort us to imitate the fine teachings. Then we rise to our feet and we pray altogether in full voice. Then bread with wine and water are brought. The presider elevates prayers and thanksgiving to Heaven for as long as he can, and the whole people acclaim in response: Amen! Then the bread is distributed and the Eucharist is divided, sending part of it to those who are absent by means of the deacons.

Why is it that faith imposes we keep a red lamp burning day and night before the tabernacle where the "reserved Eucharist" is kept, the consecrated bread not consumed by the priests and the faithful during the course of the assembly? The red lamp that the Church has made obligatory seems but a small light, said François Mauriac, but in reality, it is the most powerful of beacons lit in the darkness. It is nevertheless the only light among those that shine throughout the darkness of history, that has never gone out: "It is the *veilleuse*, the nightlight that reassures little children frightened in their room populated by disturbing shadows. And it is thanks only to that little light that, when the moment comes, we shall not fear falling asleep."

Beautiful words, and they ring true to one who shares the faith of their author.

Beauty and truth, which do not seem to be well understood and shared, given that the places where that lamp shines, Catholic churches, are certainly not full of people "giving thanks" but seem almost always deserted, when not downright barred shut to protect them from thieves.[53]

---

[53] According to data provided by the Italian Episcopal Conference (data confirmed throughout Europe and in the Americas), theft to the harm of ecclesial patrimony grows every year at an incredible rate. From the paintings to the furnishings,

ON THE EDGE OF THE PRECIPICE

Accepted or not, convincing to many or to few, it is our task to examine the eucharistic sign with renewed energy. Our project is not an escape into the Heaven of the afterlife, but to remain firmly attached to the reality of this life. And the Mass, the bread and wine at its center, the Eucharist, is it not the utmost of what one can see, hear, touch, and even eat, in this life?

The focus of the investigation must be concentrated here because the host and the chalice might reveal themselves as the concrete objects of our wager with death. Is it only common unleavened bread? Is it merely grape wine confused with something else by means of a sacrilegious, long-standing illusion? Is this not by chance something more, infinitely more?

What if the Church were right in insisting, since her infancy, upon saying the unspeakable — namely, that through the hands that become an instrument of the mystery, those common foods explode in a hidden way from within, such that, under the matter reduced to an appearance is contained, *"truly, really, substantially the Body and Blood of the Risen Jesus Christ, together with his soul and his divinity"*?

> even objects of lesser value, it seems there is nothing that escapes the looting. And it all finds an easy outlet in the thick network of merchants and the crowds of "respectable" clients.
>
> According to law enforcement, thieves are not the old, serious professionals of a former period, who knew how to choose their targets and kept respectfully clear of churches. The predators of today are amateurs, almost always youths from so-called "good families," on the lookout for a little cash to buy drugs, for the dance club, to put gas in their car, for their music, and so forth.
>
> As a result, many bishops are finding themselves obliged to close the churches outside of the hours of worship. This is no light decision: this is the first time this has happened since the time of Constantine's Edict of Milan (the year 313!). Going even further back, it is the first time in history that places considered "sacred" are no longer safe from looting, which has become a mass phenomenon, routine and widespread. This too, then, is an unheard-of fruit of "progressive," "enlightened" society, so scandalized by the barbarity of the "Dark Ages," so derisive toward the uncivilized "savages."
>
> Thus, while in the East the churches are being closed by police order, in the West they are being closed following the advice of the police. The result is the same: at any rate, have we not seen that the presuppositions of the two societies are the same? Every culture gets what is deserves. Our cultures have not only failed to express a credible hope, but have led to the closing (out of ideological hatred or out of fear of thieves) even the places where one might find hope.

And it does not stop there, because He who makes Himself present gives Himself to us as food that assures us of eternal life. Nothing less.

Here, the audacity (or the recklessness) of the faith reaches its nearly unbearable apex.

It is above all in the face of this provocation that one can measure the loss of the gift of wonder, our incapacity to react, whether to be scandalized or to kneel. Yet no religion in the world loads any of its symbols with such upsetting significance. There is nothing else under Heaven for which we are invited to make such a radical, lofty, decisive wager.

It is a wager of such importance that, if the believer is correct, the problem of death changes its perspective completely. The cards are so completely reshuffled that we might discover that we are immersed in *life*—no longer as it seems, death in the midst of life, but as it does not seem, life in the midst of death.

Beware, therefore, more than ever, because if the Eucharist is truly what the faith believes, you have before you a reality that upsets every framework and every appearance, bursting like a powerful missile the boundaries that circumscribe the world and, with it, our lives.

The example of the missile is not random, but rather gives a modern face to the image of one of the ancient Fathers of the Church: "The words of Christ, through the priest, pronounced over the bread and wine (*'this is my body,' 'this is my blood'*), are like a sword that bursts open the cage that imprisons us."

There is a precise reason why Vatican II calls the Eucharist the "summit of evangelization": after this, there is nothing left to proclaim. One can go no further.

We know well that it is not in man's power to give faith to others.[54] We do know, however, that it is in our power to indicate the content of the faith: it is possible to indicate what are the real terms of the wager with life and death that the gospel proposes.

The path has been long, the journey that has brought us to this point full of dangers and adventures. I do not presume to have been an infallible guide. Have I erred perhaps in identifying the tracks in the sand? It is certainly possible, although I insist on hoping not to have dragged you along toward a mirage, but rather to an oasis where there is "a spring of water welling up to

---

[54] Note, however, the timely clarifications we shall make in the last chapter of this book.

eternal life" (John 4:14). Having arrived at this point, the discussion is freed of the risk of subjectivity and becomes objective: it is not my personal opinion, but a concrete fact that there is in this world a community that states it can make the Messiah present, the Christ, the Son of God, God Himself; there is a community capable of being the means for transforming substances that spoil into the vivified and vivifying flesh of the very author of life. Being nourished by this flesh, we too are infected with immortality.

This is the extreme objective of our journey, threatened by the ferocity of ideologies, by the snares of philosophies, by the seductions of cultures, by the competition from other religions.

Hic Rhodus, hic salta.

Here you have arrived at the edge of the steepest of precipices found on the earth. Here you are finally forced to decide whether to retreat or to trust and leap. Would you like to turn around? You can certainly do so, as long as you are aware that nowhere else will you find a similar possibility.

By now you know that it is no use to go knocking on the door of politicians, philosophers, sociologists, scientists, psychologists, and experts of every sort — pedants all, yet condemned to death like all the rest of us, they know no more and can do no more than hang portraits on the walls of the dead or stupefy with their dialectics, carefully avoiding the theme of death.

Among religions, you can find premises of life, hopes that death shall be vanquished one day. That is something, but it is not what you can only find here: not words, but a fact; not more waiting, but a certainty of victory already obtained. Only Christianity indicates in a bit of bread and wine the possible junction between time and eternity, between human and divine, between reality and mystery.

What happens in the Mass? Are all who participate in it deceived to the point of pity? Is it not truly here that the breach is made, the opening toward another dimension, which escapes the senses but is not for this reason any less real? Why, extracting randomly just one letter from a jar containing the names of many of the greatest intellects of history, why would a lucid and modern philosopher like Jacques Maritain write, "The Mass is the most important act that can take place on earth to the point that, even supposing the worst prospects of universal persecution, God will never allow that even for one single day a Mass is celebrated nowhere in the world"?

In whatever way one might spin it, there is no middle ground here. We stand before either the greatest of mysteries or the greatest of mystifications. This is either the place of definitive joy or the place of definitive disappointment.

Hatred of Life

We shall try to point to and awaken scandal, or at least wonder. As usual, we do so with the realism of one who knows that it is not enough to note, to describe, to reason through something. Distinct from the dangerous simpletons who believe themselves to be modern, we are convinced that men are moved not only by reason but also by hidden powers, which are more insistent the more profound are the issues.

We believe that in the Eucharist there lies hidden a mystery that cuts to the quick, even under the rationally incomprehensible fury with which the world has always lashed out against that which is the most concrete possibility of hoping that death is not the ruler of this world. It is a possibility we can accept or reject, but not, as its enemies have always done, ridicule a priori with hatred and derision.

Woe to anyone who forgets that Jesus knows what is inside of man (John 2:25). There is this within man: coexisting with the impulse toward the best in each of us are suicidal and homicidal temptations, our loving "darkness rather than light" (John 3:19).

It must be for this reason that those who in every epoch have defined themselves "friends of the light" (the allegedly "enlightened") have always hurled blind abuse against whomever dared even hypothesize that "the light has come into the world" (John 3:19). It is in this stubborn refusal, this love of darkness and death that the believer sees as the disturbing sign of the devil, the "Prince of Darkness," the sign of sin and the root of death. Let him snicker who will at what seems medieval naïveté, for we shall see in the end who is truly clever.

A "monstrous superstition." This is one of the many definitions this century has given the Eucharist. The fury that ravaged Voltaire is striking, the very symbol of the new culture of luminaries, when (and he returned often to this, like a man obsessed) he writes on Christian faith in the Eucharist: "This is devilry, the last word of priestly insolence and of the imbecility of the laity. This barbarous superstition is a hundred times more absurd and blasphemous than all those of the Egyptians put together."

Usually quite ironic, detached, and playful, at the mere thought of the Mass and of what it might signify, Voltaire was invaded by such wrath that he would "go to Rome bearing arms to punish that brazen priest who took possession of the palaces of Caesar and from there continues to propagate such a vile belief."

This is not an isolated case. Not only intellectuals and polemicists, but also scholars of the comparative history of religions fight to dissolve Christian belief by plunging it into the ambivalent chaos of primitive ritual meals. In the most progressive state, California, in the most progressive country in the world, the United States, growing like mushrooms on a manure pile is the Church of Satan, whose primary aim is to profane by means of sexual orgies the consecrated hosts of the Eucharist. In the land of electronics and space voyages, one finds the phenomenon of Black Masses, in which men vent their hatred toward the Eucharist.

In the rabid, obstinate crusade against every possibility that the Eucharist is true (only faith can reach this conclusion) but also only a hypothesis that can be formulated, we see fully revealed the necrophiliac temptation that, if always present in man, has been ennobled and exalted by modern culture. We have already detected several aspects of this, but it is in the discussion on the Eucharist that this reality is revealed as truly monstrous.

We shall see how the Eucharistic solution is the logical, coherent solution of salvation history: *the maximum concentration of energy in the least amount of space in order to give life*. Has not the coherent solution of the history of the world been to reach *the maximum concentration of energy in the least amount of space to give death*? Is this not an atomic bomb?

You might suspect me of bias against this poor culture, already so harassed. I would not know how; I am not a poet who strings together sensations, nor am I a bad journalist throwing together opinions and not news. I remain faithful to the facts. And here, reflecting upon the mystery of life in which the Christian believes, the facts say that the sinister face of a world that wants to believe itself merry and jubilant stands in sharp contrast.

Here one must inevitably speak of the heart, of symbols, and of the calendar, both those of the Church and those of the world.

HEARTS, SYMBOLS, CALENDARS

Remember that the Eucharist is the heart of the Catholic Church: she "makes" the Eucharist, but the Eucharist "makes" the Church as well. Vatican II never tires of seeking words (summit, apex, source, root, hinge) to reiterate this centrality. "All the sacraments," said the council, "as all the ecclesial ministries as well and the works of the apostolate, are closely united to the Holy Eucharist and are bound to it." Looking into its essence, one discovers that the Church exists above all to celebrate, administer, preserve, and perpetuate this mystery. It is *the* heart of life. Whether it convinces or not, it is nevertheless faith in the presence of the Risen Lord, in a living man who offers His life to all.

Is not the heart of our modern, organized society (Moscow, Beijing, Washington, or anywhere else) a dead man, a cadaver? Are not perhaps the bones of a poor man sacrificed to the glory of power and transformed, certainly with his scarce enthusiasm, into the venerated "Unknown Soldier"? Is not the heart of the state precisely this tomb which, with a significant term, is called an "altar," the "altar of the fatherland"?

This is the altar on which they celebrate their liturgies, they who sent the wretched to die and now use even their ashes to their advantage. Every visit by heads of state ends in the necrophiliac rite of the crown of flowers brought to that "sanctum," while standing all around are the generals whose trade it is to make sure that this tomb is not the last one.

Giving death, at any rate, has always been the way to give life to states; declaring wars and winning them is an infallible remedy for bringing a failing administration out of crisis. And the bloodier the war, the greater the force drawn from it by the one who comes out victorious, sending others to die for him.

Let us move on. The symbol that summarizes all Christianity, the entire Church, is the image of a monstrance with the consecrated host. It is a eucharistic symbol, as believers demonstrated in the catacombs, decorating the tunnels with bread, chalices, fish, clusters of grapes, and other references to this mystery. When, in the Middle Ages, St. Bernardine of Siena wanted to give Christians a sign to place next to the cross, he drew the famous image of the monogram of Jesus on the radiant sun, symbol of the explosion of life in the host.

According to the faith, the Eucharist is the greatest possible hope of union with the Father and, therefore, of union with our brothers in humanity. Not by chance, this reality is called "Communion": communion with God means communion with all other men. "Judge for yourselves what I say. The cup of blessing which we bless, is it not a participation in the blood of Christ? The bread which we break, is it not a participation in the body of Christ? Because there is one bread, we who are many are one body, for we all partake of the one bread" (1 Cor. 10:15–17).

If the symbol of Christianity is the image of the greatest possible unity among men, is not the symbol of the state perhaps that image of division and war that is the flag? The hundreds of national flags are the sign of a divided and belligerent humanity. It is the flag that identifies armies.

Those same statesmen who call a tomb an "altar" call the place where they guard the flag a "sanctum," because one dies for the flag, under the flag, behind the flag. This holds in the East and in the West: sanguinary nationalism as we know it is a typical creation of the modern age, of bourgeois liberalism, but it was inherited by the socialist regimes that arose from internationalist utopias and which have ended in the usual, menacing cult of "patriotism."

The existence of different flags is a painful reality that, instead of being detested, is exalted with rivers of winged words. This is no surprise: "And he said to them, 'the kings of the Gentiles exercise lordship over them; and those in authority over them are called benefactors. But not so with you" (Luke 22:25). Hypocrisy is also a sign of the satanic.

Furthermore, the calendar of the Church revolves around the center, which is the Easter Resurrection, the day on which we commemorate not some fallen hero, but one who is alive and who promises the same life to us, if we unite ourselves to Him. Grouped around that "primordial Sunday" are the other Sundays of the year: "According to the apostolic tradition, it has its origin in the very day of Christ's Resurrection," Vatican II reminds us:

> The Church celebrates the paschal mystery every eight days, in what it rightly calls "the day of the Lord" or "Sunday." ... Sunday is the primordial feast that must be proposed and inculcated to the piety of the faithful, in such a way that it becomes a day of joy and rest from work. No other solemnity shall be given priority over it, because Sunday is the foundation and the heart of the whole liturgical year.

Sunday, continues the council:

> Is the day on which the faithful must gather in assembly to listen to the Word of God and participate in the Eucharist and so remember the Passion, Resurrection, and glory of the Lord Jesus

and give thanks to God through whom we have been "born anew to a living hope through the Resurrection of Jesus Christ from the dead" (1 Pet. 1:3).

Sunday, the day of the Eucharist, is thus a day of joy: the joy of being forgiven of one's sins and therefore liberated from death; the joy of participating in the banquet of life-giving flesh and blood; the joy of discovering that our life, full of suffering and anonymous in the eyes of the world, has infinite and eternal significance for Someone, a Someone who, if he had a desk, would have your picture on it. Sunday, a day of such festive glee for the full life promised and given, that the primitive Church on that day did not pray on their knees, but on their feet, ready to depart; or seated, to bear witness to the nobility of those invited to the table of Christ.

Not only Sundays, not only the "feasts," are for the Church a reference to hope and life, but every day of its calendar it recalls the memory of saints on their *dies natalis*, their "true birthday," not that which the world intends, but rather the day of their death, and so their birth into eternal life. The end transforms into the beginning.

The "new" *calendars*, those of "liberated" societies, first attempted to cancel the weekly cadence of the year, making Sundays disappear, both the bourgeois French Revolution as well as the proletarian Bolshevik Revolution. In the end, seeing the revolt of the masses (Lenin was met with harsh passive resistance when he tried to transform the week into a period of ten days, for the sake of making the people labor a few days more, to the glory of production and thus to his regime), modern societies have surrendered and accepted this Christian inheritance.

This is also an oppressive inheritance because, without the meaning faith gave them, Sundays have become as sad as an empty bottle, or worse, filled with lethal poisons. Modern Sundays are a moment for counting the fallen among those who, in the motorized escape, try to evade themselves and their unsustainable daily environments. If in Christian cultures one celebrated to remember the Risen One and the life awaits us thanks to Him, today we celebrate to forget death and to forget that we too must die. Born as a celebration of life, Sunday has become "the weekend," that idol whose toll of sacrifice we have already analyzed. By tragic irony, the statistics of traffic police throughout the West say that the greatest number of deaths occur precisely on Easter weekend, as the Church is celebrating life.

But Sundays today are not only a problem for the traffic police, but for the police in general: Sundays have transformed from a celebration into a social problem. It is the day on which apparently irrational violence is unleashed by young hooligans; it is a day of dangerous drunkenness; it is a day of hatred, of wounds if not death around playing fields, where fans vent their lust for warfare. It is a day on which more people kill than any other (by involuntary manslaughter on the roads, and by voluntary manslaughter); and it is also the day on which people kill themselves the most, a tragic fact supported by statistics that reach their highest point precisely on the days we insist on calling a "holiday."

And that is not all: over the scaffolding of the once-Christian Sunday, secular society has superimposed its own "holidays," not the celebrations of the people, but those of the elite, in which the powers in office celebrate themselves. Days that commemorate marches, liberations, revolutions, constitutions; days of speeches from a stage or from a balcony for uniformed public officials or in black suits, awaiting the day when the next group in office will impose new secular holidays. In the past century in Italy alone, the calendar has changed at least three times: in the period before Fascism, during Fascism, and then in the post-Fascist period. We resignedly await the next change. Who knows what they will demand we celebrate in the future? More disturbing still is the fact that, while many celebrations change with the regime, some resist every change because they are blessed by all regimes: war anniversaries. Those days that recall death are irremovable; they give the cadence throughout the centuries to the secular calendar, not fearing their cancelation by any government.

Nor do the powerful renounce the highest solemnity of their calendar, the military parade, with the authorities on the grandstand, decorated with flowers, and enthusiastic citizens waving flags while the air is filled with the roar of the motors of tanks and jets.

Do we need to remind you that the most solemn parade in the Christian year was the *Corpus Domini* procession, when the Eucharist was carried through the streets to recall the attention of all not to a deadly threat to those who are guilty of having a different flag, but the offer of life to every man of good will? Need we recall that the Thursday of *Corpus Domini* is among the celebrations removed by the alliance, for once peaceful and in agreement, among factory owners, union leaders, and those "Christian" politicians who dominated Italy, with such enthusiastic results for the faith known to us all?

A Refusal from Afar

On one side, we see heart, symbol, calendar, all with death in the center, and on the other side with life in the center. This is what I see as I examine the matter, not giving myself over to sensations or temptations to nostalgia for some long-lost time. I have said already and I repeat it again here: I do not believe in a golden age of history, neither in the past nor in the future. If anything, I believe in a Paradise that we begin to construct in history, but which exceeds history by far.

I know the concrete flaws of Christianity better than all my predictable objectors. But this takes nothing away from my ability to find objective superiority in the Christian, Catholic *project*, especially when compared with what has taken its place, and regardless of the deformations this project has suffered in daily practice.

But what I see as I examine the facts is also something else, unfortunately: the negation of life that leads the world to the hysterical a priori denial of the possibility that the Eucharist is what the Church says it is, and not only by the laity.

Here even the followers of other religions react violently, not content with merely denying it. Muslims, for example, concerning the Eucharist, shout to Christians to stop "being extravagant and excessive," "not to profane to such an extent the sanctity of God." This is the same protest raised in the Jewish world ever since Jesus first announced His coming.

But the rebellion, the refusal to surrender to the unprecedented scandal of a God who makes Himself food with such concreteness, involves the Christian world as well. From its very beginning, the Catholic Church has had to oppose those who assail it, renewed in every generation, those who would demythologize it, downgrade it to a simple symbol, reduce the Eucharist to human size. It will become clearer how it was Catholic realism, "materialism" almost, that saw in this bread and wine the Body and Blood of Christ, which led so much of the Protestant world to strike out against Rome with the same cries of Voltaire: "Superstition!" "Idolatry!" We shall examine the temptations that insinuate among certain contemporary Catholic theologians, who are too concerned with pinning their limits upon God, establishing what is more convenient, opportune, dignified even for Him and for us.

For twenty centuries the Church has been fighting within and without to keep her hope undiluted. For two thousand years it has been waging the war begun by Jesus Himself when He promised the Eucharist in the synagogue in

Capernaum, when those unprecedented words were first heard: "I am the living bread which came down from heaven; if anyone eats of this bread, he will live for ever; and the bread which I shall give for the life of the world is my flesh" (John 6:51).

Those whom John calls "the Jews" immediately rose up scandalized. By this name, John intends, as was his custom, not only the Jews (was he too not a member of the Jewish people?) but all men "of the flesh," who want nothing to do with *this* Flesh; the men who do not love enough to surrender themselves to hope; the men who give full reign to the temptation to love death more than life, the darkness more than light.

Those Jews, John narrates, "began to dispute among themselves, 'How can this man give us his flesh to eat?'" To which Jesus replied, renewing the provocation, tightening the bond between life and food which He Himself will become. His words are to be read with great attention when preceded by one of these "Truly, truly I say to you" prefaces that mark the most solemn declarations: "unless you eat the flesh of the Son of man and drink his blood, you have no life in you; he who eats my flesh and drinks my blood has eternal life, and I will raise him up at the last day" (John 6:53–54). He then adds, not lessening but reiterating the scandal: "For my flesh is food indeed, and my blood is drink indeed.... He who eats this bread will live forever" (John 6:55). At this point, even the Jews who follow him rebel, saying among themselves, "'This is a hard saying; who can listen to it?' But Jesus, knowing in himself that his disciples murmured at it, said to them, 'Do you take offense at this?'" (John 6:60–61).

It must be noted that it is precisely this offer of life that unleashes the most profound crisis within the group of apostles. As John continued to narrate, "After this many of his disciples drew back and no longer went about with him" (John 6:66). So profoundly were they troubled that the Master, for clarity's sake, had to ask them the radical question: "Jesus said to the twelve, 'Will you also go away?'" (John 6:67).

Simon Peter answered him with the words I have already quoted, but will gladly quote once more, words that best express the cry of us all in the face of the Gospel and that mad, extreme consequence which is the Eucharist. They are words of surrender to a reality that transcends us, that is almost incomprehensible to us, but which still has the mysterious power of the facts to which we must inevitably surrender: "Lord, to whom shall we go? You have the words of eternal life; and we have believed, and have come to know that you are the Holy One of God" (John 6:68–69).

A Hidden Love Story

Let us go forward, then, even if instead of an attentive listening followed by a profound reflection, a trepidatious search, we find only hysterical mocking and dogmatic rejection.

Forward, and I say this for the good of former believers, those Catholics who, if they do not refuse the mystery, have done something perhaps even worse: they have grown accustomed.

There are religious communities that seem afflicted by eucharistic inflation; there are daily Masses and Communions that (at least insofar as it seems from the outside) are performed more out of respect for the rules than from a spontaneous, irresistible interior exigency. In this way, the Eucharist could be considered reduced to a mere morning habit, like breakfast.

Those who go to church on Sundays know the scene of certain Masses that, judging from the faces and the voices, seem so long because faith is so short. Perhaps such Masses are covered by the deadly dust of entrenched habit, such that, bursting forth from those words and those gestures, one finds drowsiness rather than life, interrupted only by the smiling jolt at the dismissal: "Go forth, the Mass is ended." The response of the assembly assumes an ambivalence: "Thanks be to God." Giving thanks, perhaps, not for what just happened within those walls, but for the fact that it has finally come to an end? Thankful for having carried out once more what, with a demeaning term, until recent times was called the "Sunday obligation"?

I am the first in need of being aroused to wonder. It is for this reason that I am reviewing here the meaning of the word *Eucharist*. No, we are certainly not saints, those of us who perceived the blaze of life under opaque appearances and acted accordingly.

While their eyes saw, we are among those who have heard it said (Job 42:5). We do have some mitigating circumstances, however. The Sunday Mass lasts less than an hour, and the week has one hundred sixty-seven additional hours, nearly all filled with messages, stimuli, solicitations that militate in the opposite direction to what in that hour is being announced, celebrated, experienced. In contemporary society, the Eucharist is an erratic, cumbersome blockage, not in the least homogenous with the system. Given its premises, it is on a collision course with it, both when the Scriptures are read and when the mystery is renewed at Consecration. In societies that avidly consume goods and ideologies, the Mass fits in like a gay pride parade in the Florence of Savonarola.

This gives us one more reason for reviewing some of the content of the mystery, first of all for our own benefit. We shall not write a treatise on the Eucharist. This would not be fitting. I have not forgotten the warning of my former mentor: "The secret to boring people is to say everything" (Voltaire). Now, boredom is related to death, while here I would like to speak about life.

Nevertheless, the risk of a treatise is avoided by my ignorance as well as by the lack of something much more important than culture: the ability to love, which is indispensable here. Now more than ever, I ought to confess in the words of Job, "I have uttered what I did not understand, things too wonderful for me, which I did not know" (42:3).

But what I understand, and what I would like to share, is that there is something here that might show itself to be decisive. As a navigator through the nights and fogs of the sea of life, I would like to send a warning out to other navigators: Be careful. If you see little or nothing, be vigilant of icebergs that just barely emerge from the waves. Indeed, as we ought to know by now, the tactic of the Christian God is precisely to hide Himself, to camouflage Himself, to be as discreet as possible.

We turn once more to the words of Blaise Pascal, who, in the tradition of Latin Christianity, was among the first and best to understand one of the central paradoxes of the faith: the concealment of God behind the most unsuspecting disguises.

Usually, I make brief quotations because I know that the eye struggles over long passages between quotation marks and tends by instinct to race to the end. Perhaps because of our thirst for novelty, we have little patience for "used" words, already said by others, even if we have never read them before. Here is one of the exceptions to my rule. The quotation is quite long, but it must be read in its entirety.

Pascal writes:

> If God were to reveal Himself continually to men, there would be no merit whatsoever in believing. If, on the contrary, God were never to reveal Himself, there would be no faith. God, however, usually hides Himself, but at times does expose Himself. Thus, He

remained hidden under the veil of nature which covered Him until the Incarnation. Having then decided to appear, in reality, He hid Himself even more, covering Himself with the humanity of Jesus. He was much more recognizable when He was invisible than when He rendered himself visible! Finally, when He decided to fulfill the promise to remain with men until His final coming, He chose to remain among us in the strangest and most secret concealment of all: the appearance of the Eucharist. This is the sign that St. John in Revelation calls a "hidden manna" (2:17); and I believe Isaiah caught sight of it hidden under those species when, inspired by prophecy, He exclaimed: "In truth: you are a God who hides himself, God of Israel, Savior!" (45:15).[55] That of the Eucharist is truly the most secret, the most impenetrable of hiding places. The veil of nature that covered God has been penetrated by many pagans as well who, as St. Paul says (Rom. 1:20), have been able to know the invisible God from visible nature. Also the veil of humanity that covered Him, in Jesus has been penetrated by heretics who indeed, adore Jesus Christ, God and man. But to recognize Him fully in the Eucharist, under the appearances of bread and wine, is proper only to Catholics: only we are so illuminated by God to such a degree.

Clarifications need to be made regarding the "heretics" according to Pascal: to discover Christ under the appearance of the Eucharist is not only *proper* to the Catholic, but *belongs* solely to Catholics (and, to a great extent, to Orthodox as well, though with some limitations that we shall examine in a moment), to push all the way to the discovery of that presence.

The truth of Pascal's observation remains: In the Christian economy of the concealment of God, it would not be in the least surprising, but rather in conformity with all its premises, if the Eucharistic species were to be His last hiding place. I know this seems incredible. But I also know that the Bible enjoys mocking the "incredible" and the "impossible" of those who consider themselves reasonable, adult, and perhaps quite clever. "It is not very logical on your part," said Victor Hugo to the usual professors, "that what you consider strange, you conclude does not exist." And why not? After all, like the entire faith of which it is a

---

[55] Thus the authoritative Jerusalem Bible renders the word of Isaiah, while the Italian Episcopal Conference translates it: "Truly, you are a hidden God."

synthesis, the Eucharist surpasses reason but does not contradict it. In the end, not only is it not in contradiction with reason, but it is not even in contradiction with the premises of the faith. On the contrary (as we have just seen concerning the *Deus absconditus*), it is a natural outcome.

It is also the logical and natural solution, especially considering it from another point of view: placing oneself on the side of love.

I pronounce this word (*love*) with hesitation, so deformed as it is by the mellifluous emotional kitsch as to be "infamous," as Nietzsche said it rang in his ears — just as it does to my ears or yours.

But what can be done if, for some, Christianity is a mere fairytale, and for others a true story: in any case a story that one must necessarily call a "love story"? The Eucharist, however one wishes to judge it (myth or reality) is the logical climax of that affair.

Like it or not, our allergy must surrender to that word; we must confess that without making an effort to enter through love we will understand nothing of the gospel. "He who does not love does not know God; for God is love," says John in his First Letter, repeating himself immediately afterward, lest he be misunderstood: "God is love and he who abides in love abides in God, and God abides in him" (4:8, 16).

If one does not place himself on the side of love, he can understand nothing of Christianity, and even less will he be able to understand the Eucharist, which is the inevitable climax of the crescendo played in that tone.

John reminds us of this again, this time in his Gospel. Before beginning the narration of the Last Supper, the evangelist sets the scene for what is about to take place: "Jesus ... having loved his own who were in the world, he loved them to the end" (13:1). This is meant not only in a chronological sense ("to the end" of His earthly life), but above all in a moral sense: to the furthest possible extreme, to a summit unimaginable to the coarseness of our hearts, symbolized by Peter, rebel against the Messiah who wants to wash his feet.

WOMEN

I am delighted to have discovered that it was thanks to the struggle of a woman, St. Giuliana of Cornillon, that in 1264, the Church decided to include in the liturgical cycle the feast of the Eucharist, of the "Most Holy Sacrament": the solemnity of *Corpus Domini*, characterized by the procession mentioned above.

To the contrary of us men, so often blinded by mortifying mirages of power, glory, money, or even simply hindered by the filter of a false modesty, I do not believe there is a woman in the world who is ashamed of confessing that love is not only more important but is decisive, who would be afraid to say she is in love with love.

And for this reason, they have understood the gospel: the extraordinary women whom the Church has proclaimed its saints and doctors have demonstrated it, but so have the throng of anonymous women known only to God.

A constant running throughout the history of the Church has been the religious sisters and cloistered nuns of every generation, who have been three times as numerous as their male counterparts. This is a constant only in Christianity: in other religions, where monastic life exists (Buddhism, for example), women are a small minority compared to men. Christian religious life, with its vows of poverty, chastity, and obedience, presupposes the total wager of one's life on the fact that the gospel is right: a witness that the Kingdom of Heaven is already here, anticipated in the existence of the one who consecrates her life to it.

The quantitative prevalence of women is significant, therefore. But to the rightful derision of the sex of the author, it must be added that the prevalence also seems true "qualitatively": in moments of radical crisis (when the Reformation and the modern revolutions beginning in France abolished convents), the most tenacious resistance, often indomitable to the point of martyrdom, was that given precisely by female monasteries, by those presumed to be "fragile" religious. Hundreds of them throughout the centuries mounted the scaffold, rather than turn back after having set their hand to the plow (Luke 9:62).

In fact, the feminine need to give all for the gospel brought back the experience of religious life that the fathers of Protestantism had declared defunct. It was women who created communities of deaconesses, challenging suspicion and opposition, which in some way reintroduced in the reformed world the life of the nun dedicated wholly to Christ.

Was it not to a woman, the anonymous sinner, that Jesus said, "her sins, which are many, are forgiven, for she loved much" (Luke 7:47)?

I suspect that this enviable openness to love is precisely what has led for two thousand years an ever-renewed host of women to understand, accept, and wager on that love story par excellence that is Christianity.

It seems they have understood better than us men (always ready to be scribes, to tear each other apart over words, to transform religion into power) that ours is a God who, to give us an idea of His tenderness, presents His covenant with man as an impassioned marriage, as in the Song of Songs. They understood well how that God, going from proclamation to fulfillment, had displayed in Jesus what it means to love in that way, to the point of reaching that sign of extreme love that is allowing Himself to be eaten, to be united bodily with the beloved, in the Last Supper. Not incidentally, in commenting on the Eucharist, the most ancient Christian tradition refers precisely to the intimacy of the Song of Songs, nearly embarrassing for us.

This truly is a "horrible superstition" if one does not convert to the observation made again by John, "we know and believe the love God has for us" (1 John 4:16). This recognition, this belief in love, is among the most difficult things for us. So often we neither love others nor ourselves, and so it is not simple for us to recognize that God might want to do so, and to what extent. Mauriac observed that for a man there is no reality more difficult to accept than this: *"We are loved."*

It seems that for women it has been easier to convert, to believe. Is it because they have accepted more fully this dynamic that sustains and guides the entire history of God's relationship to us, and have done justice to the name *Eucharist*, truly "giving thanks"?

The exemplary fact that I recalled would seem to demonstrate this: the "Day of Thanksgiving" imposed on a proud and misogynistic male hierarchy by the humble yet tenacious Giuliana, who fought from the depths of her cloister in Liege, warning the theologians that a year without a day of explicit love for that sign of love is "like a moon that is never full." Another fact seems to demonstrate this: the almost exclusively female phenomenon of the scores of congregations exclusively dedicated to adoration, reparation, and devotion to the Blessed Sacrament in reclusion and prayer their entire lives, in thanksgiving for this gift.

No, I have not gone on a digression. I have tried to explain how the Eucharist cannot be understood if not by situating it in its dimension, in its "order," as Pascal would say. He observed that there is the order of force, which is that of kings, generals, politicians. Then there is the order of intelligence, which is that of the wise, philosophers, writers, artists. Only these two orders of greatness are seen, understood, and honored in the eyes of the world. The world does not perceive, it cannot notice the true greatness to which only the gospel opens our eyes. It is in this order that the Christian God acts, in which the logic of Jesus of Nazareth develops. The dimension in which the only values that count are love, humility, poverty, purity of heart, service, and silence.

It is within this order of agape, of *caritas*, of *amore* that the Eucharist is situated. We can only reject it, never understanding its message of life if, after having become children, we do not also become a bit "feminine," with all that this means in terms of sensibility to love.

At any rate, it was to a woman, to Mary the Mother of the Lord, to whom we must look to discover the point to which the divine agape can transform us, insofar as we allow ourselves to be loved.

Some News, a Fact

Let us not forget, therefore, that it is to this that we must compare ourselves: a story of life comprehensible only within a dimension of love.

It was a love story and a story of life from the beginning, from the story of Abraham and Moses: God who chooses a people, who enters into intimacy with them, who applies His pedagogy to them, guiding them, reprimanding them, praising them, punishing them. It is a web that grows ever more intricate until arriving at the passage from Word to Presence, from one who listens to one who touches, from intuiting to seeing. From the Father to the Son, from Yahweh to Jesus: "And the Word became flesh and dwelt among us" (John 1:14).

The Christian community understood immediately that it was involved in something new and unprecedented, a matter more of flesh than of breath, of events than of words.

The entire New Testament shows how the first preachers of the gospel did not disperse throughout the world proclaiming the "Christian idea" or the "Christian manifesto." They did not go about (at the risk of their lives) announcing above all that God is Father, and therefore we are all brothers, and thus we must love one another, and therefore we must love even our enemies.

These words are new and sublime. But they are only words. Any prophet, any philosopher could say as much. Are not the words of the corrupt teachers of our day equally convincing and inviting, at least in appearance?

More than teachings, the apostles present a person, giving news about Him that matters to us. It is news that respects the rules of journalism: Who? How? Where? When? Why?

> Jesus of Nazareth, a wandering prophet in Israel, was sent to his death by the imperial procurator in Palestine, Pontius Pilate, before the Jewish Passover in the city of Jerusalem. He remained three days in the tomb, as he promised and as the Scriptures of the Jews announced, that crucified and risen man appeared to us and we are his witnesses. As he had promised, his victory over sin and death is also ours. He had said, "I am the resurrection and the life; he who believes in me, even though he dies, shall live; whoever lives and believes in me, shall never die" (John 11:25-26).

This is the *gospel*: information on the facts, which move immediately on to their consequences. Whoever was convinced of the truth of the news given was involved without hesitation in the "facts" that extended to him as well the promised victory over sin and death: the Church informed and at the same time baptized, celebrated, and distributed the Eucharist.

Gospel, Baptism, and Eucharist appear to the first Christian generations as that which we struggle to see today: the same thing, that is, Christ dying and rising for us. The gospel tends to become irresistibly that water, that bread, and that wine: in these, the whole gospel is concentrated. Already in the letters of Paul, the first Christian writings we know of, we see how the Church is at work in Baptism, in the distribution of the flesh and blood of the Lord that the promise of the same apostle is realized: "Christ has been raised from the dead, the first fruits of those who have fallen asleep" (1 Cor. 15:20).

The Letter to the Corinthians was certainly written no later than the year 57. Yet it already shows that the celebration of the Eucharist had become a habitual rite even in those areas of Greece quite far from Jerusalem where it was practiced by the new community immediately after Pentecost: "And they devoted themselves to the apostles' teaching and fellowship, to the breaking of the bread and the prayers" (Acts 2:42).

It is this efficacious presence expressed through water, wine, and bread that fills their hearts with joy. Historians know of no other moment in human affairs as pervaded by such a profoundly impacting joy as that which spread in Christian environments in the early centuries.

For too long we have transformed the Resurrection only into an apologetic proof of *His* divinity, *His* glory, forgetting that it is also the origin of *our* hope and *our* joy.

Believing is precisely this: being able to see the link between what supposedly happened in Jerusalem that morning on the first Sunday, and the history of each one of us. It is an invisible bond, which is rendered visible and continually strengthened through the signs of the sacraments — all the sacraments, but in particular the Eucharist, which is not the only presence of Christ, but is the most intense. It is the presence that the Church calls "real" not by exclusion but because of its excellence.

It is not the exclusive "presence," but it is the summit presence.

Already Here

The Christian conscience has therefore already understood from the start that Jesus is not some extraterrestrial who, after a thousand adventures on earth and His grand finale in the Resurrection, says His goodbyes to all and takes off again in His spaceship, disappearing with His immortalized body into the immensity of the universe.

The faith has always understood why, in the first Gospel, the ancient prophets are quoted according to whom the one who is about to be born whose name "shall be called Emmanuel, (which means, God with us)" (Matt. 1:23).

This God is with us everywhere we turn. The faith teaches that the Father has entrusted to the Risen Christ complete lordship over the world and history. This gives Him an intimate, profound presence, not above matter but inserted into it. "Split wood, I am inside it. Lift a rock and there you will find me," the apocryphal Gospel of Thomas (saying 77) has Jesus say. This Jesus is with us in our neighbor, in the brethren, in the Bible. "It is He who speaks," says the Second Vatican Council, "when in the Church the Scriptures are read." Thus, the Liturgy of the Word (the reading and commentary on the sacred texts) which constitutes the first part of the Mass is not a sort of antechamber before entering the Eucharistic liturgy, the only one that counts. Rather, the Liturgy of the Word brings about a presence that is in some way "real."

The Risen Christ is present in the community of those who believe in Him: "Again I say to you ... where two or three are gathered in my name, there am I in the midst of them" (Matt. 18:19–20). He is present in a privileged way in the six sacraments, which derive from the seventh and tend toward it — that which the Church, for good reason, calls the "Most Holy Sacrament."

Thanks to this presence, the most spiritual and the most material possible, the Christian, in hope, experiences the life that is already here, although the face to face has not yet arrived. The Kingdom of God is still future, but at the same time is already present, though surrounded in mystery.

According to the Gospel of Luke: "Being asked by the Pharisees when the kingdom of God was coming, he answered them, 'the kingdom of God is not coming with signs to be observed; nor will they say, "Lo, here it is!" or "There!" for behold, the kingdom of God is in the midst of you'"(17:20-21).

Or, as the Greek text seems to suggest with possible eucharistic interpretations: "The kingdom of God is within you."

We now understand more than ever how in Christianity eschatology (an imprecise term) is not at the bottom, because *all Christianity is eschatology*: the final reality, the *Eschaton* or Resurrection of Jesus, has already come about, and the effects have already been applied, such that we already live in the last times.

We insist on this uninterrupted presence, because many believers seem to have forgotten that their faith does not await the return of their Lord who, like that extraterrestrial, will come back from the depths of space after a very long absence: nearly two thousand years by now and who knows how many still.

Faith is not expecting the return of Christ because it believes He has never gone away. Faith perceives all the promises of the Gospel as credible, beginning with the last in chronological order (attributed to the Risen Christ as He ascends into heaven) but perhaps the first in importance, because it contains all the others: "And lo, I am with you always, to the close of the age" (Matt. 28:20).

Until then, the Christian considers himself neither an orphan nor a widow: in that "end of the world" his Lord will not *return* but *reveal* Himself. The provisional system of signs and sacraments will end because there will be the passage, not from absence to presence, but from *concealment* to *manifestation*. All shall see what many did not see, yet which was already everywhere in the world, in infinite ways, but according to a crescendo, with the maximum presence being found on a banquet table.

UNITED BUT DIVIDED

If, according to the faith, the Eucharist is the extreme, coherent consequence of the history of salvation in its dynamics of concealment and of love, it is not to wonder that it is recognized by all the churches, despite the divisions.

In 1937, the representatives of the Christian confessions throughout the world met in Edinburgh. A final document of the assembly stated, "We all believe that Christ is present in the Eucharist, though we differ regarding the manner by which this presence is manifested and realized."

Vittorio Subilia,[56] director of the most important Protestant theological school in Italy, that of the Valdese, commented, "the presence of the Lord in the Holy Supper is affirmed by theological reflection and by the faith confessions of all the Christian churches, without exception." Not only the churches, but also the sects and new movements do not renounce this minimum gospel patrimony: even if they reject the concept of *sacrament* as the Catholic Church understands it, even if they dismantle every other sign of presence and union between Christ and us, they maintain nonetheless these two fundamental, primitive signs: Baptism and Eucharist.

One who claims to be a follower of the gospel can renounce it in many things, in practice as in doctrine, but he has not forgotten the two fundamental commands, which immediately characterize the community of believers: "Go and baptize the people in the name of the Father and of the Son and of the Holy Spirit" and "Do this in memory of me."

Yet, if we move beyond appearances, the reality is as usual much more bitter. Just a few years after the assembly in Edinburgh, another meeting of the sort took place in New Delhi and was able to state (without contradicting the preceding document) that "in no place are the divisions among the churches so visible and painful as around the Holy Table."

Indeed: those differences pointed out at Edinburgh regarding the "manner" by which the presence of Christ is "manifested and realized" are so profound that the faith of Christians in the Eucharist goes from extreme realism to extreme symbolism, which tends to evaporate the Real Presence into nothingness.

In this variegated front of opinions, the Catholic Church lies on the extreme of realism united to the other extreme of symbolism: the *et–et*, according to the usual fundamental law of its thought.

Here too, it is the Church that applies to the Scriptures a reading that is the most simple because it is the most literal. If her faith appears as the most scandalous, it is because she has done nothing but take Jesus' words literally. Reading the gospel, one strains to remember that its law is not ambiguity, not

---

[56] Editor's Note: Vittorio Subilia (1911–1988) was a well-known Valdese theologian.

the paraphrase and the distinction, but clarity: "Let what you say be simply 'Yes' or 'No'; anything more than this comes from evil" (Matt. 5:37).

During the Mass, at the moment of Communion, the priest shows the host to the faithful before offering it to him and says, with tremendous simplicity, "The body of Christ." The faithful respond with an equally tremendous simplicity: "Amen," which means "it is true."

Against the demythologizing temptations of the Reformers, Catholicism reaffirmed with extreme vigor at the Council of Trent the same faith that dates back to the beginning and which Vatican II certainly did not weaken but forcefully reconfirmed, though it preferred to be "pastoral," to use the positive exposition rather than the *anathema sit* imposed by the fire of ancient controversies. "If someone should deny," said Trent, "that the Most Holy Sacrament of the Eucharist contains truly, really, substantially the Body and Blood together with the soul and divinity of Our Lord Jesus Christ, and thus the whole Christ, but will say that in the sacrament He is present only in sign or in figure or in potency, let him be excommunicated."[57]

A "Cantankerous and Savage" Word

To ensure the radicality of such a faith, after much difficult work, the bishops at Trent and their theologians decided upon a word that was already four centuries old. As Manzoni called it, this word was so "cantankerous and savage" that even pronouncing it was difficult, let alone writing it on a keyboard. Its use is limited only to this case, logically, being unique in all the world the reality it attempts to describe: *transubstantiation*.

---

[57] Catholic doctrine is that of "extreme realism" concerning the Eucharist, as compared with that of the Eastern Orthodox churches as well, although the Orthodox are much closer than others to the Catholic faith, allowing the Second Vatican Council to concede, under certain conditions, that a Catholic may receive Communion in an Orthodox church. Nevertheless, for a long time now, Eastern theology has renounced efforts to clarify in what way the Body and Blood of Christ are truly present. In the Middle Ages, the East translated into Greek and seemed to accept from the Latins that word (*transubstantiation*) that we shall explain on the following pages. But for centuries the value of this term, if not entirely rejected, has been severely weakened. Furthermore, the celebration of the Eucharist reserved by rule to Sundays and the other feast days, the lack of adoration and of a consequent eucharistic worship outside of Mass, different accentuations in the concept of priesthood, all seem to render this reality less present and central in the spirituality and life of churches that are admirable, despite the Protestant and Enlightenment infiltrations of recent centuries, in the defense of the ancient faith.

Do not be taken aback, for we shall try to understand it better with a bit of effort. You can live a wonderful life and die in peace without ever having attempted to decipher what lies behind the incomprehensible words of those who, already for St. Augustine when he understood how things stood and retired from his chair in rhetoric, seem nothing more than "merchants of chatter." These types, more numerous than ever today, taking advantage of the cordiality of the people, get by on the ancient law: "The more obscure you are, the more power you can hope to acquire." Look around: how many mediocre politicians are confused for "statesmen" thanks to the ambiguous abstruseness of their speeches? How many spinners of webs and plagiarizers are honored as great writers or poets or philosophers or sociologists thanks to the impenetrable obscurity of what they write, and thanks to the conformity of the "learned" and the reverential awe of the "unlearned," such that no one dares raise the liberating shout: "The king has no clothes on"?

"Leave the dead to bury their own dead" (Luke 9:60), save your precious time and energy, because under those dark words you will only find more darkness; in any case, you would not find a spark of life, a hope of vanquishing death. But this hope of light is there under words that seem obscure like, *Eucharist* and *transubstantiation*.

"We call transubstantiation," the documents of Trent tell us, "the incredible and unique (*singularis*) conversion of all the substance of the bread into the body of Jesus and of all the substance of the wine into the blood of Jesus," such that, after the Consecration performed during the Mass by the words of the celebrant who speaks and acts not for himself but on behalf of Christ Himself, "only the species of bread and wine remain," namely the appearances, what appears to the senses. Under those species, the faith confesses that "the whole Jesus Christ is living and present."

This is a change that goes well beyond the observable phenomena: no chemistry or physics lab can say anything about this. The dimension of science is one thing; the dimension of love sustained by faith is another. The electronic microscope is blind here; the one who can truly see is the heart that abandons itself to the Word of God.

The word seems obscure, the reality it expresses can seem incredible and unacceptable. But the concept is perfectly clear, as is everything that is led by extremes, for this is in fact the most one can think happens to the matter of this world.

This extreme takes the Church to the logical conclusion of rendering the sacramental species the worship of adoration due to God alone, asking her faithful to kneel, as a sign of greatest respect, when entering and exiting a church where the tabernacle is "inhabited."[58]

THE REASONS FOR A LANGUAGE

Know that the Council Fathers at Trent, on a par with the preceding theologians who had distilled the term *transubstantiation* and with later theologians who accepted it, were well aware of the limits that always assail human language, and which are fully evident here.

They were so aware of those limits that they explicitly clarified that "this way in which Christ exists in the Eucharist," which they had sought to define,

[58] Reassuring that this is not a tract on the Eucharist but, if anything, an attempt at kerygma, at a first proclamation, I can spare the reader the questions that the manuals call "the permanence of the real presence," "adoration of the Eucharist." These topics, after a millennium of cooling, are once again hot. And there is no want of petty abbots who would like to demonize beliefs and practices as important on the doctrinal level as they are efficacious on the concrete level, given that they have contributed for centuries to nourishing sanctity. And not only medieval, Baroque or Restoration sanctity: in spiritualities considered more "modern," for example that of Charles de Foucauld or Thérèse of Lisieux, or even more recently of Mother Teresa of Calcutta, eucharistic adoration holds a privileged place.

It is evident to all that the accent placed on "adoration before the tabernacle" has caused certain spiritualities to slide into an individualist intimism that lost sight of the essentially communitarian character of the Eucharist. Having recognized the deviation, the usual Catholic law of synthesis of opposites must also be recognized, of dialectical equilibrium, that demands that action be paired with contemplation, the social with the individual, such that the Mass and eucharistic adoration are not mutually exclusive but complementary, especially in the awareness that the bread guarded in the tabernacle continues the preceding Mass and prepares the successive one. And then: a nearly magical term has been constructed out of the word "dialogue." Must it be practiced (and rightly so) with all people, but not with the Person whose presence the faith perceives in the tabernacle? It is of dialogue that Vatican II speaks when, rather than abandoning in the least a doctrine and a spirituality profoundly rooted in the Church, the Council Fathers recommend it anew: "We hold dear, furthermore, that if they want to carry out their ministry with fidelity, [they must practice] the daily dialogue with Christ, going to visit him in the tabernacle and practice the personal worship of the Holy Eucharist." The council's exhortation here is aimed at priests, but also at all believers.

"is unutterable to us in words," although "with the mind illuminated by faith we can intuit it, firmly believing that for God it is possible."

At any rate, for more than a thousand years, until the theologians of the twelfth century, Christians believed in a reality that had no need of being expressed by means of a technical term. In Christianity, the words always come after the liturgical action, which expresses the faith with the warmth of life and not the enforced frigidity of theology. To know *what* the Church *believes*, it would suffice to observe *what* the Church *does*. Here, too, the Christian logic of life prevails over that of death found in intellectual frameworks and treatises, *facts* over *words*.

As happened for nearly all of its dogmas, so too in the case of its eucharistic belief, the Church was forced to make a binding definition not for the sake of closing the mystery into a cage, but to safeguard its faith from what seemed to be dangerous errors.

Thus, transubstantiation was thrown against the already less robust, less provocative consubstantiation of Martin Luther: a "coexistence," namely of the body and the blood with the substance of the bread and wine. Put differently, while for the Catholic, bread and wine are *substantially transformed into* Christ, for Lutherans, Christ limits Himself to taking up these as His temporary abode.

Transubstantiation was thrown against the even less robust opinion of Calvin, who left untouched the substance and spoke only of a "dynamic presence."

Transubstantiation, finally, was thrown against the third branch of the Reformation, Zwingli, who took the defusing of the eucharistic bomb to its logical conclusion and took refuge in the spiritualism of the symbol: the bread, therefore, as a simple "symbol" of flesh; the wine as a simple "symbol" of blood.

Those new forms of Christianity of the sixteenth century tended to slide into subjectivity: "Yes, in the Eucharist there is, in some way, Christ; but He is there only if you believe it."

For the Catholic it is indeed necessary to believe in the presence of Christ, if communion with Him should bear its fruit. If this is the greatest act of love, how can one forget that love needs to be reciprocated? The shout is followed by an echo; a call needs to be answered; *presence* (here) seeks *awareness*.

Yet the presence of Christ is not the result of our belief: on the contrary, we believe because of His presence. An example might help here: for a Protestant, if one receives the Eucharist without faith, or worse, out of spite or mockery, one has received nothing. For a Catholic, however, this would be an act of terrible sacrilege. Concerning this, St. Paul admonishes in the sharpest of terms that go right in the direction of the Catholic thesis of the "objectivity" of the mystery behind the bread:

> Whoever, therefore, eats the bread or drinks the cup of the Lord in an unworthy manner will be guilty of profaning the body and blood of the Lord. Let a man examine himself, and so eat of the bread and drink of the cup. For anyone who eats and drinks without discerning the body eats and drinks judgment upon himself (1 Cor. 11:27–29).

The apostle does not hesitate to sound the alarm: the Eucharist is a two-edged sword, an offer of life, but for one who knowingly wants to trample it, it can transform into the opposite. The God of mercy is not for this reason to be mocked: the *mirabilia Dei* can be transformed into the *terribilia Dei*. "This is why many of you are weak and ill, and some have died" (1 Cor. 11:30). Love has to do with fire, and it is best not to play with fire.

We add, lastly, that the Reformers not only placed limits on the "substantiality," and therefore on the objectivity, of Christ's presence; they also wanted to limit its duration as well: once the supper is over, the presence ends, the bread returns to simple bread, the wine to simple wine.

There was a need, then, to react and to safeguard the concreteness of the faith witnessed by the entire tradition, even through blood. Since the mid-third century, the Church has honored as one of her saints the boy Tarcisius, who preferred martyrdom to profaning the "celestial members" (as he called the Eucharist, as recorded on an ancient inscription on his tomb) which he hid under his sleeve while taking Communion to a sick man.

This tradition was defended at Trent through the use of difficult words, though knowing that words are not to be confused with the mystery that transcends all.

What formula could ever be found to circumscribe the riches of God? With all our modern scientific arrogance we do not even know what life means, what matter means. How could we ever describe with verbal constructs the author of life contained in the profundity of matter?

Fides quaerit intellectum, faith seeks to understand, says the principle that explains and guides twenty centuries of Catholic theology. But this is true theology, truly a "discourse on God," when it maintains a sense of proportion and recognizes that God is God and man is man. When it recognizes, that is to say, that, having reached a certain point of *intellectus,* faith gives its assent and cannot be confused with presumptions of intellectual dominion.

Thus, after Consecration, the celebrant kneels, adoring something that infinitely exceeds not only his strength, but also his ability to understand and he confesses to the congregation, which affirms, "The mystery of faith!"

Caution

The Council Fathers at Trent were aware, therefore, of the limits of their efforts. But with their adversaries, the Protestants, they were certainly less aware that in their disputes and subsequent definitions, both sides were making use of concepts (substance, accident) derived from ancient Aristotelian physics, soon destined to change.

Furthermore, those theologies were led by controversy to be overly concerned with establishing the *how,* leaving in the shadows the *why* and the *for whom.* The Eucharist is a reality as such, but at the same time it is a gift *for us.* Its objectivity has a destination and a meaning that risked being forgotten in the sole emphasis on the analysis of the "contents," seen more from the point of view of experts of natural sciences rather than of theologians.

Thus, today, the word *transubstantiation* enjoys bad press among many theologians, who hasten to substitute it. Though one might want to try, he should heed warnings such as that of Pierre Riches, a contemporary writer, in some of his good-natured "notes on the catechism:"

> There are many technical words used in theology that are still used today, that the Magisterium of the Church insists on using, but which tend to irritate and confound a lot of people (for example: substance, nature, person, transubstantiation, etc.).
>
> I do not believe the Magisterium holds that these words have anything magical about them; but the concepts behind the words are so demanding that the use of particular words to express these concepts was the fruit of a long and tormented historical elaboration. Arriving at the determination of a word as

suitable (for example, the Trinity is three persons in one nature, and Christ one person in two natures), the Magisterium fears that using other words would leave even more space for error and confusion.

Out of prudence, then, there need to be well thought-out and examined reasons before rejecting the old terms to introduce new ones. I, for example, would prefer not to use the word *transubstantiation*, even though it is theologically precise, when speaking of the Eucharist, because many recent theologians have pointed out its limits, but I would certainly use the words person and nature when speaking about the Trintiy.

Words are not to be desacralized, therefore, but neither are they untouchable, immutable. They have their own reasons and their own history.

Before we throw them away, let us not forget that in the words of Christianity there are millennia of faith, of prayer (there was a time when almost every theologian, before being a man of study, was a man of prayer, and among them there was a preponderance of saints), of reflection, of intelligence, of experience. We must remember that those terms that seem to us, and often are, insufficient, have nevertheless carried out with great effect the task of sustaining the faith of many generations.

Beware, then, of those who propose to "render Christianity comprehensible," to "express it in modern categories". We know that many of them are clerics who grew up in the sacristy like flowers in a hothouse and recently converted to the world, of which they sniff and pick the latest trends like flowers with all too much excitement. But their "adaptations of theology in terms suitable to contemporary man" are often pathetic botches, even less comprehensible than the ancient formulas themselves.

THE FEAR OF BELIEVING TOO MUCH

But be careful, above all, because those "new formulas" are not only less efficacious (because even less comprehensible) — often, they are also more insignificant, imprecise, and evanescent.

Now, the true question is not about words but about content. In this regard, one must hold fast and be vigilant, in the interests of all and not only of believers, because all have the right to a proposal of hope that has not been watered down. They can pass it up indifferently or refuse it altogether, but if one day they were led to accept it, they must find it intact and sapid as the unbroken chain of Tradition rooted in Scripture has passed it down. For the believer, this is the only light that shines in the darkness: but then neither "do men light a lamp and put it under a bushel, but on a stand, and it gives light to all in the house" (Matt. 5:15).

In the tracks of those who frequented the synagogue of Capernaum, today many non-Catholic theologians seem to have become fussy, quick to be scandalized. They might be enthusiastic about a brand of dialectical materialism, guaranteed by Karl Marx and company, taking seriously their materialist rereading of the Bible, while they refuse indignantly the materialism of faith in the Tradition.

Thus, to them as well, certain words seem unbearably harsh: "For my flesh is food indeed, and my blood is drink indeed" (John 6:55).

These men, at any rate, are nothing new. They represent the Gnostic temptation that has accompanied Christianity since its origins, the temptation to transform the gospel from a person into knowledge (*gnosis* in Greek), from flesh into word.

Nothing strange, then, if today, Catholics, so often culturally delayed, have been infected two thousand years later by the spiritualism of the Gnostic sects of antiquity; or, four centuries later, by the spiritualist demythologizing of the Eucharist at work during the Reformation.

Already in the old Calvinism, the Holy Supper, celebrated at any rate with circumspect parsimony only four times per year, was preceded by the warning of the presiding pastor, "Brothers, guard yourselves against thinking that the Lord Jesus is contained in the bread and wine in the crude and carnal manner in which the papist-antichrist and the church of Rome-Babylon believe with their cursed idolatry!"

Now, it is not my irrelevant opinion, but that of the most ancient and numerous of the Christian churches, which claims its descendance from the apostles themselves, that the so-called "crudeness" and "carnality" of the "cursed Catholic idolatry" (the literal expression of Calvin himself) is nothing to blush about, but, on the contrary, should be defended tenaciously.

Change the words, if necessary, but do not diminish Catholic concreteness and realism. Do not attenuate the richness of the gift, do not attempt to cool the ardent globe of life that burns under the crust, because only if the presence is *real* can we be *really* saved, in all our reality of soul and body.

It is above all when it speaks to us of the Eucharist that, as André Frossard writes, "the gospel clashes with the avarice of our intelligence and the meanness of our heart, contracted by the fear of believing too much."

Certainly, the materiality that has always accompanied spirituality and symbolism in the Catholic faith must be defended to the bitter end, maintaining, however, the awareness of the mystery. The body that the believer perceives behind the appearances is the body of Christ risen and glorious: He already belongs, therefore, to the new and transformed world, about which we cannot presume to know too much. In fact, we know almost nothing of it. It is indeed the body of the Risen Christ that at every apparition asks for something to eat, to show His incredulous disciples that He is not a ghost, a spirit, although His body does pass through closed doors.

Yet, respecting the mystery, it must be said that one seems to detect a pessimism in the divine omnipotence in many of these Byzantine subtleties, concerned with placing our limits upon him. "If God became man, He can easily become bread and wine," reasoned Pascal, who then gushes forth, bothered by Christian sophists who today have become so numerous: "How I detest these idiocies, like not believing in the reality of the Eucharist! If the gospel is true, if Jesus Christ is God, what difficulties can there be?"

This mystery moves entirely within the dimension of love, and love always tends toward the maximum, toward extremism. I will be the first to try convincing myself that one can never err *overestimating* the confines of the love of the Christian God, while *underestimating* the limits of that love is always an error.

I tried to convert myself to the exhortations of the apostle to believe in a God who "was generous" (2 Cor. 9:9), in a God who "by the power at work within us is able to do far more abundantly than all that we ask or think" (Eph. 3:20). It is because he foresees our meanness that Paul prays that we "may have power to comprehend with all the saints what is the breadth and length and height and depth" (Eph. 3:18) the love with which He has loved us.

Why then aim at a reduction of hope? Why want to believe less than that maximum that has been offered to us, in that extreme of presence, of life, of resurrection which, changing the "substance" of bread and wine, can change our very "substance" and render it immortal?

Believing the incredible, hoping the impossible: at the same time, far from any suspicion of magic that has nothing to do with the gospel and with the authentic reading that the Church gives it. If a certain Catholic theology today tends toward demythologizing, in the past it tended toward mythologizing that created a nearly magical aura around limpid simplicity of the sign.

Magic always means esoteric, concealment, obscurity. Jesus announced on the other hand, "nothing is covered that will not be revealed, or hidden that will not be known. What I tell you in the dark, utter in the light; and what you hear whispered, proclaim upon the housetops" (Matt. 10:26).

The mysteries of the gospel, and therefore of this extreme of the Eucharist, have been given to shed light, not for increasing the darkness. They are "mysteries" that have nothing to do with the occult. The power of the Church granted to the priest presiding over the eucharistic assembly does not come from Him, as if He were a wizard, but emanates directly from God who, here as well, wants to make use of men as collaborators and mediators of His grace.

Despite the immense power granted them, the words of Consecration are not a magic formula. Perhaps to free us from any temptation to consider them such, the formula of Consecration is mentioned four times in the New Testament (in the three synoptic Gospels and in one of Paul's letters), but every time in a different way. The Church repeats them in the Mass, according to a fifth formula in which it has synthesized the other four, reserving the right to change them if it seems opportune.

There is not the faintest suspicion of hocus pocus: no magic, but conscientious and serene approval of the mystery of salvation, not distilled from some circle of the occult but proposed by an unforeseen gift of God.

Every magic is tied to the night which, according to the Gospels, is the very image of death. The Mass is instead tied to the dawn, to the rising of the sun, to the lightness of fasting, all realities that make reference to life.

INCORPORATED INTO A BODY

Defending the Catholic faith in the Eucharist as a reality both material and spiritual means defending faith in eternal life as salvation both material and spiritual, as salvation of the entire person. This means reaffirming that what the Christian expects for the future is the resurrection of the flesh.

Tell me which Eucharist you believe in and I will tell you which eternal life you hope for. For the Catholic, there is the body in the *past*, in that death and Resurrection of Christ, which is the origin of everything.

There is the body in the *future*, in the life beyond death.

There is also the body in the *present*, in that Eucharist through which one is incorporated into the body of the Risen Christ and ensures from this very moment immortality for one's body.

Uniting ourselves to the Risen One by means of what the Church calls *panis vivus et vitalis*, we are transformed into what we receive, according to the famous expression of Thomas Aquinas.

This is the intertwining of bodies to which Jesus Himself alludes with great clarity: "He who eats my flesh and drinks my blood abides in me, and I in him" (John 6:56). It is the intertwining of bodies of which the Church Fathers were not afraid: "He who wants to live has here the place from which he can draw life. Come with trust, allow yourself to be incorporated, and you shall be vivified" (St. Augustine).

As St. Ireneus explained, "The Eucharist is the medicine of immortality, it is the remedy that preserves one from death." Thanks to that medicine, that remedy, "our bodies are no longer corruptible because they have within them the seed of resurrection."

If the Eucharist were only a symbol, a disembodied presence, then it would be able to save only souls. But to save *people*, as the faith proclaims, food is needed.

The theologians of the great initial season of Christianity establish continual parallels (entrusting themselves to the words of Jesus) between Sunday food and daily food. In many ways, the Fathers teach that the bread and wine familiar to everyone give energy to continue with life day after day, but which "the fathers ate and died," as Jesus reminds us (John 6:58). They teach that there is bread and wine that, eaten and consumed, give infinite energy to continue life infinitely when earthly days will draw to an end: "He who eats this bread will live forever" (John 6:58).

A food, therefore, that, like every other food, realizes an encounter of matter, of bodies. As the solemn definition of 1439 at the Council of Florence reiterates, "All the effects that the nourishment and drink produce on the life of the body, this sacrament performs for eternal life."

But with a decisive difference: contrary to the process that occurs with ordinary food, which we assimilate into our body, this food assimilates us into His Body. In this encounter, it is not the Risen Christ who becomes mortal, to our measure; here, it is we mortals who are transformed into the measure of Christ, we who are made into the Risen Christ. He does not enclose Himself once more into the limits of time and space. But we are the ones who are forced out of those limits and projected beyond.

Catholicism has always defended the realism of this true food in its doctrine, despite the practice of centuries that saw in the Mass the nearly exclusive appearance of the "sacred ceremony," of the solitary worship by the priest, while behind him the faithful "listened," if they understood Latin. This has now been remedied by the Second Vatican Council, with the aspect of the banquet that announces the eternal banquet in the Kingdom.

The fact is that the Catholic faith perceives in the Eucharist, in the Mass, not one, but two realities: a banquet *and* a sacrifice. We shall return to this below. Yet if the Reformers had diminished the reality of the banquet, they completely rejected the aspect of sacrifice.

As a reaction, the latter aspect was then accentuated, altering (at least in appearance) the balance between the two realities present together: the altar was no longer seen as a table and at the same time a sacrificial altar, but *only* this. The Mass came to lack the familiar aspect of a festive feast, and assumed that of the sacred propitiatory ceremony, distant and abstract.

But perhaps in this imbalance, there was at work, still and always (in the unconscious), the fear that we recognize: when it is a question of moving from words to facts, there arises from within us the fear of the mystery of a God that comes to make Himself food. It is the recurrent fear of the Eucharist that in certain ages induced the Church almost to savor it, to give it to the people just a few times a year, with infinite caution that, more than showing respect, testified to bewilderment.

An Example by the Name of Mary

Whatever might be the mysterious action of that food, the faith believes it is capable of instilling in us such energy that it could be said of each of us what is said of Mary on August 15, the solemnity of the Assumption into Heaven: "The tomb and death did not have sufficient strength to hold you back."

According to the Catholic vision, Mary is an example, a sort of definitive "proof." She is the promise already fulfilled. She concretely anticipates what we too shall be, according to the faith.

In her, the carnal Mother of Christ was realized the fullest, most intimate, most physiological of incorporations with the body of Him who is "the resurrection and the life" (John 11:25). For nine months her body hosted Him who wanted to be the fruit of her womb (Luke 1:42).

First, she was with Him in one flesh and one spirit, thanks to the Spirit who fertilized her in her body and soul the day of the Annunciation: "The Holy Spirit will come upon you, and the power of the Most High will overshadow you" (Luke 1:35). For thirty years, then, she shared daily life with Him in the close quarters of their Palestinian home. It was a spiritual as well as a bodily contact, with all that this meant according to the Gospel: "And all the crowd sought to touch him, for power came forth from him and healed them all" (Luke 6:19).

For another woman, it was enough to touch the hem of His cloak, and from Him once more, "power came forth" that healed her suddenly of an illness that had tormented her for twelve years (Luke 8:43–48). And so, what became of this other woman, who was His Mother and touched His body and washed His clothes for three decades?

For the one who believes in the Eucharist and in the reality of the presence that it actualizes, what happens in the body of the Virgin Mary happens also, in some enigmatic way, in our body as well. Of her it is said: *caro Jesu, caro est Mariae*, the body of Jesus is the body of Mary. In a certain sense, something similar can be said of us: *caro Jesu, caro est et nostra*, the body of Jesus is also our body.

We still live, however, in the economy of faith, and therefore of concealment, of the sacramental sign, of an obscure light. Salvation is already here, already at work, but has not yet rendered visible all its effects. In contrast to Mary, for us the Risen Christ is still hidden behind the veil of the elements, the "substances."

Therefore, for us the victory of life over death remains hidden behind the veil of the apparent victory of death over life. For us there will still be a tomb, though provisional; there will be a cemetery, a "dormitory." In the near future there will be the dissolutions of our bodies; only faith can reassure us that this will not be our definitive future, that an omnipotent power will be able to recompose us and render us immortal.

But the adventure of the Virgin of Nazareth gives heart to the believer, witnessing that the spiral of life that involved her fully, without veils, already surrounds us as well, through the eucharistic veil, yet with the same power of the Resurrection.

Conception without stain of sin made Mary the first to be saved. But if she became the perfect object of salvation; if her person passed from earthly life to immortal life through death, even without an intermediate "pause," then this came about through her exemption from sin (the Immaculate Conception), and because no human body like hers has had similar contact, union, comingling with the body of Christ.

Mary is not, as certain primitive devotions offensive to God would have it, a goddess or a demigoddess. Mary is not an alien. She is one of our species, who bears witness to how the union of bodies and spirits with the human and divine body of the Risen Jesus is a means of eternal life, a secure means to such an extent that, at least in one creature, it has already been realized as such.

Among her words handed down to us by the Gospels, there is only one directed to another human being. The few others (like Joseph, like every other creature of God, Mary is a quiet person) are addressed to the angel of the annunciation, and to Jesus. That one word addressed to us, mortals like her, says, "Do whatever he tells you" (John 2:5).

Do we not know that the two fundamental commands of Jesus are both aimed at countering death and giving us life, namely to pour water on the head for the forgiveness of sins and to eat His body and drink His blood? *"Do whatever he tells you,"* allowing yourself, therefore, to be nourished and penetrated by the Eucharist, means putting yourself on the same path that she trod. In her exhortation, the Magnificat, she speaks from personal experience, showing by facts that the conditions of the covenant will be respected, that death will not be the ultimate but only the penultimate chapter of our biography. As her entire biography demonstrates, the journey does not end with considerations around a tomb, but with the announcement of her Assumption into Heaven.

"Cause of our joy," "our hope" she is called in the constant, indomitable veneration that is among the most amazing, spontaneous, and profoundly popular phenomena found in history. And perhaps also for this reason, Marian devotion has been so ridiculed by those who say they serve the people, but who really only serve themselves; those who claim (and maybe even believe it) to have the support of the people, but who really have the support only of their servants and jesters, and only so long as their power lasts.

Those ancient attributes (*Causa nostrae laetititae; Spes nostra*) are not gratuitous; they are not part of the exaggerations and deviations of devotion to her. Those invocations are rooted in the very dialectic of the Catholic faith, which, in the words of Karl Rahner, "says of Mary what it announces as the hope for all of us. Thus, the contested and misunderstood truth of her Assumption in body and soul says nothing else about her than what we confess to believe for each of us: *resurrection of the flesh and eternal life.*"

If, in Europe alone, people constructed at their own cost, with their own hands, something like twenty thousand sanctuaries to that little Jewish girl, it is because they intuited, in the words of Giorgio Gozzelino, that "she guarantees in her body that the Son vanquished death on Easter morning, and therefore our most audacious hopes are well founded." In this way, "if the Risen Christ present among us in the Eucharist is a pledge of our resurrection, the vision of Mary already assumed bodily allows us a taste beforehand."

If, according to her prophecy, "all generations" have called her blessed, it is because, as she herself immediately adds, "he who is mighty has done great things for me" (Luke 1:48–49). But the faithful have always heard it said that to call her "blessed" is to call ourselves "blessed," as well, because the Almighty will do the same "great things" for us as well. Is there anything greater than giving us eternal life, overflowing with joy?

Was it then to confirm our faith in our salvation, to hearten us by showing us the proof that the promise is true, was it for this that Mary is said to appear more frequently and with greater resonance than all the other saints?

No apparition is indispensable to the faith, for sure. In fact, the Gospel calls "blessed" those "who have not seen and yet believe" (John 20:29). Indeed, Marian apparitions normally do not occur to produce faith, but to confirm it. Their protagonists are not the doubting and unbelieving, but the suffering, humble, uneducated, children. They are privileged by a faith that is firm and simple.

Making herself visible in her glorified body, more than a source of faith, she seems a confirmation of faith already in action, telling us that we, too, shall be like that.

Every apparition is the encounter of a body definitively alive with a body that will become definitively alive.

What unites the innumerable accounts of the visionaries is not fear, but surprise mixed with joy and trust. For this reason, many apparitions leave behind an exemplary sign: the outpouring of springs of fresh water, the Gospel symbol of eternal life (John 4:14).

For this reason, every apparition always leaves behind one of those sanctuaries of which we spoke. What is a sanctuary, if not a building where, venerating Mary as the forerunner of our race along the paths of salvation, one adores "the God of Abraham, and the God of Isaac, and the God of Jacob," who is "not God of the dead, but of the living" (Matt 22:32)? What is a sanctuary, if not a building where the Eucharist, which has in it the power to transform us like Mary, is celebrated and kept? There is no Marian pilgrimage that does not have as its culmination participation at the banquet of the Mass.

Here we come full circle, once again *tout se tient*: taking as our model the Virgin of Nazareth, one listens to her words, one does whatever the Son says to do, and we unite ourselves to His life to live as she did.

Here we see the concatenation of realities that the visionary of Lourdes, St. Bernadette Soubirous, so lucidly intuited. Although she received her First Communion after the apparitions in the grotto, when asked if she was happier for having seen the Virgin Mary or for having received the Eucharist, the poor, uneducated little peasant girl replied as no theologian could have better put it: "I can't say, because they are two things that go together."

As always, in the Christian paradox, it is the saints (and not us scribes) who understand everything before everyone else.

Food and Victim

But the Mass, during which the Eucharist is celebrated, is not only a banquet. As we mentioned, and as the Catechism insists, the Mass is at the same time a sacrifice. In it, Jesus is simultaneously *food* and *victim*.

The Mass is also, as the Church teaches, "that action or sacramental mystery with which the Son renews to the Father and perpetuates on earth, in a non-bloody fashion, the one sacrifice of the Cross." But is not the Cross the sacrifice that has vanquished sin? And is not sin the cause of death?

In this perspective as well, the Eucharist is for the faith the loftiest promise of life. The two aspects (the living bread and the renewed cross, the food and the victim) end up being revealed as one. The former is derived from the latter, and both are for the same objective: to assure us of eternal life.

The Eucharist, as a representation and memorial of the Passion, continually renews the moment of victory over sin and its consequences, the most serious of which are sickness, aging, and death. From that representation memorial, the application of the fruits of that sacrifice descend upon us, always seeking to vanquish sin.

In every Mass, it is always Christ who expiates and intercedes before the Father that our sin be forgiven, that we might "have life and have it abundantly," which is the reason for the coming of the Word (John 10:10).

The action of "the one who gave himself as a ransom for all (1 Tim. 2:6), of the one "who did not know sin" and who God "for our sake he made him to be sin who knew no sin, so that in him we might become the righteousness of God" (2 Cor. 5:21), is repeated every day, every hour, every minute. (Playing with time zones, there is no moment in which in some part of the world the Mass is not being celebrated — is it perhaps for this reason that the world is round?)

Becoming the bread that is not the prize for the perfect (as too often the rigorist mentality considered it), but medicine for the errant, the Eucharist becomes in our flesh the "yeast of life" by applying itself as an antidote that cancels past sin and defends us from future sin; it forgives the punishment due our faults and gives two graces in particular, on which mystics and theologians have reflected: the grace of repentance, that great liberating gift of tears, and the grace of joy that opens the heart to love, which is the very opposite of sin.

There is a precise message in the fact that the Gospels present us with Jesus at table with sinners. "And the Pharisees and the scribes murmured, saying, 'this man receives sinner and eats with them,'" (Luke 15:2). The eucharistic banquet is still the "sitting down at table with Christ," the way in which the Prodigal Son was welcomed back and forgiven.

Thus, the more one tries to penetrate its mystery, the more this "thanksgiving" seems truly what St. Paul thought when he exclaimed, "thanks be to God, who gives us the victory through our Lord Jesus Christ" (1 Cor. 15:57).

Provisions for the Journey

The pages of this chapter are only notes: long in appearance, but in reality, quite brief when compared with this greatest of gifts that has been given to men to face and that, though belonging to our world, leaps beyond time and space to explode in unfathomable cosmic dimensions.

We are given hints that are not only brief, but also imperfect and sketchy, given their limited objective corresponding to the intentions of the author: to lead one to perceive at least some of the vertiginous depths that the faith reveals behind such trivial appearances, helping myself first of all to take with due seriousness the cry of the Gospel: "If you knew the gift of God" (John 4:10).

The little we have examined thus far might suffice to understand the constant concern of the Church that the faithful frequent as often as possible the table which she alone is able to set, and to understand why the greatest punishment it can inflict on one of its members is excommunication, exclusion from ecclesial communion and therefore from eucharistic Communion.

Thus, these meager hints suffice to help us intuit why the same Church, this instrument of joy and life whose leaders have done all in their powers to make it seem an ally of darkness, if not even of death, would push its solicitude almost to the point of exhaustion so that the dying are not deprived of the last Eucharist, the ultimate Communion with the bread and wine, the Viaticum to which we return now after so many pages.

With the care that justifies its attribution of Mother of the faithful (*Sancta Mater Ecclesia*), the Church establishes that in the face of an emergency, every rule is null and void, so that no one would lack this waybread at the start of the journey that has no end. In the case of need, every disposition for normal circumstances is nullified, however rigid they might be.

This is a solicitude that has existed for a very long time: in the year 325, recalling what was already considered the "ancient rule," the First Council of Nicaea reminded the bishops, priests, deacons, and laity to do all they could "not to deprive the indispensable Viaticum to the faithful who are in danger."

The dying are dispensed from every obligation. They can receive Viaticum even without first receiving absolution through confessing their sins, and can be absolved even by a priest who has been suspended *a divinis*, nor are the dispositions regarding fasting and receiving Communion more than once a day valid for him.

For the same reasons, the ancient obligation is observed with scrupulosity binding every church whose clergy cares for souls: there must always be reserved and renewed a "reserve Eucharist" to provide in moments of emergency. No one knows when death can strike, and prudence makes it necessary never to lack provisions. The conservation of hosts in the tabernacle began in the ancient Church precisely because of the necessity of providing Viaticum for the dying.

But these are extraordinary circumstances. For the ordinary, the Church never meant for the administration of Viaticum to be hurried or stealthy. On the contrary, it has always sustained (and has recently reiterated this) that this extreme liturgy must have a public, solemn character, and invites "the community of believers to unite themselves as far as possible." Here, too, with social participation, solitude is vanquished.

Never before the present did the death of a person leave others indifferent. Always and everywhere, the death of the individual involved the community. Everywhere, the painful isolation of the dying was contrasted with signs that expressed the reality that everyone is bound to everyone else.

Until now, this was true everywhere, from African tribes to Christian parishes, where the bells rang out the "agony" to warn that one of us was fighting against the enemy. When the moment arrived, Viaticum was taken to the dying person with great solemnity, such that the carrying of the Eucharist from the Church to the home spontaneously assumed the character of a *Corpus Domini* procession. It is a sign of compassion, of solidarity, which the Church encouraged to the point of conceding an indulgence to the faithful who, as they encountered that procession along the street, joined along praying for the dying person and for his victory in battle. Today the liturgy suggests, when possible, not to take the Eucharist from the tabernacle in the parish, but to celebrate Mass directly in the sick person's room. And the Mass, as we have seen, is the community action par excellence, the most resounding defeat possible for death and the solitude that accompanies it.

Despite Everything

Much more remains to be said; many other consequences could be drawn from what has been or could have been said. Among those consequences, I cannot remain silent about one that I entrust to your reflection, not able to develop it as it deserves.

If death reveals the ultimate truth of every living reality, it also reveals the truth about how we understand Christianity, our faith in the gospel. Here, one can observe the naïveté of those who would say yes to Christ and no to a community that continues in history His action of salvation. How can we reach it or be reached by it, if the only way possible is by means of the primary and universal sacrament that is the Church?

Clearly, I do not make this appeal to the many who consider this mere ranting and raving. I am addressing the growing number of Christians (I myself was once among them) who do not understand why their faith must pass through the Church.

But how can one choose the individualism of a vertical face-to-face with this Jew who lived twenty centuries ago, when everything about Him — beginning with His words, which the Church (not Jesus Himself, nor an angel) has preserved in the Gospels, *everything* — reaches us through other men, through other brethren united to us, from the faith, in a group, in a community?

To stay on topic: If those "signs" called Reconciliation and Anointing of the Sick have meaning, would you confess yourself or anoint yourself? Above all, would you procure for yourself the Eucharist? Would you consecrate on your own the life-giving bread and wine? Would you reduce what was intended as a glorious, fraternal banquet to a self-service cafeteria, where each person not only serves himself but, paradoxically, prepares his own meal? Does this seem preposterous? Indeed, for it is. But if you do not accept the Church (for as much as it might burden you), the alternative is one alone: you must renounce that food to remain coherent with your solitary vision of the faith.

We have already spoken about this, but now we can return to it with a broader understanding of the issue. The Church with its hierarchical structures can repulse, annoy, and even scandalize. The pope, bishops, and priests can get on our nerves. But if one reflects on the matter, in the dim light of what we have said, one discovers that all (clergy and laity) have their unique place within the community, which is the only means by which salvation in Christ can be made concrete and effective.

This is the extreme opposite of any nostalgia for a Church not too far away in time of which the Dominican theologian Yves Congar spoke, the Church in which the "position of the layperson" was threefold: kneeling before the priest; seated under the pulpit; with his hands in his pocket to open his wallet.

This does not mean we must be nostalgic for this Church to recognize that, in her, "each has his own special gift from God, one of one kind and one of another" (1 Cor. 7:7). In her, "there are many parts, yet one body" (1 Cor. 12:20).

Sure: the Second Vatican Council reminded us that all the baptized are "priests," given their union with the High Priest, Christ. For us laypeople, the Church can no longer reserve the cheap seats in the gallery, while on stage and in the parterre are the plush seats for "consecrated religious." But again, I refuse to take from Vatican II only what is convenient. The same council recalls in fact the traditional Catholic position: "Although ordered one to the other and participating each in its own way in the one priesthood of Christ, the common priesthood of all the faithful and the hierarchical priesthood differ essentially and not only by degree."

To arrive at what interests us most here, the Mass, Vatican II reiterates that "if all the faithful, by virtue of their royal priesthood, contribute to the oblation of the Eucharist," it is always "the ministerial priest, with the sacred authority he has been granted ... who performs the eucharistic sacrifice in the person of Christ and offers it to God." Although, one must not forget, he does so "in the name of all the people."

Their hands are, like those of all men, often dirty. But if we accept the sacraments, if we acknowledge the sacrament that is the Church, we cannot forget that within the community that brings us life, only those hands are authorized to consecrate and elevate the bread, saying in Christ's name: "Blessed are those called to the Supper of the Lamb! Behold, the Lamb of God who takes away the sins of the world!"

I will gladly leave the class struggle to others. I will not succumb to the ridiculous fashion of wanting to transpose the political categories of the moment, such as parliamentary democracy of the Anglo-American type, onto the Church.

The Church, in her essence, is much more than "democratic": she is communitarian. Her faithful are neither card-carrying members nor electors, but much more: they are members of the one Body of Christ. They are not united by party membership, a card, but by the same Baptism and the same Eucharist. I, a layman, do not feel frustrated as such by a division of roles that throughout the centuries has become more rigid.

In the end, we are the ones in the wrong if we presume to understand Christianity with the bishops and their collaborators as our starting point.

If it is truly difficult for you to accept them, begin instead with the Eucharist and from what it uniquely signifies, remembering that bishops and priests are, if anything, the price to be paid to have it. They exist precisely to celebrate and offer it, as Vatican II reiterates: "The principal function of the priest is the mystery of the eucharistic sacrifice," and again, "the eucharistic sacrifice is the center and root of the entire life of the priest."

All the rest is good, but in theory might very well not exist. In any case, everything originates with this. You can forget everything else, but not this.

In the end, it is the Eucharist that safeguards the Church from becoming a political party, or an association, or a corporation listed on the stock market, or any other human institution that can be accepted or abandoned, to which one can belong or not, according to one's pleasure and convenience. In any other setting (politics, economy, culture), a dishonest, incapable, irascible director is merely dishonest, incapable, or irascible, while a bishop who is dishonest, incapable, or irascible is not *only* that, because despite everything, he has been given a power that cannot be substituted or revoked. According to the Second Vatican Council, he is the "steward of the Eucharist, which He offers and has offered" by His priests. This is the little, immense difference.

If your political party, your labor union, your club are causing you problems, those realities are for you a problem; everything about them is up for grabs. If the church with a lowercase *c* causes you trouble, it is not the Church in the uppercase that is your problem; nothing of what truly counts is up for grabs.

Dispute and denounce whatever in the ecclesial organization needs to be disputed or denounced, with the dash of irony of one who knows that reforms are not what brings about miracles. Other churches already have what you want for the Catholic Church, and yet their temples are still empty. Do not forget that behind the façade in need of continual, energetic restoration, the essential has been there since the beginning, will always be there, and needs no reform, until history comes to fulfillment and men no longer need to be gathered into the earthly Church because they will no longer need its mediation, its sacraments. Indeed, "For now we see in a mirror dimly, but then face to face" (1 Cor. 13:12).

Obviously, I can speak only in my name. And I am not among those of whom Giovanni Papini spoke, who "accept Christ for the love of priests." Quite the contrary. Yet, for those who hate death, and I am not at all ashamed to confess that I hate death, the Eucharist in the full significance given it by Rome is among the reasons for remaining Catholic (or to become one) and for accepting the Church, because only through her can we reach that unique reality.

For those who hate that cause of death which is sin (and I hate sin, because I know its many faces, because every day I experience in the flesh its devastating power, yet every day I am darkly attracted and vanquished), the Eucharist is among the reasons for remaining Catholic, to desire to be one, to accept the Church.

Indeed, if the Church is right in its wager over the bread and the wine, Peter too is right when he says, "for there is no other name under heaven given among men by which we must be saved" (Acts 4:12).

But how can one believe in this incredible, unexpected reality that clashes violently with the gray reality that surrounds us, with the temptation of death and desperation within us? How can we bear this faith, if not resting our weakness on the faith of others, to unite and transform it into "a victory that overcomes the world" (1 John 5:4)?

In the end, how can one believe in the Eucharist that reaches us through the Church if not by means of the Church herself? Arriving at the extreme of the believable, one discovers that the faith cannot be a "solitary vice," that believing is possible only together.

Beyond any suspicion of clericalism, Hans Küng underlines this perfectly in one of his books:

> You are not alone. Christ did not call you to the faith alone. He does not expect you to face combat with all your doubts alone. If Christ has called you, he has called you to the Church. The Church is nothing but the great community of believers, conducted and sustained by the Holy Spirit. You are not alone, therefore: you are in the Church.
>
> You are in the community of believers which, since the times of the Apostles, has always sustained each of the believers, so that in his solitude faith might not become too arduous. This community sustains you too. In this community you are protected, you are united to all those who believe in Christ throughout the world. What you believe is not some particular idea of yours. It is the faith of all the Church, the faith that rests on the apostles, on the Risen Lord.

If you are truly crazy enough to believe in life in the midst of death, then your craziness is not isolated. It is a frenzy that unites you with an immense crowd that stretches throughout history and continues still today.

A strange inconsistency: never before as today have so many Christians thought themselves capable of believing while doing without the community, the Church. And never as today has it been so difficult to remain steadfast in the faith without the comfort and support of the community. Faith and Church have been dissociated right at the time when everything demands the strengthening of the sense of belonging to a people, the people of God, whose path has always been arduous, and which today is crossing one of the most arid deserts, a most inhospitable land in which there is no hope for survival without staying together.

A Short Valediction

Marana tha

ONE OF THE MOST beautiful books in the Old Testament, Deuteronomy, narrates that one day, Moses summarized for his people the terms of the covenant with God. After reviewing the contents of the faith, after the reiteration of the duties it imposed and the benefits it ensured, the greatest of the prophets of Israel pronounced the words that are uniquely opportune to reread, having reached this our provisional finish line. They are words that resound with echoes, after everything that has been said in this book:

> I call heaven and earth to witness against you this day, that I have set before you life and death, blessing and curse; therefore choose life, that you and your descendants may live, loving the LORD your God, obeying his voice, and cleaving to him; for that means life to you and length of days, that you may dwell in the land which the Lord swore to your fathers, to Abraham, to Isaac, and to Jacob, to give them (Deut. 30:19–20).

Therefore, since its remote foundation, biblical faith portrays as an adventure of life both the wager of all or nothing (*"I have set before you life and death, blessing and curse"*) and the invitation to wager on what is better for us (*"Therefore choose life"*).

Moses then sought to avoid the misunderstandings, doubts, and hesitations of those ancient nomads (doubts which we share) by saying, "For this commandment which I command you this day is not too hard for you, neither is it far off." He continues:

> It is not in heaven, that you should say, "Who will go up for us to heaven, and bring it down to us, that we may hear it and do it?" Neither is it beyond the sea, that you should say, "Who will go over the sea for us, and bring it to us, that we may hear it and do it?" But the word is very near to you; it is in your mouth and in your heart, so that you can do it (Deut. 30:11–14).

"Neither is it far off… Very near to you." This is important.

There are many books like this one that seek to denounce the insufficiencies of the present, to remind readers of the need for a life that is different and better, because it is more human. The profession of "social critic" is today one of the most popular and perhaps most lucrative.

But most of those books and those discussions end up with pathetic appeals for all sorts of utopias to be created by the efforts of some sort of "new humanity," which by some miracle has become all reason, goodness, and interior freedom.

These are impotent and sterile appeals, unrealistic flights into the future to give people a semblance of consolation, a glimmer of hope. Fortunately, the majority of those empty words disappear into the air.

I and every reasonable person with me shall do penitence and novenas, praying that no more of the "new" men be made. With recent history in mind, we see that no Hell is more concrete and terrible than the earthly Paradises that the utopians would like to construct.

As for me, I do not need to join the parade of the idealists or the hypocrites. I can avoid the exhortations that promise to give life to great revolutions, both social and moral, or elusive research into some "third way" because the others have shown themselves unfeasible.

Having denounced the suffocating present, I do not need to invoke a problematic future. I do not need to do this because I have looked into Christianity and into what it believes. It is enough to note that already, in the here and now, the faith perceives a New Man, a New Society: Jesus the Christ, His presence in the Eucharist, His action that continues through His community, the Church. It is a New Man who, if we wish, can already render us new men. This is a New Society of which we can already be citizens, if only we so wish.

As anyone who looks into the gospel, I too can say with Paul: "if anyone is in Christ, he is a new creation; the old has passed away, behold, the new has come" (2 Cor. 5:17).

We have seen that politicians, reformers, lay prophets, and philosophers have always been forced to speak in the *future* tense, to refer to a hypothetical tomorrow. Only Christians, the Church, can speak in the *present*, pointing to today.

We can do so because what really counts for us is not, returning to the words attributed to Moses, "in heaven" or "beyond the sea," nor in those utopian dreams that, if one attempts to put them into practice, become nightmares. What truly counts is already here among us, hidden to the eyes of the flesh but visible to the eyes of faith.

The Church does not *desire* what some political party might desire; the Church *indicates*. The Church does not *hope*, which is the most the others can do. The Church *verifies*.

And what it offers contains much more than a promised and never seen utopia, in which we would have to be satisfied only by a pay raise, political freedoms, and social justice. This is a lot, but it does not in the least fill the heart.

The New World that the faith says is already in our midst offers true novelty, because nothing is newer than life in this land of death. It is a life in which we find true riches, liberty, and justice — not relative and provisional riches as promised by the prophets of the world, but full, definitive, eternal riches.

Because this life, this New World, is here already but *not yet* here (according to the Christian paradox we have often pointed out), to discover it in the faith does not mean choosing immobilism, the *status quo* of history.

On the contrary, this discovery can be the premise for a radical commitment in the world: Life that is already in us leads us to assault, to crush the limits that still hinder. In union with the power of Christ who became food, we are already, according to the word of the Fathers, "citizens of Heaven." But it is precisely the concession of this passport that does not allow us to curl up in a hammock in the shade; rather, it stimulates us to throw ourselves into history, as if to force it open, to hasten the hour that the invisible opens onto the visible.

This is the tension that animated the early Christian communities, who did not sanctify the situation as they found it, but undermined and hastened the collapse of one of the most powerful and oppressive empires known to man. It is the tension expressed in the invocation that closed all the eucharistic assemblies and concludes the New Testament as well: *Marana tha*, come O Lord, manifest yourself!

Whoever Seeks, Finds

This valediction is accompanied by a question that disturbs us. We should have turned with privileged solidarity to those who believe they do not believe. The realities we have indicated here demand faith to be recognized. And is faith not a gift, similar in a way to the plague — some catch it, some do not?

No, faith is not like the plague.

Encountering many "non-believers" (for what this ambivalent expression is worth), too often one hears them accentuate in a unilateral way the character of mysterious gift that faith has, almost as if it were determined only by the unforeseeable action of some capricious divinity.

There is no need to disturb theology; just a pinch of catechism suffices to know that faith, according to what the Catholic Church affirms, is the result of the encounter of at least three factors, not one alone.

These three elements do not act independently of one another, but sustain and condition each other mutually, such that none of them can be lacking when faith is born, though none is sufficient alone.

The first factor is without a doubt *grace*, mysterious divine grace. We have insisted on this various times. To forget this would indeed mean to fall into rationalism, to trivialize, to defame faith by reducing it to evidence or to the result of man's efforts. "No one can come to me unless the Father who sent me draws him" (John 6:44) says Jesus, with words that Paul repeats: "No one can say 'Jesus is Lord' except by the Holy Spirit" (1 Cor. 12:3).

But in the mysterious genesis of faith, two other equally indispensable factors are added to grace: will and reason. To decide (will) and to reflect (reason) is within the reach of all, not only of those "called." If we look to Scripture, grace, too (namely "the Father who draws" of Jesus, "the action of the Spirit" of Paul) is in many ways within the grasp of man; it does not escape the grasp of those who seek it, of those who solicit it with an attitude of sincere receptivity.

There is in the Gospels a very consoling passage, though it is often forgotten by those who, believing they do not believe, judge it to be impossible for them to enter into what from the outside appears to be the unattainable "magic circle" of faith:

> Ask, and it will be given you; seek, and you will find; knock, and it will be opened to you. For every one who asks receives, and he who seeks finds, and to him who knocks it will be opened. Or

> what man of you, if his son asks him for bread, will give him a stone? Or if he asks for a fish, will give him a serpent? If you then, who are evil, know how to give good gifts to your children, how much more will your Father who is in heaven give good things to those who ask him! (Matt. 7:7–11).

According to the logic of the gospel, among all the possible "good things" that man can ask of God, none is better than faith, none is more certainly attainable by our asking. Is it not then suspect that if we insist on seeing in faith only a gratuitous and mysterious "grace" to surrender passively, it offers one of the many alibis contrived by that inexhaustible factory of alibis, the human heart? One of the many self-justifications to avoid the toil of searching, of invoking what one feigns to envy? Our task is not to give a response to this question; we leave to the Lord His task of being the only judge "who judgest righteously, who triest the heart and the mind" (Jer. 11:20).

As for you, whether you believe you believe or believe you do not believe, having followed me to this point patiently in this arduous search authorizes you to apply a word that a Christian says he has heard from the Lord.

It is a word that is not explicitly in the Gospels (although it derives from them), but whose truth I believe, and not only because the one who affirms to have heard it is Blaise Pascal, who, at thirty-nine, received Viaticum crying with joy, and crossed confidently the mysterious threshold, saying, "May God never abandon me."

Pascal, who, after having thrown everything into the pot, even his lucid mathematical knowledge, to demonstrate that we must wager and we must wager on *life*, perceived with humility the interlocutor by now vanquished, "If this discourse seems convincing to you, know that it was made by a man who kneeled before and after, to pray to God to whom he submits that you too might submit, for your good and His glory."

The credentials are the best, then. But if I believe in the word that Christ addressed to Blaise Pascal, it is above all because it corresponds to the little that I have intuited of the mystery of the gospel.

Says the voice of the one in whom faith glimpses resurrection and life: "You would not seek me if you had not already found me."

About the Author

VITTORIO MESSORI IS AN acclaimed Italian journalist and author. He conducted the exclusive interview with Cardinal Ratzinger, *The Ratzinger Report*, and also conducted the first book-length interview with Pope John Paul II, published under the pope's authorship: *Crossing the Threshold of Hope*. Messori is also the author of *Kidnapped by the Vatican? The Unpublished Memoirs of Edgardo Mortara*.

Sophia Institute

Sophia Institute is a nonprofit institution that seeks to nurture the spiritual, moral, and cultural life of souls and to spread the gospel of Christ in conformity with the authentic teachings of the Roman Catholic Church.

Sophia Institute Press fulfills this mission by offering translations, reprints, and new publications that afford readers a rich source of the enduring wisdom of mankind.

Sophia Institute also operates the popular online resource CatholicExchange.com. *Catholic Exchange* provides world news from a Catholic perspective as well as daily devotionals and articles that will help readers to grow in holiness and live a life consistent with the teachings of the Church.

In 2013, Sophia Institute launched Sophia Institute for Teachers to renew and rebuild Catholic culture through service to Catholic education. With the goal of nurturing the spiritual, moral, and cultural life of souls, and an abiding respect for the role and work of teachers, we strive to provide materials and programs that are at once enlightening to the mind and ennobling to the heart; faithful and complete, as well as useful and practical.

Sophia Institute gratefully recognizes the Solidarity Association for preserving and encouraging the growth of our apostolate over the course of many years. Without their generous and timely support, this book would not be in your hands.

www.SophiaInstitute.com
www.CatholicExchange.com
www.SophiaInstituteforTeachers.org

Sophia Institute Press is a registered trademark of Sophia Institute.
Sophia Institute is a tax-exempt institution as defined by the
Internal Revenue Code, Section 501(c)(3). Tax ID 22-2548708.